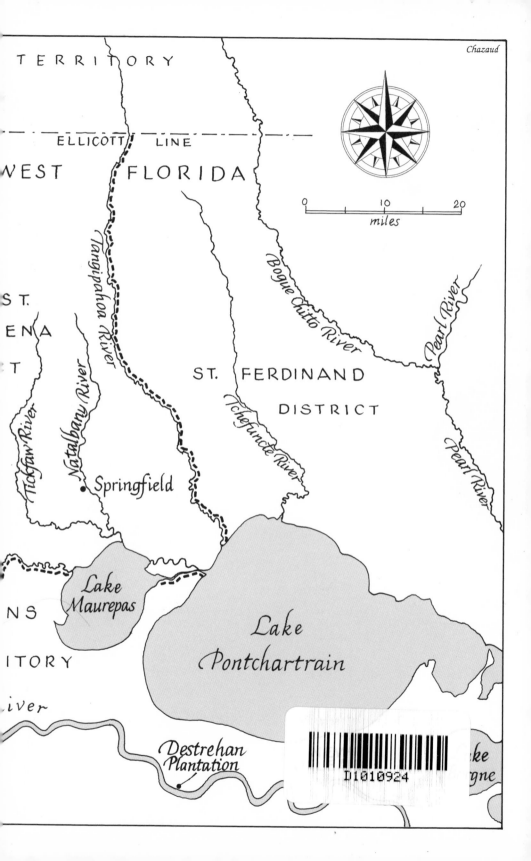

Chazaud

TERRITORY

ELLICOTT LINE

WEST FLORIDA

0   10   20
miles

ST.
HELENA
DISTRICT

Tangipahoa River

Natalbany River

Tickfaw River

Bogue Chitto River

Pearl River

ST. FERDINAND
DISTRICT

Tchefuncte River

Pearl River

• Springfield

NS

TORY

iver

Lake
Maurepas

Lake
Pontchartrain

Destrehan
Plantation

D1010924

ake
gne

THE ROGUE REPUBLIC

Also by William C. Davis

The Pirates Laffite: The Treacherous World of the Corsairs of the Gulf

An Honorable Defeat: The Last Days of the Confederate Government

*Lincoln's Men: How President Lincoln Became Father to an
Army and a Nation*

*Three Roads to the Alamo: The Lives and Fortunes of David Crockett,
James Bowie, and William Barret Travis*

*A Way Through the Wilderness: The Natchez Trace and the Civilization
of the Southern Frontier*

"A Government of Our Own": The Making of the Confederacy

Jefferson Davis: The Man and His Hour

The ROGUE REPUBLIC

How Would-Be Patriots
Waged the Shortest Revolution
in American History

William C. Davis

Houghton Mifflin Harcourt

BOSTON ✦ NEW YORK

2011

For information about permission to reproduce selections from this book, write to Permissions, Houghton Mifflin Harcourt Publishing Company, 215 Park Avenue South, New York, New York 10003.

www.hmhbooks.com

Library of Congress Cataloging-in-Publication Data
Davis, William C., 1946–
The rogue republic : how would-be patriots waged the shortest revolution
in American history / William C. Davis.
p. cm.
Includes bibliographical references and index.
ISBN 978-0-15-100925-1
1. West Florida — History — 19th century. 2. Florida — History — Spanish colony,
1784–1821. 3. Revolutions — West Florida — History — 19th century. I. Title.
F301.D36 2011
975.9'03 — dc22
2010026068

Endpaper maps by Jacques Chazaud

Book design by Dennis Anderson

Printed in the United States of America

DOC 10 9 8 7 6 5 4 3 2 1

For Bird, once more

CONTENTS

DRAMATIS PERSONAE

SOLOMON ALSTON • Captain of militia who helped put down the
Kemper revolt of 1804; participant in the revolutionaries'
kidnapping in 1805

JOHN BALLINGER • Leader in putting down the Shepherd Brown
counter-revolt, later a West Florida agent to the United
States

WILLIAM BARROW • One of West Florida's wealthiest planters and
most ardent proponents of independence from Spain

SHEPHERD BROWN • Land speculator, loyal supporter of Spanish
rule, and leader of the brief counter-revolt in the St. Helena
District

AARON BURR • Vice president of the United States from 1801 to
1805; father of an ill-defined effort to create an empire in
the Southwest

JAMES CALLER • Colonel in Mississippi Territory militia and leader
in the Mobile Society plot to seize Mobile

JOHN CALLER • Mississippi militia officer arrested with Kemper for
plotting to capture Mobile; brother of James Caller

MARQUÉS DE CASA CALVO • Spanish official who handed Louisiana
over to the United States; later expelled by Claiborne

WILLIAM C. C. CLAIBORNE • Governor of Orleans Territory and an
agent of Jefferson and Madison in pressuring Spain to yield
West Florida

ix

Daniel Clark • Irish-born land speculator, intriguer with Burr, enemy of Claiborne, and first congressman from Louisiana

William Cooper • Convention delegate from St. Ferdinand District who joined Shepherd Brown in his counter-revolt

Raphael Crocker • Corrupt secretary to Delassus; a major agent in spreading unrest among American planters in West Florida

Charles de Hault Delassus • Indecisive and largely helpless commandant of the four districts of West Florida that rebelled in 1810

Armand Duplantier • French-born planter and leader in the militia that put down the 1804 Kemper revolt

Sterling Duprée • Leader of volunteers from the Pascagoula region who raided and plundered under the lone-star flag

Thomas Estevan • Spanish captain commanding at Bayou Sara and loyal subordinate of Grand-Pré and Delassus

Vicente Folch • Governor of Spanish West Florida; responsible for defending Pensacola, Mobile, and Baton Rouge

Carlos de Grand-Pré • Spain's popular commandant of the four western districts; his removal in 1808 encouraged general unrest

Philip Hicky • Baton Rouge attorney and friend of Grand-Pré who became a leader in the convention

David Holmes • Governor of Mississippi Territory; Claiborne's partner in keeping peace and taking over the West Florida republic

Abram Horton • Leader of the gang who kidnapped and assaulted the Kempers in 1805, arousing anti-Spanish sentiment

Thomas Jefferson • President who purchased the Louisiana Territory and pressed for the inclusion of West Florida

Isaac Johnson • Major of cavalry volunteers who helped take Baton Rouge; probable designer of the lone-star flag

JOHN HUNTER JOHNSON · Owner of the Troy plantation, where the convention was born; ordered the attack on Baton Rouge

NATHAN KEMPER · Instigator of 1804 raids into West Florida that raised the first armed resistance to Spanish rule

REUBEN KEMPER · Storekeeper, flatboatman, implacable foe of Spain, and leader of the expedition to take Mobile

SAMUEL KEMPER · Partner with brother Nathan in 1804 raids; later commander of American invasion of Spanish Texas

JOSEPH P. KENNEDY · Mississippi lawyer and kingpin of the Mobile Society, dedicated to taking Mobile by force

IRA C. KNEELAND · Loyal surveyor for Spain, participant in Kemper kidnapping, and object of Kemper revenge

GILBERTO LEONARD · Treasurer under Grand-Pré and Delassus

JOHN W. LEONARD · Presumed royalist delegate to 1810 convention who became a leader in the independence movement

THOMAS LILLEY · Baton Rouge merchant; leader in the convention efforts for reform and eventual revolt

MANUEL LÓPEZ · Baton Rouge lawyer; the only Spaniard among the revolutionaries, he faced constant tests of his loyalties

JAMES MADISON · President who took West Florida without risking war by inciting the locals to do it for him

JOHN MILLS · Founder of Bayou Sara, leader in the West Florida Convention, and agent to New Orleans

JUAN VENTURA MORALES · Corrupt land speculator; Spanish intendant of Louisiana until 1803; later Spanish intendant of West Florida

JOHN MURDOCH · Bayou Sara civic leader who worked for John Smith and assisted in suppressing the Kemper raids in 1804

JOHN O'CONNOR · Early Bayou Sara settler and alcalde who was kidnapped by the Kempers in 1804 in their effort to take Baton Rouge

ROBERT PERCY • Irish privateer, bombastic blowhard, and alcalde who encouraged resistance to Grand-Pré and Delassus

VICENTE PINTADO • Spain's surveyor general and captain of militia who oversaw response to the Kemper uprising in 1804

EDWARD RANDOLPH • Mississippi speculator and merchant, close friend of the Kempers, and behind-the-scenes revolutionary leader

JOHN RHEA • Storekeeper who became president of the West Florida Convention

FULWAR SKIPWITH • Governor of the brief republic; he threatened to fight before he would allow the republic to be absorbed by the United States

JOHN SMITH • Merchant and politician who brought the Kempers to West Florida and whose feud with Reuben Kemper ignited unrest

ALEXANDER STIRLING • Respected alcalde and militia captain who put down the Kemper revolt of 1804

CHAMPNESS TERRY • West Florida planter and militia leader who played both sides of the field in the years of unrest

PHILEMON THOMAS • Semiliterate storekeeper who led the 1810 capture of Baton Rouge and became general of the republic's army

HARRY TOULMIN • Federal judge of eastern Mississippi who led the effort to prevent American filibusters' attack on Mobile

CATO WEST • Acting governor of Mississippi in 1804; later, political opponent of Claiborne and David Holmes

JAMES WILKINSON • U.S. Army general, spy for Spain, and plotter with Aaron Burr; he later betrayed Burr and others

MARQUÉS DE CASA YRUJO • Spain's ambassador to the United States and later viceroy of Mexico

PREFACE ✦ *Revolutions*

THE ESSENTIAL ingredient in a revolution is the men. So it was with America's second and smallest rebellion. Rarely can any one man be singled out as indispensable, and as with any upheaval, great or small, the men who had precipitated the crisis came to their defining moments more by accident than design. Yet there was a concurrence of events, of time and place, of accidents and intents, that made one man more than any other the father of this second revolution. Surely it would have come about without him. Ironically, after he unwittingly provided the initial spark of unrest and then nurtured that discontent toward an ultimate goal of revolt, his revolution all but happened without him, and he found himself simultaneously lionized as a hero and reviled as a traitor. And all he had meant to do was run a country store.

The turmoil of revolution gave birth to the United States of America and left in the victors an abiding sense of patriotism and pride in their achievement, even though in 1783 the new nation remained the smallest patch on the map of North America. Great Britain claimed vast areas of the north and northwest, and Spain held virtually the rest of the continent. All that unexploited land, and the opportunity that came with it, tantalized Americans. The term *manifest destiny* would not electrify American aspirations for more than half a century yet, but even as the former colonists contemplated their independence with pride and no small degree of amazement, some already envisioned the day when their western boundaries would reach to the distant Pacific.

Not surprisingly, when that Revolutionary War generation passed their heritage to their sons, they gave them an urge to emulate the Founding Fathers in their own times. No sooner was the Revolution over than the more enterprising veterans and their offspring filtered south and west into the unsettled lands, often with the permission and encouragement of European rulers, but sometimes without. Some went to escape failure, or the law, or poverty, or their pasts. Most were hungry for free or cheap land, and some sought the chance to court great fortune in land speculation. Whatever drove them to make the move, they did not go to become Spaniards or Englishmen instead of Americans. They took with them their own customs, and any adaptation they made to their new colonial masters' ways was solely for expedience. Lurking within their personal aspirations was the expectation that these colonies too must one day take shade under the spreading wings of the American eagle.

Revolutions come in all sizes, but most of them are driven by the same imperatives. All that was needed to set alight the inherited ambitions of these sons of 1776 was some real or perceived injustices at the hands of the foreign potentates now sovereign over them. A king's failure to treat an American citizen the way that American expected to be treated in his own United States could be the catalyst for rebellion, especially if the king's actions resulted in the frustration of an individual's ambitions to prosper. It was merely a question of how much injury (real or imagined) these patriots in waiting would bear, and for how long, before they took their fathers' example. A Europe in turmoil thanks to Napoleon — all its countries shifting policies and alliances, so distracted that they could not administer their colonies — created the perfect atmosphere to breed discontent and self-reliance in those provinces. The presence of the new Yankee nation just across an invisible border offered a constant temptation, and men on both sides were enticed to hasten American expansion, with prosperity for all.

Size did not matter. Despite being one of the new nation's smallest territorial acquisitions, Spanish West Florida, especially what would become known as the Florida Parishes, was one of the most significant. It controlled the Mississippi River, and whoever held the Mississippi governed the commerce, settlement, development, and defense of more than half of the continent. Battles had already been fought over it both before and during the recent Revolution, and more battles would come. The United States could not fulfill its manifest destiny without controlling that river. By 1810 all that stood in its way were those Florida Parishes and the crumbling remnants of a once-great empire, but young America was too new and too weak to take it and risk being sucked into Europe's endless wars.

As happened so often in American history, it fell to the men on the scene to shape the young leviathan's course. In Spanish West Florida, the man was that country storekeeper. He was the living incarnation of Americans' conviction that the whole continent must eventually be theirs. More than that, he was the very prototype of the Americans' image of themselves: pious, adventurous, a stickler for honesty and equity; a hard-working, self-made man with the daring to make history. In 1800, no one had heard of storekeeper Reuben Kemper. A decade later, he stood at the forefront of American folk heroes of the spreading Southwest. Though he did not start his revolution all by himself, it might not have begun as it did or when it did if his own very American spirit of independence had not clashed with an ambitious partner, and if more of his customers had just paid their bills.

I

Realm of Happiness

A FLATBOATMAN made an unlikely storekeeper, especially a flatboat-man like Reuben Kemper. Six feet tall, powerfully built, hazel eyes burning from a heavily tanned face beneath brown hair, he looked more like a backwoodsman, and he always felt most at home outdoors in the world of men of action and hard work.[1] He was no roughneck carouser like so many who plied the Ohio and its tributaries on their keelboats and broadhorns, but the life suited him and he never backed down from a fight. Still, he had ambition, education, and enough good sense to know that a boatman's life was nothing but toil with no to-morrow. He never intended to start a revolution.

He had deeply ingrained Christian values. The Kempers were all Presbyterians, and when his uncle James Kemper became the first minister of that denomination in the growing community of Cincin-nati, on the Ohio River, Reuben's father, Peter Kemper, left Fauquier County, Virginia, in 1793 to follow.[2] His five sons, who came with him, were all on the verge of manhood — Reuben, Presley, Samuel, Nathan, and Stephen. Reuben, born February 21, 1773, was the eldest and the one the others looked to as an example all their lives.[3]

The Kempers taught their sons well, and Reuben's literacy was above the average for his time and place. Certainly he and his broth-ers were well versed in Presbyterian dogma, and they helped fund the building of James Kemper's church.[4] Reuben himself may have felt an inclination toward the ministry as a young man, but the pulpit was too confining for his nature.[5] He had not lived long beside the Ohio before the river drew him, and at various times he worked as a flatboat hand or barge hand on the Monongahela, the Allegheny, and the Ohio. In time he had charge of a boat, but first he learned about bookkeeping and commerce from a friend who supplied military quartermasters.[6]

Inevitably, his close association with both the church and the river trade brought Reuben into the orbit of a figure destined to be central to his life; the revolution grew in no small measure from their relationship. John Smith of Virginia was the first Baptist preacher in Ohio. In 1790 the fifty-five-year-old Smith ministered at the Forks of the Cheat River in Monongalia County, Virginia, and then he took a new congregation at Columbia at the mouth of Little Miami River, six miles upstream from Cincinnati. Behind the large man's customarily grave expression, Smith was intelligent, bold, a born leader with intense ambition, and torn in loyalty between church and commerce. At first he worked hard to establish the Baptists in the vicinity, but in 1798 he left the ministry to manage grain mills and mercantile establishments in Cincinnati and nearby Port Royal. There he brought in European manufactures, proudly boasting profits of 100 percent on his investment. He dreamed of land speculations on the lower Mississippi, where he intended to make commercial links for his Cincinnati concerns. Meanwhile he pushed for Ohio's statehood and sought a seat in the legislature of the Northwest Territory, a step to higher office. In 1797 a visitor marveled that Smith seemed to be merchant, farmer, and parson all in one.[7] A year later Smith hired Kemper at fifteen dollars a month to work in Port Royal.[8] It was the first step on the circuitous road to revolution.

At the time Reuben Kemper started keeping Smith's ledgers and accounts, his employer was almost ready to take the bold step of starting a store eight hundred miles downriver, near the Spanish frontier post at Baton Rouge. Merchants in New Orleans faced considerable pains getting goods the one hundred miles upstream to Baton Rouge, but a barge coming from Cincinnati could let the river current do the work and cover sixty miles or more in a day. With Napoleon at war with almost everyone, European goods bound for New Orleans and upriver markets often fell prey to the privateers of several nations. That shortage could work to the advantage of a resourceful merchant like Smith. He planned to fill a flatboat with goods, sell them downriver at his usual 100 percent profit, and then return to Cincinnati in 1799 to take the seat he had won in the Northwest Territory legislature. He could not do it alone, and he decided that his Port Royal clerk Kemper was the man to help him.

That fall Smith prepared a list of goods he believed would sell quickly: linens for clothing; silks for fine gowns and shirts; cotton and silk stockings; buttons; handkerchiefs from India; high-topped shoes; watch chains; fine hats; riding boots and saddles; and ninety pounds of white wig powder for the men who still wore wigs. To furnish the planters' homes, Smith wanted to bring striped chintz for draperies; parlor mirrors and framed pictures; blankets; windowpane glass; china and flatware; candelabra for their tables; and carpets for their floors. He even determined to sell doorbells, fishhooks, and field glasses for leisure, as well as tools for all manner of work and repair. Smith's list essentially declared that rude settlers were not to be his market. His targets were affluent planters with ready cash and credit, and he meant to tempt them with everything they could want.[9]

In January of 1799 Smith gave Kemper cash and credit up to $12,000 — a sum equal to $150,000 two centuries later — and dispatched him to Philadelphia, the great emporium of the East. By February Reuben was filling Smith's order.[10] When he finished in March he had spent £3,555, 2 shillings, and 10 pence, or $9,500.38. Then he consigned the merchandise to a shipper to get it to Port Royal, which cost another $1,000.[11] On his ride back to Cincinnati, Kemper stopped in Zanesville, Ohio, and bought a large flatboat to send ahead to meet him at Port Royal.[12] By early May the flatboat was loaded, and Smith and Kemper commenced the downward passage. There were not many places to visit, and as well supplied as they were, Smith and Kemper had little need to stop. A few days after they entered the Mississippi they came to the boundary of the newly created Mississippi Territory, established just the year before, after Spain's 1795 cession to the United States. No doubt they landed at Natchez, capital of the new territory and a major trade outpost. Even though Smith eyed the Baton Rouge market, he needed to know people in wealthy Natchez as well. He would be cut off from his country in Spanish territory, and his closest link with his home would be Natchez and Governor William C. C. Claiborne.

After Natchez, Kemper and Smith needed another two or three days to reach their destination. Forty land miles south of Natchez they passed Fort Adams, and then they crossed an invisible border at latitude 31° north, the southern boundary of the Mississippi Territory. Andrew Ellicott had recently finished the area's survey, and some called the border by his name — the Ellicott line — but as Smith and Kemper soon learned, everyone who lived in the region knew it simply as "the line." Beyond the line, they entered Spanish West Florida, and before the end of the month they pulled into the east bank and ran into the mouth of Bayou Sara. Smith had been there before, when he had first secured permission to open his business from Governor Carlos de Grand-Pré, commandant and chief magistrate in Baton Rouge. He had already rented a house to use as a temporary store in the little settlement called Bayou Sara.[13]

This was a world very different from Cincinnati. Tiny Bayou Sara sat beside a leisurely stream once known as Bayou Gonorrhea, the origin of that name mercifully forgotten.[14] It lay at the foot of a mile-long crest, atop which, about a mile inland, sat St. Francisville, which the Spaniards had first called New Valencia. Smith chose the location well, for produce came down Bayou Sara from the interior to the only landing amid miles of bluffs. One good road ran from St. Francisville twenty-five miles north to Woodville, Mississippi, and Natchez; a less traveled route led northwest through Pinckneyville just across the line; and another road ran south to Baton Rouge.[15] There was money being made here. A forty-one-year-old New Yorker named John Mills and two others had founded the settlement on the landing in 1785.[16] By 1790 other settlers had come but there were still only a few dozen. Chiefly, planters raised cattle and sold sugar, tobacco, and lumber for market products. Then, in 1794, Eli Whitney patented his cotton gin; this made large-scale cotton planting commercially attractive, and the lower Mississippi saw sudden and dramatic growth. At that time the region around Bayou Sara had 287 inhabitants, more than half of them slaves, working 22,000 arpents — an archaic French measurement equivalent to 0.84628 of an acre — planted in indigo, corn, and cotton. The corn helped to raise and fatten 2,400 head of assorted livestock, much of which were sent to the New Orleans market along with more than five tons of ginned cotton.[17] Planters harvested oranges and pecans from their orchards, as well as hardwoods to sell to

New Orleans builders and boatyards. No wonder Smith the Baptist expected to sell his wares quickly.

When Smith and Kemper arrived, Bayou Sara and the immediate vicinity had forty families totaling a hundred and fifty-five people, with seventy-three slaves. More telling than the numbers of people were their names. Of the heads of families, one was a Spaniard and two were French. The other thirty-seven were American or English, virtually all immigrants.[18] Some Englishmen had come when Great Britain briefly held the territory, and others had arrived as fugitive Tories from the American Revolution; the few Spaniards and Frenchmen had filtered up from New Orleans. To become citizens, they had only to present themselves to the local alcalde or magistrate in order to secure the necessary permission.

Smith and Kemper arrived exactly a century after the French explorer Sieur d'Iberville had founded Baton Rouge, which was nestled on a bluff overlooking the Mississippi. Since 1763, it had been the administrative center of the region called West Florida, which the Spaniards divided into four districts. Bayou Sara sat in Feliciana, which meant "realm of happiness"; it was bounded by the Mississippi on the west, the Ellicott line on the north, the Amite River, which ran north to south, forty miles to the east, and a notional line between the Mississippi and the Amite some ten miles south of the Bayou Sara landing. Below that line was the district of Baton Rouge, which ran south along the Mississippi some fifty miles to the Bayou Manchac and east to the Amite. Across the Amite lay the much larger St. Helena District, extending all the way from the Mississippi line to Bayou Manchac, and eastward an average of more than thirty miles to the Tangipahoa River. Beyond the Tangipahoa lay the largest district of all, St. Ferdinand, stretching east to the Pearl River and south to Lake Pontchartrain. Springfield, on the Natalbany River, was the only real settlement in St. Helena, as almost all of the settlers lived in Feliciana and Baton Rouge, with clusters of isolated planters on the rivers in the other districts.[19]

Europe's wars and empires wrote their history on the region. La Salle claimed the Mississippi River and the vast regions in its basin for France, calling it Louisiana after his king. By the early 1700s the

French had established a few settlements on the lower river and one at Natchitoches in the borderlands two hundred miles northwest of the future Baton Rouge, but they put their colonial capital at Mobile, on the large bay of the same name at the mouth of the Mobile and Alabama rivers. In 1718 they founded New Orleans, and four years later they moved their capital to that growing city. As the century's conflicts wore on, France, Britain, and Spain traded titles in the region. At the end of the American Revolution, the territory from the Apalachicola River eastward, including the Florida peninsula, was Spanish East Florida. The Apalachicola west to the Mississippi became Spanish West Florida; Spain also held all of Louisiana west of the great river, as well as the future Mississippi Territory.[20]

When the American Revolution ended, in 1783, perhaps as many as eight thousand British fugitives from what had been the American colonies lived there. The Spanish acquisition frightened most of them away, but about three thousand stayed and found a rather benign regime. Spain allowed — even invited — Anglo settlers to apply for grants of good land or to purchase it from current landowners. The applicant had to swear fealty to Spain and profess Catholicism, the latter a requirement that was rarely if ever enforced. Grand-Pré awarded the grants, then authorized his chief surveyor, Captain Vicente Pintado, to perform a survey once the grantee had picked a plot of vacant land. The average grant was 644 arpents, but it went as high as 800 for a large family, the intent being to create a settled population that could support and protect itself. The settlers had to occupy and improve their land for at least four years, which discouraged speculation; grantees also had to serve in a militia. After improving his first grant, a landowner could apply for another. With a secured title, the land could be sold, usually for one peso — a dollar — an arpent, with an average purchase of about 240 arpents. Some people grew sizable holdings, and by 1805 most farms ranged from 31 arpents to 2,000.[21]

Some of the new Spanish grants carelessly overlapped earlier British grants that Madrid had promised to honor.[22] The usual corruption that appeared in any remote colonial administration made the situation worse. Rumors of extortion clung to Juan Ventura Morales, the temporary Spanish intendant, or governor, in New Orleans; Spain sometimes placed bored functionaries, men too lazy or venal to secure better posts elsewhere, in Louisiana and West Florida.[23] Applicants who had gone to Morales for land grants told of his demanding bribes, and surveyor Isaac Johnson threatened to resign in 1799, telling Pintado that he no longer wished to deal with the intendant, as "I am thirty years too old to be fond of such politicks."[24]

Most officials sought honest, equitable solutions to title problems, even if it meant giving new grants on vacant lands to those with conflicting claims elsewhere. The result was the spread of a dynamic planter economy in which everyone raised something, many built some fortune, and a few acquired great wealth. Spain's goal was not so much a happy population but rather a well-settled buffer to protect against the raiding Plains Indians to the north and west of Natchitoches and the new American nation flexing its muscles to the east.

Certainly the Americans eyed West Florida. No sooner did Britain cede it to Spain, in 1783, than the new United States offered to buy it for one million dollars.[25] Virginia, North Carolina, and Georgia claimed western borders on the Mississippi River. It seemed natural that sooner or later the rest of that territory should belong to the new nation. In fact, in 1795, by the Treaty of San Lorenzo, Spain acknowledged the claim of the United States to what became the Mississippi Territory: everything between the Mississippi and the Atlantic and from the Ohio to the Gulf, except the Floridas. Spain had minimal interest in East Florida at the moment, but West Florida controlled the lower Mississippi and the rich New Orleans market. The province was of little significance compared with Mexico or Texas, and Spain maintained it as a defensive buffer to protect Texas. As early as 1795 Madrid considered selling it, but not to America.[26] There were beginning to be too many Americans there already.

Two of them at Bayou Sara now had a storehouse that bulged with all the goods they had brought down the river. On June 1, 1799, their temporary emporium opened to the anticipated floods of customers. They did not come.

A boom had seen land prices rise to three pesos an arpent by 1799, but forces already at work soon halved that. In Feliciana land values did not share the drop but remained static. That made planters conservative about the discretionary and luxury goods Smith and Kemper offered. Uncertainty over Europe increased their caution. Napoleon was building an empire, and Spanish Louisiana and West Florida could again become pawns in his bargaining. French Creoles living in West Florida gave planters concern, as did English settlers hoping for Britain to regain its lost territory. With that much unease, planters husbanded their pesos more than usual, waiting to see how Europe's politics played out.

More immediately, Smith's commitment to 100 percent profits probably slowed sales, and his impatient nature did not help. He had expected to sell his merchandise within two weeks, but by early June goods were not moving fast enough, and Smith decided to leave Kemper in charge of the store while he returned to Ohio. To ensure that Kemper had an incentive, Smith proposed a partnership. He valued his merchandise at about twelve thousand pesos, and in return for Kemper's time and effort, he offered to share profits from its sale.[27] For twenty-eight-year-old Kemper, the prospect of earning several thousand dollars to remain in the Feliciana must have seemed too good to be true. He could make enough to become a planter or even to set up his own store back home in Cincinnati.

On June 12 the two framed a three-year partnership whereby Kemper was to sell the stock and then pay Smith from the proceeds half the actual cost of the goods, half what it had cost to get the stock to Cincinnati, and half of the expenses of running the store. Kemper was also to pay Smith eight hundred dollars to settle his own and his brother Nathan's open accounts at the Port Royal store. After that, all profits and losses were to be shared equally, and Smith anticipated sending more merchandise downriver once Kemper sold most of this first shipment. Smith even suggested calling the partnership Reuben Kemper and Company.[28]

The customers came, but not enough of them, and far too many did not pay for what they bought. On the frontier, most mercantile businesses were run on credit, and Kemper and Company was no different. Nathan and Samuel came to help Reuben run the store, and as the seasons passed the ledger showed sales, but most of them on account.[29] Some buyers paid in cash, but the Kempers carried more than 140 customers on credit, virtually all of them Americans. Among them the Kempers made friendships important in future years — Bayou Sara founders John Mills and John O'Connor, neighbors such as Colonel

Frederick Kimball, and Isaac Johnson, an alcalde — a kind of magistrate — who founded Troy plantation.[30] Padre Francisco Lénnàn of Baton Rouge and Father Charles Burke of Point Coupée across the Mississippi also charged with them.[31]

Kemper kept the flatboat, expecting to need it when business got better.[32] In January of 1800 he bought a forty-year-old Negro woman, which had to be an extravagance with just the three brothers in the household.[33] Then on March 25 Reuben signed a mortgage with his customer Armand Duplantier for 1,260 pesos to purchase 630 arpents nearby, bounding Bayou Sara on the north and the Mississippi on the west. It was an ideal location for the river trade, but Kemper had only nine months to pay the debt.[34] Kemper was not being prudent, and barely three weeks after he had bought the land, John Smith appeared.[35] Tired of waiting for his money, Smith had decided to close the partnership. After posting public declarations, Smith petitioned on April 24 for a dissolution. As of July 24, allowing for the notice period, Kemper had to cease doing business on Smith's behalf.[36]

Smith's action was not necessarily meant to be punitive. In fact, he retained the Kempers as employees to run the store and liquidate the partnership's assets, a muddy arrangement requiring Kemper to account for sales of goods from the partnership separately from those sold solely on behalf of Smith. It took three months for alcalde John O'Connor and Mills to inventory the assets and liabilities of the defunct firm.[37] Then O'Connor took charge of all of the assets and books of the partnership and turned them over to Isaac Johnson's son John H. Johnson, and all remaining inventory reverted to Smith. Johnson was to get a proper evaluation of the goods and collect the debts owed to the partnership for the benefit of its creditors, and then he would split any remaining balance between Smith and Kemper, though Reuben had little hope of realizing profits.[38] Still, over the winter the Kempers came to a new agreement with Smith. In February of 1801, before John Smith returned to Ohio to sit in the territorial legislature, he bought 240 acres on Bayou Sara next to O'Connor's farm and two months later sold it to Reuben and Nathan.[39] Smith employed them to sell some of his remaining goods unconnected with the old partnership and perhaps to market timber from the property.[40]

In September Reuben bought a *barcaza*, or barge, and the brothers went into business in what Reuben thought was a small way, using Smith's property and their own new parcel. Reuben and Nathan were both able river men. They could use Smith's storehouse; one of them would take a cargo downriver to New Orleans and return hauling cargo for their neighbors and goods to sell in their store, while the other would run the store itself. When Nathan married Nancy Whitaker, on July 24, 1801, Reuben took over the *barcaza* full-time so his brother could stay with his new wife.[41] He named the barge *Cotton-Picker* and made several trips a year down the Mississippi past Baton Rouge, and also up to Natchez.[42] They also sold timber from their land and had to appeal to Grand-Pré to protect them from neighbors who poached their trees and thieves who broke into their house and storeroom during their absences.[43]

For the next two years the brothers made a living but neglected Smith's affairs. Then in September of 1802 another store opened a few miles from Bayou Sara. John Rhea was rumored to be an Irishman but had lived in America for years before coming to West Florida. He owned a nearby plantation and in 1802 was an alcalde in his area, a peaceful man who liked the quiet of his family and his farm.[44] His store drew business away from the Kempers.[45]

Reuben was pursuing unpaid accounts as far away as Natchez and New Orleans, with few results.[46] Still, he made useful business acquaintances in the latter, most notably the Irish-born land speculator and politician Daniel Clark, an early settler in the city who had a thousand arpents in West Florida and plans for acquiring many more.[47]

There in New Orleans Reuben saw firsthand the latest effects of Europe's constant turmoil and its ramifications not just for Louisiana, but for his own Feliciana and West Florida. In October of 1800 Napoleon pressured Spain to cede Louisiana back to France, without specifying the territory's precise boundaries. Bonaparte promised not to sell Louisiana to any third party, but then war with Britain prevented Napoleon from taking possession. By late 1801 the retrocession of Louisiana became an open secret, presenting the new president, Thomas Jefferson, with a serious problem. He believed that anyone possessing Louisiana became America's natural foe. Spain was difficult enough to deal with, but it was crumbling under Napoleon's eagles. France represented an entirely different sort of threat.

All of this kept the smoky coffeehouses of New Orleans buzzing. Then on October 18, Juan Ventura Morales, the Spanish intendant of Louisiana, suspended the right of Americans to deposit their goods on New Orleans' wharves for shipment, a blow to merchants and planters all the way up the Mississippi and Ohio. Just two months later and on orders from the intendant general in Cuba, Carlos de Grand-Pré, the Spanish commandant of the four western districts, prohibited commerce between inhabitants of West Florida and U.S. citizens. Americans still freely navigated the Mississippi to get produce to New Orleans, but now those flatboats could not stop or sell goods in West Florida and had to transfer their cargoes directly to American vessels in New Orleans without landing so much as a hogshead on the wharf. Outraged voices in Washington called for retaliation. "If this be peace, God give us war," cried one congressman, who declared that the only question was whether it would be "a bloodless war of a few months, or the carnage of years."[48]

Jefferson hoped to avoid war but he wanted the territory and its control of the Mississippi, and he sent Robert Livingston to France to pursue a sale. A concurrent issue was whether West Florida would be included in the cession, since France understood Louisiana to include the Floridas while Spain maintained that it did not.[49] Without West Florida, however, there would be no secure American hold on both banks of the lower Mississippi. Initially, Livingston and Jefferson's secretary of state James Madison had assured the president that the Floridas were French and that they could negotiate a single price for everything.[50] All diplomacy is murky, however, and both French and Spanish authorities subsequently adopted shifting positions. By March of 1803 Napoleon was receptive to American pressure for a purchase, and on April 30 the United States acquired a territory called Louisiana for $11,250,000. Jefferson still did not know if it included the Floridas, so he sent James Monroe to Spain to negotiate for them separately.[51] The issue soon became so electric that French negotiators warned Monroe and Livingston that their even mentioning Florida would cause problems with Spain. In August Jefferson spoke of West

Florida "whensoever it may be rightfully obtained," indicating that it was acceptable to wait and press the issue later. With the constantly shifting canvas of European politics, another opportunity might well arise when Spain would feel more amenable.[52]

People in New Orleans believed that West Florida was part of the Louisiana territory, since they remembered that it had been before 1763.[53] Reuben Kemper's view of the issue was probably much the same, especially since by this time events in his own orbit had left him irrevocably opposed to Spain and all things Spanish. He had ignored John Smith for too long. Now a senator for the new state of Ohio, Smith heard from friends in West Florida that his business was not being well managed. He petitioned the commandant Grand-Pré to appoint arbiters to examine the accounts kept by the Kempers, which the commandant did. Practice called for both litigants to nominate arbiters, but Reuben stalled, and Smith suspected that Kemper's absences in Natchez and New Orleans were his means of evading Grand-Pré's orders.[54] For his part, Reuben felt Smith's claims were unjust and that Smith had too much influence with Grand-Pré. Acting on that belief, he reasoned that if he delayed a decision until after the American takeover of the territory of Louisiana, which Kemper expected would include West Florida, then an American court would give him a fairer hearing. He also relied on the custom dictating that disputes over amounts larger than a hundred pesos were not decided by the local governor but had to go to a higher authority.[55]

When Smith returned to West Florida in April of 1803 and Reuben had still not chosen arbiters, Grand-Pré allowed Smith to name them all himself. Naturally Smith chose friends, such as Isaac Johnson and surveyor Ira C. Kneeland. Johnson headed the panel and showed some concern for Kemper's interests.[56] Kneeland, however — though he was an honest man — got along with few of the Americans and feuded for over a year with the Kempers' friend and neighbor Frederick Kimball.[57] Hence it is not surprising that the tribunal found in Smith's favor. On August 20 Grand-Pré ordered Kemper to pay $5,807 and as a partial settlement gave Smith a writ for Reuben's own 240 acres. Grand-Pré gave the Kempers seven or eight months to vacate Smith's property.[58] Before leaving to assume his Senate seat,

Smith authorized local civic leader John Murdoch to take the Kempers' land.[59]

Reuben Kemper protested the entire proceeding. His specific complaint with the monetary settlement is hazy, but it was probably due to the valuation of the partnership's property. Attachment of his 240 acres was worse. He blamed Smith, but he blamed Grand-Pré and the arbiters, particularly Kneeland, even more. His reasoning is cloudy regarding the surveyor; he may have suspected Kneeland of showing favoritism, accepting bribes, or coveting Reuben's timber, but whatever the case, Kemper later characterized the surveyor's actions as "unworthy."[60] From this time forward Kemper blamed the Spaniards for putting him out of business.[61] He felt a keen and unyielding sense of justice. Years later, at the close of Reuben Kemper's life, one of his close friends remarked that he was "as sincere in his attachments as he was implacable in his resentment, when he felt that he had been injured or betrayed." And Kemper's resentment "was always felt by those against whom it was directed."[62] While Smith left for Washington having collected barely two hundred pesos, the Kempers faced ruin.[63] Reuben still had the *Cotton-Picker* and could move on, but Nathan had a wife and a nine-month-old son.[64] Since Nathan was not a party to the Smith dispute, his property would be safe from attachment, so in October he applied for his own thousand-arpent grant.[65]

In November Reuben went to New Orleans to pay a debt, which put him in place to witness the handover of Louisiana.[66] Jefferson had instructed William Claiborne, the governor of Orleans Territory, and General James Wilkinson to receive the property, but they could not arrive before France's Pierre Laussat took over from Spain, and Jefferson feared that in the interim the Creoles might try to frustrate the transfer. Late in October he suggested that Laussat and American consul Daniel Clark raise volunteers to prevent any interference.[67] Claiborne warned that a recent Caribbean slave revolt might inspire the slaves in New Orleans to seize the opportunity presented by a power vacuum.[68] Clark believed he could raise three hundred reliable men, and he began, as all American business began in New Orleans, at George King's coffeehouse, where Clark enlisted King, Kemper, merchant Benjamin Morgan, and others. He soon had between two and three hundred, virtually all of them family men except the perpetual bachelor Kemper.[69] Pinning black cockades to their hats as badges of uniform, they presented themselves to preserve order.[70] On the appointed day, they formed on the Place d'Arms while the Spanish military formed on the opposite side, and they observed the peaceful turnover. The next three nights they remained alert, and thereafter stood day and night guard. Several days of parties followed, and Kemper perhaps overenjoyed himself, for illness confined him until Claiborne and Wilkinson arrived to take possession of the territory on December 20.[71]

There was policy in Reuben's assistance in the peaceful transition. Almost certainly he acquainted himself with Claiborne and with Wilkinson, who for the moment would be governor of the new territory. Like most Americans, Kemper believed the territory included West Florida, but Jefferson had settled for a passive assertion of ownership while allowing the Spaniards to remain in possession, a policy that left the American inhabitants of the province rather uncertain. That was not a problem for most of them, for the Spanish administration suited them well enough, but the Kempers were very unhappy indeed. Claiborne and Wilkinson could probably occupy the weakly defended districts without opposition. If they did, then a more favorable American administration could overturn Grand-Pré's ruling and return their property. But the United States had to move quickly, for by the time Claiborne and Wilkinson arrived, the Kemper brothers had barely four months left to decide if they should abandon their Bayou Sara home or put themselves directly in confrontation with Spain.

Instead, Jefferson did not move at all, and Spain moved even slower than before. Though they lifted the bans on trade with American vessels, the Spaniards felt surrounded by the Americans above the line, west of the river, and below them in New Orleans. Knowing that virtually all of those Yankees also wanted West Florida only increased Grand-Pré's uneasiness, and more worrying than that were fears that the Americans in his province felt the same.[72] Spain was about to learn the danger of encouraging American settlers. They might be loyal only as it suited them, and efforts to halt more settlement could arouse the ire of those already there. Once opened, West Florida would be hard to close.

Some Americans had already caused problems with Spain's surveyors. Arthur Cobb, hotheaded friend and neighbor of the Kempers, threatened Kneeland, calling him a "damned rascal & lyar," adding that he and Pintado could both "go to hell."[73] Cobb's brother William tormented another surveyor until the man complained that "my Head is greatly deranged upon acct. of the way that I am perplexed by Cobb."[74] In such an atmosphere, getting any surveys done was difficult.[75] One surveyor spent so much time in the swamps that he quipped, "I am becoming I believe amphibious."[76] Worse, some settlers refused to obtain surveys, saying that no Spaniard should trespass on their property, and they petitioned Washington to guarantee their titles, which showed who they thought would soon be in charge.[77] Delays on surveys angered landowners who were awaiting clear title to sell, and as a result some surveyors feared for their safety; one received death threats.[78] In retaliation, in the fall of 1802, Grand-Pré backed off on grants.[79] At the same time Pintado called a near halt to surveys and further ordered his surveyors not to survey any claims subject to litigation.[80]

It seemed a poor time for Nathan Kemper to apply for a grant, but he got his thousand arpents, land on the Comite River that he had no intention of living on, for in January he leased it with the proviso that if he wished he could move to the land himself.[81] The proviso may have been a means of making sure he had a place to live if he and Samuel left Bayou Sara, though April of 1804 came and Grand-Pré's deadline to evict them from their property passed. The *Cotton-Picker* kept Reuben away for weeks at a time barging between New Orleans and Natchez, and even up the Red River to Natchitoches two hundred miles west of Baton Rouge, but surely he stopped occasionally to see his brothers.[82] May came and Smith's agent Murdoch still did nothing, so the Kempers remained with no other apparent plans.

If the Kempers hoped for action by Washington, they hoped in vain. Claiborne saw the American inhabitants of West Florida becoming restless under Spanish rule and sensed a desire for American annexation.[83] Though most of the Spanish *soldados* in New Orleans left by early April, the boundary commissioner, the Marqués de Casa Calvo, and his personal guard remained, a foreign presence that irritated Americans.[84] Claiborne and Wilkinson reiterated that the failure to press the West Florida issue did not mean the United States had abandoned its claim.[85] Officially Washington would act as if West Florida belonged to it while doing nothing overt to take the province.[86] Claiborne suspected that the local inhabitants might just do it for themselves.

Carlos de Grand-Pré missed none of this in Baton Rouge. His administrative capital sat on the first high ground north of New Orleans, a bluff thirty to forty feet above the river at high water, regarded by some as the finest town site on the Mississippi below Memphis.[87] It was hardly the finest town. A visitor described Baton Rouge as "a dirty little town of 60 cabins crowded together in a narrow street"; half a dozen better frame houses lay scattered over a plain surrounded by woods. Another visitor thought it "a right French" village, every other house being a shop selling bread, tobacco, pumpkins, rum, and the like. A Frenchman and an Irishman kept two good stores, and a widow operated the best inn, serving an excellent gumbo at her table, where the conversation ran a babble of French, Spanish, English, and "American."[88]

Fort San Carlos sat on a plain north of the village, commanding a long view of the riverbanks to the south.[89] Visitors disagreed on the shape of the bastion, perhaps because it needed constant repair. A Frenchman thought it a symmetrical six-pointed star.[90] Pintado saw the fort as a multi-angular three-sided affair entirely open on its river face. The Spaniards depended on the height of the bluff to deter any assault from the river, and thus nothing but a thin palisade of pickets protected that side.[91] In fact the ramparts were just earth from a ditch, or fosse, that surrounded the land side, with a stockade of pickets set vertically into the top. A number of small cannon, many of them in poor repair, covered both the river and the outer approaches. After forty years of peace, the Spaniards had neither the resources nor the inclination to maintain the works, and more than one visitor came away thinking it could not withstand a determined foe.[92]

Grand-Pré had perhaps two hundred *soldados* and militia to garrison Baton Rouge.[93] About ten miles southeast at Galveztown, at the confluence of the Iberville and Amite rivers, he had another small fort with only a dozen *soldados* and a few rusted old cannon.[94] Grand-Pré himself typified the tangled history of the region. French by birth, he remained and transferred allegiance in 1783 when Spain took over West Florida, and thereafter held several administrative posts. He arrived in Baton Rouge as governor of the four districts at almost the same time as Reuben Kemper, and he involved himself in the community as a citizen as well as an administrator. He made friendships, engaged in civic affairs, and raised eleven children, several of whom married Americans, and was easygoing, fair in his administration, and popular. His superior Vicente Folch, governor of West Florida in Pensacola, thought him lax, but Grand-Pré better understood the tenor of the people in his domain and helped them as he could, especially after the Louisiana Purchase left him governing a mostly American community surrounded by American territory.

Despite a few American complaints, in 1804 justice in West Florida was more equitable than in most places. Syndics dealt locally with civil cases, with Grand-Pré as a first court of appeal, but citizens could appeal to Cuba, then Madrid, and ultimately to the king. All criminal cases tried in an alcalde's court could be appealed to a governor's court.[95] Distant garrison commandants held court on suits for sums under fifty pesos, and precedent suggested that even Grand-Pré's authority did not extend beyond a hundred pesos. The accused had a right to question his accuser and witnesses.[96] Both parties in civil cases paid for the court's time, with fees for every decree and document, and those petty fees could accumulate without limit until even the victor found little left to him.[97] Some of the cases challenged fair judgment, often involving feuds like Kimball's with Kneeland.[98] Though legend depicted Spanish justice as corrupt and inefficient, it functioned well given the time and place and caused no discontent in 1804.[99] In fact, Claiborne found that Americans preferred the Spanish approach to the jury system.[100]

Little criminal activity troubled Grand-Pré prior to 1804, though with U.S. military posts not far above the line, deserters fleeing to West Florida presented a growing problem from 1800 onward. Havana wanted them arrested, but planters recoiled from reporting fellow Americans until early 1801, when deserters committed a rash of armed robberies and Grand-Pré had to raise militia to put down the "Dysorder & Scandal."[101] Thereafter deserters and criminals from above the line committed half of the robberies and virtually all arson, murder, and attempted murder in West Florida.[102] In February of 1802, when Reuben Kemper discovered a corpse in a road, the possibility existed that the man had met death by violent means. After 1803, more miscreants fled to the enclosed borderland, and violent crime increased fivefold.[103] The proximity of foreign borders encouraged West Florida's own criminals to flee, and the government's failure to apprehend a felon was a source of resentment when an American's property had been stolen.[104]

Grand-Pré also faced a problem with the introduction of more slaves, for the slave uprising at San Domingue in 1791 raised fears everywhere.[105] The proportion of African-born slaves in West Florida gave cause for concern, for they were considered more rebellious than second-generation slaves. Yet slave owners were among the wealthiest men in West Florida by 1803, holding more than twenty times the capital wealth of non–slave owners.[106] Consequently Grand-Pré balanced concern for security with the interests of his more influential citizens.

Grand-Pré's authority extended east only to the St. Helena and St. Ferdinand districts, where the Pearl, Tchefuncte, Tangipahoa, Natalbany, Amite, and Iberville rivers ran southerly into Lakes Pontchartrain and Maurepas, putting settlers there in easier reach of the New Orleans market than settlers in Feliciana were, though their plantations paled compared with St. Francisville's. East of the Pearl, extending to the Apalachicola, the country was wild, sparsely settled, and unruly. One visitor described the settlers as "poor and indolent, devoted to raising cattle, hunting, and drinking whiskey." The people impressed travelers as a wild race of few morals.[107] No more than twelve hundred people lived along the Tombigbee, cut off from Natchez by more than two hundred miles of wilderness.[108] In April of 1804 one local predicted "they will naturally become a banditti, fugitives from justice, and disturbers, of the peace."[109] They were "illiterate, wild and savage, of depraved morals, unworthy of public confidence or private esteem; litigious, disunited, and knowing each other, universally distrustful of each other."[110]

Only two real towns broke an expanse that stretched almost three hundred miles. Pensacola became West Florida's capital after the Spaniards left New Orleans, but it had little to offer. Vicente Folch, governor of Spanish West Florida, doubled as both mayor of the town and its provincial governor, enjoying neither job. With white women scarce, as attested to by there being only sixty-one married white men in the community, the four hundred white bachelors in town had little to do, meaning Governor Folch was not the only frustrated man in town.[111] The other community was Mobile, forty miles west of Pensacola on a wide and deep bay fed by the Mobile and Alabama rivers, and thereby much the more populated and prosperous settlement. Navigable streams from the interior of the Mississippi Territory brought produce down to market, while bay shipping sent consumer goods upstream, but the planters and consumers above the line lived in American territory; Mobile was Spanish. All trade depended on the goodwill of the Spaniards. People in the Mississippi Territory believed the Mobile District was included in the Louisiana Purchase, while Americans in the district were at odds with the Spaniards. American posts at Fort Stoddert on the Mobile, six miles above the line, and Fort St. Stephens, another thirty miles upstream, tried to keep peace.

Tempers flared when the Spaniards began stopping American vessels and charging duties on cargoes passing through. Claiborne predicted in April that "these proceedings will tend to settle the claim of the United States to West Florida or rather bring it to a speedy issue."[112] Meanwhile Claiborne acted as if West Florida already belonged to the United States and tried to establish its post offices, starting with Baton Rouge. Folch warned him that such an act would be an outrage and that anyone attempting to do that must look to the consequences.[113] Washington advised Claiborne to appoint Spaniards to be his postmasters, thinking that would be seen as conciliatory even while it exercised American authority.[114] Claiborne was more concerned about some of the Americans flocking to the new country. "Many adventurers who are daily coming into the Territory from every quarter, possess revolutionary principles and restless, turbulent dispositions," he warned Jefferson that May. "These Men will for some years give trouble," and "a few designing intriguing men may easily excite some inquietude in the public mind."[115]

Claiborne soon concluded that one of those intriguing men was Daniel Clark. There was a fortune to be made in land speculation, and Clark expected Claiborne and Wilkinson to help him. Wilkinson was every bit as venal as Clark, eminently corruptible, and he already had a history of playing America and Spain against each other for his personal gain, despite being a senior general in the U.S. Army. Clark gathered around himself a group of like-minded professional men whom Claiborne's brother referred to as "a certain insidious Junto," but Claiborne made it clear that he would not be a party to their schemes.[116] He told Jefferson that Clark had more capacity for good and ill than any other man in the province, but "he pants for power."[117] The fact that Reuben Kemper was Clark's friend could have suggested to Claiborne that Kemper was part of that "Junto." Even if Reuben was not, subsequent events demonstrated to Claiborne and Grand-Pré that the Kempers were just the sort of men who would bring trouble to West Florida.

2

Kemper & His Madly Deluded Party

AT THE END of May 1804, the Kempers' deadline for leaving the Bayou Sara property had passed, and Nathan and Samuel showed no sign of leaving.[1] In fact, that month one of the brothers borrowed a box of carpenter's tools, in particular planes for making cornice moldings, showing a determination not only to stay, but to decorate the house.[2] Neither John Murdoch, the man John Smith authorized to take over the Kempers' land, nor John H. Johnson, who was to evaluate the Kempers' assets, moved quickly on the business, and neither cooperated with the other.[3] John Smith returned in late April to get an order from Grand-Pré for Johnson to produce all the partnership's documents, but Johnson, who told Pintado that "I do not court the smiles or fear the frowns of any man," took his time complying.[4] He was probably preoccupied that month by the sale of his own Feliciana store for fifteen thousand pesos to the acquisitive Daniel Clark.[5]

This endless delay proved too much for Smith, and in May he petitioned Grand-Pré to remove the Kempers immediately, before Smith returned to Washington for the late fall session of Congress.[6] The governor complied, and on June 13 he decreed that Nathan was to vacate immediately and gave the order to alcalde Alexander Stirling to be served. If Nathan refused to comply, Stirling was authorized to arrest him. A fifty-one-year-old Scotsman, Stirling had previously lived some years in Point Coupée, where he married the widow Ann Alston. He later moved to Thompson's Creek in West Florida and at this point lived at his twenty-thousand-acre plantation, called Egypt, five miles north of St. Francisville; his thirty-six-year-old brother-in-law

Solomon Alston lived there with him. He was a sublieutenant in the militia and one of the most respected men in the area.[7]

Grand-Pré authorized Stirling to take an armed party, and clearly Stirling knew or had heard enough about Nathan's stubbornness that he applied to Pintado to furnish the necessary men and a militia officer.[8] Nathan had put out word that he would not leave and intended to defend himself and his property.[9] More than that, he summoned several friends, and together they barricaded the house at Bayou Sara. They were young men, most if not all of them under the age of thirty, and few besides Nathan were married, a prime prescription for impetuosity.[10] Precisely what the Kempers expected to accomplish is unclear, but they probably counted on American neighbors in the militia to balk at supporting the Spaniards against fellow countrymen. Thus, both parties were surprised when late that same day, June 13, Stirling and his twenty militiamen appeared at Bayou Sara.

When the alcalde arrived he saw all the doors and windows closed and barred. Nathan stepped out onto the high veranda carrying a rifle and demanded to know Stirling's business. Four other men stood on the veranda, all armed, and one pointed his rifle at Stirling. The Scotsman boldly ordered them to leave the house. At that, Samuel Kemper, backed by four other armed men, said they would fight before they left.[11] The Kempers now had at least a dozen men, including Basil Abrams, several of them customers and all of them friends, but they were no doubt chagrined to see the number of Americans who had come forth to assist the alcalde.[12]

Stirling had orders to arrest but not to attack, and seeing that the house was too strongly defended for him to take without his party's suffering casualties, he withdrew and established a patrol around the vicinity, hoping to catch the insurgents in the open if they tried to escape. Then another band of militia, led by Armand Duplantier, who had sold Reuben the property in the first place, arrived in the night. At this point, the "boys in the house," as Reuben Kemper called them, slipped out into the darkness and made their way north to cross safely above the line to Pinckneyville, seething and no doubt embarrassed that Grand-Pré had had no trouble finding sufficient Americans to aid in their eviction.

The Kempers decided to ride back into West Florida almost immediately. Their ultimate purpose was still apparently undefined, but they took time to consider some premise other than simple revenge. Nathan and Samuel determined to capitalize on the widespread feeling that the province had always been a part of Louisiana and that the United States would take it over. If the Kempers told people that they had authorization from Claiborne, the governor of Orleans Territory, they might persuade many to join their group and thus bluff Grand-Pré out of evicting them. One or two men in New Orleans had recently claimed they had seen a letter from Jefferson that said he would send support if the West Florida settlers raised the American flag. There was nothing to the report, but here rumors counted as facts, and the brothers hoped to start a groundswell that would intimidate the Spaniards into leaving.[13]

In New Orleans, Reuben learned of Stirling's abortive eviction attempt, and he sent the alcalde a letter chiding Stirling for trying to take his land at Bayou Sara. The tribunal's award of the property to Smith was invalid and corrupt, he argued, and Grand-Pré lacked the authority to approve a judgment exceeding a hundred pesos. Stirling found the letter threatening, and he turned it over to Grand-Pré; he thought it "insolent and bold" and complained of Reuben's contempt for his authority.[14] The letter was part of Reuben's tactic of delay. He and many others expected the United States to claim possession soon. He called on Claiborne, probably reminding the governor of his service with the volunteers, to ensure a peaceful transition of Louisiana. If Kemper mentioned the judgment against himself, Claiborne would have told him that he intended to regard rulings by Spanish courts as nonbinding on a U.S. court after a "change of dominion." If a Spanish judgment was delayed until the territory changed hands, he would refuse to honor it unless confirmed by an American court.[15]

All the Kempers had to do was continue delaying and never recognize the justice of Grand-Pré's tribunal. Claiborne gave Reuben some advice when they met, and it may have included his expectation that sooner or later West Florida would fall into the Louisiana Territory. Certainly the governor made no commitment on behalf of the United States, but Reuben perhaps implied to his brothers that such would be the result. Nothing suggests that the Kempers had a fixed determination to foment rebellion or to call on their countrymen to rise against Spain, nor that they had any idea of an eventual takeover by the United States. They were just angry and vengeful. The Kempers' claim of Claiborne's backing was simply an expedient to keep Americans in Feliciana from resisting them.[16]

Early on the morning of June 16, Nathan and Samuel and the others rode back undetected across the line to Bayou Sara, evidently with no purpose other than to release frustration and get even with anyone who crossed them. John Mills, the founder of Bayou Sara, went there that morning for some business with a man who lived in a rented cottage on the Kemper property, and they and two other men were talking in the front room when Nathan Kemper unexpectedly stepped inside, armed virtually to the teeth. A dagger hung from his belt, and a pistol was tucked into his waistband. The handle of a long butcher knife poked from a fold in his shirt, and in his hand he carried a rifle. He walked up to Mills and called him a "liar, Scoundrel, & villain," upbraiding him for interfering in his business. Mills asked just what he had done, and Nathan said he had done too much, including advising people who stopped at the landing not to go to the Kempers' store. Mills bravely admitted that he had done so because Nathan had not left the place by April and thus was in rebellion against the government. Mills felt it his duty as a syndic of the district to advise people not to trade with those who defied the law. At that, Kemper called him a rascal, declaring that were it not for his fondness for Mills's family, he would have "corrected" him some time since. Nathan did nothing more than bluster, and then he left, but as soon as he had gone Mills immediately wrote to notify the alcalde Pintado of the episode, expressing some fear that he might hear from Kemper again.[17]

The Kempers and their followers occupied their old house and remained in the area that day and the next, clearly preparing for a fight. The house stood eight feet above the ground on pilings for protection from high water, an elevation affording an advantage in defending against an assault. They borrowed or demanded firearms at nearby homes, and some neighbors aided them by riding into the country at night to collect more. On Sunday, June 18, they openly cast lead bullets and cleaned their weapons, obviously wanting word of their preparations to intimidate those who might come against them. Late that night news of this reached Stirling, and he called for Pintado to send military force to subdue them, though unless Pintado had a cannon to intimidate the insurgents, Stirling feared an attack would be bloody. Stirling heard rumors that the Kempers' followers were many and determined, leaving the loyal people in the vicinity alarmed and apprehensive.[18]

Stirling sent local planter Champness Terry and three militiamen to ride through the nearby settlements to stop any suspicious persons on the roads, and John Smith, still in West Florida, carried the order. If a person did not satisfactorily explain himself, Terry was to arrest him. Thereafter Terry and two others rotated patrols, sending Stirling reports at the end of each day.[19] On June 19 one of the patrols stationed at the Bayou Sara bridge captured some of the Kempers' outriders, and John Mills rode to the bridge under Pintado's orders to take custody and escort the men to Stirling's plantation. Mills had just reached the bridge, shortly before 10:00 A.M., when the Kempers' band suddenly rushed out from cover along the bayou; they took Mills and the patrol entirely unawares. Without a shot being fired, they captured Mills and all the guards except one, who ran away. John H. Johnson was one of the guards, and he must have felt apprehensive being in the hands of men who had little cause to wish him well, but the Kempers merely took the guards' arms, freed their friends, and then released the militia. Writing so hurriedly that he failed to put on his spectacles, Mills scrawled a note to Pintado stating that he needed a substantial body of armed men quickly or "certain individuals will be made to suffer soon."[20]

For the next several days the Kemper band lay unmolested in their house-turned-fortress. Stirling watched them and kept the governor apprised, while Grand-Pré and Pintado sent out a call to raise a force sufficient to put them down.[21] The governor found the inhabitants alarmed and restive, and on June 20 he appealed to the governor of Spanish West Florida, Vicente Folch, for reinforcements to deal with these *bribones* — "rascals." He suspected the United States' intentions toward West Florida lay behind this uprising. Knowing Spain's overextension in the province, Grand-Pré complained that the Americans were "inclined to insubordination and prone to insurrection" and suggested banning strangers from the province so no one would come in and stir unrest. A day later he sent a cannon to Stirling and warned

Folch of the danger of delaying an expedition against the rebels, asking for a gunboat to blockade the mouth of Bayou Sara to prevent the Kempers from communicating with or receiving aid from Natchez or New Orleans.[22] On the scene, Grand-Pré told Pintado and the alcaldes to watch all roads, stop all travelers trying to enter the province, and watch for the Kempers' associates, especially around the mouth of Bayou Sara, where several *soldados* stood guard. Mindful of how far the threat might extend, the governor set men in Baton Rouge to work repairing the crumbling fort's walls and emplacing a cannon to cover the gate.[23]

The inevitable delay in getting an expedition mounted very nearly realized Mills's prediction that people would suffer soon. Smith called at his friend's home on June 23. Mills was standing on the front gallery talking with Smith, who was sitting in the fenced yard, when Samuel Kemper and Ransom O'Neil, a teenager and the youngest of the raiders, suddenly rode up to the fence. Kemper had a cocked pistol pointed at Mills, while O'Neil carried a pair of pistols on his saddle and a cocked rifle in his hands. Mills happened to be holding a double-barreled shotgun when they came in sight. Kemper said he had come to take Mills down to the mouth of the bayou, but Mills, no doubt brandishing the shotgun, replied that he was prepared for Kemper and told him to leave at once, making it clear that if he dared to step into the yard, Mills would shoot him. Kemper defiantly dismounted but did not test Mills's resolve by going any farther; instead he tried to disarm Mills with talk.

Samuel lied to Mills, saying that he came with Claiborne's protection, and he again asked Mills to come with him to the bayou where Samuel promised to convince him that Claiborne had authorized their actions. The Kempers probably intended to punish Mills with a whipping, but Mills bluntly said that Samuel was not an honorable man and he would not trust him. Kemper angrily left, warning that his party was well prepared should Grand-Pré send *soldados* against them and that the local militia, virtually all Americans, would take no part against them; obviously, the brothers still believed their fellow Americans would not oppose them. Samuel and O'Neil left by 10:00 A.M., and Mills sent Smith off with a hurried and somewhat panicked message to Pintado telling him that his situation at Bayou Sara was critical. Clearly the Kempers had marked him. He saw no course but to leave the area until he could return safely.[24]

Prior to this time, Grand-Pré had offered the Kemper band amnesty if they left the territory and did not return. Spanish colonial administrations used amnesty liberally as a policy to rid themselves of undesirables, but in continuing their raids, the Kempers went too far, and they may have refused the offer anyhow. They made it clear they did not intend to leave peacefully.[25] Consequently, on June 25 Grand-Pré sent Pintado another order to arrest the band. He also issued a statement to the people of Feliciana thanking them for their help in defeating the attempt of the *piratas* to raise an army against the government. Now he required aid to apprehend these *bribones* and *revoltosos*, whom he additionally called "protégés of the American Government." Responding to Samuel's claim that he had backing from Claiborne, Grand-Pré emphasized that the United States was not going to support or protect the rebels, whose actions he now embellished with unspecified, and fictitious, murders, though to date not a shot had been fired.[26]

Stirling spent two days raising a real force of volunteers, and by June 25 more than sixty men stood at his command, many more than he had expected on such short notice. That afternoon he and their immediate commander, the Kempers' old customer Bryan McDermott, took them down to Bayou Sara within sight of the Kempers in their barricaded house, but they arrived too late in the day to act. Stirling planned to keep the house under watch through the night, and if the miscreants did not launch a night attack, he intended to storm the house at dawn and capture or kill the lot of them.

Nothing happened that night, and in the morning the entire command volunteered unanimously to assault the house. Champ Terry and a small company had arrived during the night, and Stirling let Terry pick nineteen of Stirling's men to add to his command. Terry then led the men down to the Mississippi bank, and they moved on the house from the river side. They reached the building without a shot being fired, only to discover that the Kempers had escaped undetected, taking everything portable with them, including all the arms seized from locals. Stirling scoured the vicinity and finally determined that the band had escaped by rowing across the river to Point Coupée. Almost immediately he suggested that magistrate Julien Poydras, one of the most influential planters on the American side of the river, be asked to arrest the fugitives. As Stirling's men rode back to Bayou Sara, another twenty volunteers arrived, making more than eighty men, plus Terry's small company. Stirling discharged all of them, except ten under Terry, with the proviso that they reassemble if called. The Scotsman had nothing but high praise for all.[27]

After the escape of the raiders, Grand-Pré coordinated the pursuit personally, establishing guard posts and patrols with the assistance of the locals, almost all of whom were Americans. He especially did not want the *bribones* to get away to the Louisiana coast, for then they might never be apprehended.[28] He knew Reuben was still in New Orleans, and he feared that Reuben had formed a secret compact with influential men there to aid his brothers. Grand-Pré believed his initial proclamation against the Kempers had been popular, as the volunteer turnout showed, and it was important now to arrest all of them.[29]

For several days information came in to Baton Rouge. Militia captured two men on July 2, the same day that the alcalde John O'Connor learned that the Kemper brothers were back in Pinckneyville, supposedly having announced that their intent was to go to Baton Rouge and kill indiscriminately.[30] Informers in Pinckneyville gave the names of some of the other raiders, and they also stated that Nathan's wife had crossed the line and rejoined her husband.[31] Along the line, some of the Kempers' followers began a series of cross-border incursions, sometimes going no more than a hundred and fifty yards, to taunt the patrols on the other side.[32]

Poydras interviewed some of the Kemper men at Point Coupée late on July 5; he found them insolent but could not detain them.[33] The next day a few of their associates still roamed north of St. Francisville.[34] Stirling felt too uneasy to leave Bayou Sara just yet, and he ordered storekeeper John Rhea to take command of the district and mount foot patrols to arrest anyone suspicious. Significantly, Grand-Pré and Pintado turned repeatedly to Americans rather than their own *soldados* to quell the disturbance, and so did Stirling. All understood the need to focus on maintaining the peace without allowing ethnic tension to cloud the business and play into the Kempers' hands. Stirling cautioned Rhea to choose men who would not abuse their authority, who would not insult or unduly interfere with legitimate persons, and who would use firearms only for self-defense. Anyone behaving otherwise could face criminal prosecution. Stirling learned the names of two of the fugitives and ordered their arrest and the seizure of their property.[35]

Stirling remained at Bayou Sara to inventory what the Kempers had left behind when they had abandoned their house in the night. He and his men found bits of furniture and some remaining stock from the old store, but no evidence of any plan for an extended occupation. The brothers' billiards table still had all its balls and cues. Elsewhere they found assorted cookware, several barrels of tobacco, flour, sugar, and coffee, a case of gin, and a quantity of grindstones. They also found the borrowed carpenter's tools, five shotguns, and a pair of pistols the insurgents had commandeered in the vicinity, and some shot and powder; all were to be held until claimed by their rightful owners.[36] Down at "the Pointe," where the bayou flowed into the Mississippi, they found millstones and, nearby, a small flatboat the Kempers used to ferry goods across the bayou. All of this Champ Terry turned over for safekeeping. Six prisoners apprehended by the patrols were being held, among them the Kempers' old friend Henry Bradford Sr. Within a few days the patrols took two more and placed them all securely in custody for Grand-Pré to examine.[37] Pintado maintained the patrols and, apparently intending to keep guarding the roads for some time, issued rations of hard biscuits and beef to sustain the men. Terry promised to "Ecert my self to Effect the Arest of the persons Mentioned."[38]

With the Kempers and most of their men having escaped, Grand-Pré did not rest easy. They had fled once before, only to return. On July 2 he issued a proclamation that the brothers — he erroneously included Reuben — had "had the audacity to Rebel with an armed force against the Government" and had brought with them "a sett of Vagrants whom they deceive by causing them to believe that they were protected by the American Government." They were all pirates and highwaymen, he said, the sort who "sowed confusion in Order to Rob and Escape." Everyone had a duty to help apprehend them, for "it cannot be doubted that when they have committed the grossest Crimes so easily a thousand others will follow." No one should give the rebels aid or succor. Grand-Pré ordered alcaldes to have public criers read his proclamation, which he had issued in English for that purpose, even though finding a translator had presented a problem.[39] Still, the proclamation reached Bayou Sara that same day, and Rhea read and posted it at once.[40]

Pintado soon reported that the proclamation produced a good effect, though none of the *bribones* had yet turned themselves in.[41] The day after the proclamation, the first news of the disturbance had reached readers in the United States. On June 27 a man in Baton Rouge sent a letter to the *Natchez Mississippi Herald and Natchez Gazette*, attributing the origin of the uprising to the Kemper-Smith suit. He garbled news badly, as first reports often do, and predicted erroneously that Americans would not respond to Grand-Pré's call to mobilize. "In fact," he wrote, revealing his own bias, "the circumstance has created great *alarm* to the Spaniards, and much amusement to the Americans." He had heard talk in Baton Rouge convincing him that Kemper — he seems to have thought it was Reuben — would find many friends to rally to him and could repel any attack. Unaware that the Kempers had fled their house the day before, the anonymous correspondent expected a fight at Baton Rouge, saying that "a few days will, in all probability, terminate this most extraordinary affair."[42]

Grand-Pré sent an express to the Spanish official Marqués de Casa Calvo; it reached him June 26. Quite coincidentally, that same day Claiborne wrote to Jefferson that he saw "much disquietude and a spirit of disaffection to the Spanish Authorities" among the people of West Florida, especially those living on the Mississippi, and he believed they would stay unhappy until the American government took over.[43] Persistent rumors that much of the Louisiana Purchase west of the Mississippi was about to be returned to Spain enhanced that disaffection, and Casa Calvo did not help matters by not refuting the stories.[44] The ink on Claiborne's letter had scarcely dried before Casa Calvo appeared to complain of the riot in West Florida. Casa Calvo demanded that Claiborne cooperate in preserving order, and with some pleasure Claiborne turned the Spaniard's own arguments around by reminding him that with the borders of Louisiana still unsettled, he, Claiborne, lacked the authority to take any action in disputed territory. The next day Claiborne wrote to Secretary of State

Madison about the uprising and the meeting with Casa Calvo, hinting that the Kemper affair might help hurry Spain to the table to settle the West Florida matter at last.[45]

Yet Feliciana showed little support for what English settler John Mears called "Kemper & his madly deluded party."[46] More than forty American militia guarded the Kempers' modest log cabin, more insurgents were arrested, and the words *dead or alive* were heard in connection with the rest. The anonymous American writer in Baton Rouge moved to the safety of Pinckneyville and wrote another letter complaining that "we have been flattered with a hope of participating in the blessings of your government, as being included in the cession: if it is really the case — in the name of God, why are we left exposed to the despotism we daily experience?" When that appeared in the press on July 3, it made him the only person thus far who had publicly declared sympathy with the Kempers.[47] Meanwhile, O'Connor posted patrols at each of the roads entering Feliciana from the Mississippi Territory. John H. Johnson, also a colonel in the militia, believed the danger was past by July 4, with virtually all the miscreants either captured or escaped. Days of searching failed to turn up the only two reportedly still at large below the line.[48] But then a few days later, a patrol spotted and chased several of the gang back above the line, firing a volley that wounded two and ended with their capture.[49]

By this time, the authorities knew that Basil Abrams and possibly Samuel Kemper had made their way to New Orleans, presumably to meet with Reuben and plot more trouble.[50] More of the raiders, they learned, had escaped by way of Bayou Tunica, taking refuge in a house just half a mile from the line.[51] Then on July 8, in the vicinity of the recent shooting, Stirling's brother-in-law militia captain Solomon Alston took a man identified as one of the Kemper party.[52] At about the same time, when Pintado left to escort the two wounded prisoners to Baton Rouge, unseen men set fire to his house, which was narrowly saved. He had no doubt that it was retaliation for Grand-Pré's decree and for his own efforts to capture or expel the lawbreakers.[53] No longer certain that the Kempers were gone, Pintado set patrols on all the roads and small bayous that the fugitives might use to pass above the line, and Grand-Pré gave unequivocal orders to take them dead or alive.[54] The Kempers had changed tactics, though again with

no clear long-range purpose. From Pinckneyville they launched a series of raids over the border, often no more than a few men at a time,
preying on the plantations of men who opposed them and stealing
horses, slaves, and other goods.[55] Mainly they took pistols, swords,
and knives, a warning that they were rearming for something bigger.
During one raid, Samuel Kemper and others even took over a planter's home for a night to hide out.

Rumors circulated that the rebels had nearly a hundred rifles and
pistols, any number of sabers and hatchets, and even artillery hidden
in a house on the Point Coupée side of the river three miles above
Bayou Sara. Several men in the vicinity of Bayou Sara were said to
be spies for the Kempers, and this seemed to be confirmed on July 17
when Nathan brazenly rode past O'Connor's home in the company
of two others, spent the night at a woman's house above Bayou Sara,
and then came to the landing to see his empty house and declare that
he would return to defend it.[56] He left just hours before Grand-Pré
arrived in person to see the state of things. The spreading rumors had
done well the work of raising apprehensions, and the almost daily
incursions from above the line encouraged mounting fears, prompt-
ing Grand-Pré to issue a proclamation declaring the Kempers state
criminals. He did not need to embroider this time with false stories
of murders, for now the actual crimes against the property of Americans worked against the Kempers.[57] Grand-Pré decreed the brothers' remaining property in West Florida forfeit if they did not surrender. They could never live or do business in Feliciana again unless
cleared of charges or pardoned, neither of which were now very likely.
Having made all Kemper property liable to seizure, Grand-Pré forgot
the grant to Nathan just a few months earlier and made no move at
confiscation.

Grand-Pré named thirty-eight men who had acted with the Kempers.[58] With the exception of one Frenchman, all were American. Nathan owned land. So did the Bradfords, Nathan and son Henry, and
Samuel Kirkland and Lemuel Bradford, all men Grand-Pré deemed
the most dangerous. Then there was Arthur Cobb and his sons William and Arthur Jr., troublesome citizens for years now. Nearly a third
of the men were related to one another, and except for Arthur Cobb
and Nathan Bradford, most were under thirty. The majority were

bachelors. Those without property Grand-Pré branded vagrants, and some, such as William Cobb, actually lived above the line.[59] He confiscated the property of the rest, which would be restored only after their surrender and proof of contrition.[60] Grand-Pré hoped the possible return of property would divide the band and turn them against one another, and he promised to grant "very celebrated excellent pardon" to all except the Kempers and Abrams. Those men he might pardon, but only if they left the territory forever.[61]

Claiborne gave the governor well-intentioned assistance. When word of the earlier outbursts reached New Orleans on June 26, Reuben Kemper called on Claiborne, who probably asked what Kemper knew of the extraordinary events. Kemper would have told him, truthfully, that he knew no more than the governor, since it had all happened in his absence. No doubt Claiborne remonstrated with Reuben, reiterating the delicate situation between the United States and Spain, and then sought to win his influence with his brothers by proposing that leniency might defuse the situation. Acting in his capacity as governor of Mississippi and now of Orleans Territory as well, Claiborne promised pardon to all inhabitants of those territories who had been involved in the recent outrage if they peacefully returned to their homes outside West Florida. He then sent his father, William Claiborne, to Baton Rouge armed with a power of attorney to meet and act on his behalf with Grand-Pré.[62] Whatever his private suspicions of Reuben, Claiborne remained cordial, presumably told him of his intentions, and advised him to keep his brothers quiet until everyone calmed, at which point a means might be found to allow them to return to West Florida.[63]

Within a few days, Claiborne's and Grand-Pré's policy seemed to bear fruit. Henry Bradford and another man agreed to cooperate and received pardons.[64] Then the post commandant at Galveztown complained that Claiborne's offer of pardon raised fears among the loyal planters that the United States was behind the Kempers' acts, virtually confirming Samuel Kemper's boast to Mills. It seemed to hint to others in the American territories that there would be no repercussions if they joined the Kempers. Grand-Pré suddenly feared that his policy of pacifying unrest might only fan its flames.[65]

His proclamation was barely known before O'Connor stepped out of his home on the evening of July 20 to find Nathan and Samuel Kemper and half a dozen well-armed men. They claimed they had been pardoned and their property returned under Grand-Pré's proclamation and now they were returning to take possession of their home at Bayou Sara. They announced that the militia had all gone home, likely a ploy to get O'Connor to reveal militia movements at the moment. He refused to comment, but he did allow them to read a copy of Grand-Pré's proclamation to see its stipulations, and then he called on them to turn over their arms. They refused, then spoke a few minutes more before riding on almost to St. Francisville, crossing Bayou Sara, and riding back north on the road to Woodville. Clearly it was a reconnaissance to sound remaining militia strength in the vicinity and to learn the whereabouts of O'Connor, Pintado, and Stirling in particular.[66]

In Pinckneyville the Kempers persuaded some locals to join yet another, stronger raid across the line, this time with a fixed and bold plan. They would capture Pintado, O'Connor, Stirling, and other American leaders to disrupt the militia command, take more arms, shut down communications between the Spaniards and the militia, and then descend on Baton Rouge. Knowing that Grand-Pré and most of his officers lodged in the town rather than in the fort, they would take Grand-Pré by surprise and then hold him hostage for the surrender of the fort. However aimless and spontaneous their previous actions had been, this was revolution. Nathan and Samuel had nothing to lose, really. They could never move back to West Florida. If they raised enough men to bluff or drive the Spaniards out of Baton Rouge, then perhaps Claiborne would send militia to take possession before Folch in Pensacola sent reinforcements. Should they fail, they would be no worse off than they were now, so long as they did not lose their lives.

Nathan and Samuel acted on their own, for Reuben was still in New Orleans and knew nothing of their new plans.[67] Unknowingly, Reuben contributed to the heightening tension by writing more letters to Stirling advising him in a tone that the alcalde found threatening to leave Nathan and Samuel alone.[68] That Reuben approved his brothers' scheme seems unlikely, for failure would leave no remaining hope in his continuing dispute with Smith. Even if it succeeded and the United States came in, the people's experience of the American takeover in Mississippi and Louisiana showed that new authorities usually avoided reversing extant judgments in land disputes.

Nathan and Samuel did meet with a close friend of Reuben's in Pinckneyville, however. Thirty-one-year-old Edward Randolph came from Augusta, Georgia, and first settled in the Spaniards' Natchez District and took the oath of allegiance in 1789.[69] Ten years later, already having business ties to West Florida, he married in Baton Rouge, and he now lived in Pinckneyville, where he ran a store in partnership with the ubiquitous Daniel Clark.[70] As recently as May of 1804 he had acquired property in Feliciana to open a store of his own at Tunica on the next bend of the Mississippi above Bayou Sara.[71] The Kempers may have met him in the course of business at Bayou Sara, but more likely Clark introduced them, commencing what Reuben called "my good will and friend ship towards Edward Randolph."[72] The other brothers met at Randolph's home and probably lodged with him for a short time, which exposed them to his persuasive influence.[73]

Randolph had his own agendum, which was probably influenced by Clark. They sold goods to Indians in the Mississippi Territory from their Pinckneyville store. If the United States took over West Florida, they could then trade with the natives at their Tunica store as well.[74] Daniel Clark wanted more land in West Florida, and land would be more open for speculation under the United States than under Spain. If Randolph hoped to join in exploiting that land, an American takeover worked for both their interests. In their haphazard way the Kemper brothers stirred some unrest in Feliciana, even though close to a hundred or more American planters volunteered to quell the disturbance. Clearly the majority of Americans felt insufficient discontent with Spain to be insubordinate, but observers on all sides agreed that given the choice, the Americans preferred to be a part of the United States. That preference simply had not yet moved more than a handful to action.

Now the Kempers produced a genuine, carefully crafted plan to return to Feliciana, capture Spanish leaders and disrupt communications to prevent mobilizing the militia, and then take Baton Rouge without a fight. If the Kempers gathered a hundred followers, or even fifty, they could take Grand-Pré by surprise and force a surrender.

Randolph probably influenced their plans, playing on their anger and frustration to instigate their return to West Florida.[75] Before long an American planter named Thomas Hutchins, loyal to Grand-Pré and Spain, declared that "Randolph is well known to be a man of the most infamous principles; capable of doing every thing but a good action."[76] Whether he manipulated the Kempers or not, all of them surely realized that if they hoped to persuade some of the planters in Feliciana to rally when they crossed the line, they needed to offer some object other than causing mayhem. They were all sons of the Revolution. Their fathers rallied to the call of the Declaration of Independence; these men needed their own declaration. Randolph put pen to paper.[77]

He wrote with no specific model, but clearly the Declaration of Independence influenced him. "For a people to be free, it is sufficient that they will it," he began. Then he jumped immediately into a statement of causes. "The despotism under which we have long groaned, has grown into an insupportable burden," he said, but unlike the authors of the 1776 declaration, he failed to state any specific grievance. He paraphrased Jefferson by asserting that "as it is long since admitted, men are born with equal rights," but again he offered no instance of Spanish denial of equity to Americans. Instead, he went straight to his ultimate point: "We the undersigned inhabitants of that part of the dominion called West Florida, have resolved to throw off the galling yoke of tyranny, and become FREE, by declaring ourselves a FREE and INDEPENDENT PEOPLE."

Saying nothing of the "sacred honor" cited by Jefferson, Randolph did aver that the signatories supported this declaration with their lives and property. That said, he issued an invitation to all "fellow sufferers" to flock to their standard for their mutual emancipation. In return he promised to avoid shedding any but Spanish blood and pledged that private property would be protected, though judging from the recent raids across the line, that referred only to the property of sympathizers. Any fellow Americans, Britons, and Frenchmen who opposed them would be regarded as enemies like the Spaniards and treated accordingly. Randolph concluded by stating their ultimate purpose: as soon as they took over "we will offer ourselves to some government accustomed to freedom."[78]

It was a peculiar manifesto. It complained of grievances and inequities but cited none. It spoke of tyranny and despotism but gave no example. It invited fellow planters to join with them, then virtually threatened the lives and property of any who did not. It proclaimed independence, but stated a determination to surrender sovereignty as soon as possible to someone else, the United States being the implicit beneficiary. Randolph would win no awards for his prose. The document was hurried, repetitive, and worse than vague. To any but its author — and perhaps even to him — it read as a cynical pretext of legitimacy for what the Kempers and their band were determined to do anyhow. Randolph made several copies of his document, and then it only remained for the Kempers to ride into West Florida to post them publicly and start their revolution.[79]

3

The Late Insurrection at Baton Rouge

ON THE MORNING of August 7, 1804, Nathan and Samuel Kemper and about twenty followers, some of them Mississippians and some from West Florida, gathered at Pinckneyville and pinned blue and yellow cockades to their shirts. Most brought their own provisions, but William Cobb filled out their rations from his own storehouse.[1] Then they mounted and rode south, all well armed with rifles and pistols. In minutes they reached the line, halted briefly, and then blew hunting horns as a summons to more men in the vicinity. One of the riders boasted to a passing traveler going to Natchez that they would take the fort at Baton Rouge within twenty-four hours. Someone else indiscreetly revealed that the men intended to capture the alcaldes along the way.

Then they crossed the line. When first cut, the line was a forty-foot-wide swath through the forest and undergrowth, but the woods had since encroached due to neglect.[2] The Kempers unfurled a flag most likely made for them by Randolph's wife, Polly, and which their followers now saw for the first time. Four white stripes alternated with three blue, with a yellow field with two red stars in an upper corner.[3] The symbolism, if any, is elusive. The four white stripes may have stood for the four districts of West Florida. The three blue stripes could represent the three principal towns in the province, Baton Rouge, Mobile, and Pensacola, or even the three Kemper brothers. The two red stars may have been meant to suggest the United States and West Florida. One of the Kempers read Randolph's declaration aloud for the first time, the brothers clearly having waited until they were on West Florida soil to reveal their intentions, and now the Kempers and their lieutenant Basil Abrams promised that more than three hundred would join them before they reached Baton Rouge.[4]

The party included some new men and some familiar names, including Abrams, the Bradfords, the Cobbs, O'Neil, and more.[5] Several of them had shopped with the Kempers.[6] The banner and the declaration surprised some and perplexed others, for prior to this moment the leaders had given some men one reason for their expedition and others a different one. One young man had believed that the Kempers had no settled plan.[7] The Cobbs said that they were moved to act solely on their own behalf "for the injustice and Ill usage they had received from Gran Pree the Spanish Governor." One of the Cobbs felt certain that before they marched, not a word had been said of receiving any encouragement from Jefferson. The men did it on the expectation that the United States would soon take over anyhow and also to regain the property of which they said Grand-Pré had unjustly deprived them.[8]

Another man knew nothing of Randolph's declaration, and several knew nothing of their leaders' actual objectives. The Kempers said they wanted to release prisoners from their earlier raids who were being held in Baton Rouge, and several men admitted that they joined without mature reflection on the hazard of their conduct. When one man saw the flag, heard the declaration, and found himself in arms against the government, he did not know what to do and was afraid to go back. The declaration's promise of retribution against those who did not aid the cause was even more sobering; several of the riders secretly agreed among themselves that if they succeeded, no one would be injured for opposing them, though they would arrest the government in Baton Rouge.[9]

Abrams enlisted at least one man by telling him that the Spaniards in Baton Rouge intended to execute as many as eighty Americans in the night, hinting that the enlistee might be one of them. "For myself I thought I might as well be killed in battle as murdered in my sleep as out of more than eighty persons to be killed I thought the danger to me was as great as to any other," the recruit reflected. Besides, Abrams promised that the whole country would rise against the Spaniards to prevent the massacre. Only later did Abrams and the Kempers admit their plan to take Baton Rouge and hand it to the United States.

They forced no one to join, but some later felt they had been seduced by false reports against the government, while more than one simply acted without time for reflection only to be "very sorry for it" upon learning that the leaders planned to cast off Spanish authority and "establish Liberty and Independence."[10]

Another young man met the Kemper company by accident, heard their story of releasing prisoners, and yielded to the impulse of the moment without reflection; he soon lamented his error.[11] Abrams and Nathan lured several by telling them that morning that Champ Terry and his militia would change sides and join them and that Kneeland's nemesis Colonel Frederick Kimball had promised to be their leader, with two hundred men due to join them by the time they reached Baton Rouge that night.[12] The men took heart from that promise of major support, which encouraged them to remain.[13] Nathan declared the whole country would join them, including many from above the line, and if they took the fort, even the Mississippi militia would come.[14] One or two recruits felt skeptical, especially after hearing that Terry offered only to lend the moral force of his position as a militia leader in return for five hundred dollars, one man remarking that Terry was "a character on whom no dependence was to be placed."[15]

Only one man understood unequivocally that the Kempers planned to change the government and establish independence.[16] Beyond that, no one knew if the Kempers intended to confiscate the property of opponents or to reward followers with appointments in any new government.[17] Either the leaders simply did not think that far ahead or they kept their immediate plans closely guarded. By the time everyone realized that the Kempers meant independence, the recruits were already on West Florida soil and to some degree committed. They were all young men, and a few who wanted out nevertheless remained in order to avoid looking like cowards to the rest; at least some of them actually feared reprisal if they withdrew.

Their route to Baton Rouge followed the wagon road from Pinckneyville to St. Francisville, then across Thompson's Creek to a wide level area known as Buller's Plains that stretched about seven miles above Baton Rouge.[18] Along the way they passed Kimball's plantation, but there was no sign of him, which almost immediately raised apprehensions over the Kempers' promises. Soon they came to Solomon

Alston's plantation; fortunately he was absent, or he would have been the first hostage. However, they found the sixty-year-old O'Connor at home, as they no doubt had anticipated. People knew him as a respectable old gentleman who got lost without a pocket compass.[19] They took him without resistance, having a purpose in mind for him when they reached Baton Rouge. O'Connor had just enough warning to get an express rider off to Baton Rouge, but the Kempers had wisely sent men ahead on the road, and they stopped the messenger.[20]

With one of their targets in hand, they turned next to Pintado.[21] They sent riders ahead and out on the small side roads to intercept anyone attempting to spread the alarm, and the main group rode to Pintado's; they took him without resistance. Just three days earlier he had complimented the American militia, promising them that his report of their recent conduct would go to Grand-Pré and from him to Havana and even Madrid. He also passed along a reward from Governor Folch, a lifting of the 6 percent duty being charged on import and export commerce with New Orleans.[22] Before Pintado rode away with the raiders, he saw his house and cotton gin in flames, and this time no one would put them out. The Cobbs held a standing grudge against Pintado's surveyors, and Pintado himself owed William Cobb an uncollected debt. Perhaps to exact payment, Cobb took one of Pintado's pistols, and others removed a set of cased pistols from the house before they set it alight.[23] Unlike O'Connor, Pintado was a Spaniard, and the treatment he received made it evident that the declaration meant what it said about dealing with the enemy. That made a few of the riders uneasy, and they counseled their comrades to use care handling all prisoners.

When the riders came to the bridge over Little Bayou Sara, they arrested two men, took their pistols, and then released them on their promise not to warn Baton Rouge or take arms against them. Along the way they met one or two travelers as well as a mail rider, all of whom they let pass since they were headed away from Baton Rouge.[24] What they did not encounter were Kimball, Terry, and the two hundred to three hundred volunteers the Kempers had promised. Still, the plan to keep word of their coming from spreading seemed to be working thus far, and neither O'Connor nor Pintado had been able to alert local militia. Now the main party rode on to get Alexander

Stirling. Unlike O'Connor and Pintado, Stirling had no intention of going peacefully when Samuel Kemper confronted him at his plantation. The Scotsman put up a fight at first, and Kemper struggled with him, trying unsuccessfully to tie him with a rope until finally Stirling yielded.[25]

Before nightfall the riders and their hostages came within a few miles of Baton Rouge, but despite all their precautions John Mears had alerted Isaac Johnson that the Kempers intended to attack Baton Rouge and that they had a proclamation of independence and even their own flag. By 7:00 P.M. Grand-Pré knew of the danger.[26] No doubt it came as a shock, for just a few days before he had told Folch that Feliciana was quite tranquil. Nathan and Samuel had declined the offer of pardon and exile, and he anticipated no more trouble from them.[27] Now came word from Mears, who exaggerated the Kempers' strength to two hundred men instead of no more than thirty. Grand-Pré put the garrison of the fort on alert and called nearby militia to assemble immediately. He posted a picket of twenty men in advance of the fort to warn of the Kempers' approach, and the next morning at 5:30, when the revolutionaries were several hundred yards from the fort, the picket guard hailed them and ordered them to halt.[28]

The Kempers had not expected this. It meant that word of their coming had slipped through after all, and it killed the plan of taking Grand-Pré hostage and bartering for the evacuation of the fort. All they could do now was make a show of force and see what advantage might be gained. The Kempers replied to the challenge with a ragged volley that wounded two Spaniards and sent the rest retreating to the fort.[29] Excited at the first "victory" over the Spaniards in spite of the failure of their original plan, the leaders considered what to do next. They could have attempted to take the fort, but if they thought about that option, they quickly dismissed it. Even though the fort's cannon were in bad repair, the fort's armaments and garrison outnumbered them, making an attack futile. Still, the revolt might not necessarily be over. When word spread of their victory, even in this minor skirmish, they might withdraw into the country and hope for volunteers to rally to them. If they could demonstrate that they had won something from the governor, their case would be even stronger.

Consequently, at noon, Nathan, who had been in charge throughout, sent O'Connor with an offer to Grand-Pré. If Grand-Pré freed the prisoners he held from the June raids, the Kempers promised to release O'Connor, Pintado, Stirling, and a few other hostages. The governor wisely refused to negotiate. Doing so would have given them some standing or recognition. Moreover, Grand-Pré understood the American majority of his citizens. Pintado, a Spaniard, might be at some modest risk, but Stirling and especially O'Connor were not. For the Kempers to harm either of them risked arousing the enmity of the rest of the Americans and Englishmen living in West Florida, exactly what the Kempers did not want. Grand-Pré felt sure that none of the hostages were in danger, and he was right.[30]

The governor's refusal left Nathan with no choice but to attack or retreat. He defiantly kept his men on the outskirts of Baton Rouge for the rest of the day, and the next day they left to return to Bayou Sara. Nathan and Samuel, and probably Abrams as well, considered their next move. They were not defeated, only stymied in their initial aim. They expected Grand-Pré to start calling out militia immediately but still hoped many Americans would refuse to muster. One way to influence matters toward that end was to make Randolph's declaration public, so they sent riders out to post copies in public places in the vicinity. Interestingly, only Abrams put his signature on the document, stating that he "signed for all."[31] More conscious of security than ever, they stopped anyone they encountered on the road who they felt might be a spy for the Spaniards, but carelessly they let at least two men pass them, one of whom may have been carrying Grand-Pré's militia call.[32]

Unfortunately, the Americans began taking horses and more weapons from local planters, no doubt to equip volunteers as they came in, but it won them no support.[33] They also started taking more prisoners and their weapons.[34] No one practiced intimidation to enlist men, but the mere presence of the party was intimidating in itself, especially the prospect of being made prisoner. One young man decided to join rather than become their captive.[35] Not far from the home of Reuben's friend Bailey Chaney, one prospective recruit stepped out from behind a tree and said he wanted to join but he first wanted to be made their prisoner so he would have an alibi should he later face Spanish justice.[36]

That evening they reached William Cobb's plantation on Bayou Sara and stopped for the night. Their plan had not looked beyond capturing Grand-Pré, and as far as the men could tell, the Kempers were improvising now; no one knew of any support promised from outside West Florida.[37] Nathan made Cobb's place their headquarters for the present and tacked a copy of the declaration on an inside wall.[38] Randolph's draft ended with the date they began their operation, August 7, 1804, but still only Abrams's signature pledged life and property. They had hoped to add many names to that list, but though men like Chaney gave them arms, only a few youths enlisted. Apparently even those planters who wanted to see the back of Spain did not want it enough to risk their own fortunes.[39]

Nathan had to address the growing number of prisoners, for now, in addition to Pintado, O'Connor, and Stirling, they held half a dozen others, and Grand-Pré's refusal to bargain made them worthless. Nathan assembled them in front of the command and formally paroled them, some for thirty days or for the duration of hostilities, and the rest on their promise not to take arms against him.[40] At this point Champ Terry finally appeared, but only to give a rifle to a recruit.[41] Many of the men felt betrayed when Terry failed to join them, but it appears that Nathan had invented the whole story of his support, for Nathan arrested Terry too, and then paroled him with the rest.[42]

News of their actions had reached Natchez in a rumor crediting the party with three hundred men, a story possibly planted by Randolph to encourage volunteers from above the line. Some believed the raiders meant to take all of West Florida up to the Mobile River and that they flew the Stars and Stripes. Instead of stirring up sympathy, however, the news aroused indignation that a party of U.S. citizens had violated the soil of another nation.[43] Certainly Grand-Pré wasted no time responding to the outrage. While the governor's friends congratulated him on escaping "the trap planned by a handful of brigands," Grand-Pré called for 125 Feliciana men to come forward by August 15.[44] He instructed Captain Duplantier to take command of those on foot, and Grand-Pré's future son-in-law Major Samuel Fulton was to lead the mounted men of what became known as "the Expedition against the Kempers."[45] The first response brought over three times the number of men requested to Baton Rouge to reinforce and occupy the fort. Duplantier organized the volunteers to operate in rotation to guard the fort, hold strategic bayou crossings, and patrol the region toward Bayou Sara. They strengthened the main gate of the fort, and planters loaned twenty-five slaves to repair and bolster the eroding earthworks. Virtually all the volunteers came from the Amite and Comite settlements, but very few from Feliciana itself, and Grand-Pré's sons Luis, Carlos, and Enrique, all cadets in the Regiment of Louisiana, helped with the work and took command of defending the fort. Some Americans, such as prominent attorney and friend of the governor Philip Hicky, took part as militia officers.[46]

Less than a week after the Kempers retired from Baton Rouge, 109 men stood ready to march, and sent Fulton's party out a day early, on August 14. Two days later the governor addressed more new militia in front of the fort, gave them a flag of their own, then sent them off to patrol the Feliciana roads near the line under Captains Duplantier and George de Passau, a Baton Rouge planter and alcalde. Grand-Pré also sent two gunboats up the Mississippi to the mouth of Bayou Sara, hoping to prevent a repeat of the Kempers' June escape to the Point Coupée side. Finally, with a possible long-term campaign in mind, Grand-Pré sent a call to St. Helena for militia to guard the roads along the Mississippi border. He appealed to Folch for five hundred more rifles and bayonets, warning Casa Calvo of his fear that Cato West, acting governor of Mississippi Territory pending Claiborne's replacement, encouraged the Kempers in their perfidious designs.[47]

At the headquarters of the insurgents, confusion and disintegration set in. Time on their hands and uncertainty worked against the Kempers. Some of their men began plundering in the area, in a few cases just to feed themselves. No more volunteers came to join them, and sober reflection led to remorse among some of the younger West Florida men; others who had come from above the line simply returned home. After no more than three or four days, the Kemper brothers, Abrams, and three of the other leaders admitted that the rebellion was a failure, and they decided to try to salvage what they could of the situation. On August 16, Nathan wrote to Daniel Clark stating their willingness to lay down their arms and return to their homes if Grand-Pré would grant pardons. Clark may have been in Pinck-neyville with Randolph at the time, and Nathan may have handed the letter to him personally.

On August 19 Clark called on the governor in Baton Rouge. He presented Nathan's letter, signed by himself and five others, and asked for pardon on condition that they commit no further acts of hostility or plunder. Grand-Pré had been lenient with these men once, and they had repaid him by plotting against his person. He was not about to forgive a second time. He upbraided Clark for coming to him with such an entreaty, told him he suspected Randolph was partly behind the raid and the declaration, and reminded Clark of the arson, robbery, and kidnapping committed by the Kempers. Grand-Pré probably did not tell Clark that he believed he was just as much involved as Randolph.[48]

By now the disintegrating band at Cobb's were on the run. Fulton and his command came within a few miles of the Kempers on August 14 and believed the raiders intended to make a fight.[49] He was wrong. The Kempers stood their ground for a day or two, probably hoping to hear something from Clark, and Fulton did not press ahead, waiting for Duplantier with about fifty more militiamen. On August 20, seeing the desperation of their situation, and perhaps learning of Clark's failure, the remaining raiders rode back across the line to Pinckneyville. Fulton and Duplantier followed them to Arthur Cobb's home just below the line, and there they made headquarters for their self-styled "Corps of Operations in Feliciana." The next day they sent a demand to Pinckneyville for the local authorities to hand over "the vagabonds who infest this territory." The only authority in the village at the moment was a lowly magistrate who protested that he could do nothing without a decision from the chief magistrate, and in response to further demands he protested that he could not arrest citizens of his town without evidence of their guilt. All Fulton and Duplantier got in the end was a vague promise to punish any citizens who violated Spanish sovereignty.[50]

In New Orleans the news of the incident seriously upset Marqués de Casa Calvo. Reflecting on the events of June and July, he feared that the movement for insurrection, given a little time, would destroy Feliciana. He asked that the *Vigilante* be loaded with men and mate-

riel and sent to Baton Rouge as soon as possible. The Spanish intendant Juan Morales took his time, but by August 15 he had the vessel
ready to go.[51] Casa Calvo protested to Claiborne that Spain had been
lenient to the Kempers at Claiborne's urging, but now he had learned
that "Nathan and Samuel Kemper are always going about with arms
accompanied by men of their party threatening every body." He cited
Grand-Pré's false report of murders and assumed that Reuben's letters to Stirling and his correspondence with Randolph abetted the
mayhem.[52] The whole district was in a state of insurrection, he complained, citing Randolph's declaration, and he demanded that Claiborne order Cato West, the acting governor of Mississippi, not to
give asylum to any of the rebels. As for Reuben, Casa Calvo insisted
that Claiborne reprimand and even jail him if he did not stop his
menacing letters to Stirling.[53] Claiborne did not rush to satisfy Casa
Calvo. He waited a fortnight, then simply denied giving encouragement to the raid and promised to speak with Reuben Kemper and
instruct his subordinates not to aid the raiders in their bailiwicks.[54]
Even then Claiborne waited another two days to send out his orders.[55]
That same day, August 30, he wrote Madison that the unpleasant affair was "fast approaching a close."[56]

Claiborne failed to reckon with the impact that recent events would
have elsewhere in the Union. The Natchez newspaper carried news
only a couple of days old, thanks to travelers from West Florida,
though it was not always accurate; from the outset, the *Natchez Mississippi Herald and Natchez Gazette* provided most of what the outside public read. It could take a month for an issue to reach the East
Coast.[57] Consequently, reports of the events of late June and early
July did not reach New York until mid-August, where the news appeared under a headline proclaiming a "ludicrous account of an affair of some singularity." It may have seemed at first just an amusing
frontier story, but within days newspapers in every major city from
Boston to Richmond printed extracts. Readers everywhere saw that
someone named Kemper had led a harebrained incursion into Feliciana with no apparent objective. Letters with further details arrived in
the East, written by men in Natchez and Pinckneyville, some of them
eyewitnesses, as did subsequent issues of the *Mississippi Herald*. Five
times more eastern presses covered the story in September than had

done so in August, and, most important of all, on September 15, the text of the Randolph manifesto that had first appeared in the Natchez paper saw print for thousands of readers in the East.[58] At the same time, some eastern readers heard the rumor that the Kempers had actually captured Baton Rouge.[59] Press coverage waned in October but remained brisk, confusing Nathan with Reuben and attributing the outbreak to the older brother, whom for some reason the press began calling "Colonel Kemper." A few tried to find hidden motives behind the abortive attempt at uprising, including a suggestion that British gold backed the Kempers.[60] And the editor of the *Norwich (CT) Centinel* commented sarcastically that France had its Napoleon, the new black republic of Haiti was about to get an emperor, Jefferson seemed to be building an empire that America did not need, "and Kemper by the appearance of affairs, means to be Emperor of Louisiana."[61] Virtually all denied that any man on the raid was a U.S. citizen, which was manifestly false.[62]

By year's end, the story had left the press entirely, but not before the aimless and inept episode gained a notoriety out of all proportion to the facts.[63] Moreover, the name Kemper for the first time achieved recognition beyond the confines of Bayou Sara, and tens of thousands read the manifesto of independence. Citing that declaration, some editors thought it obvious that the West Floridians wanted the United States to take over. The province, said one, "is more valuable to us than all Louisiana, excluding New-Orleans," Spanish rule was obviously oppressive, and the desire for freedom unanimous.[64] Right or wrong, an impression of discontent and insurrectionary sentiment in West Florida gained currency in the United States, and in some quarters people suspected that the Jefferson administration encouraged that for its own ends. During the height of the press coverage, with Spain getting decidedly the worst of it, Spain's minister to the United States, the Marqués de Casa Yrujo, unwisely offered a transparent bribe to a Philadelphia editor to buy favorable comment, and this so outraged Jefferson that Madison demanded that Spain recall the minister, leaving Spain with no ambassador.[65]

Meanwhile, in Pinckneyville the raiders attracted no little attention. Neighbors complained that they seemed perfectly at ease and that local magistrates were doing nothing to stop them despite their armed raids on the Spanish government.[66] When he learned that the party had eluded pursuit, Casa Calvo provided to Claiborne the names of those he could identify and asked him to exercise his authority as governor of Mississippi Territory to order their arrest.[67] Again Claiborne stalled, replying that as bad as the Kempers' behavior had been, they were citizens of West Florida and he had no authority to arrest foreign nationals.[68]

Judge Thomas Rodney visited Pinckneyville not long after the fugitives arrived, and he spoke with Nathan and Samuel and one of the Cobbs. The last, whom Rodney termed "a pretty intelligent man," said he and others resented presumed past inequities and wanted only to regain property lost to Spanish justice. Arguing that the invasion had been foolish, Rodney told them they should stay quiet and wait for the excitement to die. He discouraged any renewed attempt on their part by assuring Cobb that there would be no hope of success, warning that they could not again get away with using Mississippi as a base. The Kempers promised to try nothing more.

Rodney left, convinced that the Americans and everyone but the few Spaniards were eager for a change of regime. The Kemper raid had failed only because most Americans there were too prudent to follow the brothers.[69] "A spunk has been made in some papers about Kemper and his party," he observed, "but that was a More private quarrel with a few Individuals." The Spaniards intended to hold on to "West Floraday," though he believed it could be taken quickly, "for the Spirit of the western people is very high on that Subject. — Indeed they would rejoice perhaps at an Opertunity of not stoping short of the City of Mexico."[70]

He may have been right, but the Spaniards exaggerated the significance of a minor episode that would have had little chance of success even if the Kempers had captured Grand-Pré. By the end of the month more than nine hundred volunteer militia patrolled all the main roads and bayous from the Mississippi to St. Helena. They kept a special eye on the home of Arthur Cobb, which had been a rebel rendezvous in the past. As concerned citizens of Baton Rouge looked on, Grand-Pré improved the antiquated fort's walls and raised more militia.[71] One Spaniard in town, or a loyal American friend, damned the escapade as the act of bandits "headed by a poor trifling wretch, and whose object was plunder."[72] The fact that Mississippi authorities took no action to punish them only convinced people the more that the United States condoned or even assisted in the act, and Grand-Pré actually believed Randolph to be an officer in the Mississippi territorial militia.[73] Loyalists in Baton Rouge felt determined to make a desperate resistance if the Americans interfered. "The people of this country are heartily attached to their Government," declared one. If they saw any new preparations above the line to threaten their tranquillity, "we will not wait for the invaders, but boldly advance and meet them on their own ground, and risk a battle."[74] In fact, revealing that the raid had raised belligerent feelings in Baton Rouge, he warned the Americans to look to their own crumbling defenses at New Orleans, which might start to look as attractive to the Spaniards as Mobile did to some Americans. "We have nothing to fear," he concluded. The Spaniards expected up to twelve regiments of *soldados* at Pensacola, and once they arrived "we shall rather rejoice at the approach of a rupture than dread it."[75]

That letter, with its rattling of the war saber, gained wide circulation in the press, though fortunately not until late November and early December, after the rest of the coverage of the Kemper raid died out and the crisis faded. Some thought it written by Casa Calvo himself, though he denied it, and the common assumption was that a Spanish officer in Baton Rouge was the author. A Philadelphia editor declared that whoever wrote it, it was the work of a foreign or domestic enemy.[76]

Meanwhile people wrestled with the seeming proliferation of Kempers. Most of those outside West Florida continued to assume that Reuben had led what one editor called "the frolic."[77] Garbled reports got it right that Kemper had worked for Smith but said that the merchant came from Tennessee rather than Ohio, and that Kemper had come to West Florida to escape debt.[78] Anyone knowing the circumstances of the Smith suit knew that this described Reuben, not Nathan, while other accounts depicting Kemper as "formerly a merchant at Bayou Sara" clearly meant Reuben.[79] A widely circulated statement spoke of "Col. Kemper" as "a planter of eminence, a daring, persevering character," adding to the confusion. The mysterious promotion to colonel reflected nothing more than the honorific often given to any leader of an armed party of men in the South, but ironically it attached itself to Reuben, not Nathan, for the rest of his life.[80] Clearly Kemper — any Kemper — was an unknown quantity. Papers in the East, which watched with amused interest, did not know what to believe of the mysterious revolutionary. One New York editor dismissed him by asking "if all the noisy demagogues in the world were collected together, how many of them would prove to be patriots of the same rank in which Smith has put Kemper."[81]

The Spaniards, like the Americans, made good use of the episode, each group for its own ends.[82] Claiborne thought that "Kemper's Riot, for it cannot fairly be called an Insurrection," had garnered far too much attention, and he condemned Yrujo and others for using it as a pretext to attack Jefferson; he blamed Casa Calvo for failing to advise the Spanish minister that America was not involved. In Madrid, the name Kemper even came before King Carlos in dispatches.[83] Still, by year's end Claiborne believed that the late insurrection at Baton Rouge had subsided and "would not be renewed."[84] In New Orleans and Washington, as in Pensacola and Havana, most just wanted the episode to go away.

Residents of West Florida were not fooled by the liberty rhetoric. Even the Kempers seemed uncertain of their motivation, operating from a mix of aims that shifted with circumstances. Violence was a problem throughout the Spanish colonies from 1785 onward, and occasional raids driven by motives of loot, revenge, and sometimes glory occurred all along the border from East Florida to Texas. The rhetoric of liberty more than once masked a thirst for plunder, and the efforts of American settlers to halt such activity shows how little most of it had to do with American nationalism.[85] The raiders, whatever their initial motivation, were opportunists, with too many lies and too much plundering to sustain an image of freedom fighters. Most Americans in West Florida already had as much freedom as they wanted, and more than they would have if the United States took over, at least when it came to deserters, fugitives from civil justice, and debtors hiding from creditors. Some preferred Spanish indolence and inefficiency in government to the more active justice system that might be imposed by the Americans. Land was still cheap or even free and easily available from Spain, whereas in the United States' territories, the speculators seemed to get the best tracts first. British inhabitants of the province and the Tories who had fled there from the Revolution were already conditioned to be loyal to a distant monarch, so Spain's king represented nothing unusual; what the Kempers offered would only return them to the political system they had come there to escape.[86] Men act in self-interest, and the Kempers learned the hard way that the interests of most Americans at the moment simply did not mirror their own.

4

Birds of a Feather

THE OUTBREAK in Feliciana surprised many who had expected it elsewhere, as very real confrontations constantly imperiled relations between Spain and the United States. Mobile was a constant hot spot, distracting Vicente Folch's attention from West Florida. Even before the Kemper episode, Folch had warned William Claiborne, the governor of Orleans Territory, that any attempt he made to exercise authority in West Florida would be an outrage against the rights of Folch's master, the Spanish king, and that any agent acting under instructions from Washington must beware the consequences.[1] Customs duties the Spanish exacted on American shipping through Mobile Bay were the sore point, and though Claiborne ordered them paid to avoid confrontation, settlers above the line strenuously objected.[2] They were a different breed in the Tombigbee settlements. In May of 1804, an American at Fort Stoddert complained that the area had long afforded an asylum to fugitives from American justice. His neighbors were "illiterate, wild and savage, of depraved morals, unworthy of public confidence or private esteem; litigious, disunited, and knowing each other, universally distrustful of each other." Justice there was corrupt, and he questioned "how long a rude people, who have been in the habit of redressing themselves on all occasions, will, under such circumstances continue quiet and peaceable."[3]

One of those scheming people was John Caller; he and his brother James, along with a large family and several slaves, had settled on the Tombigbee in 1799. When the new territory was created, John Caller had gained appointment as judge of the Washington County court, while his brother became a colonel of local militia.[4] In late August, just as Baton Rouge began to return to normal, the Callers complained loudly enough about the duties that the Spaniards feared they might raise discontent above the line to the boiling point, especially when rumors reached Pensacola that the Callers threatened to capture and burn any Spanish vessel they caught coming up the Tombigbee.[5] Caller and other judges like him decided their cases according to the laws of the states they had come from, each holding the laws of the others in contempt.[6] If these men felt so little regard for the statutes of their own country's states, Spain could hardly trust the Callers to respect the rights of another nation. The Kempers' march on Baton Rouge might inspire others, such as the Callers.

After the June standoff at the Bayou Sara house, Folch sent fifty *soldados* from Pensacola to Mobile to cut a road from there to Baton Rouge in case he later had to lead a reinforcement to Grand-Pré. In late August when he got word of the Kempers' incursion, Folch decided to act, boarding armed schooners with fifty dragoons, a company of grenadiers, two companies of fusiliers, twenty artillerymen, two small six-pounder cannon, a dozen officers and cadets, and even his band, and they all set sail for Lake Borgne, which connected to Lake Pontchartrain immediately north of New Orleans. There he picked up the new road to Baton Rouge, ordering the commander of the Mobile garrison to be watchful in case the Kempers should appear in his front.[7] Once ashore Folch found the new road as yet incomplete, which slowed the advance of the foot soldiers and artillery; Folch rode ahead with some dragoons on such existing roads as they could find. On Sunday, September 30, they reached Baton Rouge. The next Saturday the rest of the column bivouacked at a nearby plantation, and the following morning, October 7, people in Baton Rouge heard military music approaching town. At 8:00 A.M., led by a dozen musicians and drummers, the column marched into the fort accompanied by a seven-gun salute from its artillery. That afternoon a relieved Grand-Pré held a fine outdoor dinner for the new arrivals, followed by the military band accompanying a local woman for several songs, and then a ball lasting until midnight.[8]

Relative quiet reigned in Baton Rouge. The Kempers had not reappeared, and Grand-Pré finished an investigation into the uprising. He wisely treated the raids as simple outlawry, not as an international incident, and so did Marqués de Casa Yrujo, Spain's ambassador in Washington; they made no formal complaints to the United States, which they would have done if they had thought there was American backing or encouragement. A number of West Floridians who had joined the Kempers came to their senses and turned themselves in, and throughout September a board composed of Stirling, Isaac and John H. Johnson, Mears, and others — not a Spaniard among them — deposed the men and presented findings to the governor. Concluding that these participants were "infatuated by the pernicious and inflammatory insinuations of the Kempers," the board exonerated each man who posted a five-hundred-dollar bond, allowing them all to return to their homes in Feliciana without molestation. As for those who fled the province, chiefly Abrams and the Kempers, the board pronounced them outlaws.[9] By the end of the year almost all of the West Floridians in the gang had gained amnesty and returned to their homes except for the Kempers, Abrams, and one other, all of whom were by that time known to be in Pinckneyville.[10]

Normal business resumed. Pintado opened the surveyor's office again, and legal affairs that had been suspended for three weeks in August resumed by the end of the month.[11] Officials sold effects left behind by the Kempers, including a horse of Samuel's, to recompense planters for their expenses in repelling the revolt.[12] In fact, the area returned to quiet so quickly that Folch may have regretted the time and effort spent to bring his reinforcement to Baton Rouge, but the governor was not to be lulled by the current calm. Within a week he openly avowed that he feared another attempt to take West Florida.[13]

Claiborne believed Folch expected war with the United States and was preparing Baton Rouge accordingly.[14] When Folch summoned the Floridas' Spanish officials to Baton Rouge for a consultation, it raised apprehensions. Some welcomed confrontation, and Judge Rodney in Washington, Mississippi, just outside Natchez, thought locals preferred war to Spain's keeping West Florida, making him fear that if a conflict started, the United States could not keep westerners from overrunning Texas and even Mexico.[15] Folch's consultation did not happen, for after just two weeks he had neither provisions nor money to sustain his command at Baton Rouge any longer. He left only twenty *soldados* and two officers to augment the Baton Rouge garrison, which hardly sounded like he feared immediate danger, and sent the rest of his command home, though he got permission from Claiborne for himself and his staff to travel by way of New Orleans.[16] Folch no doubt wanted to see the city's defenses and look for signs of military preparations, while Claiborne wanted to take the Spaniard's measure.[17]

Renewed complaints of the Spaniards' actions at Mobile fed the discord. The Spanish stopped every American vessel coming to or sailing from Fort Stoddert and charged 12 percent duty on its cargo, with the Spaniards doing the valuation. Looking on from Fort Stoddert was forty-four-year-old Harry Toulmin, newly appointed superior court judge for the Tombigbee District of the Mississippi Territory, the highest civil official in hundreds of square miles of wilderness. This friend of Jefferson and Madison was a character in his own right. The English native began as a Unitarian minister, then became president of Transylvania Seminary in Lexington, Kentucky. His 1804 enrobement made him postmaster, superintendent of roads, local diplomat, and judge; he also performed weddings and worked as a physician, in spite of his having no medical training. At the same time he was writing the fabulous story of Maurice Griffith, a Welshman who said he had been captured by Shawnee in about 1765 and taken to a Missouri River settlement of thousands of white Indians who spoke Welsh. Toulmin hoped that Meriwether Lewis and William Clark, then exploring the Louisiana Territory, might discover if there was anything to the tale, which of course there was not.[18]

Toulmin wrote constantly to Madison protesting the Spaniards' duties as "the source of perpetual heart burnings and contention" between Americans and Spain. He warned of repercussions and came near to being right as American vessels started running past Mobile without stopping.[19] It led to sharp words between Mobile commander Francisco Maximiliano de San Maxent and Toulmin's future son-in-law Captain Edmund P. Gaines at Fort Stoddert, who refused to cooperate.[20] Maxent threatened to seize vessels, cargoes, and captains who tried to evade paying duty, and he began work on a gunboat to force them to stop on demand.[21] By October of 1804 the authorities were unloading cargoes to make sure they charged duty on everything. If that continued, Toulmin warned, the settlement would be abandoned, for impatient planters could not give up one-eighth of the value of their imports and exports.[22] "They are born amidst the clouds of ignorance," said Toulmin, and with few churches in the area, even religion could not restrain them.[23]

Claiborne took the matter to Governor Folch, asking for the interference with American shipping to cease. He warned Folch that if he reinforced Baton Rouge, Washington might have to strengthen its garrisons in the area, escalating an already charged atmosphere.[24] Folch finally agreed to stop collecting duties at Mobile when Claiborne confirmed that Spanish vessels taking goods to Baton Rouge paid no duty when they passed New Orleans. The problem, of course, was that such agreement constituted an acknowledgment that West Florida was genuinely Spanish territory.[25] The climate remained tense; Claiborne believed that a war over West Florida could be averted, but even an incident as trivial as the Kemper episode could change that. Claiborne was conciliatory when he called on Casa Calvo, whom he detested, and agreed to allow American mail passing through Baton Rouge to be examined. That eased Spanish fears, since the Spaniards could intercept any seditious correspondence.[26]

Then Folch inflamed Americans again when he issued two decrees before he left Baton Rouge on October 28. The first said that no American owning land in West Florida could sell it until he had actually occupied and improved it for ten years, instead of the usual two, and the second decreed that no new settlers could come into the province without prior permission from the government. Folch meant to halt further American settlement by either grant or purchase, just in case of war, which American settlers saw all too well. His act may have been defensive, but it looked like preparation for war, and it made the Americans feel almost as isolated as the Spaniards.[27]

No sooner had Folch left than Grand-Pré, no doubt acting on his superior's orders, issued a decree calling on planters in the area to turn over one of every five slaves to go to work on Folch's road. Some planters feared their slaves would not be returned, but in fact Grand-Pré encouraged the importation of more slaves from Africa into his districts, causing Claiborne to protest that if they came through New Orleans it would violate the prohibition on foreign slave trade in American territories.[28] Thus far, slavery in West Florida had provoked little contention other than protest over the occasional forays below the line by Mississippi owners chasing runaways. However, in the current atmosphere, any threat to the planters' property could lead even those planters who had put down the Kemper uprising to rise on their own. Their loyalty to Spain was always a matter of convenience and never ran deep, as Grand-Pré well knew, and it did not help that Point Coupée citizens had just uncovered a slave insurrection plot. Mindful of the horrors at San Domingue, they petitioned Claiborne for protection.[29] No wonder Judge Rodney found the slave owners below the line restless and uneasy and feared an eruption if Grand-Pré did not return the blacks when they finished the road.[30]

Folch's stop in New Orleans unwittingly added to the tension. While at Baton Rouge one of his captains had arrested an American citizen suspected of some disloyal act, but the fellow escaped, went to the superior court in New Orleans, and obtained a writ for the officer's arrest, probably for abduction. When the captain refused to appear in court, Claiborne sent militia to arrest him, only to find the captain surrounded by friends with drawn swords, ready to resist. No blow was struck and the captain surrendered himself, but Folch and Casa Calvo demanded his immediate release or else the latter would leave the territory and would not be answerable for "the *consequences* and *Revolution* that might ensue." Claiborne, who would have been delighted to see the back of Casa Calvo, refused to interfere in a judicial matter, said he would deal with the Spaniards' demand when he found it convenient, and happily promised to give Casa Calvo a passport to depart at any time. That same evening he had to send militia to disperse a mob of about two hundred gathered in front of a shaken Casa Calvo's residence.[31] Madison later fully approved Claiborne's conduct. Folch was allowed in New Orleans solely as a courtesy and had no cause to expect immunity from territorial laws. As for Casa Calvo, he was in New Orleans as a private citizen and had no authority to demand anything of anyone.[32] In fact, thereafter Claiborne simply left Casa Calvo's letters unanswered.

The Kempers' resistance the previous summer had set all this in motion. Their raid briefly broke down law and order, provoking a response that aroused anger at the authorities.[33] The atmosphere did not cool after Folch and his officers left New Orleans in mid-December.[34] Almost simultaneously, Claiborne and Cato West received instructions from Washington to prevent further expeditions originating in American territories from violating those "possessed by Spain," an interesting choice of words given Jefferson's posture that West Florida belonged to the United States.[35] Possession was not the same as ownership, and thus the president acknowledged Spanish occupation of the province but not Spain's title to it. The Kempers had forced even Jefferson to act.

Claiborne found himself under fire from one of Reuben Kemper's friends, Daniel Clark. Any cordiality between the two men had ceased some months since. Clark, along with Edward Livingston, an influential attorney and speculator, wanted immediate statehood for the Orleans Territory, most likely to advance both his political and speculation ambitions.[36] When Clark found an obstacle in Claiborne, he began writing anonymous attacks in the city's press. Clark had ties to another enemy of Claiborne. In October of 1804 Congress formally established the Territory of Orleans as all of the Louisiana Purchase below the thirty-third parallel, designating the rest of the vast country spreading north and west to the Pacific as the District of Louisiana. Jefferson appointed Claiborne governor of the new territory, which meant that he could no longer govern Mississippi Territory as well, so the president appointed Robert Williams to that post. Until Williams took office, however, Cato West continued as interim governor. West was allied with a group in the territorial legislature whom his foes called "the clan," all of them opposed to Claiborne.[37] Clark could cause little direct harm to Claiborne, for Jefferson and Madison stood thoroughly behind the governor, but his connections with would-be speculators and with men like Randolph and the Kempers positioned him to make trouble.

With the new year, tensions gradually escalated. Both Washington and Madrid discussed what Madison called "the affair of Kemper," and Jefferson maintained steady, though muted, assertion of the United States' right to West Florida. Since Folch had run a road through West Florida to Baton Rouge without American permission, Jefferson directed in March of 1805 that a new post road be run from Nashville to New Orleans, which necessarily had to cross West Florida.[38] Madison anticipated no Spanish resistance, for even with a slightly bolstered garrison of two hundred at Baton Rouge, fewer than one hundred at Mobile, and perhaps another six hundred at Pensacola, Folch was too weak to risk a confrontation, and Claiborne's sources told him that Spain could not depend on the West Florida Spaniards, especially in Baton Rouge, that a general spirit of disaffection possessed them and that they had a great desire to become Americans.[39] Visitors noted the area's isolation and weakness and its recent history; a French traveler remarked that the Kempers, striking by night from Bayou Sara, "almost succeeded in seizing the Spanish post at Baton Rouge."[40]

Word also spread of mounting discontent over land policy, for now Grand-Pré prohibited Americans who came to West Florida to take the oath of allegiance, become citizens, and obtain land grants. That meant that relatives of current settlers could not join them unless they found a landowner of more than ten years' residence willing to sell at a fair price, both rarities in 1805. Soon the few who qualified to sell their land began to speculate, sometimes doubling their investment, but in Feliciana, values stagnated at their 1805 level. Elsewhere, prices started a rise that saw them more than triple by 1810. At the end of that same period, Feliciana land was worth less than it had been in 1802. Late in 1805 when Morales resumed land sales, he sold almost a million acres between Baton Rouge and Mobile but not an arpent in Feliciana.[41]

Once again the Kemper raid lay at the root of the problem. With Feliciana barely more than a mile from Pinckneyville, few buyers wanted to risk locating close to that haven of mayhem.[42] Morales's resumed sales led to a rumor that he meant to dispose of all remaining vacant land in West Florida before any United States takeover. That would leave nothing for new American settlers to occupy, and no revenue from its sale. When Casa Calvo confirmed the rumor, Claiborne refused to allow Morales to conduct any further business in New Orleans.[43] That effectively stopped Morales for the moment, though he remained in the city for some time.

Meanwhile, Pintado all but shut down operations, telling his surveyors nothing could be done for the present.[44] When one of them was slow to comply, Pintado sternly warned that he would take any necessary steps to prevent disobedience.[45] Quick and efficient surveys came to a halt, and some grantees blamed the Kempers, but more blamed Spain.[46] The Spanish law requiring anyone with fewer than two years' residence in the province to leave their land if they were unable to prove legal title made matters worse. Little or no land was actually lost, but grantees now unable to get the surveys to secure legal title felt serious concern.[47] Grand-Pré tried to dampen unrest by rewarding those Americans who had helped to repel the Kempers. In March he offered land grants to men who had put down the uprising, and at the same time he began to deprive suspect men, such as Champ Terry, of the unsurveyed land on which they had made improvements.[48]

The situation arising from the Kemper episode justified Folch's and Grand-Pré's actions, yet everything they did seemed only to irritate those whose loyalty they most needed, making the Kempers' cause of expedience seem closer to a reality. When the Spaniards encouraged the two-year-old rumor that West Florida might be traded to the United States in return for the rest of Louisiana, they did so to weaken the loyalty of American settlers west of the Mississippi around Natchitoches, but unwittingly they also sent mixed signals to the people of West Florida, implying that Spain did not care about them in spite of their loyalty during the recent crisis.[49] Now accusations of corruption in the administration of justice emerged. John Mills accused Alcalde Stirling of misappropriating property entrusted to him by the court, and a jailed debtor alleged that Stirling overcharged him and others for their provisions and used the man's seized property for private speculation and profit. When Grand-Pré ordered Stirling to surrender the man's property, Stirling refused.[50] It was out of character for the respected alcalde, but even false accusations of corruption could do damage among the Americans.

All the while, the Kempers looked on from Pinckneyville. It was "a straggling village of ten houses, mostly in decay, and some of them uninhabited," according to one visitor; it had a church, a store, a tavern, and a post office. It sat on a pleasant sloping plain of good soil, fine plantations, and prosperous planters, and it extended down to Thompson's Creek.[51] The Kempers did not prosper, however. Neither Samuel nor Nathan owned a home. Instead, shortly after being driven from West Florida, Nathan leased a building next door to Randolph, and with his wife and two young sons, he began operating a tavern with no property to his name but a slave and a brace each of horses and cattle. Samuel owned nothing but three slaves that he had spirited out of West Florida before the raid, having lost his horse in fleeing. Only Reuben had the cash or credit to buy property next to Randolph, who probably sold him the twenty-eight-foot square frame house and three half-acre town lots in Pinckneyville where Samuel and others lodged with Reuben's one slave while he was working on the rivers.[52]

Although the brothers stayed out of West Florida, Reuben never abandoned his determination to settle his dispute over the award of his 240-acre parcel to Smith. Kemper persuaded George King, the New Orleans coffeehouse keeper, to buy the unpaid mortgage on the property from Duplantier, with the understanding that King would transfer the title to Reuben when he paid the $2,100 outstanding.[53] Having the title in King's name would presumably place the land beyond seizure.

However, some believed that Reuben had bold plans beyond this one lot, plans involving the whole region in international intrigues that might well see a new flag flying over Baton Rouge, all seeming to stem from events and plots gestating half a continent away. On July 11, 1804, even as the Kemper band traded shots with Pintado's patrols, Vice President Aaron Burr mortally wounded former secretary of the Treasury Alexander Hamilton in a duel. Burr knew that killing Hamilton ended his political career in the United States. His term of office expired in March of 1805, and his Federalist Party waned in the face of Jefferson's growing Democratic-Republicans, leaving Burr little hope of fulfilling his towering ambitions. For nearly a decade he had eyed the Floridas, Texas, and Mexico, often boasting that he could take them away from Spain. That put him in the mainstream of American expansionists, but he did little more than dream until May of 1804, when he met with General James Wilkinson. They had been friends for years, and no doubt Burr suspected or knew that Wilkinson had been selling Spain confidential military and political information for some years but was willing to turn on his Spanish masters, just as he had on his own government, if he stood to profit. For his part, Burr might have planned to rebuild himself in the Southwest, though then and hereafter his precise plans were cloudy: did he want to take an empire away from Spain to rule himself; wrest it from the

Spaniards only to hand it over to Britain; or take Orleans and even Mississippi and dismember the Union? Possibly his plans extended no further than seizing huge tracts of land west of the Mississippi for speculation. Unquestionably he envisioned armed Americans taking Texas and the Floridas, and since Jefferson maintained that the latter belonged to the United States, that meant that whatever Burr and Wilkinson planned was treason.[54]

Burr met with British minister Anthony Merry in Philadelphia, and Merry came away believing that Burr proposed to aid Britain in taking all American territory west of the Appalachians, though Burr probably overstated his intentions to get British support for his real, though less ambitious, scheme. With Britain and Spain then at war, it was implicit that any new British empire in Louisiana and Mississippi would leave the Floridas isolated and easy prey. Burr tried to visit the provinces in the fall of 1805, but he had gotten no farther than St. Simons Island on the Georgia coast before bad weather turned him away, though not before the press buzzed. On September 15 one editor speculated sarcastically that Burr meant to become "emperor" of St. Simons. That same day the eastern press published Randolph's declaration and details of the Kempers' raid. "Perhaps Mr. Burr has a notion to become the Kemper of St. Simon's," the editor went on. "Possibly he means to join Kemper, and act as lieutenant-general of the *commonwealth of Florida.*" St. Simons was on a direct line with Bayou Sara, "the head quarters of the gallant Kemper." Perhaps Burr intended to join the Kempers and together spread their treason. "New Orleans and its vicinity seem to be the load-stone to the intriguing, the dangerous, the discontented, and the worthless," observed the editor. "To raise rebellion in this quarter against the government would complete Mr. Burr's Catalinian character." Reminding readers of the cliché about birds of a feather, the editor added that "Kemper and Burr, however, may differ, and a quarrel among the generals of the camp become fatal." To readers who that very day had read the declaration about people being free if they willed it, he concluded that "Mr. Burr found that *willing* was not sufficient, and I rather think Kemper will by and bye be of the same opinion."[55]

The generic rebel Kemper had briefly become in the eastern mind the equal, and even potential superior, of Burr as a plotter. Quite coincidentally one paper ran a small notice of Burr's arrival at St. Simons immediately beneath a comment on the West Florida uprising, noting that Kemper "was confident of success, calculating on the common credulity of the multitude to stories of liberty and equality."[56] It was a description that aptly fit Aaron Burr as well, who spent the next several months enlisting confederates, raising money, and establishing contacts with some influential men. Yrujo saw what he was doing and warned Folch that he should arrest Burr if he in any way got involved with local dissidents. With the Kemper raid still a recent memory, he did not need to remind Folch that some men near them would be happy to oust Spain.[57]

At least five of those men lived in Pinckneyville. The Kempers made three, and Burr traveled with Wilkinson's introduction to Clark in his baggage. Clark was a major planter with 130 slaves on his plantation near Pinckneyville.[58] Of course, he also had a partnership with Randolph in their mercantile business, and he was part of a new organization calling itself the Mexican Society of New Orleans, made up of as many as three hundred merchants and professional men, including lawyer Livingston, Judge James Workman, militia colonel Lewis Kerr, and more. If Clark was in the society, then Randolph likely was as well, and possibly even Reuben Kemper. Claiborne warned Madison that Clark was deeply involved with Morales in speculation on West Florida land and posed a danger to relations with Spain.[59] At that moment Clark planned a trip to Veracruz to acquaint himself with the military strength of the Spaniards. Though Burr had not met any of the Pinckneyville five as yet, his ties to Wilkinson tied him to them.

Rumors reached Baton Rouge of secret meetings at Randolph and Clark's store below the line at Tunica, where the owners employed a man as both clerk and agitator. Frederick Kimball met with the group, as did Randolph and the Kempers, especially Reuben. Alleged specifics of their plans emerged when a Feliciana planter named Thomas Hutchins visited Pinckneyville on April 20.[60] Someone, probably the Kempers' near neighbor Abram Horton, recently relocated from his Feliciana tavern, told Hutchins that during the first week of April, Reuben, Arthur Cobb Jr., and another man sailed from New Orleans for New Providence in the Bahamas. They expected to get commissions in the British army for themselves and others back home, and then return in an armed vessel to Lake Pontchartrain and go from there up the Amite River, with authority to raise what Hutchins called a "body of Brigands." Supposedly at that very moment confederates on the coast waited to catch sight of their vessel, whereupon runners would return to Pinckneyville and West Florida to assemble their associates. Kemper would march from the Amite while the other band would descend from Pinckneyville in a repeat of the raid of last year. In fact, Hutchins warned, "a Band of these Brigands is already formed to perpetrate the most diabolical Deeds."

The columns would converge on Baton Rouge "with a view to plundering all, of massacring many, and if supported by the English of conquering the District for them." The men marked for assassination made a budget of the Kempers' grudges — Grand-Pré, Pintado, Fulton, Kneeland, and Murdoch, who currently rented Horton's tavern at Bayou Sara. Then everyone at Tunica was to die, and several more who lived on Thompson's Creek, the victims' property to be plundered and removed to the ship moored in the Amite. Only fear of arousing the United States and having Mississippi and Orleans militia cut off their retreat restrained them at the moment, said Hutchins. If Kemper got English support they would be ready by early June. Hutchins heard whispers in Pinckneyville that these "Partizans" were confident of success.[61]

The story was almost pure invention based on wild rumor, exaggeration of a few facts, and the animus of informants toward the Kempers and Randolph. Reuben was absent that April, but instead of leaving New Orleans the first week of the month, he was in the city during the last week arranging for King to buy his old mortgage. While Burr might have entertained British involvement in his West Florida enterprise, every act of Reuben's revealed a single purpose: to see the province come under the American eagle. Moreover, the supposed plot had no ultimate or permanent goal but was rather a raid for plunder, with some murder thrown in. The raiders would just load their booty and flee.

Hutchins sent warning of the plot to Grand-Pré or Casa Calvo or both on April 22, and in a few days Casa Calvo brought it to Claiborne's attention. "Kemper and his adherents are attempting to renew their Hostile designs," he stated, asking Claiborne to alert Governor Robert Williams in Mississippi and entreat him to keep Kemper and the rest above the line.[62] Claiborne promised to prevent Kemper from gaining any assistance in U.S. territory, doubting that the British would have anything to do with such a scheme, but if Reuben did show up with a British ship, Claiborne would prevent any violation of American neutrality.[63] He clearly regarded the story as nonsense, telling Williams that it was an exaggeration even as he put him on the alert.[64] All the same, he reinforced Fort St. John, which guarded Lake Pontchartrain.[65]

Claiborne left almost immediately for a two-week visit to Baton Rouge. Ostensibly, this was an inspection trip of upper Orleans Territory across the river, but the real purpose was to assess the situation in West Florida. Grand-Pré received him cordially, but the Spaniards were nervous.[66] Claiborne's order to reinforce Fort St. John had led to a rumor that troops were being set in place to seize West Florida. Claiborne tried to put Grand-Pré at ease, which he did, but some in Baton Rouge expected to be attacked at any moment.[67] Grand-Pré ordered more repairs on the fort and put his garrison, now down to 120, on alert, and he moved from his house in the village to the protection of the fort's walls, there to remain for the next few months.[68]

It was not a good time for Aaron Burr to appear in New Orleans. He reached the city on June 26 and began meeting with members of the Mexican Society, passing considerable time with Livingston and Clark in particular.[69] He also met with Morales, seemingly confirming his connection to the speculators.[70] Burr left in mid-July, crossed Lake Pontchartrain, and then rode across country through Feliciana to Natchez. To cross the line, he had to pass through either Woodville or Pinckneyville; the latter route was more direct, and Burr would have wanted to meet Randolph and the wealthy Dr. John F. Carmichael, who would later figure in his plans. Surely he would have wanted to meet the Kempers as well, the men who had already led one attempted uprising and still had some following in West Florida. If Burr had heard Hutchins's story, then he could see that Reuben had plans with Britain that overlapped with his own. And he had to know that the eastern press compared him to one of these Kempers. Such men, few though their adherents were, could be useful allies in his grander schemes.

If Burr met with any of the Kempers, later events suggest that Reuben was not one of them. In fact, he was probably still in New Orleans, where his friend George King sold the mortgage on the Bayou Sara property without waiting for Kemper to pay it off, a serious blow to Reuben's efforts to retain some hold on the land.[71] Still, the conjunction of Burr and the speculations of his designs, together with Reuben's supposed plan for massacre and pillage, the growing discontent in West Florida over halting land surveys, cessation of American settlement, complaints of corruption of justice, and more, only reawakened old fears. Amid such heightened tensions incidents were inevitable. The first came in midsummer, when a West Florida man killed another man in an altercation. The killer took his wife and fled to the home of a nephew just half a mile above the line, in Wilkinson County. On the afternoon of August 21, two American lieutenants and a dozen Spanish militia rode across the line without permission and tried to intimidate the fugitive's relatives into revealing his whereabouts. Sabers were drawn and pistols cocked, and when one of the family said the party had no authority in Mississippi, a lieutenant declared, "Damn the line," and said he would use his authority on either side as he wished. The militia left only when it was apparent that shooting was about to commence.[72]

Instead of recrossing the line, however, the party kept looking, and they finally found the fugitive and took both him and his wife below the line, where they released the wife. Riding deeper into West Florida, the militia then robbed their prisoner of his horse and saddle at gunpoint and let him go, making it apparent that the arrest was simply an act of plunder much like those the Kempers carried out the year before. Their victim believed most of them were in fact deserters and refugees from the United States who had fled to Spanish territory.[73]

Claiborne probably learned of the incident when he stopped in Baton Rouge four days later on a second visit to Grand-Pré. It would be up to Williams in Mississippi to make any formal complaint, but it was evident that there were men in West Florida quite willing to return the favor of unlawful incursion and mayhem. Though Grand-Pré gave his visitor a fine dinner in the fort that was now his home, his unease was apparent, as was his weakness. Claiborne concluded that despite the fort's recent repairs, it would take a thousand rather than Grand-

Pré's mere 120 *soldados* to defend the place, especially since poor location put it at the mercy of higher ground barely four hundred yards distant.[74] Grand-Pré did not tell Claiborne that he had something in mind to redress this weakness, but even as the governor left for New Orleans, plans were being made, possibly with his knowledge or even at his instigation. If the Kempers presented a hazard to West Florida, then West Florida would have to remove the Kempers.

5

You Have Ruined Our Country

ONE OF THE KEMPERS' neighbors had already warned them to move away for their own safety. The plot against them originated with Abram Horton.[1] He was one of the more prosperous settlers in Wilkinson and the eighth-largest slaveholder.[2] Before moving there he had been a loyal vassal of Spain in West Florida for more than fifteen years.[3] That alone gave him cause to resent the Kempers. With land prices stagnant, he stood to lose money, while unstable conditions along the line discouraged people from buying even the land that he and others could sell. Men on the supposed death list, such as the surveyor Ira Kneeland, were Horton's friends, and John Murdoch was a tenant in his old tavern on Thompson's Creek, where more men were supposedly marked for murder. Though there had been no serious disagreements between them, as far as Horton was concerned, the Kempers were ruining the country. Others agreed, some of whom were virtually next-door neighbors of the brothers. The merchant Minor Butler lived just three houses away from them, and he was fed up with the way the brothers attracted vagabonds and encouraged lawlessness on the border. Unable to get local authorities to curb the Kempers' activities, he was happy to act with Horton and the others to deal with the problem themselves.[4] Kneeland's brother John lived nearby.[5]

Below the line, others nurtured their own causes for grudge. Solomon Alston's father-in-law, Alexander Stirling, was on the death list. His lieutenant William Barker and another man had trouble getting grants confirmed, thanks to the ban on surveys.[6] Some were just friends of John Smith.[7] Ira C. Kneeland, of course, felt a very per-

sonal reason to want the Kempers out of the way: they had supposedly threatened his life despite his recent marriage to their friend William Cobb's widow.[8] Several former residents of the Natchez District
moved below the line after Spain gave up Mississippi, simply preferring Spanish rule. Many of them resented the Kempers' efforts to oust
the Spaniards.[9]

Grand-Pré had the most cause of all to hate the Kempers, since the
brothers had raided and robbed along his border, plotted his kidnapping, and supposedly planned to kill him and plunder his province.
Every night he spent in the cramped quarters of his fort rather than
in his comfortable home in town he could blame on them, as he could
all of the growing unrest in his districts. Nothing would make him
happier than to see the Kempers and their friends removed from the
scene, and a preemptive strike might do it. Even if the governor did
not instigate the effort, he still might have communicated to Captain
Alston that he would not be displeased to see "the Partizans" disappear. Grand-Pré may not have had to give an order for his friends to
decide to take action against the Kempers, and in fact it was better for
Grand-Pré if they acted without his involvement.[10]

Two separate parties would be involved, one from Pinckneyville,
and the other from Feliciana, and they may or may not have been coordinated. Horton's group planned to surprise the Kempers in their
homes by night and take them to the line, where they expected to
meet Alston commanding one of the border patrols. Horton either
arranged it with Alston or simply took advantage of knowing that Alston regularly rode the line after dark. If Alston was in on the plan,
then he arranged to have a pirogue waiting at the Tunica Bayou landing to take the prisoners down the Mississippi and thence to Baton
Rouge, where Spanish justice could deal with them or send them to
Havana for trial as traitors. One uncertainty remained. Reuben Kemper worked on the rivers, only occasionally staying in Pinckneyville.
The plotters had to wait for his next visit.

Reuben certainly never made the voyage to New Providence and
was in Pinckneyville by early September. Those watching for him
learned that he intended to stay long enough for them to launch their
scheme. On Monday evening, September 2, Horton and his sixteen-
year-old son, James, brought seven of their slaves to a rendezvous

with Minor Butler and others, while at the same time Henry Flowers, Bryan McDermott, and other men from below the line crossed over to join them.[11] Ira Kneeland, stopping at Pinckneyville for the night on the way home from business at Fort Adams, bumped into the party on the road and rode along with them, or so he claimed.[12] There were twenty to twenty-five of them, and the whites blackened their faces, hoping to look like Negroes. Since Samuel stayed at the tavern when Reuben was home, and Nathan and his family lodged with Reuben on the outskirts of town, the Kempers could not all be taken together. Horton divided his gang. Five men rode to the tavern, while the bulk headed for Reuben's, evidence that Horton expected the most resistance from the two older brothers.[13]

There were other men in Reuben's house that evening, including two who had been with the "boys in the house" the previous year, either a coincidental visit or evidence that Nathan planned some new action. All of them had retired by 11:00 P.M. when they heard a shout outside. The calls awakened Reuben from his sleep on a mattress on the floor of his bedroom. He went to the door and asked repeatedly who had called; he got no answer the first two times he spoke, but then the man on the other side said he was their old friend Basil Abrams and he wanted to come in. When Reuben unfastened the latchstring, several men armed with pistols and clubs rushed in shouting at him and immediately began choking and beating him so severely that he could barely rasp, "I surrender." They dragged him outside, tore off his nightshirt, and started beating him about the head and face, while one man cut a deep gash across his cheek with a knife. Meanwhile, others rushed inside and grabbed Nathan in his bed by his arms and legs and carried him out; one of the slaves pushed his wife down on the floor and held her there. As he was carried outside, Nathan heard someone behind him in the bedroom say, "If the bitch utters another word, put her to death." Then he heard the sound of a blow being struck, and his wife did not answer when Nathan called to her. They took Nathan outside, where he saw James Horton "stomping" Reuben's face, and then they tied up both of them, all the while cocking and uncocking their guns and pointing them at the brothers. When Nathan asked to see his wife, they refused to let him, and when she tried to leave the house, they restrained her roughly. Dazed and bewildered, Nathan asked why they were doing this. "God damn!" one of them growled. "You have ruined our country."

Their captors set guards at both doors to the house and ordered all the people inside to identify themselves. When any of them approached the door, including Nathan's wife and sons, the raiders pointed cocked weapons and warned that if anyone tried to come to the brothers' aid, they would "blow the first one through." Meanwhile, the beating of Reuben continued, leaving him with more severe gashes on his face and chin, and blood on the ground all about him. Thanks to a full moon, he recognized the Hortons, Butler, and Kneeland through their hasty disguises, while some of Horton's slaves he knew by name. The assailants let Nathan don some overalls but allowed Reuben neither hat nor shoes, and with the brothers firmly bound and their mouths gagged with sassafras roots, someone, probably Horton, yelled, "Forward, march," in military fashion and they set off.[14] Most likely they had hoped to take Randolph too, but he must have been away. Their lack of interest in others in the house suggests that they came with specific targets in mind rather than a general purge of Kemper associates.

Meanwhile, the other party approached the tavern where Samuel Kemper lay sleeping. A recent visitor regarded area taverns as rendezvous for "the idlers of the countryside, the drunkards and the gamblers," and Kemper's may have been no different.[15] On this night he had three lodgers: Arthur Cobb and two other friends who had ridden with Nathan the year before; they were local cronies and no doubt regular patrons. About midnight Samuel heard a knock at the tavern door. Down with a fever for several days, he called from his bed to ask who was there, and he did not distinctly hear the reply that it was friends who wanted whiskey. He asked again, and suddenly the raiders broke down the tavern door and rushed into his bedroom. Before he got out of bed they were upon him, and when he tried to rise one of them hit him with a double-barreled shotgun. The assailants dragged him out by his hands and into the tavern room, where he put up a struggle as they began beating him with clubs.

Awakened by the commotion, one of his friends started to rise, only to have two men with blackened faces push him back into his mattress, threatening to kill him if he moved. Cobb awoke and heard

Samuel yell "Murder and robbers" as loud as he could while struggling with the assailants. When Cobb saw a few more armed men with rifles and pistols, he decided to get out by a back door and call for help. Soon another man escaped, leaving only the third, who somehow slept through it all until Samuel was dragged outside. Looking out the door after them, that man saw five men beating Kemper on the ground with clubs, Samuel still yelling "Murder," hoping to arouse neighbors and warn his brothers. Samuel recognized all but one of the men surrounding him, including two neighbors, two of Horton's slaves, and two more from below the line.

Finally they bound his hands and tied a rope around his neck, then dragged him about a hundred and fifty yards before they allowed him to stand. When he shouted "Murder" again they hit him on the head with a pistol butt then took the rope from his neck and tied it to his arm, mounted their horses, and made him run alongside them for perhaps a quarter mile until they felt secure enough to halt and put Samuel up behind one of the mounted men. Even then, as they rode away a slave ran alongside holding the rope tied to Kemper's arm.[16] Again they did not interfere with Samuel's friends in spite of their involvement in last year's mayhem. This mob wanted only Kempers.

The party with Samuel took the main road south from Pinckneyville. The larger group with Reuben and Nathan were ahead of them, having stopped briefly at Abram Horton's home. This certainly gave away his identity. Horton and the others did not care if the Kempers identified them and more likely wanted the captives to know who took them, meaning they had little apprehension of legal or personal reprisals. Indeed, Horton laughed frequently during the trip, even as others occasionally beat Reuben's face even more. Clearly they did not expect the Kempers ever to return to Mississippi and perhaps did not expect them to live long enough to cause trouble. They quickly departed Horton's and then left the road and went into the woods just short of the line, where they waited a few minutes until they heard their confederates approach. The reunited raiders then rode the remaining few hundred yards to the line.[17]

That evening the dozen Americans in Alston's patrol rendezvoused as usual and checked the paths along the line until they stopped to rest at a widow's home on the Pinckneyville road by the west bank of Little Bayou Sara, barely a thousand yards from the line. Nathan Kemper had been crossing at this point, and the widow's house may have been where he had been staying during his incursions, so naturally they kept a close eye on her place. About midnight the men remounted and rode toward the line, and within a couple of hundred yards of it they saw movement ahead of them.

"Are you Captain Alston?" a voice cried out from the moonlit shadows.

"Yes," Alston replied. Perhaps not knowing who was there, he ordered his men to look to their weapons.

"The three Kemper brothers are prisoners," said the voice.

"Come closer, *muchachos*," Alston yelled back.

The riders approached to within fifty yards or so, just across the line, and Alston's patrol saw that they had three men bound and gagged, and at least one of them was being led by a rope. The captors said nothing more but simply abandoned the Kempers there in the road and quickly dispersed into the woods, though not before several of Alston's men thought they recognized most of them as Negroes. When the patrol rode up to the Kempers, they saw that two of them appeared to have been badly beaten.

If Alston had been in on the kidnapping, then this was what he expected. If he had not, then it was too late to go after the kidnappers, and meanwhile he found himself with three very much wanted men on his hands. The only recourse seemed to be to take them to Baton Rouge. With the Kempers mounted once more, Alston led the patrol to Tunica Landing; it was not much over nine miles distant, but with no good road, it took until an hour before dawn for them to reach the bayou.[18] In the gathering light, the Kempers probably recognized a few of their new escorts, especially Alston and William Barker. Samuel likely still believed that they were all to be murdered, and Alston may have treated them roughly, considering Reuben's presumed threats to Stirling the year before and the story of the death list that past spring. However, when the brothers saw the bayou and the pirogue waiting for them, they realized they were not to be killed just yet, if at all.[19]

Alston's men went to Randolph's store at the landing and found him absent. They gave his clerk and others in the house an hour to leave and probably ransacked the store, meaning that even if Alston was not in on the kidnapping plot, he quickly decided to further its aims.[20] At least one of the men thought it suspicious that a pirogue happened to be conveniently available as Alston ordered the Kempers put into the boat and placed Barker in command of a party of six men to take them to Baton Rouge. Alston gave Barker strict orders to give the captives no opportunity to escape. The Kempers were all still bound, but as a further precaution Barker tied the three of them together. Reuben recognized all of the men holding him, for they made no effort at disguise, and they freely told the Kempers that they were to be handed over to Grand-Pré.[21]

Barker cast off just after dawn on September 3, and in less than a mile rowed out of the bayou into the Mississippi. Baton Rouge lay about eighty river miles downstream, and the bank on their left was Spanish territory all the way, so they had little to fear as long as they stayed close to that side. Adding the power of their oars to the current, they could make five or six miles an hour, perhaps more, and if there was no mishap, Barker expected to reach Baton Rouge before dark. At first the voyage passed uneventfully, but when they rounded Raccouri Point they began to pass plantations on the west bank above Punta Cortada. The river current coming off Raccouri must have pulled the pirogue closer to that shore, near enough to the Louisiana bank that the boat's occupants could be seen and heard.

Reuben indicated to Barker that he wanted to speak to him. With his gag removed he told Barker he had a boat back above the line that he wanted to sell to Dr. John Fowles, whose plantation they were just then passing. Would Barker steer close enough to shore that he could hail the doctor? Unaware that Fowles was the post surgeon for the United States garrison at Point Coupée, the credulous Barker steered toward the bank. The brothers yelled, and Fowles left his bed and stepped outside. As soon as they believed he could understand them, they shouted, "We are the Kempers taken on the other side of the line and these Spaniards are taking us prisoners to Baton Rouge."[22]

Within minutes, Fowles saddled and mounted a horse, and soon the men in the boat saw him speeding along the river road toward Point Coupée, some five miles downriver. If Barker knew the Kempers had been heard, he should have put in to the Spanish bank, but he kept on his course. Fowles covered the distance to Point Coupée much faster than the pirogue, and he rushed to tell Lieutenant William Wilson in command what he had heard. Wilson immediately manned a barge of his own just as the pirogue was passing, and he gave chase. Before long he overtook the pirogue and demanded to know whom Barker had tied up in his boat. Barker answered that he had the Kempers, and after a brief show of resistance he surrendered and pulled to shore shortly before noon, at which point Wilson took all of the occupants into custody, the Kempers and their captors, until he could sort out the situation.[23]

The lieutenant scarcely knew what to think. He ordered depositions taken from all of the Kempers and from Barker, and he sent an express to Colonel Richard Sparks, commanding at Fort Adams, asking for some reinforcements, and another to Claiborne, who was then in Natchez. Wilson feared that the kidnapping of the Kempers might be part of some larger conspiracy or that the Spaniards might move against him in retaliation for his stopping the pirogue. "My force is weak, and I expect an attack from the other side of the river," he warned Claiborne. "I shall, however, give them as hearty reception as the situation of my force will admit."[24]

Wilson's appeals reached Fort Adams and Natchez the following day. Since the initial attack on the Kempers had taken place on Mississippi soil, Claiborne ordered all of the prisoners to be sent there for Governor Williams to deal with. He calmed Wilson's fears of a Spanish attack, assuring him that the militia could be called out if necessary.[25] Sparks hurried a detachment to Point Coupée on September 7, and two days later Williams ordered the Kempers and other prisoners sent to Fort Adams.[26]

Word of the outrage had spread quickly from Pinckneyville. The morning after the attack, witnesses who had fled came back, only to find Samuel gone from the tavern and a lot of blood on the ground outside Reuben's home. Other witnesses remained to testify of what they saw, and though none seemed to have recognized any of the assailants, Cobb found a pistol belonging to Ira Kneeland left behind at the tavern. That same day they all went to the county justice of the peace to give depositions, as yet uncertain whether the Kempers were alive or murdered.[27]

Even while the witnesses told their stories, a man from Pinckneyville arrived in Natchez on September 5 with the first sketchy news of the affair, reporting only that Reuben and Samuel were taken and that it was done by "a party of armed Spaniards."[28] The next day, his brief statement appeared in the Natchez press, soon to be on its way all across the country. Once the Kempers reached Point Coupée they also began telling their story to eager ears. Just two days after their rescue, a full narrative based on their accounts was on its way to appear in the *Mississippi Herald,* and soon it too traveled to the presses in the East.[29] Meanwhile Williams ordered 106 men from the territorial militia to rendezvous at Pinckneyville and commence patrolling the line, stopping to examine all suspicious characters who passed over from below, especially those crossing after dark, and arresting any who were armed. If there were any further attempts at violence to either citizens or property, he told them, "force must be repelled by force."[30]

Pinckneyville was already in a stir, alarmed, enraged, and apprehensive, especially since rumor said that most of the party had been slaves. Any time blacks assaulted whites, there was bound to be fear of a servile uprising in the background. The patrols soon eased those fears, though the citizens all appeared to be on the alert, "no man considering himself safe where a few designing bad white men can exercise an influence over the blacks." Before long they knew that most of the raiders had been whites, a fact confirmed when at least two of the men recognized by the Kempers — probably the Hortons — fled below the line to evade Mississippi law. The Kempers' neighbors wanted justice for the assailants and waited to see how far Grand-Pré would try to go to justify the act.[31]

Governor Williams wanted to know the same thing. As soon as he learned of the outrage he wrote to Grand-Pré, on September 6, that "this conduct, sir, does not comport with that good understanding and friendly disposition supposed to exist between our Governments." It could not be tolerated. He put the Spaniard on notice to prevent any further such outrages against Americans and demanded an explanation of the conduct of Spanish subjects, some of whom appeared to be officials of the militia subject to Grand-Pré's orders.[32] Responding almost immediately, Grand-Pré claimed that he had known nothing of "the extraordinary event" until he received Williams's letter, averring that he could not imagine the intentions of the kidnappers. But then he unwittingly gainsaid himself by adding that he had actually learned of the event on September 5 from Alston, whose patrol was charged to protect the line from incursions by "that turbulent banditti, headed by the Kempers." If Grand-Pré faithfully related what Alston told him, then the captain gave him a basically accurate account, claiming not to have recognized any of the kidnappers in the darkness. Nothing in it indicated how Alston's patrol happened to be at the line just as the captors arrived with the Kempers or why a pirogue was waiting at Tunica.

Grand-Pré promised to look into this singular occurrence, but then he immediately launched into a complaint at the catalog of past incidents: "disorder, confusion, violations, outrages, plunder, insult to the magistrate; dragging him by a rope round his neck; attempts on the flag of the King, my master, and now the violations committed with the Kempers, (authors of all the above mentioned)." Some of his accusations were a bit obscure, especially the reference to roping a magistrate and other current violations involving the Kempers. Perhaps he blamed recent cross-border incidents of cattle theft and shootings near Mobile on the brothers, and they could have been involved, which would explain the presence of several of their old companions from the 1804 incidents in Pinckneyville. Grand-Pré felt no inclination to be apologetic. He demanded the release of Barker and his men and insisted that the Kempers too be handed over. In so doing he came close to an implied admission that he knew of the intended raid all along.[33]

Much depended on what the authorities learned from the men sent to Fort Adams. The Kempers and their captors arrived under escort on September 20, and Governor Williams immediately ordered that they all be handed over to Judge Rodney for examination. If no evidence emerged that Barker and his crew committed offenses in Mississippi, then they could be taken to the line under guard and released. As for the Kempers, Williams assumed they would be dealt with according to the law. Since they were victims, he did not expect them to be culpable of anything, but knowing their past record, he ordered that they post bonds for good behavior toward Spain.[34]

By September 25 Judge Rodney arrived from the new territorial capital at Washington and began hearings. He concluded that since the men manning the pirogue had committed no offense above the line, there was no alternative but to release them. None of the Spanish citizens involved in the actual kidnapping were in custody, so he could do nothing about them. He concluded that two parties of men acted in a conspiracy, but in such a fashion that neither committed an invasion of foreign soil. As for the Kempers, he required their bond to keep peace with Spain and do no injury to anyone below the line.[35]

Williams approved Rodney's findings and informed Grand-Pré of them, telling him also that he had ordered Barker and the others to be escorted to the line and freed, despite his feeling that Grand-Pré's explanations were equivocal. He had no intention of turning over the Kempers, however, because he knew they likely faced imprisonment or worse should they come into Spanish hands. Instead, he freed them after they posted their bond. Then Williams reminded Grand-Pré of recent Spanish outrages against American citizens and asked for an explanation.[36] Grand-Pré launched his own investigation into the kidnapping and began hearing statements on September 25 from the members of Alston's patrol. All denied knowledge of a prearranged plan, as they also denied knowing the men who kidnapped the brothers. A few gave statements so nearly word-for-word identical that some prior collusion on their testimony is probable, though that was no assurance of a prior plot. One man thought Ira Kneeland had foreknowledge of the capture, but he testified unconvincingly that he just happened to be passing through Pinckneyville at the time, and McDermott denied any involvement until after the brothers were dropped at the line. Grand-Pré made no conclusions from the statements and merely forwarded them to Folch, but clearly he found no fault with Alston or his men.[37]

Claiborne had intended to pause at Baton Rouge for a courtesy call on Grand-Pré on his return to New Orleans. On the way he stopped at Point Coupée to speak with Lieutenant Wilson and no doubt examined the several depositions. As a result, he concluded that Grand-Pré not only approved of the kidnapping and assault but knew about it beforehand. A few days earlier he had received a warning from a friend that Grand-Pré might take Claiborne himself as a hostage for the release and return of Barker's men and the Kempers.[38] It was hardly likely, but still Claiborne decided not to call at Baton Rouge.[39] He notified a military commander that the kidnapping of the Kempers on American territory had excited outrage in the region, and their recapture afforded equivalent satisfaction. He already dreaded hearing from Casa Calvo, for "I assume it will furnish grounds for a long Correspondence."[40]

Once again, events swirling around the Kempers charged an already tense situation. Rumors swarmed that Williams threatened to use force to free the Kempers.[41] The unexplained disappearance of an American mail rider led to accusations of his murder by the Spaniards.[42] At the same time, stories of the forced removal of other Americans from Mississippi to West Florida hit the press, and then readers learned that Spanish militia from Texas was committing similar outrages near Natchitoches.[43] Folch chose this moment to send a reinforcement to Baton Rouge, leading Claiborne to respond that the United States might reinforce its own posts in a further escalation.[44] Again the eastern press seized a Kemper story, mixing fact and exaggeration, as readers digested the Kemper interviews and Judge Rodney's finding.[45] In December the State Department released all of the documents in the matter to the press, and Madison handed it all to a select committee of the House of Representatives. The story's coverage did not wane until the end of the year, and even then its echoes continued into May of 1806.[46]

Several points gradually became fixed in American minds, regardless of exaggeration. The Kempers were kidnapped by a body of "armed Spaniards" numbering as many as fifty, rather than by fewer than two dozen whites and blacks, most of them residents of Mississippi.[47] The outrage, some editors maintained, was supposed to have been encouraged by the Spanish government while the Kempers were under the protection of the United States.[48] American soil had been invaded — barely — and American citizens taken captive and removed from their country. That is how it read when the affair came to the floor of the House of Representatives the following spring in a secret session discussing relations with Spain. Armed Spaniards violated American sovereignty by riding into Mississippi in a "riotous pursuit of a family of the name of Kemper."[49]

President Jefferson himself complained over the Kemper episode.

"Our citizens have been seized and their property plundered," he declared in his December 1805 message to Congress.[50] He demanded an explanation from Yrujo, whose response was aggressive rather than apologetic. No Spanish officers crossed the line, he said, and besides, the real outrage had been the Kemper raids of 1804. Unfortunately he tripped over his own words, accusing the Kempers of being American citizens in 1804 when they invaded West Florida, but then saying they were Spanish citizens when kidnapped in 1805.[51] Besides, it was Americans who took the Kempers in Pinckneyville, so there had been no violation of sovereignty, and thus no cause for further explanation or apology.[52] That simply was not good enough for people in the United States. One New York editor echoed the sentiment of many when he declared that the time had come for war. The Americans would likely be in conflict with Spain as soon as Britain defeated Napoleon and his Spanish allies anyhow, the editor felt, and that being the case, the United States had better commence the fight when Spain had not the power to defend her colonies.[53] The Kempers had some of their countrymen calling for war.

Frustrated as they must have been at the release of Barker and the others, the Kempers soon learned that the court back in Wilkinson County would do no more. The Hortons were indicted for a felony and bound over for trial in November, but they apparently fled and forfeited their bond.[54] Most of their slaves remained, yet through a legal technicality the judge there could not try any of them. Simple assault was not a felony under territorial statutes, and neither was forcibly taking the Kempers below the line. If that was not felonious, then breaking into their houses to take them could hardly be a felony either. In fact, all the justice the brothers got was the demand that they each post a one-thousand-dollar bond.[55] The local authorities probably did not want to take action, remembering the difficulty the Kempers had caused the year before. It seemed that the Kempers would find no justice for their cuts and bruises. If they were going to have redress, they must get it themselves, and that they intended to do in their own time.[56]

The episode soured Samuel Kemper on West Florida, a place that had brought him nothing but upset and controversy, and now battery and a fear for his life. He would remain in Mississippi a little longer, but only to press an unsettled land claim preventing him from purchasing clear title to land he squatted on and had improved.[57] After joining many other settlers in petitioning Congress for preemption rights to their squats, he left. He may never have set foot in West Florida again.[58]

Reuben suffered the worst injury in the assault and carried deep scars on his face and chin for the rest of his life.[59] Old festering wounds now reemerged to add to his discomfiture. His mortgage had changed hands yet again. Josiah Taylor, the man to whom George King had sold the mortgage in spite of his agreement to hold it until Reuben could pay the debt, sold it in turn on October 24 to none other than Reuben's nemesis John Smith.[60] Now Smith had possession not only by Grand-Pré's decree but also by holding the original mortgage itself. Worse, an agent sent by Smith to examine all the books of Kemper and Company found a discrepancy of nine thousand dollars in Reuben's favor, no doubt the same issues that formed the basis of his effort to reopen the case. The agent believed that the errors invalidated the seizure of Kemper's own land at Bayou Sara and so informed Smith; he should have reported it to Grand-Pré, who would have had to restore Reuben's property. However, Smith apparently said nothing to anyone, and Reuben may never have known.[61]

Still Reuben Kemper was not done with John Smith, nor, especially now, was he done with the Spaniards. Already people on this frontier knew how inflexible Reuben's sense of justice to himself and to others was, and people all across the continent had read enough to know that all of the Kempers could be implacable, even violent, when they felt themselves abused. Years later one of Reuben's close friends observed that "even in his resentment, which was always felt by those against whom it was directed, he displayed a nobility and openness rarely witnessed in other men."[62] Fifty years later people on this frontier still heard stories of a man "of gigantic frame, noble, open countenance, frank and gallant bearing, kind and courteous, but firm, and, when aroused by a sense of injury, fierce and vindictive," a man with a bitter prejudice against Spain.[63] Others recalled that as "men of strong frontier sense, with a pleasing appearance and fine address, the Kempers were well suited to the times and were dreaded by the Spaniards."[64] Even after a century, the memory of their feud with Spain was so ingrained that men in Baton Rouge still said of them that "they were implacable in hate."[65]

The Kempers might have been bloodied and battered. Samuel might have given up on West Florida, and Reuben had seen his land taken by means that he at least thought unjust. Their neighbors in Mississippi might have turned against them. But Reuben and Nathan were not beaten. There were scores to settle, and now unwittingly they were already starting their vengeance against Spain, for all across America the story of their assault and kidnapping made their names synonymous with Spanish cruelty and tyranny. Their names had disappeared from the press by the end of the year, but the inextricable linkage of Kemper to West Florida and Spanish injustice remained indelible.

6

Live Hogs, Bees-Wax, Coffee, Etc.

THE NEW YEAR brought no one in West Florida any great relief. Grand-Pré sent such gloomy estimates of the situation that the Junta de Guerra, the Council of War in Havana, authorized him to surrender if he found himself attacked by an overwhelming force on the condition that he and his garrison be allowed to withdraw to Pensacola.[1] In New Orleans Claiborne found that the continuing talk of the Louisiana Purchase territory west of the Mississippi being traded back to Spain encouraged a more belligerent attitude in the Spanish officials still in his city. Priests seemed to make it worse by telling uninformed outlying settlers the same thing, warning them that if they obeyed American laws, the Spaniards would not be gentle with them when they returned. The terms of the Purchase allowed Spanish officials to remain only three months after the takeover to clear their personal and official affairs, and they had overstayed their welcome by more than two years now. Claiborne wanted an order to force them, especially Morales and Casa Calvo, to leave, but Washington hesitated to take any steps that risked further confrontation.[2]

Despite all the war talk, the frontier grew noticeably quieter for a while, disturbed only by the usual irritants of runaway slaves, army deserters, and the paying of duties at Mobile.[3] The Spaniards stopped all traffic past Mobile, including U.S. mail, for a time, in effect cutting off the Mississippi forts and settlements from supply, while Congress tried to secure claims on the border to keep settlers in place in case war came with Spain.[4] Then tensions eased microscopically when the Spaniards agreed at least to allow mail from New Orleans to pass Mobile to Fort Stoddert.[5] Mirroring international affairs, John Smith even made what seemed like a peaceful overture to Reuben Kemper. Smith planned to lay out a new town on his Bayou Sara property, but further trouble from Kemper could risk clear title. The dilatory John Murdoch who worked for John Smith had not communicated with Smith since August of 1805, so early in September, Smith revoked his power of attorney and moved it to a New Orleans firm, instructing them to collect all money and papers in Murdoch's hands. They were also to manage Smith's lands and all other affairs, which included any continuing difficulty with Kemper.[6] Murdoch should have known of his dismissal by October at the latest, yet he acted as if he did not. On February 22, 1806, he appeared in Pinckneyville before Justice of the Peace Joshua Baker with a proposal to settle all differences between Smith and Reuben. Present to hear the proposal were Reuben Kemper, Murdoch, and Dr. John F. Carmichael, perhaps the leading man in Wilkinson County and a person already on the fringe of Burr's plans for West Florida.

The document was certainly generous. In sum, it would release each party from all claims against the other and settle $340 and the slave Maria on Reuben, plus return to him his own seized plot at Bayou Sara. Since Reuben could never sue in a Spanish West Florida court, and no American judge had jurisdiction to interfere, it represented more than he could have hoped for. No wonder he shocked the men in Baker's office when he entirely dismissed the proposal.[7] Kemper was shrewd and well informed. He knew that Smith was selling lots for his new town on their original joint Bayou Sara plot, and Reuben expected that the property would be worth many times what he had paid for it as the town grew. He was not about to relinquish his equity in that land just to be acquitted of his mortgage debt on it.[8]

Reuben knew that he required the best legal counsel. He needed to go to New Orleans anyhow on business, and now, prodded by this proposal's implication that Smith owed him more than the arbiters allowed, he hoped to engage New Orleans district attorney James Brown to sue Smith in New Orleans.[9] Just to keep the controversy bubbling, Reuben, who certainly enjoyed taunting his enemies, sent Murdoch the latest in a series of notes, all in what Murdoch thought an insolent tone.[10] On March 7 Kemper reached Point Coupée, almost within sight of his old place at Bayou Sara across the river, and took the opportunity to tweak Smith and Murdoch once more. In March of 1805 Major John Ellis, a Virginian and recent arrival to West Florida, formed a partnership with merchant Christopher Stewart and leased Kemper's old warehouse and store from Murdoch.[11] Following the abortive August 1805 raid, Nathan and Samuel had threatened to destroy the buildings in revenge against Smith, and Ellis rather boldly rode to Pinckneyville and asked them not to molest his business.[12] Feeling no animus toward Ellis, they agreed, and he became friends with Reuben, who referred to him ironically as his "tenant."[13]

Now at Point Coupée, Reuben risked crossing the river to dock at Bayou Sara.[14] When Ellis stepped aboard, Reuben handed him a letter; Ellis stepped off, and Reuben immediately cast off downstream.[15] In the letter Reuben apologized for not visiting sooner, asked his tenant to take good care of his property for him, and then told Ellis to present his respects to Murdoch. With pointed reference to Murdoch's shock at the refusal of the settlement proposal, Reuben added: "I am informed that the weight of the Gentlemans brow since the 22 ult. Has been allmost unsupportable. pray let him know that every man has his price & if he comes to mine I am his, but I am not yet a Spanish Don that seven or eight thousand dollars should to me be an object as a bribe."[16] Ellis went immediately to Murdoch and asked if he wanted to see Reuben's note, but Murdoch had had enough of Reuben's gibes and refused to look at it, believing it contained nothing but insults.[17]

When Reuben reached New Orleans he met Samuel and found it would be days before he could meet with the attorney Brown. However, Samuel said he had recently met Richard R. Keene, a lawyer whose father-in-law, Luther Martin, was one of the greatest attorneys in the East and a confidant of Aaron Burr. Keene had suggested that the brothers call on Lewis Kerr, formerly sheriff of Orleans and about to become major and fourth-ranking officer in the territorial militia. When Reuben asked why, Samuel replied only that he thought his brother would be game for what they would discuss. That same evening they called on Kerr, who wanted to swear them to secrecy before he told them anything. Reuben refused to take any oath until assured that Kerr intended nothing hostile to the United States. Kerr promised that it was nothing of the sort, asserting rather that he was backed by men in the highest offices in the United States, which Reuben took to include Jefferson himself. Satisfied, Reuben took an oath "to use all lawful means to aid and assist in effecting the emancipation of Mexico and Peru" and the rest of Spanish America.[18] Kerr then told them that Americans in the city were forming a society for the purpose of taking Baton Rouge and the Floridas. Kerr cited the Kempers' hard fate at Spanish hands and expected they would favor a move to free West Florida, and he had no doubt that Jefferson ultimately wanted the same and more, including Mexico.

Kerr's associates wanted to send agents north to raise volunteers to accomplish the task, and he told the Kempers they would be offered the job. Reuben immediately pointed to two obstacles: he and his brothers had neither the qualifications nor the money for the job. Kerr dismissed their inexperience and said his friends had *"money at will,"* and would provide not less than five thousand dollars to each of them, with power to draw more, up to a hundred thousand dollars at least. Kerr dropped the names of well-known New Orleans merchants enlisted in the cause as evidence of the society's access to money. Thus assured, Reuben said that men from Mississippi and the Floridas themselves could take West Florida without needing outside volunteers, but Kerr told him that taking that territory was only the start. They would have to build forts and have enough men to protect the territory until the United States could take over. Once West Florida was secured, the Kempers would be entitled to millions of dollars in addition to their monthly pay from the United States. Reuben argued that Americans who enlisted would lose interest after the territory was taken and would have little stomach for digging ditches and building forts, but Kerr said that they need have no concern about the hard labor, for they would take scores of slaves from Judge Poydras and others. Kemper knew Poydras was one of the most influential men at Point Coupée, with a very large plantation.[19] He doubted they could just take the man's slaves without its being robbery, but again Kerr dismissed his objection, noting that armies seized private property all the time for the good of all.

Reuben promised to talk with Kerr again, but Kerr warned that all of his associates met only in private to avoid attracting attention. After the brothers left, Reuben felt uneasy, somewhat confused, and a bit anxious. He knew that everything was not always as it seemed when it came to land and politics. Kerr's plan might not be as patriotic as it sounded, and Kerr might not have given them all the facts. Reuben wondered who lay behind the whole business. If the name Burr did not occur to him right away, it did soon. Over the next few days, still unable to meet with the attorney Brown, the brothers often discussed Kerr's proposition, agreeing that it seemed suspicious. They decided to approach Benjamin Morgan, a man they knew and trusted, the president of the New Orleans branch of the Bank of the United States and a leading merchant.

Before Reuben met with Morgan, however, he dined alone late one evening at the City Hotel, and after other diners left the room, "a man of genteel appearance" entered and approached him. The man asked if he could meet the Kemper brothers, whereupon Reuben identified himself. The gentleman introduced himself as James Workman, a former newspaper editor in Charleston, South Carolina, and now the recently appointed superior court judge of Orleans; he was a talented man, according to some, "but a villain."

Workman said he had heard much of Kemper and sympathized with him in his misfortunes. He sat down, they talked while Reuben finished his dinner, and then Workman suggested that they repair to a private room. There he brought up the Mexican Society of New Orleans, of which he was president, and said that most American civil and military officers were members and were already making musket cartridges for the great enterprise.

Workman wanted to know how many in the Mississippi Territory could be raised for the expedition. Reuben estimated that five hundred to a thousand men would turn out if the United States required them to take Florida, but when Workman asked how many Kemper thought he could raise himself, Reuben replied that he did not know that he could raise any. After all, his standing in Mississippi was as mixed as in West Florida. Asked if he would be willing to go to Ohio and Kentucky to raise volunteers, Kemper said he would like it well enough if he could do the job and was properly equipped. Workman told him that he thought the brothers the right men for the job, and he felt sure all the chief members of the Mexican Society would agree, and they should expect soon to be offered the appointment. The flattery raised Reuben's suspicions, and he concluded that Workman was not entirely sincere. "I fancied he discovered my want of relish," Reuben later told Samuel, for Workman immediately invited Reuben to come with his brother to Workman's home for dinner the next day so he could introduce them to more of his associates and discuss their plans under the guise of an innocent supper party. Kemper promised that either he or Samuel would attend.

Later that night he rehearsed the discussion with his brother and suggested that Samuel go to the dinner, since Reuben had an appointment with Morgan and wanted to learn what the merchant knew of the plot before he spoke again with Workman. The next day Reuben called at Morgan's, and, in what he thought "a very awkward manner," he indirectly pumped the merchant for information. He got almost nothing but evasion. All Morgan would say of Workman was that he was "a fat, chuffy little fellow" and "a damned smart active little fellow considering his size" and that he was believed to be honest and well informed and was respected as a judge. Finally Kemper dropped all guile and asked if Morgan knew anything of Aaron Burr's plans, revealing that he suspected all this business was connected with Burr. Morgan testily replied that Burr was not in the habit of informing him of his plans. He did say he had heard that Burr was working on a revolutionary idea of some kind with Mexico in view, though Morgan had laughed at the idea. When Kemper called Burr "an intriguing character, who would stop at nothing," Morgan agreed, adding that Burr had too much sense for that sort of intrigue. Reuben thought this ridiculed his own questions and left, thoroughly weary of cat-and-mouse.

Meanwhile at Workman's dinner Samuel met several people, including a young Mexican revolutionary, twenty-seven-year-old José Bernardo Gutiérrez de Lara, whom he would meet again some years hence.[20] Workman and his associates immediately took Samuel into their confidence, giving him details on the volunteers they were to raise, their pay, rations, and the promise to each of a thousand acres of West Florida land. They also unveiled a means for secret correspondence between them and the Kempers. Using the fictitious name Patrick Roy of Pinckneyville, the brothers were to write to an equally fictitious James Jenkins at New Orleans in care of Lewis Kerr. Then

Kerr, as Jenkins, would respond to Roy in care of the Kempers. They had code words for men, arms, ammunition, and more. *Bees-wax* meant "muskets," and *best bees-wax* meant "muskets in complete order." *Coffee* meant "common gunpowder," while *coffee, in bags* stood for "best-quality rifle powder." *Live hogs* meant "men," and *live hogs fat* meant "men equipped for duty." Since couriers from New Orleans might need to meet in person with agents from West Florida, the lakes and bayous seemed the safest places, and they devised signals for lights on boats to summon a meeting.

When Kerr arrived, he and Workman asked about the defenses of Baton Rouge and the Red River country and what resistance the Spaniards might make there. They also asked about the route from Baton Rouge to Mobile. Throughout they implied that the United States supported them; it also appeared that most of the leaders were Freemasons. Yet Workman at the same time contemptuously called Governor Claiborne "a mauled bitch," suggesting that Jefferson's top man on the scene was not with them. As for financing the operation, contrary to what Kerr had said to Reuben, Workman told one man that they would get all they wanted by robbing the New Orleans banks, though he said it with enough of a smile that some thought he only joked. Workman said he could take Baton Rouge with twenty-five men, and once that was accomplished he would marshal the volunteers the Kempers were to raise in the Mississippi Valley and march to Lake Pontchartrain, where British vessels from New Providence would transport them to take Mobile. It was an echo of the story of Reuben Kemper going to New Providence, evidence that the plan may have been genuine, though rumor confused the protagonists. Kerr and Workman promised to plunder another two hundred thousand dollars when they took Mobile and then sail to take Texas. Daniel Clark vowed to raise support in Congress when he took his seat that fall as the first elected representative from the Orleans Territory.[21]

When Samuel reported on the dinner party, Reuben paid scant attention to the details because he still felt uneasy over the business. He had been over a week in New Orleans, daily encountering people claiming to be in the society and asking if he had met Kerr and Workman yet. Yet the only way anyone would have known of the brothers' involvement was to hear it from the conspirators, which added to his confusion. Soon the brothers doubted the legitimacy of Kerr and Workman, especially since the former implied Claiborne's support while the latter did not. "I knew that Mr. Claiborne detested even the ground I stood on," admitted Reuben; "he had in many instances very materially and unjustly injured me by reporting things that never did exist." If Claiborne had said anything, Reuben thought, he would have warned Kerr and Workman to have nothing to do with the Kempers.[22]

Finally the brothers returned to Pinckneyville, Reuben perhaps hoping to hear no more of it. He was already branded a rebel and outlaw in West Florida. Involvement in an affair that would be unlawful without official approval, and treasonous if Burr's goal was more than just Spanish territory, would make him an outlaw everywhere else. Then other niggling matters gradually unfolded. The society's tentacles reached everywhere. Josiah Taylor, who had sold Kemper's mortgage to Smith the previous October, was in fact the adjutant of the Second U.S. Infantry and a close confidant of Wilkinson, having been involved with the general in a brief scandal over expenses two years before.[23] Did that mean that Smith was also involved with the society and Burr?

Soon after Reuben returned to Pinckneyville, news came that Spanish cavalry had crossed the Sabine River for the second time that year to occupy a disputed piece of territory between the river and Natchitoches. American forces converged to make them leave as before without violence, but on April 3 an anonymous letter went from Pinckneyville to Baltimore complaining that the United States kept putting up with Spanish affronts. "I have myself been a great sufferer," it said, which sounded like Reuben, though more likely it was Randolph, whose agent had been scared out of Tunica during the Kemper kidnapping six months earlier. Whoever the author, he spoke for the Kempers and several others above the line when he went on to say that if a fight with Spain should come, "no one wishes it more than I do."[24]

Weary of his confusion, Reuben tried to concentrate on his claim against Smith, but he could not escape the Burr business. He went to Justice Baker, who reluctantly gave him a copy of the Murdoch proposal, and Reuben sent it to Brown on April 7 to engage him as counsel. Reuben particularly asked if Smith's sale of lots from the disputed property would be valid if there should be a subsequent change in regime in West Florida, taking into view what he called "my situation with that government and its present organization." His recent conversations in New Orleans obviously prompted the question. A positive answer from Brown could persuade him to work with Burr. If Kemper had any inkling that Smith was involved with Burr, though, then a negative response from Brown was motive to prevent Burr, and thereby Smith, from succeeding. Reuben knew he could never sue in Baton Rouge, but if his claim against Smith was on record in a New Orleans court before the United States took over, then he could rationalize that any sales Smith made would be invalid after the change. But he freely confessed that "in these things I am greatly at a loss," which was why he needed Brown.

Kemper had another reason to need a powerful attorney. He and Nathan had already hired a firm of Natchez attorneys to pursue civil damages suits against Horton and his son for assault and battery. Each brother sued for twenty thousand dollars, and hearing that Brown would be in the territorial superior court at Washington in May, Reuben hoped to enlist him as their advocate. The two brothers themselves were the only prosecution witnesses thus far, but Reuben had letters from others who had been in the surrounding houses the night of the attack, as well as circumstantial evidence connecting the Hortons and some of their slaves to the crime.[25] Before Kemper could send his letter to Brown, however, he had a visit from Lieutenant William Mead, brother of Cowles Mead, the secretary of the Mississippi Territory. The lieutenant handed him a letter from Kerr — as "James Jenkins" — to "Patrick Roy," in care of the Kempers. While Mead quietly looked on, the brothers read the letter. Kerr wanted to know their progress collecting "live hogs, bees-wax, coffee, etc.," and one of them wrote a response reporting they had collected none, and asking for more information.

A couple of days passed and two visitors arrived; one of them was William Mead again, and his companion was none other than Lieutenant Josiah Taylor. Taylor told the brothers that he was in the enterprise "at all hazards," mentioning that Smith's friend Dr. John Carmichael was in the fold. This only added to Reuben's confusion. Carmichael and Taylor were both close to Smith. Could Kemper trust either of them, especially since Taylor had sold the mortgage to Reuben's Bayou Sara property to Smith? If nothing else, the Kempers had demonstrated that they were men of action who would take risks, if not always prudently, and they had at least a small following who could be counted on to join them. The growing discontent and unease among Americans in West Florida might attract more to their guidon now than in 1804; if Smith was involved with Burr, might he seek to use them to aid himself by aiding Burr? Who would they really be working for, and to what end? And whether it worked or all came to nothing, would they be left out or worse?

As soon as the lieutenants left, the brothers went to the office of Justice Joshua Baker, whom they believed they could trust. They told him of their visitors, of what had happened in New Orleans, and of their belief that Taylor was intimate with Carmichael, whom Jefferson had appointed assistant collector of revenue in Mississippi in 1803 and who presumably enjoyed the president's trust.[26] Taylor was close with at least one of their kidnappers, Minor Butler, which worried them. Since Baker, Carmichael, and Butler were friends and neighbors, the justice might be in a position to ask the others what they knew.[27] In the weeks following, Reuben and Samuel often asked Baker if he had spoken to the other two, but Baker always evaded the question, which made Reuben more anxious. "I scarcely spent thirty minutes either in company or alone without thinking on the subject," he confessed. Finally he concluded that Baker would never speak with the men, which upset him, since it suggested that Baker was party to the plot. The involvement of Minor Butler, with his connections to the kidnappers Horton and Kneeland, troubled him all the more.

Amid that mounting uncertainty, shortly before 7:00 A.M. on May 18, people in Pinckneyville watched the sky to the southwest turn black; this was followed by a heavy downpour and then hail. Trees swayed menacingly, betraying a tornado's approach. The funnel came and went in a minute. It swept the church more than a hundred feet from its foundation, and it reduced the new log home of Thomas Lilley from Baton Rouge to a stone chimney around which the Lilleys huddled for safety. The tornado swept the roofs from the home of Abram Horton's son John and one of Randolph's warehouses; next door, the tavern he rented to Nathan Kemper and every building on the lot lost its roof, though Kemper and six other people somehow survived.[28] The funnel missed Reuben's house, and most likely he and Samuel worked with Nathan to get a new roof on the tavern, Reuben's anxiety over the Burr affair mounting all the while. The Kempers had collected no funds and as yet done nothing to raise any men locally. When letters came from Jenkins for Roy, they equivocated in their response, still asking for more information. Reuben wanted to know first if the plot really had official backing in Washington or if it was just a private scheme. In the end he concluded that the only way to be certain was to ask Jefferson himself. Leaving Nathan behind with his family and the tavern, Reuben and Samuel set out overland in June for the nation's capital. If any of the Burr men in their neighborhood wondered at their leaving, their route through Tennessee, Kentucky, and Ohio looked like a trip to raise "live hogs" and "coffee."[29]

By this time much had happened. Burr met with Wilkinson, his plans still unclear even to some of his associates, then spent some time with Smith in Cincinnati, seeking information on West Florida and Smith's cooperation in supplying an expedition. For his part, Smith seems to have believed the insinuation that Jefferson supported the scheme, since he knew firsthand that the president wanted the province. Weary as he was of the Kempers, Smith was likely the one who alerted Burr that the brothers might be useful. Burr also solicited support from Britain, asking for naval and military aid for his plan, with Clark as his agent in New Orleans. He told the British envoy in Washington that he had ample funding from influential men, as well as assurance that the people of West Florida wanted their independence. Burr even declared that the people of New Orleans were wild to be free of the United States, and a revolution in the entire region could be accomplished bloodlessly if Britain would act. If it did not, the people would ask France to step in and take over.[30] Unfortunately, Burr's was the worst-kept secret in America, and as early as August of 1805 speculation on his intentions became common in the press. Meanwhile, the slippery Wilkinson and Clark began to waver, and both commenced efforts to make sure they had a foot in each camp in case something went wrong. When Workman and Kerr met with the Kempers, Grand-Pré got wind of it, and as a precaution he started to require passports of all U.S. citizens passing through West Florida.[31]

Grand-Pré felt even more isolated when Casa Calvo and Morales finally left New Orleans. But then Morales reestablished himself in Pensacola and resumed selling titles to unclaimed land, making Claiborne fear that if the Morales titles were upheld after a U.S. takeover, the Americans would probably not have one acre of vacant land fit for cultivation left for sale.[32] Morales started licensing planters in West Florida to import slaves through Pensacola and then overland to Baton Rouge, thereby avoiding any hazard of their being stopped in New Orleans.[33] Few men in the region objected to slavery, as all of the larger plantations depended on slaves. Still, by this time all but one of the states had abolished the importation of foreign slaves, well ahead of its constitutionally mandated demise in 1807. The abolitions reflected moral antipathy to slavery as well as belief that the slave population was self-sustaining, that natural increase would meet future needs without lowering the chattels' value. If the Spaniards introduced an unlimited supply into West Florida, and the Americans subsequently took over, both moral and economic interests would be compromised. Slavery itself never divided the Spaniards and the Americans in West Florida. Some in Grand-Pré's districts welcomed new field hands, but with land values stagnating or declining, every new slave that reduced the value of existing blacks was a blow to the planters' pocketbooks.

The Kempers likely thought about none of this on their trip. Reuben pondered more vital matters. Having decided to call on Jefferson personally, he wondered now how he should broach his mission to the president. "On my route, I had planned a thousand ways of introducing the enquiry," he wrote later, expecting that Claiborne, Smith, and others had misrepresented him to Jefferson and that he would have a hard time overcoming that. Finally Reuben decided on an indirect approach. He would present himself as an applicant for the contract Jefferson recently announced for improvements on the Natchez Trace. Then in conversation he would introduce his real object. If Jefferson disavowed the project, Kemper intended to ask him to assign a company of soldiers to protect Pinckneyville from Burr's designs.

They reached Washington in July, perhaps just in time to catch the president before he left for Monticello to escape the summer heat. Jefferson gave him an audience but it did not go well, and it probably got off to a bad start when Reuben opened with subterfuge rather than forthrightly stating his real reason for coming. "In the whole I think myself I rather bungled the business," Kemper confessed. The two men were cagey with each other. Jefferson knew something of Burr's activities and the Kempers' reputations, and he tried to find out as much as he could without giving anything in return. Reuben, leery of going too deeply into dangerous waters, remained circumspect. In the end he obtained no information, "and I suppose gave but little." When the shadowboxing concluded, Kemper left feeling that "the president though[t] he had received a novel visit, and I thought he treated his guest in a novel manner."[34] Just weeks later, when Jefferson received his first confirmation of Burr's activities, he said it fit with what he heard from other sources, but he had heard none of it from Reuben Kemper.[35]

The brothers left the East in late August, unaware that on their way home they followed Aaron Burr as he started assembling money and supplies. When the Kempers reached Cincinnati on September 1, they actually arrived a few days ahead of Burr. John Smith was in town and learned they were there almost immediately.[36] News of Reuben engaging lawyer Brown to handle his suit did not worry Smith, who declared that "I do not fear the pretended reclamations of Mr. Kemper."[37] He knew, as Kemper probably did not, that James Brown was himself on the outer periphery of the Burr circle and probably expected him not to try too hard to disappoint Smith. In fact, when he learned of the brothers' arrival, Smith urged his agents to press on selling the new town lots, since, with the Kempers at Cincinnati, "they cannot make much noise down there."[38] In fact Smith was more concerned with his mercantile interests, having gotten a contract to provide supplies to military posts in the Orleans and Mississippi territories. He sought Wilkinson's help to get his goods through West Florida, for "if anything is to be done with the Spanish government he can handle it and he will handle it."[39]

Burr reached Cincinnati on September 4 and stayed with Smith, giving out varying stories to explain his passage through the region. The Kempers learned of Burr's visit only a day or two after he left; rumor said he was going to New Orleans, or Point Coupée, or Louisville, where he and Smith had a plan to build a canal around the falls of the Ohio River, which would help finance their grander de-signs. "Whenever I heard his name uttered," Reuben said, "*I thought of their toasting him at Workman's at dinner.*" Kemper's antipathy to-ward Smith only made him more suspicious of a man associated with his old nemesis. Reuben called on the commandant of the army post at Newport Barracks, across the river in Kentucky, who told him that Burr had asked a number of questions about the arms in his keeping, leaving with the cryptic promise that at the proper time Burr would have "a subject of importance" to discuss with him.

By this time Reuben Kemper felt weary of rumors, evasions, and uncertainties. There seemed only one way to learn the truth before the brothers got in too deeply, and Reuben decided to catch up to Burr on the road and confront him. Reuben rode to Lexington, Kentucky, only to find that Burr had gone to Louisville. Thereafter Kemper was always a day or two behind Burr, sometimes spending the night at the same inn that Burr had left that morning. Reuben found that everyone thought Burr a clever fellow and a great friend to the West when in fact he had incited them to join his enterprise by telling them the East drained their region of its money, dooming them to poverty. Fi-nally at Nashville the brothers learned that Burr was just ten minutes ahead of them on his way to the home of Colonel Andrew Jackson, commander of the Tennessee militia. With no idea how long Burr would remain at Jackson's, they decided to go home rather than wait.

By October they were back, and based on what they had seen and heard, neither felt any confidence in the uprightness of Burr's proj-ect. Soon "Patrick Roy" sent one more letter to "James Jenkins." In it Reuben said that since no one in New Orleans gave them the infor-mation and assurances that they had asked for, they could take no ac-tion to raise men. "Jenkins" never responded, and the brothers had no further communications with Workman and his confederates. After that, as Reuben put it, "the story grew old."[40] The Burr story faded for them not least because upon their arrival in Pinckneyville they found West Florida in a greater uproar than ever before. Discontent with Grand-Pré's government had escalated dramatically, and at the same time the Spaniards had invaded Louisiana west of the river once more to threaten Natchitoches. Spanish actions might be about to achieve Burr's ends and foment revolt in West Florida.

7

A Second Edition of the Kemper Attempt

BEFORE LONG the Kempers had cause to congratulate themselves on staying out of the Burr business. Randolph may have influenced them, for if he had ever been enchanted with Burr, it wore off. He wanted West Florida to go to the United States and not some private empire. Even as the brothers were returning home, Randolph became the agent in Mississippi for the new journal *Western World*, published in Frankfort, Kentucky, a paper devoted to American expansion in the Southwest and the exposure of Burr and Wilkinson.[1] Meanwhile, warnings of Burr's plot reached Washington from Claiborne, Judge Rodney, and others.[2] Jefferson knew enough by November 27 to issue a proclamation calling on all involved in the scheme to cease and ordering authorities to arrest those guilty of complicity.[3] With his own interest in mind, Wilkinson betrayed his coconspirator, warning Claiborne that Burr would be in Natchez by mid-December on his way to capture Baton Rouge; on January 1, 1807, Claiborne ordered a flotilla of gunboats upriver to arrest Burr, though not without firing the customary salute to Spain as it passed Baton Rouge.[4] Claiborne issued his own proclamation about the plot, as did Governor Williams.[5] Then the arrests began. Richard Keene, who had brought the Kempers into the scheme, fled to Jamaica to avoid justice.[6] Workman soon resigned his judgeship, and before long loyal New Orleanians, including some of the most prominent citizens, condemned "Workman and Co."[7] In February, indictments appeared against Kerr and Workman, with more to come, and no one could tell how deep the conspiracy ran.[8]

Still Burr pressed on. He reached Natchez in January of 1807, aware that in Kentucky an effort to indict him for insurrection had just failed. Now he sent two men to meet with Carmichael and learn the Spaniards' numbers at Baton Rouge, any weaknesses in the fort, and what U.S. forces might be at Fort Adams. Carmichael equivocated and refused to go to Baton Rouge to reconnoiter the fort, even though Alexander Ralston told him that Burr would be near the following evening, waiting for reinforcements, and that he intended to take Baton Rouge, raise his flag, gather ten thousand from Kentucky and Tennessee, and then march on Mexico. When Carmichael told his visitors of Wilkinson's arresting sympathizers in New Orleans, the news startled them, and they asked what it could mean. Had Wilkinson betrayed them, or was he simply doing it to conceal his own involvement and mask the greater interest?[9] Could they trust Carmichael himself, who had spent time on Wilkinson's staff as a surgeon and was on somewhat intimate terms with him?[10] The two men Burr had sent decided to seek information elsewhere. Somehow they learned about "Patrick Roy" in Pinckneyville. As soon as they finished with Carmichael, the two appeared at Reuben's house.

Just when the Kempers decided that Burr was up to no good is cloudy, but they could not ignore the mounting chorus of rumors swirling around the Southwest, and Burr's connection with Smith hardly gave them confidence. By the time they returned home from Washington, they had concluded that it was a bad business and passed on to Justice Baker what they knew from their own experience and from the rumors they heard. When Wilkinson began making arrests and all but took control of New Orleans by martial law, they realized that the danger was now apparent to everyone, and there was no further need for them to warn the authorities. Then Burr's two emissaries appeared at their house and provided almost verbatim the same account of Burr's position and intentions that the two had given Carmichael, unaware that Carmichael even then was on his way to New Orleans to give a deposition about their visit and thereby mask his own peripheral involvement.[11] In another week Burr and the mere hundred and fifty men with him would be under house arrest at Natchez. A territorial court failed to return an indictment, but an infuriated Judge Rodney ordered Burr's arrest all the same, and the adventurer fled. Wilkinson sent Carmichael to arrest him, both of them avidly trying to protect themselves now, and on February 19, not far from Fort Stoddert, a party of soldiers found and arrested the fugitive.[12] Judge Rodney contemptuously dismissed Burr and his plot. "It seems like a second Edition of the Kemper attempt," he declared, "and Burr only appears the greatest Don Quixote of the two."[13]

After John Smith passed through West Florida bringing a load of army supplies downriver, he wrote to Jefferson that he thought the Burr plot would soon "evaporate in smoke."[14] Others saw nothing at all foolish about it. Claiborne believed that if Burr had reached Baton Rouge in mid-January, Grand-Pré might have been forced to surrender.[15] Now Governor Folch responded by once more coming to Baton Rouge with a reinforcement.[16] A few weeks later, with distrust epidemic, Grand-Pré arrested his own executive officer on suspicion of complicity.[17] Governor Williams meanwhile advised the president that the Burr business left "the Country as it were in an uproar."[18]

More than Burr had upset the frontier. When an American exploring party left Natchitoches and traveled up the Red River some little distance into Texas, word got to Spanish authorities that the Americans had raised their flag on Spanish soil. Spaniards made a foray to cut down the flag, whereupon Washington ordered Wilkinson to protect the vicinity and maintain the United States' claim to the area. Finally on August 5 the Spanish governor of Texas sent *soldados* to establish a camp in Orleans Territory about fifty miles from Natchitoches, the third incursion that year. At almost the same time Grand-Pré received reports that other American military patrols were seen surveying on the Spanish side of the Pascagoula northwest of Mobile.[19] By this time the Americans in Mississippi and West Florida had already been in a state of excitement for months. Mississippi sent a memorial to Congress seeking protection, and Judge Rodney saw mounting discontent.[20] A Mississippi militia captain found the country in a fervor, virtually up in arms, many of them men who felt they had suffered greatly at the hand of Spain. All they wanted was the order "to raise the hand of vengeance."[21]

The latest rumblings from Natchitoches only enhanced the sense of urgency. "This Country is Strong and I believe the Inhabitants could defend it against any sudden force the Spaniards can send," Rodney observed early in September.[22] Americans in West Florida openly avowed that when the first gun sounded, they would take Grand-Pré's fort, which Kneeland found raised quite a stir in Baton Rouge. Grand-Pré pressed to get yet more repairs done on the hopelessly moldering old fort and its cannon, and he called out militia to reinforce his garrison.[23] When Wilkinson arrived at Natchitoches on September 22, he suggested that if he had to attack the Spaniards to drive them out, as long as he was in the vicinity he might as well take West Florida too. Pensacola's four-hundred-fifty-man garrison was too small to reinforce Grand-Pré; Mobile's defenses were weak; and Baton Rouge's fort was all but falling down and surrounded by a disaffected population that could easily rise up and overwhelm the feeble garrison. He wanted his small command at Point Coupée to be ready to take Grand-Pré and his garrison at a moment's warning.[24]

For reasons of their own, the Spaniards left Orleans soil without incident on September 27, 1806, but that hardly calmed leaders in West Florida. Several met at the Bayou Sara plantation of Bryan McDermott, one of the Kempers' kidnappers; among the men were Solomon Alston, Father Lénnàn, Grand-Pré's tax collector Gilberto Leonard, and scores of others. Discussing the general feeling that the United States wanted hostilities with Spain as a pretext to overrun West Florida, they concluded that they needed to prepare against attack. They pledged to defend the government at the risk of life and property, all of them bolstered to some degree by a rumor that New Orleans militia sent to Natchitoches had stopped by Baton Rouge en route home and offered to fight for Spain.[25]

Aroused fears and passions on both sides had kept West Florida's population on edge all year. Was the United States going to trade them to Spain for Orleans? Was Burr going to come as a liberator or a conqueror? Was Spain with Burr or against him? Now the Spaniards looked set to be invaders themselves. Could planters capitalize on any upheaval by gaining more cheap land, or would a new regime threaten their existing titles? The Burr episode widened the cracks in their conditional loyalty to Spain as it demonstrated that Spain could not protect them from outside force, while the incursion toward Natchitoches raised fears that Spain might risk a war with the United States that could see West Floridians and all their property swallowed in the conflict.

The constant irritants at Mobile escalated too. The settlers lived in wretched conditions, unable to get produce past the Mobile blockage to market, which left them unable to pay for their land.[26] The discontent there was much greater than in Feliciana, and it prompted Washington to order the commander at Fort Stoddert to tell the Spaniards that Jefferson did not sanction any hostile acts that might occur and to ignore any order to attack that he might receive from American military officers in the region.[27] Meanwhile, protests did not stop the Spaniards from charging duties on American shipping, even after Claiborne sent proof that no duties were being levied on Spanish vessels passing New Orleans.[28] In fact, the anger over duties worked to the advantage of Jefferson and the expansionists. They wanted no war with Spain, but if locals rose and peeled off bits of territory that Spain would not fight to keep, then so much the better.[29]

It was a hazardous game, and the administration's fence-sitting created problems of its own. If Mississippians marched on Mobile too soon, or if they and the West Floridians moved against Baton Rouge before Washington was ready, the acts could precipitate the war Jefferson hoped to avoid, especially with Spain now allied with Britain in their own war against Napoleon. Conflict with Spain could bring British warships and soldiers back to the Floridas. Jefferson's policy also caused problems for his friends in the region. Crippling factionalism emerged in Mississippi as outspoken opposition to the administration grew. In October of 1807, when Governor Williams dismissed Claiborne's brother Frederick as a militia colonel, the rest of the officers disintegrated into acrimonious partisanship. By March 1, 1808, it grew so bitter that Williams dissolved the legislature. A year later he would dissolve them yet again and himself resign as governor pending the election of an entirely new assembly.

In a state of confusion largely resulting from the unsettled status of the territory's southern border, authorities sometimes ignored the demands of justice in the face of the sentiment of their citizens toward Spain; in one instance they refused to extradite a Mississippi man who had beat a slave to death on the road north from Baton Rouge. Though the killer deserved punishment, Williams and Madison feared that if an American met hard justice at Spanish hands, Mississippians all along the line might explode.[30] At least the Kempers got a measure of justice at last, which kept them quiet. In December, soon after the brothers returned from Washington, Reuben's attorneys persuaded a civil jury to find the Hortons guilty of assault and to award Reuben six thousand dollars in damages. That was far from the twenty thousand claimed in the suit, but it was virtually all Horton had. When John Smith learned of the judgment, he told Jefferson that "this will set him a float again," and the president must have wondered anew at that novel fellow who had called on him the past summer and whose name kept coming across his desk.[31] The finding for Reuben made success in Nathan's suit a foregone conclusion; since Horton had no remaining assets other than five hundred arpents along Bayou Sara near Pinckneyville, the court later awarded that to Nathan.[32]

That spring Smith returned to Bayou Sara to survey and sell his town lots, but by early August the work was still going slowly. Business in the country stagnated and nothing could be done expeditiously, he complained, but until the surveys were finished he could not complete his sales.[33] Then one day a newspaper stunned him with its announcement that he had been indicted in the Burr business. Protesting his innocence, John Smith went to Natchez and surrendered to Governor Williams on September 19. Thereafter he scrambled to prove that he knew nothing of any conspiracy, that his meetings with Burr were largely accidents, and that he had never done anything more than contract to provide provisions. He may have been telling the truth, and to support his story he named Murdoch and Ira C. Kneeland as character witnesses.[34] It availed him nothing, and Smith became the first member of the Senate ever to be indicted for a crime. Though he would finally be acquitted, he was a ruined man. He resigned his seat less than a year later, then saw his Cincinnati business fail and his property go to creditors.[35]

Reuben Kemper probably played some small role in Smith's discomfiture, for that July in New Orleans he wrote a lengthy deposition detailing his encounters with Workman and Kerr, the trip to Washington, and his knowledge of Burr's visit with Smith at Cincinnati. On August 8 he gave it to the court at Point Coupée. It likely had no influence on Smith's indictment and may not have appeared at the trial. In fact, Kemper may have written it to get his side of his story on record as a preemptive measure in case Workman or others tried to implicate him, though in all of the subsequent testimony in the colorful history of the Burr trials, the name Kemper remained virtually unspoken.[36]

Much to Grand-Pré's relief, the name all but disappeared from West Florida too. For more than two years after Reuben's brief stop at Bayou Sara in March of 1806, if the brothers made any visits, they were quick and unobserved. Samuel had moved west of the Mississippi, Nathan ran his tavern, and Reuben worked his barge. Surely they watched events with interest, but for Reuben, his *barcaza* often took him places where West Florida news arrived weeks late. The brothers' absence did not leave the province any more tranquil, however, for land and settlement policies continued to be irritants. Even when Grand-Pré began issuing land grants again, the recipients could not get surveys fast enough to confirm their titles. Grantees continually appeared at Kneeland's door demanding surveys that he could not immediately perform, and he complained that some refused to leave "as they are in every sense of the word land mad."

What they said disturbed Kneeland, for it was the old story that the Americans were sure to take the country.[37] In the St. Helena District, between the Amite and the Tangipahoa, he found the settlers "a damned poor set" who cursed both Grand-Pré and Pintado over the increased cost of surveys and threatened that if the rates were not lowered, they would revolt and all unite against all Spaniards.[38] Kneeland alone had a hundred and fifty survey orders on his desk but inadequate resources to do the job. Hurry meant that newer surveys sometimes conflicted with older ones, and the errors were compounded by inadequate maps and the surveyors' unfamiliarity with the backcountry.[39] Some angry planters accused the Spaniards of blatantly piling one survey on top of another without regard for the consequences.[40] Often applicants had to go to Pensacola to get grants and then return there again later to study existing surveys to see where claims could be located. Many accused the surveyors of overcharging, and Kneeland found people much more willing to trouble him than to pay him, telling Pintado that they cursed "me, and you, and every one else."[41] It did not help that all of the American surveyors wrote only in English, while Pintado wrote mainly in Spanish.[42] All the while the fear of war on the western border fed unrest, and Wilkinson's signing of the Neutral Ground Agreement on November 5, affirming that title to the land along the Sabine would be decided by negotiation, did not settle nerves.

There could not have been a worse moment than November 1 for Madrid to suspend all further surveys and decree that all future land sales would be at two dollars per arpent and that henceforth Anglo-Americans were ineligible for grants. The orders were actually eight months old, but Havana enforced them only then in response to the mounting friction with Americans.[43] Now Kneeland had to tell disappointed applicants that an American could not possibly even claim the land under the new regulations, and the resulting outrage was no surprise.[44] The decrees only made things worse for the surveyors, but they suspended operations nevertheless.[45] Soon Kneeland told Pintado of "a total Stagnation of Business here, no money here nor is it possible to collect any."[46] Settlers openly defied surveyors trying to collect the money due for past surveys or for land purchases, and they complained that Pintado set the surveying fees and then shared them with the surveyors, intentionally profiting by overcharging.[47]

The discontent became more belligerent in March of 1807 when the alcalde of the fourth division of Feliciana, Robert Percy, became openly defiant. A former lieutenant on a British privateer and, according to Kneeland, a "loud mouthed Irishman," Percy had a reputation for self-importance and bluster. Now he harangued landowners about Spanish injustice, calling it "Damned Chicanery" to raise land to two dollars an arpent. The people were "damned fools" if they paid any surveying fees, and he vowed not to pay his own. Moreover, he declared that he would not enforce orders to make others pay, even for work already performed. He would see Kneeland and Pintado and even the governor "Damned" first, for he announced that Grand-Pré "would Decree any thing for two Dollars." When Kneeland told the governor of Percy's insubordination, Grand-Pré did nothing, leading the surveyor to complain of his timidity. Grand-Pré was not a timid man, but he found his position increasingly difficult. Surrounded by American territory, with constant agitation outside and growing discontent inside, entirely dependent on Americans for the administration of justice and civil order, he dared not act against even an Irishman without hazard. His hesitation led even loyal friends such as George Mather to conclude that Grand-Pré was "no judge of such business." When Percy refused to pay for his surveys, others said that if he did not pay, then they would not either. As a result, in the first quarter of 1807 Kneeland collected less than thirty dollars for his surveys and had to file suits to get his fees, which only heated tempers more.[48]

Land policy was doing what the Kempers' 1804 raids had not: galvanizing a variety of fears and resentments into a larger and focused irritation with Grand-Pré and Spain. It was not a good time for Daniel Clark to be promoting speculations in his Orleans holdings in the eastern press, touting "the richest land in the world" for as little as two dollars an acre.[49] Seeing Orleans acreage being offered at double the value of West Florida land, which could be sold only after expensive surveys and then only to non-Americans, just drove the thorn deeper into planters' sides.

For those waiting for the United States to take the province, no joy loomed on the horizon. Rumors of a purchase continued to fly, exciting Rodney to exclaim in June that possession of West Florida would quadruple the value of the Mississippi Territory, for it would then control all the outlets to the Gulf that passed through the province.[50] It was a false expectation, for Spain refused all attempts at purchase or negotiation. Congress appropriated money for a purchase in February of 1806 when it seemed that Napoleon would intervene, but it all fell apart. Jefferson's consul at Paris, Fulwar Skipwith of Virginia, tried to smooth the negotiations, but in the end Napoleon, to whom Spain was now little more than a vassal state, agreed to let Spain part with the Floridas only if the price was right for France. By July West Florida was no longer for sale, and Jefferson gave up entirely in June of 1807. It was the biggest failure of Jefferson's administration, and no people were more disappointed than the Americans in West Florida itself.[51]

Nothing seemed to be going well that year, and the result was predictable. While land values steadily rose elsewhere in West Florida, a gradual rise commencing in 1805 came to a halt in Feliciana, and that was after a 50 percent drop in 1803 to 1804. At the end of the year men with land to sell saw the beginning of what would be another 50 percent collapse as Americans, the largest potential market of buyers, were banned from immigration and purchase, while planters already there refused to pay the two dollars an arpent mandated by Madrid to get more land. Spain was hitting the men of Feliciana in their pocketbooks.[52] By July of 1808 Kneeland was so fed up that he wanted to quit surveying entirely. No one paid for anything, and Grand-Pré tried to placate his American inhabitants by taking their side and decreeing that no one could be made to pay $2 an arpent for land until Havana agreed to confirm their grants on the original terms of $1.50. Much as he liked the governor personally, Kneeland thought him naive and gullible, complaining that "I have often with astonishment beheld him led away and imposed upon, time after time, by designing, artful, and Intriguing men."[53]

That made people resent all the more those artful men who prospered, for they all seemed to have Grand-Pré on their side, and none more than John Smith. As soon as he learned of the order for his arrest, Smith transferred all of his assets in West Florida to Murdoch to protect them, not least from the New Orleans attorneys whom he had not yet paid.[54] Then in February of 1808 Murdoch transferred the land to Smith's son Ambrose Dudley Smith, which put the land back in his father's control but out of reach of federal authorities, and also out of reach of Duplantier, who still had not been paid for the original land and now commenced a suit against Smith.[55] The following spring, Ambrose began promoting sales in what the Smiths called New Valencia, and he forthrightly referred to Grand-Pré's role in turning the land over to his father. If anyone shared Reuben Kemper's belief that the arbiters were unduly influenced by Grand-Pré or by bribes from Smith, the son's advertising inadvertently fed that suspicion.[56] That Grand-Pré was among the earliest purchasers of New Valencia lots might have added to the suspicion, though he paid the same price as other buyers.[57]

One newcomer seemed particularly good at steering the governor in his favor. Fulwar Skipwith, who had failed to promote Jefferson's interest in West Florida at the French court, took an interest in the province himself, sight unseen. His brother-in-law William Herries bought substantial property north of Baton Rouge from Daniel Clark, with the backing of Skipwith himself as security for the mortgage. Probably with Skipwith as a partner, Herries planned a town of his own, to be called Montesano, complete with steam saw and gristmills and other enterprises.[58] Herries all but bullied Clark into selling him the land, then repeatedly pressed Grand-Pré for orders of survey that extended his boundaries farther back from the river into vacant land, in effect taking more property than he had purchased. When Kneeland protested, Herries threatened to use his influence with the governor against him, and the surveyor concluded he was motivated by "Insanity or Rascality," while losing more respect for Grand-Pré.

Nor was Herries alone in stirring animosity. Robert Percy never stopped his public railing against the government, and Kneeland heard him proclaim constantly that everything the government said was false, and that the land price increase was just a scheme to swindle the people out of their money. Kneeland thought Percy "possessed of all the Haughture, Tyranny & Ignorance Imaginable"; Grand-Pré knew of Percy's fulminations but allowed the rot to spread by doing nothing. To Kneeland, Herries and Percy were two of a kind: "Both are assuming, artful, ambitious, envious insinuating men, Inveterate enemies, and make it their sole object to carry every point with the Government." Even if the regime had no other enemies, "they are sufficient and have many tools & pimps to support them." By August of 1808 Kneeland feared that complaints from Percy and others had made the people so suspicious that nothing would satisfy them.[59]

Meanwhile, in St. Helena rival factions headed by two alcaldes emerged.[60] People complained that one of them took bribes in civil suits, and as so often happened, the accusation of corruption became its own proof.[61] The notion of justice for a price fit into a patchwork of other grievances against Spain that were exaggerated by every subsequent instance, real or imagined. From the fringes of that same irritable region, James Caller introduced a resolution in the Mississippi territorial legislature declaring that the ties binding citizens of Spain's American provinces were now too weak "to restrain the Oppressed from making one last and desperate effort to rid themselves of their oppressors."[62] It passed handily, a warning that the Americans surrounding West Florida thought nothing of taking arms if a pretext arose. No wonder that in June Folch sought permission from Claiborne to send arms up the Mississippi to Baton Rouge.[63]

A siege mentality was taking hold in West Florida, and it was fostered by men who simply had never felt any fealty to Spain in the first place. To them the times looked suited to speaking their mind. One of them was Reuben's "tenant" Major John Ellis.[64] He drank and swore and spoke intemperately of Spain and the Spaniards, but his chief transgression may have been his spurning the affections of his partner Christopher Stewart's wife, Matilda. She began watching and cataloging his movements, collecting rumors, and making note of visitors to his store whom she thought suspicious, mostly because of his relations with the Kempers. His habit of vocally condemning Spanish justice gave her even more fuel, especially when he went so far as to say that a handful of Americans could seize Baton Rouge. A few more drinks and he may have slurred that he himself could lead his militia company to join Burr in taking the fort.[65] Matilda Stewart did not fail to note that Ellis seemed to know the whereabouts of Captain George de Passau, who had served against the Kempers in 1804 but was now himself a fugitive from justice, and that was cause to make Ellis suspect.[66] The growing signs of unrest and the idle talk of revolt became too persistent to ignore, and by May of 1808 John Ellis had had one confrontation too many with Matilda Stewart. In fact, she actually physically assaulted the hapless major more than once, and then reported him to Baton Rouge, including his supposed threat to use his own sword to kill Grand-Pré and "send him to Hell" with all his officers.[67]

All this was too much for Grand-Pré, especially with half his garrison of two hundred unfit for duty and many of the cannon useless.[68] On June 6 the alcalde arrested Ellis as he returned from Pinckneyville, where it was believed he had met with Randolph and Passau.[69] He sat in the Baton Rouge jail for the next six months while Grand-Pré's subordinates collected testimony in his case, much of it prompted by people's personal dislike of the man. The allegations even included his secretly possessing an American flag and the ridiculous claim that his house was full of artillery.[70] The testimony of more prudent men, such as that Ellis did not have "enough influence to arm even a negro," was ignored.[71] Alcaldes ordered militia arms moved from storage and put into working order to meet the feared crisis, and again Spaniards' eyes turned toward Pinckneyville and the Kempers as the real agitators. Some thought there had been a plot but that the schemers did not live in West Florida, a suggestion that the outside agitators were the Kempers and their friends across the line.[72]

Almost immediately another outspoken planter found himself under suspicion for his association with the Kempers. Men gathered at the home of Patrick Vaughan for an evening of drinking, and one of them was Joseph Moffat, who had been with Horton in the Kemper kidnapping. Vaughan warned Moffat to avoid Pinckneyville, but Moffat scolded him in response because the Kempers "had put this country to a great deal of trouble & expence by their rebellion." Vaughan defended the brothers, saying that they were "as much the Gentleman as any person in the country" and "damned clever fellows," even though he himself had condemned the brothers' past violence and in 1804 served in the picket that first halted the Kempers' approach to Baton Rouge.[73]

What was important was not the exaggerated and fictional accusations being made against those with real or presumed connections to the Kempers. Rather, the fact that even speaking sympathetically of the Kempers could lead to investigations by Grand-Pré showed the state of mind among Spaniards feeling themselves increasingly isolated and surrounded by an ever more hostile population. The antipathy toward the Kempers that was revealed in some of the Ellis and Vaughan depositions also showed the polarizing force of the memory of their activities, even though probably not one of the brothers had voluntarily set foot in West Florida recently except for Reuben's one certain stop at Bayou Sara in 1806.[74] Meanwhile, continuing problems with American deserters festered, especially when Mississippi militia crossed the line without permission to apprehend them. Claiborne suggested a cartel between the United States and Spain for the reciprocal delivery of deserters, and late that year Washington agreed to the proposal, but it did not stop the problem.[75] A Bayou Sara hideout was popular with fugitives from Fort Adams, who had lived there for years, and now locals caught them plotting to rob a merchant vessel in the stream, meaning that even deserters to whom Spain had given haven now joined the Kempers and internal dissidents to pose a threat to public order.[76]

Late in August Ira Kneeland ventured out into that raw backwoods in St. Helena and observed there the "audacious conduct of a certain set of inhabitants" that he believed demanded Grand-Pré's attention. The "evil minded" Champ Terry seemed to have great influence over a weak and ignorant local population who menaced surveyors repeatedly. When men started running surveys on the Bogue Chitto, Terry and his crowd came at them from the woods with butcher knives and guns, threatening blood if the agents did not leave. "He is a bad man," Kneeland said, and many men like Terry would do violence before allowing surveyors to interfere with the land where they squatted.[77]

There were any number of men now openly flaunting the waning authority of the Baton Rouge government, and less than a month after Kneeland's warning to Grand-Pré, the surveyor found himself facing the lash of their anger.

8

Our Tribunal Cannot
Be Men of Business

IT MAY HAVE been Ellis's problems with the Stewarts that started the troubles. Surveyor Ira Kneeland had been eyeing the timber on Reuben's Bayou Sara property for some time. The mortgage on it passed through several hands — Smith's, King's, Taylor's, and more — and by the end of 1807 it belonged to a Mississippian who ironically gave his power of attorney to handle the land to Reuben, who still claimed actual ownership.[1] But Reuben was an outlaw, and Spanish law made his property in the province forfeit, so Kneeland thought the plot was clear of encumbrances.[2] He petitioned Folch to get the tract by either donation or purchase.[3] Then in January of 1808 the defunct partnership of Ellis and Stewart mortgaged their interest in the land to Murdoch and Kneeland as surety for a loan.[4] The bad feeling between Kneeland and Reuben already went back some time. They had been neighbors at Bayou Sara. Kemper's friend Arthur Cobb had feuded with Kneeland, and the surveyor's favoring of Smith when he acted as an arbiter in 1803 and then his involvement in the Kemper kidnapping two years later did not endear him to Reuben. Now he sought to get Reuben's property at Bayou Sara.

A few hours past midnight on August 29, a slave named Cupid saw the house on that property ablaze. The Stewarts were in Baton Rouge giving depositions in the case of Ellis, so no one was at home, but Ellis himself became the prime suspect when Cupid said — or was made to say — that Ellis told him Matilda Stewart's house would not be standing when she returned from testifying against him. Ellis denied the accusation and asked what rational cause he could have to destroy the house when he owned three-fourths of it himself as majority partner.[5] No one ever knew for sure who set the blaze, and Grand-Pré finally released Ellis on November 21 with no findings against him, whereupon the major settled accounts with Stewart and left the country.[6]

Some may have wondered if the Kempers set the fire. Reuben had no need to injure Ellis but every reason to thwart Kneeland, and with no American takeover in sight, he may have despaired that a civil action would ever recover his property, in which case a fire at least prevented anyone else's using what he had built. Surely people recalled rumors of the brothers' threats to burn their old buildings a few years earlier, and, as events were to show, they were contemplating revenge that summer. Most likely the Kempers had nothing to do with the fire, and the timing of the event with what followed was only coincidental. News that Kneeland tried to get his hands on the property may have been the catalyst, or perhaps it was the arrival of their twenty-eight-year-old brother, Presley Kemper, on a visit from Ohio.

By this time Samuel lived in Rapides Parish on the Red River, but Reuben and Nathan were still in Pinckneyville, and they had already had their revenge on Abram Horton lawfully in the Mississippi territorial court.[7] Bankrupting the man was better than assaulting him, which would have made them liable for prosecution. Kneeland, however, lived beyond the reach of American courts. Given the surveyor's part in the original decision that cost Reuben his land, the Kempers probably regarded him as the chief author of their subsequent misfortunes. If they took action against him, however, they would have to make a quick dash across the line and an even faster return before an alarm spread. Their timing probably resulted from a raid on Pinckneyville by a gang of men who crossed the line without warning on or about September 20 and committed unspecified outrages that terrorized the inhabitants before returning below the line. Details are murky but Randolph told the new territorial governor David Holmes that the origins of the affair lay in the attack on the Kempers in 1805.[8]

Holmes, a forty-year-old Pennsylvania native, spent a decade representing Virginia in Congress before Jefferson appointed him to replace Williams, on March 3, 1809. In fact, it was one of the president's last official acts, a reward to an unwavering Republican. Holmes reached Washington, Mississippi, early in July, and thereafter governed with commendable courage and evenhandedness. If not brilliant, he had excellent political instincts in handling the problems of land policy and the conflicting grants from Britain, France, and Spain that had bedeviled Grand-Pré. Almost from the first, he also acted as intermediary between the Americans of West Florida and the United States. Now the Kempers and the line were his problem.[9]

Citizens protested the outrage to the governor, but he could do nothing other than commence a patrol to catch any of the raiders should they set foot above the line again.[10] Whether or not the Kempers suffered directly from the raid, its genesis lay in that earlier outrage against them and provided enough motive to prompt their retaliation. Kneeland participated in the raid, then gave perjured testimony in defense of the Hortons at their civil trial. Before dawn on September 23, no more than three or four days after the raid, Reuben, Nathan, Presley, and three other friends took the public road south over the line. When they got within a mile of Kneeland's house the Kempers rode into the woods while two companions posted themselves at some distance as lookouts.[11] The third rode on to Kneeland's. When Kneeland came to the door the caller said he was traveling with a friend who had suddenly become terribly ill, so sick, in fact, that he needed someone to write down his will, and a local man had suggested Kneeland.

Unsuspecting, Kneeland agreed and the two left at once, the caller all the while spinning more of a story to lull him. After about a mile the three Kemper brothers suddenly rushed out of the woods pointing pistols. Kneeland recognized Nathan and Reuben, and when he asked who the third was, Presley Kemper introduced himself and said he was there in his brother Samuel's place. Kneeland feared for his life, for he could see the scars on Reuben's face, some of which he may have put there himself, and Reuben said if he attempted anything they would kill him on the spot. Then they gagged him with a handkerchief, put a sack over his head, and dragged him into the woods, where they stripped him and tied him by his hands between two trees.

All three of the brothers took out whips and for the next half hour without letup they flailed at him, all the while shouting insults and releasing three years' pent-up anger. Reuben assured Kneeland that they would not kill him but that he was being punished for his role in the "unworthy arbitration" of the Smith matter. They also shouted threats of what they would do to others in the area who worked for the Spaniards. When they put down their whips, they punched him a few times and called him a "lousy dog," and then one of the three, probably Reuben, drew out a sharp knife. While the others held Kneeland's head, he cut a slice out of each ear just as a planter notched the ears of livestock to signify ownership. Then they cut Kneeland down, remounted, and rode back across the line.[12]

Battered and bleeding profusely, Kneeland struggled to remove the gag, then dragged himself to the road and started the painful trip back to his house. Along the way he met Henry Flowers, who had participated in the Kempers' kidnapping in 1805 and was lucky that the Kempers had not recognized him just minutes earlier as they raced past.[13] Flowers got Kneeland home and then went for two doctors, who examined Kneeland and found him suffering a high fever as well as considerable loss of blood.[14] The Kemper party made no attempt to hide as they raced back to the line; they were seen and identified by several people they passed.[15]

The surveyor lay ill for three weeks before he could rise and dress, and not until October 24 was he well enough for two alcaldes to come to his house and gather depositions from him and others. Grand-Pré sent transcripts to Governor Holmes with a protest at the outrage, but he should have saved his ink.[16] Grand-Pré had protested that he could not take action against his own citizens when they committed a felony across the line, and Holmes now used Grand-Pré's same argument against him, so the matter died there. Folch passed all of the documents on to Havana, but unless the Kempers were caught on Spanish soil, there was nothing anyone could do.[17] Kneeland did not return to work until December, and eventually the attack passed, much confused, into frontier lore.[18] For a time, however, the reality of it was there to be seen by patrons of the Kemper tavern in Pinckneyville. In a bottle full of spirits, the slices cut from Kneeland's ears were displayed, preserved as a memento of Kemper vengeance.[19]

Vicente Folch had long suspected Grand-Pré of being unequal to his job, citing the way he put up with insolence and insubordination from Americans, and now the forays at will into Feliciana and assaults on the king's employees. Men preached sedition and suffered no penalty, and Alcalde Percy openly vowed resistance. Most of the Americans liked Grand-Pré personally, but Folch concluded that few respected his authority any longer. He may have been the victim of an impossible situation, but by the fall of 1808, especially after the latest Kemper incident, he was too compromised to stay in office. Even events across the Atlantic worked against him. By this time the merrygo-round of European politics and Bonaparte's ambitions had resulted in Spain's King Charles IV being deposed by his son Ferdinand VII. Napoleon then occupied the country, made both father and son prisoners, forced Charles to abdicate to his son formally, and then made Ferdinand renounce his own right of succession. That done, Napoleon installed his own brother Joseph as monarch, which unleashed a popular uprising on May 2, 1808, that commenced years of vicious guerrilla warfare. The distraction at home made Spain's always loose control of its provinces yet more lax. Morale that was already low among colonial officers sagged even more as they were compelled to pay allegiance to Joseph.

Americans and other settlers in West Florida shared an antipathy toward France that now was common in the United States, and all but a few resented being ruled by Napoleon through his brother. That actually gave them common cause with Grand-Pré and the Spaniards, for they all preferred Ferdinand VII, and on October 19, 1808, a number of American planters avowed their support for Spain and the "independence and glory of our Sovereign," ending the document "Viva Fernando 7."[20]

Now, however, the fear of imposition of French rule in West Florida disrupted allegiances that for the Americans had always been slender and conditional. Claiborne heard that Spanish commanders in Mexico and elsewhere vowed not to submit to Bonaparte and had told Folch that the Floridas were no longer important to Spain and ought to be ceded to the United States. Sources told Claiborne that Folch agreed and asked permission from Havana to evacuate Pensacola.[21] Spain's hold seemed to be slipping, thanks to France, which made it a bad time for the French-born Grand-Pré to entertain a Frenchman suspected of filibustering ambitions in Texas. When the visitor left behind a trunk in Grand-Pré's care, Folch suspected that it might contain proof of Grand-Pré's collusion with the man, and he seized the occasion to recommend something he had had in mind for some time anyhow.[22]

Just before he sent the alcaldes to take the Kneeland depositions, Grand-Pré received orders to report to Havana for an investigation. The news dumbfounded a friend in Pensacola, who thought Grand-Pré had exercised great prudence in maintaining peace in his isolated domain, while in Baton Rouge a French Creole grumbled "God only knows" about the affair.[23] Even among the Americans, Grand-Pré had his defenders, and twice in recent months residents had sent him compliments on his administration, affirming their loyalty to Spain and Ferdinand VII, regardless of the usurper then on the throne.[24] Uncertain when or if he would ever return, Grand-Pré took care of multiple affairs, beginning with the marriage of his daughter Hélène to Major Samuel Fulton of the militia light cavalry.[25] On December 23 he sold his town lots in Baton Rouge, including a house still under construction, and five days later, as his last act before leaving, he wrote his will.[26] More important, however, he enlarged the militia and secured a renewed oath of allegiance to Ferdinand VII from its officers.[27] And on December 3, with several leading citizens of the area as witnesses, he opened the Frenchman's trunk and found nothing more seditious than some innocent books. However anticlimactic the opening, it was the first time all of the witnesses had come together officially, and that gave some of them an idea.

One of the witnesses was Thomas Lilley, who had lived in Baton Rouge on and off since at least 1799 and returned following the destruction of his Pinckneyville home by the tornado. He was a man of considerable education who sometimes tutored orphaned children, and he was also something of an engineer, having built a 163-foot-long bridge over Monte Sano Bayou some miles outside the village.[28] Now he petitioned Grand-Pré to call the alcaldes and syndics in his districts to a consultation on means to dampen growing discontent. The governor agreed, and on December 7 they met, along with a number of invited leading citizens. Lilley took the chair and conducted an open discussion of grievances as well as expressions of support for Grand-Pré. They drafted a memorial to Havana asking that Grand-Pré remain until the unsettled times passed, or at least until his successor had enough experience in the region to understand its dynamics.

Then the convocation proceeded into territory Grand-Pré had not anticipated. The men wanted to hold discussions on import duties, how they should be charged and what should be done with the income. They also spoke of paying their governor's salary from the receipts, which would save Havana the expense. More important than the details of their discussion was the fact that they envisioned managing the financial affairs of their part of West Florida themselves, something vastly beyond their mandate as minor officials and citizens. They did not call themselves representatives of the people when they adjourned, but they had the taste of power in their mouths as they closed by calling for a larger assembly at Murdoch's home in a fortnight. Such a meeting, now to include militia officers and an even wider representation from men of influence in the area, afforded the best potential for addressing the means to keep the peace and calm the population.[29]

Lilley sent Grand-Pré copies of their proceedings, and the governor quickly realized he had allowed the meeting to go too far.[30] As so often in the history of the province, when a door cracked open for the Americans, they immediately tried to open it wider. Grand-Pré thanked them for their friendship and support as he approved their report, but time got away from him as he tried to postpone or stop a second convention, and soon it was almost too late.[31] He ordered one of his chief subordinates, Captain Thomas Estevan, to stop the meeting at Murdoch's home, and on December 20 Estevan sent Murdoch instructions not to let it proceed.[32] The members of the new convocation were already gathering on the appointed day when Estevan's order arrived. Though just convened, they dutifully adjourned immediately and without protest. Thus one of Grand-Pré's last acts halted, if only momentarily, the advance of a sudden groundswell toward a representative assembly seeking to fill the administrative vacuum created by Spain's pitiful condition at home and abroad.[33]

Grand-Pré relinquished his command just a few days later, handing it temporarily to Estevan. Behind him he left his newly married daughter and three sons, including sublieutenant Luis de Grand Pré of the Regiment of Infantry of Louisiana, just twenty-one years old and keenly sensitive to the stain on the family honor caused by his father's recall.[34] If apparent indecision and an unwillingness to take decisive action for fear of upsetting the delicate balance in his domain marked the governor's later years, still Grand-Pré served civil law and justice well. If there was inefficiency, even corruption, it was isolated and not a consistent policy. Moreover, Grand-Pré left behind a network of friendships and loyalties with leading American planters and businessmen. With virtually all his alcaldes and almost all his militia officers Americans, this Frenchman serving Spain won the goodwill of most of the people most of the time. "He had the talent to satisfy every heart by the unselfish way he dispensed justice," said a friend. He "knew how to rally people to his government."[35] When he left, those loyalties left with him, breaking yet another of the slender ties binding the inhabitants to Spain.

Ironically, his replacement was another French-born officer in the Spanish service. Colonel Charles de Hault Delassus had been lieutenant governor of the upper Louisiana Territory before the sale in 1803, and he later served in the Pensacola garrison.[36] He took his new position as civil and military commander on December 27. Baton Rouge did not impress him; visitors thought its modest one hundred houses made a very indifferent appearance.[37] If that was bad, what he found in the most vital part of his command was dismaying. Despite repeated efforts at repair, the fort lay dilapidated to near ruin.[38] Pensacola was still too far away for speedy reinforcement, but at least Folch was in the final stages of pushing through a road to Baton Rouge by way of Pascagoula. Like Grand-Pré before him, Delassus found very quickly that he was going to be isolated and would have to rely primarily on his own resources if he was to succeed.

Success depended in large part on the leading Americans who had thus far remained loyal to Spain. They were a mixed bag. The new man had no way of knowing just how deep their allegiance ran, but he was going to be hearing a lot from some of them in the difficult days ahead. In particular there was Philip Hicky. He was perhaps the most distinguished of the lot and one of the very few genuine natives, having been born in the area thirty years earlier at Manchac, once the most important Spanish post in West Florida. He had enjoyed Grand-Pré's full confidence, and he had earned it. When the governor borrowed money to keep his administration going during a long lull in payments from Spain, he entrusted Hicky with the funds.[39] Another

West Florida native was the planter William Barrow, whom one visitor described as "one of the most opulent inhabitants of West Florida." He had a handsome house and four hundred acres of cotton on Alexander Creek that were worked by a hundred and fifty slaves. He did not try to hide his attachment to the United States, but his good character, and perhaps his wealth, made him a man of influence.[40]

The most colorful man destined to haunt the new governor was Philemon Thomas, a forty-six-year-old Virginian who had fought in the American Revolution as a teenager, gained a commission, then went on to sit briefly in the state's general assembly and rose to the rank of general in its militia. He moved to Kentucky and held a seat in its legislature from 1793 to 1803, then two years later bought a thousand arpents not far from Baton Rouge. He actually lived in town, where he opened a grocery and an inn, and soon became close friends with Lilley and other leading citizens.[41] Almost entirely illiterate, he acquired a wide reputation for the unusual orthography of the signs he posted outside his shop on St. Ferdinand Street. Customers found him offering "coughphy for sail," while he promised weary travelers "akomidation fur Man & Beest."[42] A close friend maintained that he "was gifted with great good sense" and that "in all his transactions, he was the same plain, honest man," though some thought he carried with him an air of superiority, as all the Virginians did.[43] People addressed him as General Thomas.[44]

Delassus inherited subordinates fated to influence his relations with the Americans. His revenue collector Gilberto Leonard was puffed up with self-importance. An Irishman, he damned England, said Spain would never shake off Bonaparte's yoke, and habitually kept people waiting if they had appointments with him just to impress upon them his own significance.[45] A dozen years earlier he was secretly involved in a private commercial enterprise with Wilkinson that would have cost him his job, or worse, had word of it reached Baton Rouge.[46] Then there was a new alcalde on the Amite, a Virginian named Shepherd Brown, who settled first at New Orleans and built a fair fortune before moving to West Florida sometime after 1805 to become a planter. There he fell in with a set that his enemies called "notorious sharpers," blamed for much of the turmoil of recent years. He was also a purchasing agent in West Florida for a New Orleans speculator, which gave him a good motive for preferring a disorganized Spanish regime to an American takeover.[47]

The appearance of new officers changed the social and political picture in the province, but the departure of old ones altered that dynamic even more. In April of 1809 another of the Kemper kidnappers became deathly ill. One of the Kemper brothers referred to him at the time as "a poor trifling wretch, who calls himself captain Alston."[48] Solomon Alston had been a planter in Feliciana for years and had more than fourteen hundred arpents.[49] In 1805, when he led the patrol that received the Kempers, he was a respected man of some influence, not least because he was the alcalde Alexander Stirling's brother-in-law. He was only forty when his health seriously declined, in March of 1809, and in less than a month he was dead.[50] Later lore said he died of tuberculosis, which may have been correct.[51] Myth said the Kempers were responsible for his demise, though even their considerable powers could not give a man a disease.[52]

Alston's death brought an unanticipated consequence. Stirling had died just the year before, following over thirty years in the province. Now Alston was dead too, and after just as long a connection to West Florida. An alcalde and a militia officer, both widely respected, both of long residence, and both unwaveringly loyal to the regime, were gone. As these and other longtime residents passed from the scene, the continuity they represented left with them. In their place came newer men such as Delassus and Brown who won little trust among American planters, and some of the remaining older leaders, such as Percy, were unreliable in their attachment to Spain.

Meanwhile, when Grand-Pré arrived in Havana, he was already in ill health from some unknown cause, and by November he was dead, leaving his old friend Hicky to settle his substantial estate in Baton Rouge.[53]

Without these men, the old social and political balance in the province was knocked askew.

Delassus was not the man to retie severed cords. He seemed to be indecisive in nature, some of that indecision no doubt justified by his being thrust into an unknown and to some degree unfriendly situation. On taking office he found several unpublished decrees by Grand-Pré aimed at temporarily mollifying some grievances, but Delassus ignored them. He also ignored a petition to stand up to the defiant Percy and make him pay his debts.[54] Afraid that he would err no matter what course he took in these matters, he did nothing, and within a week of his arrival some in Baton Rouge believed his appointment had been a mistake.[55] Months later, in June, he still had not announced any official policy. He would not compel anyone to pay his surveying fees, but neither would he refer the matter to higher authority. "Surely our Tribunal cannot be men of Business," Kneeland moaned, wondering whether Delassus was simply afraid.[56] By this time some residents openly ridiculed the orders that he did issue, though not to his face, evidence that his opportunity to win the respect of many of those working for his administration had passed.[57]

While Delassus dithered, Jefferson's successor, James Madison, and others carefully watched. The new president sent an agent to West Florida to assess the situation, and he reported that 90 percent of the population were American, and five out of six would welcome annexation by the United States, adding that Baton Rouge and Feliciana, the wealthiest of the districts, "are as ripe fruit; waiting the hand that dares pluck them; and with them all Florida."[58] At that point, in April, Folch came to Baton Rouge to perform his own assessment. He kept his opinion of Delassus to himself, though when he learned that Claiborne happened to be at Point Coupée, Folch invited him to a private dinner without including Delassus. The Spaniard did not want his French-born subordinate to hear him tell Claiborne that he believed none of Spain's colonies in America would ever submit to Napoleon and moreover that he expected they would all break free from Spain. As for the Floridas, they were important only to the United States and must eventually fall into its hands. Folch even offered a toast to "the Liberty of the new World; may it never be assailed with success, by the old world."[59]

As the year closed another new man arrived, one destined to leave his name as inextricably linked to West Florida as the Kempers'. He brought excellent credentials as a Virginian, a friend of both Jefferson and Madison, and an American expansionist. The forty-four-year-old Fulwar Skipwith had finally come to his Montesano. He had never lived anywhere permanently until he moved to Baton Rouge. A teenager in the Siege of Yorktown in 1781, he later went into the tobacco business, then moved to London and made and lost a fortune before he virtually fled to escape creditors. His friend Secretary of State Jefferson gave him a consular appointment, and by 1794 he was in Paris, where he remained as consul or commercial agent — and sometime promoter of negotiations to acquire West Florida — until 1809, when he all but fled once more in the face of accusations of corruption. His marriage to William Herries's sister led to Herries backing the purchase of Montesano, and when Herries could not manage it, Skipwith decided to come to Baton Rouge "to retrieve something of the remnant of my Fortune."[60]

Over six feet tall, a fascinating if garrulous conversationalist, widely read, and unfailingly dignified, he loved nothing more than holding an audience rapt with his recollections of meeting Napoleon, Danton, Robespierre, Talleyrand, and more.[61] Supposedly an intimate friend of Thomas Paine and a cousin of Jefferson by marriage, he was also a devoted partisan of the Jefferson and Madison administrations and their Republican Party.[62] He became at once the most distinguished inhabitant of the province, though he lacked the two years' residence required for citizenship. While Delassus cordially welcomed the new arrival, Skipwith found it ironic that several Americans there were citizens by virtue of having deserted from the army some years before.[63]

As these new men arrived, another of the first agitators departed the scene. With no property in Mississippi and too many Kempers around for comfort, Horton moved to the Baton Rouge District and sought a grant, pleading his poverty and his years of looking out for Spanish interests along the line. He had lost his home, he said, "for motives of political sentiment and devotion to the government of Spain, by the particular meanness of the Kemper Brothers and their partisans," saying nothing about a court taking his property for a felony. Captain Estevan and Padre Lénnàn provided testimonials that Horton had suffered at the hands of the Kempers, as if being opposed to the brothers was in itself a high recommendation among the Spaniards.[64] But like Horton, Nathan Kemper was also done with Pinckneyville. The tavern may not have flourished, and in any event he only rented it from Randolph. Nathan had mounting debts, and no sooner did the court award him Horton's property than the sheriff sold it to satisfy Nathan's creditors. Reuben bought it for the six thousand dollars that he had gotten from Horton, thus making Nathan solvent enough to move across the river to the Attakapas country of Louisiana, some thirty miles west of Baton Rouge.[65] Meanwhile, Samuel took over a building in Alexandria, on the Red River, and opened Kemper's Inn, where he promised victuals and accommodation for "Genteel Travellers."[66]

That left only Reuben in the vicinity of West Florida, and the assault on Ira Kneeland seemed to have vented enough of his resentment for the moment. Now he owned substantial plots at Pinckneyville, plus his river-barge business, so there was plenty to keep him busy. His suit against John Smith still warmed his temper, but all he saw of West Florida was its bank as he plied his new barge, the Go By, to New Orleans.[67] Though the name Kemper temporarily faded from the ears of West Floridians, it was still heard in faraway Washington and was ever associated with the possibility of war. John Randolph of Virginia continually used the brothers' kidnapping to remind Congress that American honor had been sullied. Another Virginian, John W. Eppes, told the House of Representatives of how "the territory of the U. States was violated and two persons of the name of Kemper seized within our territory and forcibly torn from the bosom of their family, by persons known to be agents of the Spanish government."[68] Six months later a third Virginian, John G. Jackson, brought up the Kempers. When Randolph complained that the country had submitted to the "hostile tread of a foreign nation" in the kidnapping, Jackson reminded the House that the Kempers themselves had committed an outrage in 1804 and then fled to Mississippi. The next year, fellow American citizens took them and handed them over to Spaniards. "And was this the cause of war?" he asked.[69]

They were all very close to finding out.

9

The Spirit of Independence

I F CHARLES DE HAULT DELASSUS was to be believed, the conditions he found in West Florida made a breakdown of Spanish authority and the area's eventual independence inevitable. The fort was so hopeless, despite Grand-Pré's repairs, that in February of 1809, and again in April, Delassus warned Folch that the building was completely useless. He soon saw the dramatic shift in loyalties that had occurred since the Americans had supported the government against the Kemper raids in 1804. The loss of old leaders, the continuing agitations of the Kempers and others, and economic strains and continuing fears of a French takeover all agitated the population. That made the United States an increasingly attractive haven for many, and even for those who did not find it attractive, independence still promised more security and prosperity than an emasculated Spain. In proof of that, Folch replied to none of Delassus's complaints about the fort, and Havana was — and would remain — months behind in pay for the garrison. With only a few score *soldados*, Delassus would have to depend on Americans to fight Americans if there was an uprising, and he had little hope of that. They might help subdue a common threat that came from malcontents, but it was hardly likely that Americans would combat one another to maintain Spanish rule.[1]

Then there was an unexpected legacy from Grand-Pré. He had stopped the meeting at Murdoch's, but immediately after Delassus's arrival, Fulton and others requested another one. As a result of the labyrinthine diplomacy surrounding Napoleon's wars, Jefferson had temporarily imposed an embargo on shipping from American ports to foreign nations. That closed New Orleans to West Florida planters and hit them hard in their pocketbooks. They thought it might be possible to bypass New Orleans via Lake Pontchartrain from the Gulf, to Lake Maurepas, and then up Bayou Manchac — also known as the Iberville River — to a point just a few miles below Baton Rouge. Such a route was in everyone's interest. Delassus agreed to appoint Fulton, Hicky, and others to a committee to investigate the possibility, and on January 11, 1809, they reported a feasible route.[2] Encouraged by that, Delassus created a larger "industrial council" to make more detailed recommendations, and he staffed it with the original committee, the alcaldes and syndics of the four divisions of Feliciana, including the original four committee members, and several other leading citizens.[3] Delassus himself presided over their meeting on January 25, which seconded the idea of the alternate route and appointed the original committee to oversee the work, raise contributions to cover the cost, and monitor expenses.[4]

The symbolic import of the meetings far outweighed their temporal acts. An assembly exclusively of Americans had been allowed to meet, deliberate, make decisions, and raise money for a public project. They were not elected, but they acted like a legislature to perform functions previously reserved for the Spaniards. These men already knew one another. Several had worked together to stop the Kemper raids, though Pintado and Estevan commanded them overall. No Spaniards sat in this deliberation, however, and it put the taste of representative government in their mouths.

At the same time, Delassus allowed another taste to spread, a bad one. Grand-Pré had run a clean and honest administration, and the many protests over his recall testified to his integrity. Not a single complaint of corruption seems to have gone to his superiors. Nevertheless, the myriad court fees caused mounting irritation. In a single 1808 case, fees consumed 672 pesos out of a 1,627-peso award, and the fees were all legitimate.[5] Sadly, that legitimacy departed with Grand-Pré, and the agent of change was Delassus's new secretary Raphael Crocker.[6] He had come with the new commandant, his previous history a mystery, though he was a captain in the Louisiana regiment, and hence Delassus put him in command of the garrison at Baton Rouge for several months.[7] The title of secretary scarcely gave a true idea of Crocker's powers. Everything relating to land — grants and titles, surveys, appraisals, and more — passed across his desk. He issued all passports, oversaw commercial manifests, and created or approved virtually every official document in a culture that thrived on paperwork.[8]

Every document had its cost, and while Grand-Pré had kept the fees stable, under Crocker they became increasingly capricious. Yet without paying those fees, planters and merchants could not do business, plaintiffs could not sue, grantees could not confirm their lands, and men could not travel abroad. It created a perfect opportunity for extortion and bribery. Delassus was an honest man; Crocker was not, and unfortunately his commander dismissed complaints against his associate as coming from malcontents and troublemakers. Crocker took several months to get the feel of his situation before he began pursuing his dark calling aggressively. If someone needed a document speedily, he had to pay Crocker a bribe, and if he refused to pay, then the business somehow got buried, and might stay buried until the applicant changed his mind. Steadily, Crocker's demands became more blatant and exorbitant, even reckless, as he rushed to get as much as he could, perhaps sensing that Spain's rule and his opportunity were waning. He was ecumenical, extorting money from Spaniard and American alike, and even made prisoners in the fort's jail pay bribes for better food or speedier trials.[9] "No affair was transacted except through bribery," complained Grand-Pré's friend Pierre-Joseph Favrot, who regarded Crocker as nothing but "an escaped extortioner."[10] Crocker demanded from one creditor a two-hundred-dollar bribe to seize a merchant's goods to satisfy that creditor's claim, then Crocker suborned arbiters to appraise the goods at half their value and bought the merchandise himself at their devalued price, thereby profiting some three thousand dollars above the original bribe.[11]

Even people who had been loyal to the Spanish government for twenty-five years or more were not exempt from his avarice, and one grasp in particular inflamed outrage across boundaries of class and nativity. Everyone respected the late Alexander Stirling and held his son Lewis in equal regard. When Lewis Stirling appeared with a petition, Crocker kept him waiting for four days, then sent a servant to demand money for speedy service, adding that he would perform the service without the bribe, "but it would not be so well done." Stirling indignantly confronted him. "Señor Secretary, I dare you to demand the eleventh part of this," he said, but Crocker dared and demanded. Stirling decided to take his business directly to Folch in Pensacola, despite the time and expense.[12] Unfortunately, he needed official copies of documents on file in Baton Rouge, and Crocker was the only one who could provide them. Miffed at Stirling's refusal to pay the first bribe, Crocker now exacted six times the normal fee for each document, and when Stirling had insufficient immediate cash for the fees, Crocker demanded a beautiful horse valued at five hundred pesos or more.[13] To get his business done, Stirling had no choice but to yield, though the animal was worth many times the legitimate cost of the copies. Then Crocker did nothing to speed the documents after all, and when Stirling finally got them to Pensacola, they were rejected for being improperly executed, leaving it to be done all over again.[14]

The story of Stirling's treatment by Crocker soon became notorious in Baton Rouge, and Favrot protested, "Everybody is indignant." Crocker's cupidity became increasingly frequent, yet Delassus did nothing, and Favrot believed the commandant was so inattentive that he did not even know of Crocker's activities.[15] For his part, Crocker met the outcry aggressively, saying it was all trumped up by outside agitators and what he called "embryo insurgents" within to divert attention from their real purpose of revolution.[16] Every complaint against Crocker reflected on Delassus, and soon more direct accusations emerged against the commandant for arbitrary government, inefficiency, and maladministration of justice. In almost every instance those complaints had their origin in Crocker, as people lumped the two together into a single symbol of corruption and tyranny, often adding Captain Estevan as well.[17]

While Crocker upset the American population, the continued stresses over France and Napoleon aggravated the Spaniards. In April of 1809 a rumor appeared that Spaniards in Pensacola were plotting to massacre French residents, including the Spaniards' commandant Maxent, who was French by birth.[18] French inhabitants responded by mounting volunteer patrols of their neighborhoods. A month later Delassus and Folch discussed the possibility of evacuating Louisiana if the Americans ceded it back to France, and by August, Folch feared Cuba might fall to Napoleon and at the same time raised apprehensions that U.S. troops might come into West Florida.[19] Watching from New Orleans, Claiborne asked Washington what to do if the Spaniards banished the French inhabitants from West Florida as a precaution. If they sought asylum in New Orleans, it risked introducing a disruptive element into a society where French Creoles were already too sympathetic to Napoleon.[20] Then Creoles in Quito, Ecuador, called for independence, the first in the chorus of rebellions that would explode in the next few years. It appeared that Spain was disintegrating at home and abroad, a fact not lost on West Florida.

In October the junta of Cadiz, representing those loyal to the deposed King Ferdinand, sent one of their most experienced diplomats, Don Luis de Onís, to Washington as their minister to establish Spain's claim to the Floridas. Madison refused to receive and accredit him; with the Spanish crown in dispute between Ferdinand and Joseph Bonaparte, Madison could not recognize an emissary from either. That was a blow to those in West Florida still attached to Spain, for with Bonaparte in control of most of Spain, and Madison unwilling to deal with Ferdinand's representative, the people of the Baton Rouge and Feliciana districts felt perilously isolated. It also made Delassus even more autonomous, which meant that Crocker could continue his dirty business.[21] Once more West Florida was intertwined with the chaotic affairs of the larger world.

All of which only exaggerated the mounting internal problems. Americans made up 90 percent of the population in the Baton Rouge and Feliciana districts, and St. Helena and St. Ferdinand were so wild and remote that Delassus could scarcely exert control there. Indeed, by 1810 real Spanish authority barely extended beyond Baton Rouge, Bayou Sara, and St. Francisville. U.S. militia continued crossing the line to catch deserters, disregarding Spanish claims of sovereignty.[22] Land values in Feliciana fell to their 1805 level, the land worth less than it had been in 1802, while in Baton Rouge, prices doubled every few years.[23] Surveys were slower than ever before, even without Crocker's involvement, and administration juddered almost to a standstill. In 1809, plaintiffs filed ample litigation, but on January 9, 1810, civil suits came to a near-permanent halt, and after New Year's Day not a single criminal case was tried. When land sales — but not prices — suddenly rose in volume, it reflected fear and uncertainty and the owners' decision to get what they could for their property while they could.[24] Unfortunately they did not get much from their cotton. "Our friends here are generally well struggling against the bad times occasioned by the low price of our staple commodity," Alcalde McDermott complained.[25] Strained planters could not pay for their surveys even if they were willing to, and the embargo made it worse.[26] Kneeland told Pintado in June that business was moribund and money scarce, but the chief surveyor knew that very well himself, for Alcalde McDermott now refused to pay him for land recently purchased.[27] Leaders in the community were no longer honoring their commitments, perhaps especially debts owed to Spaniards.

The sloth in Delassus's office did not help. Pintado, now posted to Pensacola, complained that "Public business is a Sacred Thing & therefore must be done in a competent & legal way." He thought he could remedy the problems if he returned to Baton Rouge, but he failed to grasp just how deeply the rot had set in around Delassus.[28] Even Kneeland, generally honest despite his involvement in the Kemper business, accepted payment for a survey but refused to do the work, and then turned around and surveyed the same property for another man.[29] Once-reliable civil servants were looking out for themselves now.

Perhaps the most ominous sign to date came on April 20, when Samuel Fulton wrote a letter to Madison. Reminding the president that he had served in the U.S. Army until 1803 and now as a Spanish citizen was adjutant of West Florida's militia and commander of its cavalry, he confessed doubts that Spain could hold out much longer against Bonaparte. Should Spain fall, "we must of Course Change our Masters here." He believed most in the area would choose to come under the cloak of the United States, and being a lifelong opportunist, he wanted the president to remember his name.[30] It boded ill that the senior-ranking American in West Florida's militia had a moistened finger testing the breeze. If Delassus could not depend on him, then the militia who followed him were not likely to be any more reliable in a crisis.

In another part of the world, Bolivia joined Ecuador in revolt, and within days of Fulton's letter came the news that on April 19, a junta in Caracas, Venezuela, had declared its independence. A few weeks later another junta in Argentina took the first steps toward a break, and the signs of disintegration could not be concealed. That left William Barrow, one of West Florida's wealthiest planters, deeply troubled.[31] What was to happen to West Florida amid the dissolution? On the fourth of June he told a friend that he felt more alarmed at the situation than he had at any time since he had come to West Florida. They were at a loss as to what to do. Spain seemed close to collapse, his friends saw little hope of the United States taking over any time soon, and there were no able men in the province to give them sound advice on what course to pursue, while their own internal political divisions left even the Americans divided.[32]

Hope was not lost in the United States, however. Claiborne was in Washington meeting with Madison just then. This president had never felt the compulsion to gain West Florida that his predecessor had. Congress's purchase appropriation had expired, and Madison could not negotiate effectively with a fractured Spain. He knew of the settlers' complaints of bad administration and the irksome Mobile duties, but he wanted no risk of a war with Spain and its puppet master, France. He based his West Florida policy on international events rather than on local matters in the small province. "When the pear is ripe, it will fall of its own accord," he said. When reports arrived of the revolts in process in South America, he concluded that the fruit had ripened. He did not want an independent West Florida, but he hoped the settlers would rise like other juntas had, take control, and then accept absorption by the United States. Claiborne's being in the capital made it easier to reach for the fruit, and on June 14 Madison asked him to write a letter.[33]

Fortunately Claiborne knew just the right name for the address. William Wykoff had been a successful merchant in New Orleans since before the Purchase and then had moved to a large plantation on the Mississippi opposite Baton Rouge. Men of influence listened to him, and Claiborne thought him much esteemed in the region.[34] Now Claiborne asked him to go to Baton Rouge and the other districts and encourage them to call a convention to decide their future course. The people of West Florida must look to themselves for their future security and prosperity, he was saying. Schemers and intriguers would court them, and England and France both might try to lure them into alliance or more. Should they choose on their own to separate from Spain, Madison waited to embrace them. "To form for themselves an independent Government is out of the question!" Claiborne told Wykoff. They had neither the numbers nor the proximity to support to sustain themselves, while "nature has decreed the Union of Florida with the United States." Wykoff was to sound the more influential men, particularly Hicky, Lilley, Barrow, and others, and give them direction, cautioning them to be wary of French or English influence. They should call a convention to set their course, but it should represent every area as far as the Perdido. Madison could take West Florida with Spain now so weak, but he and Claiborne urged that "it would be more pleasing that the taking possession of the Country, be preceded by a Request from the Inhabitants." Claiborne made it clear that Wykoff's mission was to obtain that request.[35]

A week later, Madison instructed Senator William H. Crawford of Georgia to send a similar mission to the Alabama and Tombigbee settlements. The president wanted a general uprising all across West Florida, for even as weakened as they were, the Spaniards might fend off uncoordinated efforts.[36] Crawford sent George Matthews, former governor of Georgia, but he would not reach East Florida until well after events got ahead of them all. Madison was implementing a new kind of foreign policy for the United States, a sort of passive imperialism aimed at gaining territory with the least exposure by inciting the inhabitants themselves to take the risk. The term *manifest destiny* would not be coined for almost thirty years, but Madison, like Jefferson before him, embraced the idea that the Floridas were fated by geography to be a part of the new nation. The idea first expressed as a policy in Claiborne's letter to Wykoff would spread its shadow across the entire continent before the century was done.

Beneath the political surface, the inhabitants verged on racing ahead of Washington. The Spaniards still stopped ships at Mobile and imposed duty.[37] As a result, the Mobile Society was almost ready to act unilaterally, since it was better organized than any resistance movement in the Baton Rouge area. On June 7 Joseph P. Kennedy secretly sent a letter into Mobile for Zenon Orso, a young Mobile native well connected by marriage to leading Mobile families of all nationalities. Kennedy had already courted him to aid the society. "I know that you are an American in heart," he said. "Now is the important moment." Spain was a dying empire, and King Ferdinand was irrelevant. He had at his command men and resources, and if the Americans in Mobile were willing to resist, then Kennedy wanted to meet Orso and unfold his plans. Unfortunately Captain Cayetano Perez in the Mobile garrison had been watching Orso and arrested him.[38] After he read the letter, Perez warned Folch and Maxent.[39] The latter sent a protest to the Kempers' friend Colonel Richard Sparks, now commanding at Fort Stoddert, advising him that Kennedy had formed a society above the line that called itself "Expedition of Mobile," its object the pillaging of Mobile.[40] Sparks promised to prevent any action by Americans that could hazard relations between the United States and Spain.[41]

While that stymied action above Mobile briefly, events in Feliciana took the lead. Physicians there, including Samuel Flowers, Cornelius French, Dudley Avery, and Martin L. Haynie, occasionally gathered at a Bayou Sara tavern to discuss professional issues, and other locals, all Americans, sometimes joined the conversation.[42] The talk increasingly strayed to complaints of Delassus's government.[43] Someone suggested a more formal meeting specifically to address the crumbling rule in Baton Rouge. After all, Delassus had sanctioned the convention to deal with the embargo.[44] A petition soon circulated in the vicinity inviting prominent landowners to gather at John H. Johnson's Troy plantation, near Bayou Sara, a community that by now Delassus regarded as the place "from which all alarming News appeared to come."[45]

On Saturday, June 16, most of the planters in St. Francisville gathered at Troy.[46] Complaining of the virtual moratorium on justice, some suggested that judicial power be taken from the governor and entrusted to juries. They spoke of creating committees of safety and an elected legislature to work with the governor, and they argued that they must get legal affairs out of Crocker's hands before he ruined them. "When a man has been so often bribed as to consider justice on either, or neither side of the question," one complained, "it must be hard for him after a few years, to know on which side it really does belong." If they could remove Crocker from the chain of justice, they might "find men who are not so completely blind, and who still know something of probity."[47] John Leonard of St. Helena spoke for many when he condemned the tyranny and despotism that they endured. They could not afford to wait longer for reform.[48]

They decided to call another larger assembly representing all of New Feliciana, and they drafted letters inviting the other divisions to send delegates to deal with the virtual state of anarchy.[49] They suggested meeting on June 23 at Stirling's old plantation Egypt, now the home of his son Lewis, whose notorious travails with Crocker had helped generate these meetings.[50] The new convocation would not be a legislature, for they had no such power, but a committee of safety to adopt and propose to Delassus some measures to keep harmony and get justice moving again. There was a consensus that Delassus would grant some concessions, and if he did so, then existing Spanish laws would be continued in force. If he refused, however, then "the people will consider themselves at liberty to act in their own best interest."

There was little doubt what that meant, for one of the most discussed subjects at the Bayou Sara meeting was that alternative, yet after the meeting adjourned one delegate thought the public mind seemed more tranquil now that something was being done to address their grievances. Spain could do nothing for them, and the idea of France coming in raised horror in their minds. That left their neighbors to the north. "If the United States still pretend any claim on this place they must not refuse it when it is offered," he said, but if Washington dawdled, then "the spirit of independence is still gaining ground."[51] One of the doctors present, looking at the weakened condition of Spain's rule, quipped to the others that "the imposthume [boil] was ready for the lancet."[52]

Some thought the meeting placed too much faith in the United States; a New Orleans editor warned that they ought not "to be too sanguine on this score." Madison's caution could leave them on their own if they rose up, a rather accurate summary of the president's position.[53] The Spaniards did not know that, of course. Estevan was in Bayou Sara during the meeting but ill and confined to his bed, and he did not learn any details until Johnson and others came to his home after the adjournment and strode into his bedroom. They presented a petition for him to approve the call for the June 23 assembly.[54] Estevan tried to delay, but they insisted, and finally he signed. His pen still handy, Estevan wrote to Delassus as soon as they left. He neither liked nor trusted these Americans, and he warned that the planters were conspiring against the government, embellishing his account with hints of collaborations with the foreign enemies of Spain.[55]

Word of the Troy meeting spread quickly. "The business has assumed a serious shape," wrote a New Orleans editor, averring that the inhabitants seemed to be considering forming a new government.[56] Governor Holmes advised Washington that Spanish authority in West Florida was collapsing, and locals took care of their own law now by forming a "neighbourhood police" that was inefficient and sometimes unjust. Factions had emerged, each with a different object. The English natives wanted Britain to take over, while the Americans wanted the United States, though many would not act to throw off Spain unless they were certain of success, for fear of reprisal. Holmes thought much of the population there were rabble, and if they overcame the respectable people, that could open the door to slave insurrection, and the anarchy could spread to Mississippi and Orleans. Whatever was about to happen in West Florida, he told Secretary of State Robert Smith, it would be something interesting to the United States.[57]

Now the French specter arose more menacingly than ever when Delassus learned that Frenchmen were gathering secretly in Baton Rouge to discuss their course in case France attempted a takeover. In mid-June Delassus heard that other Frenchmen visiting in West Florida might be there to foment an uprising among the Creoles. Under Delassus's nose in Baton Rouge a Creole merchant supposedly tried to arouse sentiment for Joseph Bonaparte, and soon Delassus maintained surveillance on French visitors, to whom he assigned code names. He had little doubt that they meant to agitate the Creoles into attacking Baton Rouge and Pensacola in order to take the province for France, and they would do it with aid from countrymen in New Orleans. Delassus sent word of his apprehensions to Pensacola, knowing all too well that he was so weak that a well-organized revolt, even by the minority of Frenchmen, might succeed. He complained again that his fort was completely useless, and his superiors sent him no instructions or resources to repair it. With barely two hundred and fifty soldiers to hold Baton Rouge, Bayou Sara, Galveztown, and other tiny garrisons, he could not stop vagrants, bandits, and agitators from annoying the law-abiding people. On June 20 he warned that his situation was critical and assistance was essential.[58]

By that time, Delassus had at last taken a decisive step on his own. On or around June 10 he issued a decree giving all Frenchmen in the Baton Rouge District three days to leave, making no distinction between visitors and residents. Virtually all obeyed, since they could have little recourse to Spanish law.[59] Delassus's eviction of the French naturally angered them, and threats reached Holmes's ears that the dispossessed would reinforce themselves and return to get revenge. They went across the Mississippi to Iberville Parish, where their angry fulminations sufficiently alarmed Delassus that a few days later he put the militia on alert and dispersed them equally throughout the district.

Distracted by all of this, the governor may not fully have comprehended the import of Estevan's message about the forthcoming meeting and Estevan's less than voluntary endorsement of it. Estevan wanted militia redirected to St. Francisville as a precaution, but Delassus regarded the danger from the French as greater than that posed by the planters' meeting at Egypt.[60] Still, aware that any assembly could be an opportunity for outside agitators, including the recently banished French, he ordered all militia detachments to be in position when the meeting convened.[61] Then Delassus sent Philip Hicky and his brother-in-law George Mather to Bayou Sara to summon the inhabitants, inform them of the French peril, impress on them that any internal discord now abetted the schemes of a foreign foe, and encourage them to renew their fidelity oaths.[62]

Hicky and Mather reached St. Francisville the very day of the assembly and carried out their mission. When everyone returned from Egypt, they met with Estevan to get his assessment of the situation, and also with Lénnàn, who himself sent Delassus a hysterical warning that the meeting was a diversion to hide a plot to take Baton Rouge. Then they spoke to some of the planters, and soon Hicky and Mather concluded that Estevan and Lénnàn had overreacted and that there seemed to be good cause for a protest meeting.[63] Thus satisfied, they returned to Baton Rouge to assure Delassus that he had nothing to fear from the meeting, though whether they served the governor's ends or those of the planters at this point is hard to determine.[64] One of Hicky's friends who was clearly aligned with the new movement thought he knew where Hicky stood and congratulated him on "the happy issue of your mission."[65]

Almost five hundred men assembled at Egypt, a few miles east of St. Francisville, and Estevan and a troop of cavalry were there to keep the peace. The organizers of the Troy meeting had worked hard in the past week, and they were ready now with a draft plan of action to present. Some there thought it Skipwith's work, but he had only just taken over the Montesano plantation in late April.[66] Besides, what they proposed required no seasoned statesman. They presented a straightforward catalog of means to address the situation before them: The people should elect a governor, a secretary, and a council of three to rule the province on behalf of Ferdinand VII if he was restored; should Napoleon remain in power in Spain, then these officials would hold office for life; the governor could appoint all alcaldes, syndics, and militia officers and remove them at will with the concurrence of a majority of the council. A man from Point Coupée who happened to be in St. Francisville that day regarded it as nothing more or less than "an elective monarchy."[67]

The plan generated extended debate, which many in the large crowd on Stirling's yard could not hear. Men complained at length about Crocker's corruption and that Delassus and his administration burdened them with tyranny. There had to be a change, most agreed, but this proposed new mode of operation seemed worse than what they already had, ending ineffective appointive rule at the risk of imposing inefficient administration for life. Consequently, with only eleven dissenting voices, the members of the crowd concluded they would support the current administration until something better could be framed.[68] Then they adjourned, planning to reconvene on Sunday, July 1, by which time they hoped to have another plan to consider. The company of mounted militia saluted Estevan and gave a cheer of "God save Ferdinand the Seventh," which left the captain somewhat taken aback since he had come expecting his own men to arrest him and go over to the crowd in their treason.

"Thus it seems the present attempt will not succeed," a man from Point Coupée wrote the next day, "but it is evident that in less than two months a change will take place in the government of Florida." Men at Egypt told him they would be delighted to be absorbed by the United States but did not expect it after Jefferson had let the Spaniards stay on following the turnover of Louisiana. They saw the same lack of determination in Madison, and some seemed to favor approaching Britain. The whole country appeared to him to be in a state of rebellion. Of course, this meeting was only Feliciana men, and other districts might have different views. If they did, then he feared that civil war would commence without delay.[69] The meeting left Feliciana citizens no more secure than they had been before, and political affairs assumed a gloomy cast, with seeming hazards at every turn. The French threatened to take the province, and some feared that if they tried they would succeed. "We are very weak," lamented one attendee. They had no organized force to defend themselves against France, and the fort at Baton Rouge was crumbling, with few serviceable cannon and reportedly no more than fifteen healthy soldiers. They had lost hope of the United States taking them under its wing. It seemed that all they could do for the moment was keep meeting, and soon there came a notice to convene again to address means for assuring the safety of the country. If they managed to do nothing else, these planters were going to talk.[70]

"As we find the people so much divided, we have been at a loss what to do," Barrow soon wrote Madison. "We found it was necessary to do something to appease the minds of the people & strengthen the Government for our own security."[71] Consequently, on July 1 another assembly from all four divisions of the New Feliciana District gathered at Egypt, and this time Johnson and the other organizers came better prepared.[72] By the time they adjourned, they had drafted and agreed upon an address to all citizens of the district. Acknowledging that they were a country of varied languages, manners, and customs, as well as the novelty of such a diversity of people trying to participate in the administration of a government, they still warned of unnamed agitators trying to sow seeds of anarchy among them. A corrupt and crumbling Spain could not help them, and they had no alternative but to adopt measures for their own welfare and security. In a veiled reference to the French threat, they maintained that people in their midst wanted to raise another flag, and claimed that this danger was why they had convened this meeting.

They proposed to call on Madison for aid, acknowledging that he could not receive them if they were rebels against Spain without himself risking war with that country and its allies. Hence they asked everyone to ignore calls for revolt. They should remain loyal to Ferdinand VII and hope for the United States to absorb them peacefully, but meanwhile they needed regulations to stabilize the present, for issues and dangers confronting them here and now required immediate remedy. Fearing that "the most enormous crimes may be committed with impunity," they felt it their duty to recommend a plan. They proposed that each of the four districts choose one delegate from each of its internal divisions — four from New Feliciana, two from Baton Rouge, three from St. Helena, and one from St. Ferdinand — and send them to Baton Rouge to counsel Delassus on the current problems facing them and adopt means for redress.

Most urgently, they needed measures for safety and defense and ways to give force to the existing laws. Each division should choose its own delegate, but the meeting's members counseled that inhabitants look to men with long records of proven fidelity to the government and declared themselves opposed to innovations or "changes lightly made." The nominated delegates from each district should confer within three days and report their deliberations to the other districts, then they should all meet to compile a digest of their recommendations to present to Delassus. Before they adjourned, the members of the meeting chose Barrow, Johnson, Mills, and Rhea as delegates from New Feliciana. Copies of the address were completed, 139 men signed each of them, and off they sped.[73]

Now they began to lay the groundwork with Delassus. Two days later a copy of their address went to Hicky and Mather, since Delassus had already made them his informal representatives, and also to two others whom the governor trusted, Lilley and planter Richard Duvall; they asked Hicky to lay their address before the governor and seek his permission for similar meetings in the other districts. The convocation recommended these measures as the only means of tranquilizing the minds of the people at this moment, and urged everyone to use every exertion to prevent "all Spirit of Revolt." Johnson and the other leaders well knew that Hicky, Mather, Duvall, and Lilley were already in their camp. Whatever their former attachments to Grand-Pré, none of these men felt personal loyalty to Delassus. In fact, Duvall's home was to be the scene of the next assembly, if there should be one.[74] They couched their appeal to the governor in expressions of loyalty and the best interests of Spain, but they were still talking of electing a popular assembly.[75]

No die was cast as yet, but the men of Feliciana could feel it in their hands. Hicky and the others would make the best representation of their appeal to Delassus, though none could say how he would react. Some felt he would go along. After all, what choice did he have? They could field at least five hundred dissatisfied citizens to frame a protest, while he had only a handful of regular *soldados* and a militia composed overwhelmingly of Americans, many of whom had attended the Egypt meetings. The threat was implicit, while at the same time if the prospect of a French attempt at attacking should prove genuine, Delassus could not defend his province without the aid of these same planters. His interests as well as theirs depended on his giving them some freedom of action.

The day after the meeting one man in Bayou Sara reflected that "in this distracted state of things, without law or government; the people have thought proper and prudent too [sic] hold meetings to consult for their generrl [sic] safety," their only guidance their "principles of *self preservation*." Being overwhelmingly Americans, they naturally looked to the Northeast for succor. West Floridians would cheerfully become citizens of the United States, he believed, and he saw a commendably unselfish spirit in their deliberations thus far. If their future deliberations showed that same spirit of unanimity, he believed they would achieve their aims.[76]

Yet many thought this talk of reform only masked rebellion, and in fact most men in the assemblies probably entertained private goals that varied from their published expressions. A friend of Barrow in Nashville wrote Madison that "a revolution of some kind may be attempted," for he gathered that a large majority there wanted to become American citizens.[77] At the same time stories reached New Orleans that Bayou Sara and Baton Rouge had decided on independence, which disturbed those fearful of entanglement in war with Spain.[78] On July 4, appropriately enough, Natchez got word that the West Floridians were about to act for independence and seek American protection.[79] Just five days later news arrived that a junta in Caracas had declared independence on July 5. An editor there expected Mexico to follow soon, and declared that "our little neighbours (we hope this appellation will not offend them) the Floridians, have anticipated the good cause, and this day, we are informed, they intend declaring themselves free."[80]

That expectation gained more and more currency. On July 6 Thomas Bolling Robertson, secretary of the Orleans Territory, warned Washington that the people of West Florida appeared to be nearing revolt. He heard rumors of a new republican constitution being drafted, and of July 4 being selected retroactively as the birthday of their independence.[81] A delegate from Feliciana reported the real facts of their meetings, but then added that he expected that Delassus would not agree to their reforms, saying that "if so, something more serious will be apt to take place." Their only recourse would be to lay their grievances before President Madison and seek his protection.[82] From Mississippi, Holmes sent Washington more reliable details, and according to him the assembly had proposed to create a council with general powers to deal with dangers foreign and domestic. They did not address the status of the existing Spanish officials, but it was tacitly understood that the new council would keep them in office if they submitted to control by the council's enactments. The Floridians were going to change their government fundamentally if they could. "You may readily conjecture," Holmes told Secretary of State Smith, "how this business will ultimately eventuate."[83]

It was the perfect moment for William Wykoff to receive his instructions from Claiborne at last. Sometime around the end of that first week of July he crossed the Mississippi, mounted his horse, and set out, as Skipwith put it, to "stimulate the Inhabitants of Florida to declare themselves Independent."[84]

10

A New Order of Things

WHEN GOVERNOR DELASSUS received the petition to allow assemblies in the several districts, he knew that without money, more men, and resources to repair the fort, he had virtually no choice but to grant it. Even now the contractor who provided meat for his garrison told him that there would be no more beef until his bill was paid. Delassus and others strove to get credit to buy provisions locally, but no one advanced them a peso. A few locals gave them written orders on New Orleans banks to provide some liquidity, but beyond that Delassus had no income but the interest from an estate succession that Hicky managed for him, and he held that as a last resort. Another plea for reinforcements went off after the June 23 assembly, but they would not arrive — if they came at all — for some weeks yet.[1]

All he could do was forestall more radical acts by giving the dissidents what they asked for until he felt strong enough to meet the challenge. On July 6 Hicky, Mather, Lilley, Skipwith, Fulton, and three other men from Baton Rouge called on him.[2] They presented a petition to choose delegates for the next assembly, and Delassus assented without objection.[3] "Man is a sociable animal," he told them. They all wanted the same things — peace, security, prosperity. Divided though they were by religion and language, still all of the inhabitants of West Florida honored the blood of heroes and were loyal to Ferdinand VII, as the petitioners had said themselves. He welcomed the delegates' desire to work with him. After all, he had approved the June 23 assembly, and so now he approved the next meeting. When it concluded, he invited them to meet with him in Baton Rouge to implement the remedies for their common benefit. Still, he enjoined them to use "firmness and resolution," to "guard against bad counsel and dangerous remedies."[4]

The one thing Delassus could do was make these men liable for treason if they went too far, so he issued a decree requiring all inhabitants to take an oath of loyalty to Ferdinand VII. That only spawned a rumor that Ferdinand would cede the province to Britain, and their oaths would bind them to accept his act.[5] The people discussed this along with their other fears and grievances when they assembled to take their oaths, which brought home to residents of limited acquaintance just how widespread the disaffection with Spain had become. At the same time, it gave many a sense of the strength of their own numbers on the eve of selecting delegates for the coming convention.[6]

The men in Baton Rouge lost no time. That same afternoon eight of them met at a village home, among them Baton Rouge businessman Manuel López, the only native-born Spaniard of the group.[7] They sent expresses to the other three districts that included copies of the July 1 Feliciana proceedings, Delassus's decree authorizing a consultation, and an injunction that no time be lost in assembling their inhabitants to select their representatives in time to meet the other delegates on Wednesday morning, July 25. "The exigency of the case seems to us to require energy & promptitude," they urged.[8]

Over the next two weeks the districts selected their delegates amid renewed rumors of a French attack and stories that somewhere in the backcountry Americans had already raised the flag of independence.[9] Men tried to influence the color of the coming meeting. The day after Delassus consented, Fulton drilled his militia cavalry in Baton Rouge and took the occasion to harangue them twice on the need to appoint the right delegate. "With all that assurance attendant on low weak minds," wrote a member of the troop, Fulton "imperiously dictated a person *proper* to fill that important position," but his choice was unpopular with men from below Baton Rouge. "Ignorance is always dangerous in public characters — they are the tools of designing men," the militiaman continued, and some felt that Fulton's favorite was a Bonapartist, more than enough to disqualify him. As for Fulton, the writer shared with Hicky his alarm and "sentiments of indignation & disapprobation which the temerity of an illiterate demagogue has inspired."

Fulton's efforts worried others in his troop as well, and they looked to Hicky for guidance. A public meeting in Baton Rouge on July 14 would choose its three delegates. Should it be by ballot or voice vote? Would proxies be allowed? Were all male residents to vote? If not, what qualifications were necessary? These were not just niggling details. These Floridians had never voted before on any public issue in their districts. For some it would be the first vote of their lives, and every man who stepped forward took his small part in the creation of what all assumed would be some form of representative government, however modest. They took this vote very seriously and resented any effort from any source to unduly influence their choices. "I swear never tamely to submit to the intrigues of designing French men or a Yanky faction," the complaining militiaman told Hicky. Accusing Fulton and his friends of using underhanded means to influence delegate choices, he suggested that Hicky and others interested in being selected should keep their intentions secret until the actual day of the vote.[10] It was probably wise advice, since the election took place at Fulton's home.[11] When it was done, Fulton's favorite was ignored; the voters also ignored the instruction to choose three delegates. They picked five: Hicky and Lilley, Edmund Hawes, who had been a resident since 1801, John Morgan, and López. That done, Hicky sent word of the selections to Bayou Sara, where Feliciana residents chose Barrow, John H. Johnson, John Mills, and John Rhea.[12]

Farther eastward, it did not go so smoothly. Brown, both alcalde and militia commandant in St. Helena, did not approve of a convention. For that matter, many did not approve of Brown and the aroma of bribery and speculation clinging to him.[13] If he bribed Crocker to get land, then any threat to Spain threatened his pocket. His adherence to Delassus probably lay behind anonymous letters recently sent to him, taunting that there was a *"nuevo orden de cosas"* coming — "a new order of things" — from which he could no longer profit. Delassus's authorization for an assembly stunned Brown, and at first he thought the governor had been coerced. He sent to Baton Rouge that same day to see if Delassus acted freely, adding an assurance that St. Helena wanted no change in the old order and that he had five hundred militia ready to march on Baton Rouge to fight for Spain.[14]

However much Delassus appreciated Brown's support, he knew

that the claim of five hundred willing to fight was hyperbolic. If he had to use force to resist the movement confronting him, he knew he could not depend on American militia. He would need *soldados*, and until he got them he was powerless. Rather than say that to Brown, Delassus responded that the citizens had respectfully requested the assemblies, wished him goodwill, and pledged their *fidelidad* to Ferdinand VII, and he had cheerfully assented.[15] Baton Rouge and Feliciana delegates were all ready when Brown received the governor's reply, and he had to hurry to get delegates chosen and off to the July 25 consultation. He divided St. Helena into four sections, allocated one delegate to each of three and two to the fourth. That done, he exerted his own influence with considerably more success than Fulton, and when the elections were over he boasted to Delassus that he had secured *"cinco fielos Vasallos"*—"five faithful vassals"—who would do as he told them.[16]

The main portion of St. Helena would be represented by Brown's agent Joseph Thomas, a man little known and not very highly regarded, and John W. Leonard, a former lieutenant in the U.S. Navy who had moved to St. Helena in 1805 and become a prominent planter and merchant in partnership with a Spaniard.[17] Two of the outlying districts chose William Spiller and Benjamin O. Williams, men of whom virtually nothing was known. Because St. Ferdinand, sometimes called Tangipahoa, was so distant, Brown organized its election as well. The voters chose the alcalde William Cooper, one of the Tories who had fled there during the Revolution, leaving behind him a reputation for cruelties against his North Carolina patriot neighbors.[18]

By this time William Wykoff had called on men in the Feliciana and Baton Rouge districts. He certainly failed to keep his mission confidential, for it was soon known to Skipwith at least, and the garrulous Virginian kept no secrets.[19] From afar Madison instructed Governor Holmes to monitor affairs in West Florida and have his militia ready to act if necessary. If Holmes suspected an internal convulsion or saw foreign powers about to interfere, he was to act to protect the United States' right to West Florida. The president told Holmes he wanted to acquire the province by internal revolt, without risk of war, so that Holmes could assist in "diffusing the impressions we wish to be made there."[20] With Claiborne still in the East, Holmes was the senior official in the region and Madison's most trusted source of information through the coming summer and fall.[21]

There was much to report. Just as they had a proposal for the June 23 meeting ahead of time, some Bayou Sara men prepared a constitution and code of laws to put before the coming convention. Delassus might stop the meeting if he did not like its direction, so having a charter to submit to the delegates immediately would take less time than framing one in open assembly. It would also give the Feliciana men, leaders of the movement from the first, a certain high ground with the rest.[22] They might have been working on the document even before Delassus gave his permission, and certainly they finished no later than July 14, and probably earlier.[23] As such declarations do, it began with a statement of grievances:

> When the sovereignty and independence of a nation have been destroyed by treachery or violence, the political ties which united its members are dissolved. Distant provinces no longer cherished or protected by the mother country, have a right to institute for themselves such forms of government as they may think conducive to their safety and happiness.

Spain was in the hands of a usurper, and its colonies had to look out for themselves. In a clear warning to those who might scheme to bring the province under French control, they swore to "by all means in our power, resist any tyrannical usurpation over us of whatever kind, and by whomsoever the same may be attempted."

With Jeffersonian references to their "domestick tranquility," they framed articles preserving all existing laws regarding property and maintaining all currently serving civil and militia officials. They called for an elected governor, secretary of state, and council of three, this time with no mention of life incumbency. The governor remained the supreme executive and commander in chief of the militia, but now he would need the advice and consent of the councilors in all appointments and the dismissal of current or future magistrates. The council of three was to act as a legislature, but the governor must approve any laws it passed. He could convene them at will, and they were also to act as a court to decide all matters civil and criminal; their judgments would be final.

The governor was to be a president and congress all in one, with virtually all the powers exercised by those branches of the Washington government, even to entering into confederacy with other states, with council approval. Looking to the future, they provided that no more than three years after taking office, an elected convention should meet in Baton Rouge to frame a constitution, choose a future capital, and oversee the expiration of the powers of this provisional constitution. Finally they provided that when a majority of a district's inhabitants signed this proposal, it should take complete effect there, along with any laws made under it, and that effect would extend to the rest of East and West Florida when a majority of the people signed. The proposal concluded with its only direct quotation from the Declaration of Independence, saying that "we mutually pledge to each other our lives, our fortunes, and our sacred honour."[24]

The remarkable document teetered between loyalty and revolution. It neither professed nor implied loyalty to the deposed Ferdinand VII, speaking only of the necessity for Spain's colonies to look out for themselves. It acted as if Spain no longer existed, and as if West Florida had complete sovereignty. Though it retained a governor and secretary, the proposal otherwise recast the administration of the province, took any unilateral power from the governor, and placed real authority in the innovative three-man legislature. The grievances over slow justice, corruption, and property that had brought them to this pass were fully represented. It put the money power squarely in the hands of the council, and it gave the people of West Florida, in convention, the power to frame a permanent constitution. Nothing indicated an inclination of the West Floridians to become a part of any other power, but neither did they declare themselves independent. What they should do if Ferdinand VII regained his throne was not said.

The authors circulated it among leaders in Feliciana and Baton Rouge, and while the latter generally approved, concerns emerged in the former. Some wanted an outright declaration of independence. More thought they ought to support Ferdinand VII still. The majority, though, wanted to go directly into the arms of the United States. No one from St. Helena or St. Ferdinand saw it before it appeared in the Natchez press on July 17.[25] Once it hit print, just a week before the upcoming convention, however, the document must have generated far more negative reaction than the authors had anticipated, for it simply disappeared. It was too far-reaching, too revolutionary in its administrative provisions, and too close to an outright declaration of independence, with all the hazards that entailed. Putting it before the July 25 assembly risked provoking Delassus to dissolve them. Just as he needed time to resist this tide, so they needed time to resist him.

Thus it stood as July 25 approached. Two days before the delegates were to convene, a Natchez editor observed that "it is an awful crisis for that people — their future freedom and prosperity, or enslavement and consequent ruin, depend upon the measures adopted at the present crisis." They faced three major alternatives: remain loyal to Spain, declare independence, or seek aid from the United States. They could no longer bind themselves to the unhappy fate of Spain, and the influence of France promised nothing but evil. Their boundaries, their climate, the fertility of their land, and the trading prospects of their coastline gave them all the requisites entitling them to be a nation, but were they strong enough to seize their independence, and would the Americans or the British recognize them if they did? Much depended on the coming convention being composed of the best men available.[26]

When the day came, the delegates assembled early at Duvall's plantation at what the Spaniards originally called Las Praderias, "the Plains." The English native Duvall and his wife were noted for their hospitality, and she provided meals as the delegates gathered under the moss-laden oaks.[27] "We were in a measure strangers," said Barrow, but others were well acquainted.[28] John Ballinger, a Kentuckian and a former colonel in the U.S. Army, was a recent immigrant, yet he knew virtually all of them.[29] He thought they represented the more moderate faction of the old Spanish royalists, men of wealth and long residence, several of them native to the region, including López and a few other Spaniards; if any harbored republican aspirations, he prudently kept that to himself. Having seen revolutionary juntas form in Spain and in the New World colonies, Ballinger thought this group seemed more conservative than radical in their appeal for a redress of grievances.[30]

Revolutionary movements often turn to moderate men, and so these revolutionaries did when they elected John Rhea to preside.

The Bayou Sara merchant was a retiring sort. It took persuasion from friends to tear him from private life, but people admired his character, amiability, and well-informed grasp of the issues. He was widely respected and allied to neither the Kemper radicals nor the Brown conservatives. The group saw in him a man to win the confidence of the populace.[31] They chose three secretaries to keep complete minutes of their convention: Mather and Doctors Samuel S. Crocker and Andrew Steele.[32] That done, the delegates faced an immediate challenge. One of them, perhaps López, who had close ties to Pintado and Kneeland, proposed that they swear allegiance to Ferdinand VII.[33] A few objected, and only one man argued strongly in favor, so the motion died, but Barrow thought they had learned a lesson.[34] Opinions were unsettled and could shift, making it perhaps dangerous to be too open even with one another as yet. Someone spoke of an immediate declaration of independence, but Cooper and others declared that they intended to support Spanish sovereignty.[35] Seeing these divisions, Barrow, probably the strongest proponent of the United States, joined with a few others to conclude for the moment not to say much upon any subject.[36] Instead, they adjourned to allow a committee to draft rules of order.

That afternoon a letter from Natchez advised them that some men in Mississippi were ready to assist them if they declared independence, though Holmes thought it all talk. It sounded like an echo of the Kempers of earlier days, but Nathan and Samuel were elsewhere, and Reuben was only occasionally in Pinckneyville. Ironically, after his pivotal role in years of the agitation that led to this convention, he seemed now to be entirely absent from the stage, yet some had to wonder whether he and Randolph and their other cronies were hovering above the line, ready to descend once more with guns and whips to throw fuel on the embers of resistance. The letter caused a stir among the delegates, and, emboldened by the prospect of nearby support, some spoke more forthrightly, one even asserting that "Lassus trembles for his situation." But they turned circumspect again when they heard that Delassus might have spies there, one of them possibly López.[37]

They reconvened the next morning inside the house behind closed doors in secret session and adopted rules of order to preserve civility and dispatch their business quickly.[38] Leonard introduced the first resolution, affirming their wish to preserve the safety and prosperity of the province and correct abuses, following with another resolution affirming Delassus's authorization to advise them on grievances and redress. The members then detailed a catalog of complaints, seemingly covering everything from the lack of uniform weights and measures, to incomplete statutes and capricious legal fees, to giving asylum to deserters while denying settlement to law-abiding immigrants from the United States. They approved each grievance unanimously, then chose Johnson, Lilley, Leonard, Hicky, and Mills to draft a plan for redress.[39] It was all probably prearranged, and it revealed that Delassus and Shepherd Brown had misjudged some of their supposedly compliant friends. Leonard proved to be a leader, and Spiller seconded several grievances, while the lone Spaniard, López, advanced one motion.[40] The leaders realized that their points would weigh more with Delassus if they were advanced by moderates and presumed Spanish sympathizers than if they were proposed by outspoken Americans. They might be new to representative government, but they revealed sharp political instincts nonetheless.

It had been a long day, the delegates meeting for ten hours straight without stopping for one of Mrs. Duvall's meals.[41] Visitors shut out by the closed doors found the delegates reticent about their deliberations and learned little of the secret debates. All the delegates would reveal was that there was great diversity of opinion, some members being for independence and others for supporting Spain, while a few expected they would close their meeting without doing anything decisive.[42] Holmes had an observer at the Plains, and he reported that same evening that delegates were afraid to appeal to the United States for fear that Delassus's spies would get word to Havana before American help arrived. That would make them rebels, and the Spaniards would surely arrest them and confiscate their property, which must lead to resistance and "anarchy and bloodshed."[43]

When they convened in the morning, Hicky went on to issues that would make their efforts revolutionary if successful. With Spain distracted and weakened, West Florida could reduce the strain by freeing her of the financial burden of supporting a colonial administration.

Hence he moved that they raise locally the money necessary to administer and defend the province. That meant levying taxes and controlling their own purse, a major building block of self-government. Lilley followed with a proposal that they, not Spain, should pay Delassus's salary, making Delassus a public servant. Then Leonard stood once more and proposed a resolution that encapsulated virtually all of the remaining powers of a nation: Since they were delegates elected by the people, meeting with consent of the governor, he moved that they should assume power to create civil and criminal tribunals, raise militia, and otherwise act for the public safety. That was done, and they appointed Rhea, Leonard, and Spiller to give Delassus an address informing him of the result of their deliberations. They chose Johnson, Lilley, Leonard, Hicky, and Mills to draft a plan for redress to report to the convention when it reassembled on August 13, and they created a standing committee to receive any communications from Delassus in the interim. Spiller then prudently moved that no member of the convention was to be arrested by any civil process while serving as a delegate.[44]

Finally Leonard presented the address to Delassus that had been drafted the night before. With thanks to Delassus and due reference to "our beloved King Ferdinand," they remarked that instead of sending him a full record of their deliberations, they wanted to call on him and present a suitable digest. One resolution only did they detail in the letter, and that was one expressing their wish to act in all things with the approval and support of the governor and promising him their support in return. When they reconvened, they expected to have a plan for redress and defense drafted and ready to submit to him. Then they concluded the meeting, and except for those on the standing committee, they all went home.[45]

"Their proceedings augur well," a man at the Plains wrote that evening. The delegates had been wise and prudent. Would-be demagogues might seek to influence them in the days ahead, but if they remained faithful to their charge, they would gain honor for themselves "and secure a free and equitable government to their posterity."[46] Success with Delassus, of course, depended on how far they pushed him and how far they distanced themselves from Spain, for as soon as details of the meeting spread beyond West Florida, people could not help but notice, along with a Boston editor, that "*it will be remarked, that these Deputies of a Spanish Province all bear American Names.*"[47]

While the committee began drafting their report, it appeared that others were moving rapidly toward a more violent redress of their grievances. Despite the exposure of the plans of Kennedy and the Mobile Society, the basic goal of ejecting the Spaniards remained alive, and that kept Mobile in a constant state of anxiety. Rumors abounded that the Spaniards would enlist hundreds of Creek and Choctaw as allies in the event of an attack, and that raised fears above the line, where Judge Toulmin warned that if Indians hit the Alabama and Tombigbee settlements, "then nothing will stop retaliation and peaceable men will be drawn into the wicked machinations of the lawless."[48]

By July 12 Colonel Sparks believed that "*a general, and powerfull, combination*" planned an attack on Mobile and Pensacola, and that the plotters intended to seize his garrison's arms to keep him from intervening. There was no question that Kennedy was the ringleader, nor that he was using "every art that intrigue and policy can invent" to enlist supporters. Kennedy enjoyed influential connections. His wife was the daughter of a Georgia senator and a sister of an American diplomat. He had youth, education, and popularity, and with them ambition and a penchant for intrigue, though Sparks doubted his ability to lead effectively. He harped on the duties charged at Mobile and targeted recent immigrants who arrived angry after being taxed on their passage through Spanish territory. The result, said Sparks, was "a sudden union and friendship between a number of turbulent ambitious men who have heretofore exhibited unanimity in nothing but their aversion to the *Spaniards.*" The plotters were men gifted in arousing discontent, and they took counsel of their own desire for position and wealth. They had been too successful, he lamented. He did not know when they intended to act, but when they did he felt that it would be universally acceptable to the people of the country. He begged for reinforcements, especially since he believed the Spaniards were reinforcing the Mobile garrison and engaging Indian allies.[49]

Kennedy lived up to Sparks's estimate, combining charm with a braggadocio that compromised the confidentiality of his movement. In mid-July he called on Judge Toulmin and openly admitted the Mobile Society's intention to take Mobile. American law was no obstacle, since Congress forbade incursions into domains of foreign princes and governments only. Since Washington recognized neither Ferdinand nor Joseph Bonaparte as legitimate, Florida belonged to no acknowledged government. A few days later, Kennedy called again and said he was going to Georgia soon to meet with its senators to see if Congress would accept Mobile if he should take it. If they would, he intended to launch his campaign as soon as he returned, having already delayed it too long. The society numbered more than four hundred, he boasted, and acknowledged that James Caller would lead the expedition, even though years before that same Caller had defeated a similar design by his own brother John. Toulmin said Congress would not go for such a scheme and expected that the society would find itself on its own and facing federal charges if it acted. That did not faze Kennedy, who replied that if so, he and his men would be before sympathetic local judges and juries on whom they could rely, and he expected the president to overlook any laws broken to gain Mobile. Kennedy meant to inform Holmes of his plans and would schedule the attack on his return from Georgia. Toulmin warned Madison that "his whole manner indicated a sanguine calculation upon general support, and a perfect confidance in the success of the enterprise."[50]

Kennedy took the same approach when he learned of the arrest of his agents in Mobile. Boldly he told Perez that his society had its origin in Spanish oppression over a country that "the Supreme law of the State has declared to be ours." The Floridas rightfully belonged to the United States, and they wanted what was theirs. He tried to help Orso by denying that he and the others were in the society's confidence but did not deny a plan to attack Mobile, instead promising that the people of Mississippi would not proceed without Washington's approbation. If Madison authorized such a move, he promised that he would give Captain Perez timely notice before he acted, adding that he was leaving for Georgia, not to return before October.[51]

Perez and Folch believed the society could muster from four hundred to two thousand men, including most of three regiments of Mississippi militia, augmented by any number of "vagrants and tramps." They thought the society was more properly a confederation of bandits and knew that Kennedy intended to meet with influential congressmen as well as to bring volunteers to Fort Stoddert on his return. The Spaniards also feared that the society was allied in some fashion to the malcontents in Feliciana.[52]

Judge Toulmin could not decide whether the society meant to hand Mobile to the United States or affiliate itself with Britain. He feared the militia's involvement, for it wielded considerable moral force on the frontier, and now Toulmin could see that several appointments in the militia may have been made to put the right men in place so they would be there when the time came to move against Mobile. He doubted that loyal militia would be strong enough to stop either Kennedy or Indians and *soldados* from Mobile should they strike. Toulmin saw no evidence of concert between the society and the men in Feliciana, however, for there was little communication between the two. If Kennedy really had the support he claimed, he might succeed, but Toulmin concluded that he probably did not have as many followers as he boasted. The judge actually wondered if Kennedy had told him so much because he knew he had weak support and revealing the plan to a local authority could justify his backing out of it. Toulmin found it hard to divine anyone's real motives, for "every thing here is done by private intrigue."[53] Meanwhile, James Caller resigned as colonel of the Sixth Regiment of Militia in order to clear himself for the move against Mobile, even as Holmes, unaware of Caller's involvement, begged him to keep his commission and gather information on the society.[54] Soon enough Holmes learned what Caller was really about, for in August, as Kennedy had said he would do, he sent Holmes a broad hint at the Mobile project.[55]

By then a false rumor of the surrender of Mobile had stirred a brief hope that peaceful means might abort the scheme. Still, most people at Fort Stoddert were frustrated that the United States had not taken Mobile and were convinced that many civilians and even *soldados* in Mobile would yield without a fight. When American gunboats appeared off the bay resolved to pass up to Fort Stoddert, the Spaniards let them by, but then a reinforcement of U.S. soldiers in Mississippi raised fears anew. Holmes got them to watch the line over the western districts, but some thought they were there in readiness for a swoop on Mobile or Pensacola.[56] No one really knew what to believe.

II

Thus Has Terminated the Revolution

HICKY, LÓPEZ, and Thomas called on Governor Delassus the day after the adjournment and presented him with the convention's address,
assuring him of their loyalty to Ferdinand and their desire to work in
tandem with him. Two days later Delassus sent them his lengthy response.[1] After the customary expressions of respect and support, he
said he looked forward to receiving their budget of grievances, but
then he launched into a protest at the continuing false rumors and
"seditious Pasquinades" disturbing the people with tales of uprisings
and declarations of independence. They must report the authors of all
such iniquitous falsehoods, he said. As for their grievances, he promised that if he could agree to remedies, he would do so and happily,
though anything beyond the limits of his authority must be referred
to Havana. He politely declined their offer to pay his salary, since
only the king was his employer. Approving their decision to reconvene on August 13, he complimented them on their zeal for the general good.[2]

The response reached the committee on August 3, and though
Delassus's forced goodwill was evident, Mills believed the convention
would find it satisfactory.[3] Meanwhile, absent members confronted
broader concerns. A week after the adjournment, Barrow saw that
people of the district were much confused. Ignorance of what to expect from Washington did not help, though by this time Wykoff had
met with several of the delegates and hinted that Madison would welcome West Florida. Hints were not enough, though. "They have held
out to us, that they have a claim on us," Barrow said on August 5 after
talking with Wykoff. "Now is the time to make it known to us." With-

out a definite promise of real support from the United States, Barrow considered them absolved from allegiance to the mother country. Of course they must eventually join the other states, he believed, and to speed that end it might be best for the people to form a temporary independent government, even including East Florida if it wanted to join. They knew little of events east of the Pearl other than false rumors that *soldados* might be on the way to Delassus from Pensacola. Barrow hoped it was not true. As regularly appointed delegates, he and his colleagues could not allow the people to be mistreated. They would fight first, which must have ill consequences for all sides. He hoped for now that the present plan of seeking redress would quiet popular discontent while the convention members sought more information on Madison's policy so they could know what to do next. Fortunately, he saw that great harmony still prevailed among the delegates.

How much harmony remained to be seen. A Natchez man believed the August 13 gathering would likely be much more interesting than the last, not least because of growing fear of the French, even though genuine French efforts were never more than desultory. "If the deputies are faithful in Florida," wrote a Natchez editor a week before the convention, "they will acquire for themselves immortal honor, and secure a free and equitable government to their posterity." The peoples of the United States and Florida shared the same blood and interests, he said: "Never must they permit this hallowed haunt of liberty to be polluted by the followers of the Corsican." Rather, Congress and the Floridians must cooperate to present a united barrier to French aggression on the Gulf.[4] Herries shared the almost hysterical fear of the French and stayed at the Plains after the July 27 adjournment to watch for any who might try to sow anarchy and confusion such as the people remembered from the French Revolution. By August 10 he believed he saw sufficient danger signs in the vicinity to warn the committee that "I have not been mistaken."[5]

Governor Holmes felt no illusions about either Delassus or the convention. He believed Delassus was too weak to resist and agreed to a convention rather than risk a futile battle, while the delegates wanted much more than mere redress of grievances. He could see that the delegates felt the fear common to people who thought they were about to resist absolute power and took seriously those rumors of Folch preparing to march from Pensacola. Under such conditions, the convention could hardly issue a frank declaration of its sentiment, he believed. Like Barrow he agreed that they would not act on their own without assurance of American aid, adding his conviction that the United States could at that moment gain West Florida "without incurring an additional expense worthy of consideration or at the loss of a single man."[6]

Delassus entertained almost the same thoughts. When he agreed to the July 25 assembly, he simply lost heart, fatalistically waiting for either Folch or a revolt. Official business in Baton Rouge slowed almost to a halt.[7] Sickly *soldados* populated the garrison and several had recently died.[8] Seemingly threatened on every front, Havana could not send help to one colony without weakening another; the government was so stretched for manpower that when Delassus sought a replacement for a deceased drummer, Folch instead ordered him to get rid of the drum. If the inhabitants chose to revolt, Delassus would be almost powerless to resist.[9]

No wonder men on all sides looked with anticipation to August 13. Everyone realized that the first session had been only prelude. As the delegates gathered at Duvall's, a group of eighteen men of St. Francisville prepared a statement to their representatives in which they forthrightly gave their views. They wanted a change both in men and measures in government to address the real interests of the country. At this moment, with the mother country helpless, these delegates were the only avenue to secure redress and justice. Going even farther than any public resolution to date, they said that Spain's situation forced them to act for themselves. Therefore, they considered their delegates empowered to act independent of any other authority if that authority refused to adopt or sanction the measures they thought necessary for the general welfare. The clear suggestion was independence or revolt. Among the signers was Dr. Martin Luther Haynie, and it seems probable that he principally authored the document.[10] A native of Baltimore, Haynie moved there sometime after 1802. Even now he courted the late Alexander Stirling's widow, Ann, whom he would marry a year hence.[11] An early proponent of outright independence, he declared that "the disturbances & grievances which actuated the country could never be settled until the *government* was changed," and that the change "must be to a republic." Excepting only the futile and inept efforts of the Kempers six years before, no one had come out for such a radical shift. Now, said Haynie, "I commenced a plan of exciting the public mind into action, with the view of freeing the country from oppression & injustice in all its forms."[12]

Haynie's hand was evident in another document that day. After the body formally convened and heard Delassus's July 30 letter read, the committee charged with framing a plan to address grievances reported a bill. Upon its being read, they tabled it and then adjourned until the next morning, while the individual members spent the rest of the day at lobbying prior to debate on the bill.[13] That same evening, just hours after the St. Francisville men sent their memorial to their delegates, someone posted copies of an anonymous broadside signed "A Friend of the People" around the village. The next morning John Murdoch found one pinned to a tree on the Bayou Sara road. Leaving it in place, he went to report it to the village constable, but meanwhile Padre Lénnàn took it down and brought it to Estevan, who immediately forwarded it to Baton Rouge.[14]

"The time has come for us to look out for ourselves," it said. The body should declare independence just like their cousin colonies in South America. Ferdinand was helpless, and the Spaniards offered no justice compared to that of the United States. It was time to seek union with the Americans, which would bring more trade and new settlers, increase the value of their property, and elevate the character of their people. They took one step toward self-government in electing delegates to the convention. Now was the time to take the next one. They must shed Spanish oppression and adopt a form of government that best suited them. While the convention met, the inhabitants should form committees of correspondence to keep everyone informed and assure the convention that the people stood behind them. The delegates already heard from those loyal to Spain. They needed to hear now the voices of those who were not. The independence party was growing. The United States would embrace Florida's return to liberty and pure republicanism, and they should start now by electing an independent legislature of their own. The unknown writer closed by exhorting them all to liberty, equality, and justice.[15]

If Haynie did not write the broadside, the two documents of such similar sentiments appearing in the same place within twenty-four hours poses quite a coincidence, the only difference between them being the broadside's more radical tone. Others could have written it. John H. Johnson was still at home unwell at the moment and near enough to post the sheet. Reuben Kemper might be anywhere, and the broadside certainly echoed his sentiments. The document frightened Estevan, who complained to Delassus of "*la critica situación*," the critical situation in which he and the four isolated soldiers with him found themselves. He begged that they be removed before they became victims of public vengeance, at the same time suggesting that the broadside be published to expose the treasonous intent of supporters of the convention.[16]

As Estevan sent his plea to Delassus, a man in Pinckneyville, possibly Kemper, commented on the situation in West Florida. He hoped the people took possession of the fort before rumored reinforcements from Pensacola could arrive.[17] That meant revolution. At the same time the ailing Johnson wrote to Holmes frankly admitting that he and the reformers had used somewhat devious methods to get around the more passive elements in their society. The population needed wise leadership first before that leadership could then go the next step and lead them to independence and union with the United States. He asked if Madison would embrace them if the convention broke with Delassus, and for the first time he proposed stipulations "of consequence to us but not interesting to the United States" that could not wait until after annexation. Interestingly, Johnson said not a word about reform of law and justice. Rather, his overriding concern was property, making sure that current planters could keep what they had and be able to acquire more.[18] He too anticipated independence, and perhaps revolt, and frankly admitted that he and others played a temporizing game until the broad population was ready for the big step.

When the delegates convened again the morning of August 14 a few surely knew of the Friend of the People broadside, while Johnson's confidants already knew his views. Still they kept independence out of the debate. The next day the first real sign of internal division appeared when López rose and announced that he objected to some articles in the bill but withheld announcing which ones. Then, with the bill completed, they adjourned to reconvene in Baton Rouge on August 22. A committee was to send the governor a copy of the bill, and once again they selected conservative men — Leonard, López, Spiller, Thomas, and Williams — to personally present the bill to Delassus and ask him to adopt it as law.

This time they made no pledges of fealty to Ferdinand VII or Spain. Rather, their letter pressed Delassus to adopt their plan on his own authority without waiting for Havana's assent, adding that when they reconvened on August 22 they expected to hear his decision. They wanted their plan to take force as law from the day they met, and they warned him of the danger of delay. Their propositions offered the only means to save the country, and to punctuate that, they closed with a recommendation that the governor immediately arm the militia against outside enemies, promising that "no sentiment prevails among the inhabitants hostile to the Wise Laws and Government under which they have lived so happily."[19]

Delassus might well have wondered why, if the people were so happy, he had received that anonymous broadside. He could only conclude that it was belligerent and wrote back to Estevan telling him to stand fast, remove any more broadsides, and watch the roads until reinforcements from Pensacola arrived, though the governor had no certain knowledge of their coming. Within hours the committee from the convention called on him with their bill. Just to impress them that the fort was ready to meet any threat, he had his artillery exercise their guns and also reinforced the guard. He sent an advance party to Spanish Town, a settlement started by Grand-Pré in 1805 less than a mile east of the fort. There the Bayou Sara road crossed Bayou Gracie, and Delassus's advance split in two to watch all who came to the crossing and send back word of any large body approaching the fort.[20] If the outpost was there early enough, they might have heard gunshots, though not from approaching insurgents. Two attorneys from Point Coupée crossed to St. Francisville that afternoon to settle a personal difficulty, and one went down with a bullet in his heart, expiring instantly.[21] For the next several nights the party watched through the dark hours and returned in the mornings with nothing to report, though the guards heard occasional rumors of stirrings of the people at Bayou Sara.[22]

Delassus kept hoping to hear from Folch, and on August 18 Morales appealed to the Marqués de Someruelos in Havana to strengthen Delassus, but even if the Spaniards wanted to reinforce Delassus, two weeks could be lost just in correspondence to achieve a decision.[23] Meanwhile, all he could do was feign cordiality and cooperation, realizing that any sign of resistance from him might drive the hotheads of Bayou Sara to trade their words for weapons. He held several dinners that week, trying to win friends among small groups of delegates and citizens, and hosted a ball for the convention at his house in town on August 19, ordering all of his staff to be there in full uniform finery. They concluded the evening with a twenty-one-gun salute to Ferdinand VII from the fort's artillery, even though the magazine keeper had protested privately to Delassus that before long they might need the gunpowder for better uses.[24]

Delassus got more bad news late on August 20 when a day-old letter from Shepherd Brown arrived. He no longer trusted all his militia officers in St. Helena, and he had lost faith in all the delegates he helped to choose for the convention. He feared their actions would have a bad influence on their constituents, though he still believed most of the inhabitants in his area were loyal. Still, word of the unrest in Feliciana unsettled them, and false rumors from Pensacola of a military commander coming to impose martial law upset his people and might drive them to the rebels' side.[25]

The news Delassus hoped for, word from Folch of reinforcements, never came. People who knew the content of the convention's proposal to Delassus thought it unlikely that the governor would assent without permission from his superiors, yet they realized the consequences should he refuse.[26] So did he. On the morning of August 21, with no reinforcement and the delegates convening the next day, he called an officers' meeting in his headquarters.[27] Delassus did not mince words. Their position was "dangerous and delicate." From the day he had assumed the command, he said, he had anticipated this moment, but his warnings to his superiors had availed nothing. The deputies might plead devotion to Ferdinand VII, but he knew that if he did not agree to what were essentially demands rather than suggestions, an armed reaction would result, one that he could not oppose with an over-whelmingly American militia. He could not even properly man the fort, and its artillery was almost useless. There was no money, the meat contractor had finally cut them off, the treasury owed all of them back pay, and he had exhausted the estate succession bequeathed to the garrison. "I can foresee that at the least movement of opposition to what has been proposed, the rioters will rise together," he warned. Vagrants would join them, loyal residents would be pillaged, and he could not stop it, especially as he had learned that some officers in the militia were on the verge of revolt.

He felt compelled to accept most of the convention's proposals, and perhaps buy time that would save the province and avert "the horrors of anarchism." However, if the rebels dropped their pretense of loy-alty, then he promised to defend the fort as long as possible. After a discussion of two hours or more, he announced that since the depu-ties' proposal showed no intention other than loyalty to Ferdinand, "and to avoid the progress of those forces opposed to the monarchy," he would yield to their requests. He knew it was a rationalization and that he acted now because he simply could not resist the forces of the convention.[28] He solicited no advice. Some of his officers disapproved of his allowing the convention to meet at all. In a previous council one had criticized the governor's course so severely that Delassus angrily retorted, "If I do not rule to suit you, take my baton and govern!"[29] Now he simply told his officers what he was going to do.

The next morning at nine o'clock, the deputies filed into the gov-ernment house, where Delassus awaited them. With Cooper still on his way from St. Helena, traveling with Shepherd Brown, they were thirteen. They stood while the flag of Spain went up over the fort and then sat. Rhea spoke first, his words betraying his expectations, for instead of announcing that they came to hear Delassus's decision, he said they were there to get his approval. Delassus replied by accept-ing their framework, demurring only in the matter of a salary and minor procedural matters. Rhea bowed in acknowledgment and then said the convention wanted the power to pardon those engaged in re-bellion, past or future. The governor balked, pointing out that such an act could look as if it came from fear, so Lilley proposed that they make only retroactive pardons, which would affect the Kempers, for instance, but would not apply to any future disturbers of the peace. To that Delassus gave his assent, no doubt reminding them that all of this pended approval from Havana.[30]

The convention retired to another room where they voted the plan into law. It was an ambitious ordinance. In five articles and 108 sections, they covered virtually everything in the governance of the province. They reopened West Florida for settlement while prohibiting deserters, felons, and fugitive slaves. They organized the militia and the criminal courts and civil justice, creating a supreme tribunal with the governor to preside. Again they sought to gain financial control over the governor by providing him a three-thousand-dollar salary, then they reformed land policy to deal with the years of backlog of unsettled claims. The final article assumed the money power, decreeing a census as a basis for taxation. They even set rates for retail licenses and assumed the power to borrow on behalf of the government. Not surprising with so many physicians among the leaders, they also provided for the creation of a medical society.[31]

Their final vote would not be unanimous. Manuel López refused to sign, stating that though he accepted the ordinances and regulations in the plan as having the best interests of the province at heart, the convention violated the sovereignty of the king in assuming to itself the appointive and taxing power and in taking over the power to grant or sell lands from the royal domain. López's demurral made no difference of course, and with the plan now adopted as law, the delegates voted to send to Someruelos a copy of their new constitution. Far from wishing to raise the standard of revolt at this moment, they told the marqués, they wished only to ensure peace and tranquillity at home and relieve the financial and managerial burden on an embattled Spain. "Hitherto we have been burthensome without being useful," they averred. Now they wanted to assume their own financial responsibilities as a small offering to testify to their good wishes. To do this it became necessary "to exercise the legislative power to a certain extent." In all of this, they aimed to make as little change as possible in the existing laws, saying nothing of their revolutionary innovation of taking over administration of a royal province.[32]

At the same time the convention issued an address to the people, signed by Delassus and every delegate present including López, announcing their action and enjoining the inhabitants to preserve peace and good order. They added that they had no desire to condemn the authors of the disorders of earlier years, a clear though veiled reference to the noticeably absent Kempers; however, thereafter anyone emulating such behavior would be punished with severity. Having achieved this much peacefully, and all but taken over the government without — so far — a sign of resistance or retaliation, they did not want hotheads pushing Spain too far and spoiling it all. Their revolution was almost accomplished, but no one wanted a sudden confrontation with Spain before it was determined what the United States would do and when.[33]

The delegates lodged that night at Valentine Foelkel's hotel, then reassembled in the morning to begin staffing their new administration.[34] Delassus entertained them again that afternoon at the government house, the dinner lasting until nightfall with toasts to Ferdinand, Someruelos, Folch, the delegates, and one to Delassus.[35] The atmosphere of forced cordiality evaporated later that evening when Delassus received a two-day-old note from Estevan warning him that before leaving for Baton Rouge, the Feliciana members of the convention, Johnson, Barrow, Mills, and Rhea, had held a referendum of "obreros, Bodegoneros y Mercantes, Capitanendo por los enemigos de Gobierno" — "laborers, Saloon keepers and merchants, captained by the enemies of the Government." Suspecting the governor would not approve their plan, the delegates wanted to know if the people would support stronger action. Estevan also learned that Johnson had instructed his company of militia cavalry to be ready to ride to Baton Rouge if summoned. For Estevan, this was the "levanter de la máscara" at last, a "lifting of the mask," revealing what their real intentions had been all along.[36]

Delassus could do little or nothing about it if true. Events had moved all but out of his control now. On August 24 the convention began to put forward their appointments, their first choices a bit puzzling. They picked Percy, Brown, and Skipwith to compose the superior court — one an officious blowhard, another a suspected opponent of their movement, and the third a resident of barely a year who did not want the job. Still, the selections gave conventionalists a two-to-one majority on the high court. All but one of their appointments of sheriff and registrar of the land office and civil commandants or magistrates for Baton Rouge, Feliciana, and St. Helena went to conventionalists, putting the convention safely in control of all civil authority. John H. Johnson, Gilberto Leonard, and Shepherd Brown were the only presumed friends of Delassus, and no one objected to any of them except Brown, for whom some showed marked antagonism.[37] When they organized the three regiments of militia, the convention members again retained firm control, with Philemon Thomas brigadier general and overall commandant, and two of the three regimental commanders convention supporters, one of them a kinsman of one of the Kemper raiders of 1804.[38] They made James M. Bradford, fresh from several years of publishing the New Orleans *Orleans Gazette* and suspected of involvement in the Burr plot, public printer for the moment, and they put him to work preparing copies of their new ordinance and blank commissions for future use. In the broadest stretch of their newfound muscle, they provided that the area known as St. Ferdinand, or Tangipahoa, which had been administratively a part of St. Helena, should now become a separate district.[39]

Again they moved quickly, most of this no doubt already settled before they had convened on August 22. They had to move fast and maintain the appearance of unanimity, which, but for the absence of Cooper and the reluctance of López, they did. Secretaries often failed to note the names of those making or seconding motions, either from haste or to conceal the identities of the most dominant men, since they expected to publish their proceedings. It appeared to work, for the only reports coming out of Baton Rouge spoke of the convention working hard behind closed doors and acting in a manner suggesting that the utmost harmony existed between the governor and the convention. Observers found that many in the community felt the new arrangement would "tend to the peace, happiness and prosperity of the country."[40]

On August 25 the delegates sent conservatives Joseph Thomas and John W. Leonard to the governor to present their appointment nominations.[41] With them they sent an ordinance stipulating that militia members with no arms of their own were to be armed from the public armory as soon as they organized the new regiments, a measure that would in effect arm regiments commanded by conventionalists, something not lost on Delassus.[42] There was a dinner that night, the delegates the hosts this time, with all the usual toasts, and one of the delegates naively thought it a "dinner of union."[43] Still, after the desserts, Delassus ordered another artillery salute, just to remind them that he still had the biggest guns.

The delegates had at least an outline of Delassus's reply before they dined, and though he gave almost complete satisfaction, he did not yield everything. Delassus was no fool, and he was not about to create an armed militia at the beck of the convention by issuing weapons from the arsenal as soon as the regiments were organized. He agreed only to equip unarmed militia after being informed in detail of who needed rifles and implied that even then he would do so only in the face of a genuine danger. Otherwise he generally approved their militia arrangements and their slate of officers, both civil and military, with two exceptions. Skipwith, to whom he offered no personal objection, could not hold office because he met neither of the two requirements: he had not lived there for two years and had not sworn an oath of loyalty for citizenship. Moreover, Skipwith told Delassus in person that he did not want to be a judge, so they must nominate another in his place. And since Spain's military did not recognize the rank of brigadier general, Philemon Thomas could be commissioned only a colonel, though he could still command all militia with that title.[44]

Delassus's reply arrived Monday morning, August 27, and the next day they approved a respectful, but insistent, rejoinder to his objections. They did not quibble over Thomas's rank, but the crisis justified deviation from the current laws where it concerned Skipwith. To gain the services of a man of his capacity and experience warranted bending the law, they argued. That said, they adjourned, anticipating the next day to be the last of the session, and so it was. They renewed their resolution that the convention could borrow money with the governor's assent, then decreed an election in their newly created district east of the Ponchatoula. In one of their final actions they asked Delassus to relieve Ira Kneeland of his position as special surveyor, the only specific case of the convention's demanding the displacement of an official. Even Crocker still held his office for the moment, though the new ordinances deprived him of virtually all ability to continue his abuses.[45] When they called on Delassus again, he approved their entire slate of nominees, including Skipwith.

Their business concluded, they planned to reconvene on November 5 at the Plains, appointed a standing committee to handle daily affairs in the interim, and adjourned.[46] Naturally there had to be another dinner followed by the inevitable salutes from the fort's guns, but now the chief of artillery, Lieutenant Juan Metzinger, was so outraged over the waste of powder that he mutinously refused to fire any more.[47] None could deny that it had been a momentous few days that August. With virtually no resistance from Delassus, the convention took over the judiciary, the militia, the money power, control of land policy, and more. Though future actions under their framework of government required the governor's assent, he was almost a toothless tiger now. They had accomplished this without confrontation, admittedly because Delassus himself knew he was too weak to resist. Both sides strove to maneuver short of an eruption, while each yet worked against the other. Delassus, Gilberto Leonard, and Crocker still held the three chief offices in West Florida, and Spain still held dominion at least in theory, but it was a revolution all the same. The challenge now was to keep it from turning violent, which meant both sides must continue to deal in good faith, which neither intended to do. Whoever felt most betrayed first was likely to break the peace first.

Showing a sophisticated grasp of the need to massage the public mood, the convention issued a statement, careful to discard inflammatory expressions about corruption, bribery, and "Chaos and Anarchy."[48] They confessed that to a certain extent they had exercised legislative powers but without "innovation" in the existing laws. Now the laws would be administered by judges of their choice; every man could press his suit without unnecessary expense or delay, and the unprincipled would be deterred from crime by the speedy punishment of offenders. No more would a planter be denied his claim due to bribery or improper conduct of officials. For the present, they suspended the power of granting vacant land in the royal domain so that no established settler would be injured by grants made after this date and to keep men like Morales from selling land to enrich a few unethical strangers. To cover expenses they passed a property tax with one rate for residents and a heavier rate for nonresident landowners, again to discourage speculators; they hoped to craft a comprehensive tax policy later, meanwhile taxing only land and slaves. Now the convention placed its work before the people to invite public reaction.[49]

Each member no doubt had his own feeling about the course of the session. One or two made enough noise in the debates, and even more out of the sessions, to make outsiders think they were a majority, but in the end they came away with nothing.[50] Those of English birth who had hoped for an alliance with Britain left disappointed.[51] John W. Leonard, whom some had expected to be among the most conservative, believed the assembly showed firmness, moderation, and loyalty. He applauded their unanimity in almost every resolution and their achievement in providing for speedier justice, going on to say that "the Mutual Exchange of Civilities between the Governor & the Deputies seemed to give an Earnest and Confirmation of perfect good faith on both sides."[52] On the opposite side of the political aisle, Barrow defended the convention's laying taxes and making laws, then hinted that he saw their work as a stopgap, averring a few days later that they were firm Americans "and only act now as they do, to preserve peace & harmony, untill times justify other measures."[53]

One man in Baton Rouge certainly reacted unequivocally. "Thus has terminated the revolution in West Florida — a reform effected without tumult and without bloodshed," he wrote the day after the adjournment. Spain still ruled, but the courts were reestablished as close to the U.S. model as Spanish law allowed; a land office was to be opened, a new militia regime inaugurated, alien immigration regulated, deserters from armies of lands friendly to Spain prohibited, and a printing press established. "Perhaps so great a triumph was never gained by a people over their prejudices without disorder," he declared.[54] Within a week at that seedbed of discontent Bayou Sara, one planter thought that confidence seemed to be restored and the people could feel secure in their persons and property, for the proceedings of the convention thus far seemed to give universal satisfaction. He believed that soon the new mood of happiness and peace would transform Feliciana into the garden spot of the Floridas. Just the reopening of immigration was felt barely ten days after the adjournment as new men of means appeared and land prices shot up almost 50 percent.[55]

Above the line in Mississippi a watchful observer agreed that tranquillity had been restored. The new system of rule approximated a republican form of government, and though the delegates used Ferdinand VII's name in public acts, they openly avowed a wish to become a part of the United States.[56] When Holmes's agent Joshua Baker returned from Baton Rouge, Barrow went with him and forthrightly told the governor that many if not all of the delegates hoped for immediate annexation and asked Holmes if he had authority to intervene if they asked for his aid. The governor replied that much as he sympathized with their aspiration, his current instructions from Washington allowed him to do nothing more than observe and act as a conduit of information.

On his own Holmes stood amazed that Delassus had gone along with the convention's proposals. As he saw it, little remained of the governor's authority but his title and the salary the delegates proposed to pay him, and that tacitly, if not explicitly, Delassus had been given the choice of going along with the convention or being forced out of the country. Because of that coercion Holmes doubted that harmony would last long. Weighing the sentiments of the Floridian leaders and knowing their ultimate objective was to join the United States, he also doubted that this settlement could last for long, nor did he believe the majority really wanted an independent government. They loathed France and looked rather more kindly on Britain, but most wanted to become American citizens.[57]

In Baton Rouge even Skipwith seemed moved by the result and, believing that the United States would not back a revolt of greater extent, changed his mind and accepted the appointment as associate justice.[58] John Ballinger believed that Delassus's approval of the new ordinances satisfied the moderates and spread a momentary feeling of tranquillity. Even the republicans like Barrow thought they had gained much and seemed content for the moment, and friends from above the line suggested that while their next step might be to establish a "seperate [sic] and independent government," they should stay quiet until Congress met in the fall, when West Florida would naturally become a topic of debate.[59] Holmes's caution disappointed them, and when Barrow reported this to the committee, they decided that they had no choice but to continue working with Delassus. They had expected him to reject their requirements, which would leave them facing the option of stronger action, but being weak, he gave in to buy time. That surprised them, and also left them wary that he would keep his word. But what Ballinger called the "violent Aristocrats" and the old American Tories, such as Cooper and Brown, only felt inflamed.[60]

Cooper, who finally arrived for the last three days of the meeting, wrote directly to Folch to tell him of "the dangerous situation of the jurrisdiccion of Baton Rouge." The people of Bayou Sara were virtually in revolution, and he warned now that having taken all authority onto themselves, the convention intended to overthrow the Spanish government. Most of the people in Tangipahoa opposed the rebels, he believed, and daily prayed for Folch's arrival with reinforcements, "as our governor is put it out of his power at present to give us any protection."[61]

Murdoch was even more emphatic in his disgust. He informed Pintado of "the recent metamorphosis of Persons and things in our Quarter."

> Within a few weeks past, under the pretext of adding Vigor and Energy to the Government and to procure a more summary mode of administering Justice, a number of Individuals, in New Feliciana were assembled, and a Mock Election of Representatives took place, in other words a nomination. These were met by others from Baton Rouge, Tickfa & Santa Helena, at Duvals in the Plains, and in a very few days after their meeting, their Vision and designs were sufficiently unfolded. Instead of giving strength or assistance [to the] Government they have as far as possible endeavored to annihilate it, and a Compleat change has taken place in the order of things in this part of the Province.

All the rest of what he called the *canalla*, or riffraff, of republicanism was to be decided by the people, and to support this, he groaned, "this Inspired legislature find it necessary to levy very considerable taxes."[62]

Shepherd Brown was not happy either, and he spoke for many loyalists when he complained to Metzinger that the proceedings would have been better "if a little blood had been shed." He meant convention blood.[63] His sentiments echoed others' who hoped it would all be for nothing if Spanish reinforcements came, and one Maryland editor quipped that Folch would soon honor the convention at its next sitting by "visiting it" with five hundred *soldados*.[64]

In Baton Rouge, Grand-Pré's old friend Pierre-Joseph Favrot reflected on Delassus's administration and Crocker's corruption and concluded that "this is what destroyed everything and changed the course of the affair."[65] On too many sides now the talk was of war and revolution.

12

A Battle for the Freedom of the World

THOUGH THE convention had been adjourned, its work continued, and with no letup of pressure on Delassus. The call for election of new alcaldes throughout the several districts gave them another opportunity to nudge Spanish sympathizers out of positions of authority. The delegation from each district was to organize the election in its bailiwick. In the Baton Rouge District, where the convention left Hicky, Lilley, and López to handle its business, Hawes and John Morgan joined them on September 4 to plan the choice of their eight alcaldes. The vote tally was to be complete no later than September 25.[1]

To date, the usually loquacious Fulwar Skipwith had remained virtually silent other than his later-withdrawn demurral to his judgeship. Now however he became more active, contacting a French refugee from Guadeloupe who enjoyed some influence among the French in West Florida. Skipwith asked him to sound their sentiment in the shifting political winds and soon learned that all seemed to be opposed to Napoleon and willing to support the new convention. They preferred independence under the Americans to adherence to a countryman dictator and said they would fight to free themselves from all foreign powers, hinting that generous land grants might attract even more of them, including important men who had fled to Orleans from the recent upheaval in San Domingue, to the convention's cause.[2] Most just wanted a safe place to live, and all regarded England as their foremost foe. Thus self-interest naturally dictated that they side with the American majority.[3] The presumed support of many of the French removed them as a threat and strengthened the convention against Delassus and the Spaniards.

Delassus's frustration at his progressing loss of power showed. On September 12 he approved the laws adopted by the convention but tried to share the responsibility by saying he had acted under the "declaration" of his August 21 council of officers and from the assurances of the people through their delegates that this was the only way to preserve the peace against both foreign and domestic enemies. Of course, Delassus took no poll of his officers but simply told them what he had already decided to do. Now the weight of that decision bore on him relentlessly. He said he felt imperiously compelled to approve the convention's acts, pending sanction by Someruelos, and was encouraged by the delegates' oaths not to molest the authorities. Still he refused the proffered salary, and he objected to a clause in the ordinance that in the case of his absence or infirmity, the senior judge of the tribunal was to act in his place. That would remove the last vestige of Spanish authority, and very likely once an American judge took over, it would become permanent. Delassus reminded them that the civil governor was first and foremost a military officer, the two positions inseparable. Hence, if he could not govern, his position must devolve onto the next senior military officer.[4] The committee responded by pointing out that the governor was to preside over the superior court. Despite his being a colonel, they seemed to regard him as only a civil official, and they objected that if one of his officers should succeed him, it would place a military man as presiding judge, which violated their separation of powers and touched on one of the fundamental causes of their discontent. Since the tribunal was not to sit until November 12, Hicky proposed that they defer the matter for the convention to decide. Delassus did not entirely give in but said that if a vacancy occurred in the interim, he and the committee would choose the successor. That said, on September 14 he declared the new laws to be in effect. They had not addressed the question of vacant land, and the failure to confront such an important matter hints that neither the convention nor Delassus expected the current state of affairs to last long enough for the issue to be a problem.[5]

Delassus still stalled and avoided direct confrontations, the only course he could pursue until Folch sent help. When Folch heard of the June meetings he thought Delassus should have put the movement down at the outset rather than allow it to continue, but communications were slow, and Folch spent much of the summer in Havana, returning to Pensacola in mid-August to find Delassus's June dispatches. For months Folch had ignored his subordinate's pleas for money for repairs and soldiers' pay. Now Folch promised money as soon as Spain sent more, meanwhile asking for a current statement of the situation. A few days later, when Captain Luís Piernas arrived from Havana with funds, Folch sent him to Baton Rouge with six thousand pesos and instructions to report back on Delassus and the situation. Folch also sent a letter to Delassus telling him to feign sickness and leave Baton Rouge for a few days to come to a meeting at the mouth of the Tchefuncte River on Lake Pontchartrain so they could confer.[6]

What he did not send was *soldados*. Sending men to Baton Rouge meant weakening Pensacola while fresh threats appeared there daily of the Americans in Mississippi moving against Mobile, rumors that Madison took seriously too, advising the military in New Orleans that it might have to march in the late autumn to keep the peace.[7] While working to discourage the Mobile Society plot, Holmes heard that Folch was assembling Choctaw from above the line to defend Mobile, and he sent a hot letter reminding Folch that he should contact Holmes himself if he feared an attack from Mississippi, not stir up Indians who were subjects of the United States.[8] Holmes asked Toulmin and Sparks to discover if the Mobile plot was still alive with Kennedy away, and he ordered his militia to be ready to put down any such activity, which was as well a subtle hint to them not to get involved. Then on September 16, Holmes gave militia officers direct orders to suppress any attempt to take Mobile, not knowing that even then Toulmin was writing to tell him that signs indicated that the Mobile Society had abandoned its plans for the moment.[9]

Aware that Delassus had only a few dozen dependable men to face a population that had been rebellious and insubordinate for six years, Folch kept the bulk of his force in Pensacola, where it could reinforce Mobile in about two days by vessel; it took several days more to get any succor to Baton Rouge by water and overland. Folch let the potential menace of men with guns in Mississippi distract him from the greater hazard of men with pens in Baton Rouge, while his growing lack of confidence in his one-time friend Delassus led him to underestimate the dire conditions he reported. Of course Folch did not yet know of the new ordinance or its succession clause, but when Piernas arrived in Baton Rouge with Folch's summons, Delassus knew he dared not leave for a meeting without risk of the committee choosing his interim successor, with potentially fatal results for Spain. Indeed, Piernas's arrival probably prompted Delassus's objection to the succession section. When Piernas spoke with others in the garrison, he learned that many thought their commander gave away too much too easily, making Delassus even less eager to leave his post briefly. If he met Folch, he might well be relieved of his command on the spot. He still wanted reinforcements. With enough men and guns he could reestablish his authority, dissolve the convention, and clamp down on insurrectionary sentiment, especially in Feliciana and troublesome Bayou Sara.

Others agreed. Cooper wrote to Folch on September 12 that he believed when the convention reconvened in November "these ill dis[ig]n'd men intend at the next meeting to deny the Spanish government." At the coming election they would likely get rid of the remaining alcaldes still loyal to Spain. Arguing that he thought a majority of the people objected to current events, he appealed to Folch to bring reinforcements before the November session.[10] A day later Murdoch sent his own dire report to Pintado in Pensacola. Some people had concluded that the convention had no power to make new laws, much less to levy taxes, and told Murdoch they would shoot the new sheriff if he tried to collect taxes. "It is more than probable that on that point we shall have a Dance," Murdoch wryly added. The better-informed inhabitants were deceived by the artifices of scheming men, he lamented, for the delegates were appointed to aid and assist the government, not to bring it down. Any moment he expected to receive an order to hand over the archives of the post at Bayou Sara to the standing committee, just one more symbol of the convention's growing assumption of power.[11]

There was no mistaking the signs of gathering collapse. After a lengthy absence, George de Passau brazenly returned to Feliciana, all but daring Delassus to try to arrest him.[12] Days after Piernas's arrival, Delassus still had not paid his officers, and on September 15 a despairing Metzinger sent a friend to Pensacola to try to collect his pay for him there. Metzinger's power of attorney was the last official document Delassus would sign.[13] A day later all business and justice in Baton Rouge reached an impasse. The flag of Spain still flew and men in the fort still loved Ferdinand, but thanks to what a visitor called "the revolution of the Americans," nothing could be done.[14] López tried to collect money for Pintado, and on September 18 Gilberto Leonard wrote a receipt for money received for land, but the documents sat on Delassus's desk as activity came to a halt.[15]

Delassus and his few friends counted on delay now. Shepherd Brown spent three weeks finding one reason after another not to take his oath for the superior court. Men complained that Brown procrastinated with a constant smile on his face, making many in the convention think that he was with them.[16] If Brown did not accept his judgeship, then the superior court could not convene, which might somehow defeat the convention's making one of the judges Delassus's successor during an absence. As for the governor himself, some felt that he promised everything and performed nothing.[17] By September 18, Delassus had run out of delays and out of patience waiting for Folch. With Piernas due to leave for Pensacola that day, the governor sent with him a long, despairing letter. He was helpless to keep the convention from going too far, and an uprising almost certainly would have crushed his command. Even now he dared not leave to meet Folch or people would think he had run away from the convention's mounting power. If only Folch would come with reinforcements, it was not yet too late. With his letter, he enclosed one from Cooper containing its own entreaty for help and a warning that at the next session the convention surely would declare independence.[18]

Meanwhile Delassus stalled. September 20 was the date appointed for the election of the new alcaldes in Baton Rouge, and he tried to delay the voting by an appeal to technicalities, leading one observer to accuse him of donning "the *Spanish stilts*," referring to a ritual dance involving spinning and whirling to avoid opponents. According to one person, he declared that he was tired of acting under the threat of force and would no longer sanction the convention's proceedings at all.[19] That was unlikely, but Delassus's frustration was certainly apparent, just as his delays and pretenses of amity became more and more transparent. The day of the election Delassus sent an order to Estevan at Bayou Sara to turn over all arms, military stores, and property immediately and retire with his command to Baton Rouge.[20] Even though Estevan and his four *soldados* made a pitiful reinforcement, Delassus was strengthening the fort's garrison with what he had. That same evening he held yet another banquet for local convention leaders and their associates, to preserve the guise of amity. López and Mather, along with Philemon Thomas and others, joined Delassus, Gilberto Leonard, and Crocker at the table, where the governor tried to mollify them with renewed expressions of friendship, more toasts, and the inevitable salute from the now critically short powder magazine.[21]

Thomas and the others were pretending too, as they knew more than Delassus realized, or thought they did. They knew that Delassus had written to Folch, and they believed the governor was arranging for his superior to bring five hundred *soldados* to shut down the convention, rescind the ordinance, and arrest the leaders to send them to Havana for trial. Now they heard the rumor of Folch enlisting Choctaw, only this time the Indians were to march on Baton Rouge. One story even said that Folch was raising slaves to help in suppressing the convention. "Our Country was to be pillaged, given up to the horrors of civil War, heightened by Savage cruelty, & all the revengeful passions of the enslaved Africans," Skipwith declared.[22] Shepherd Brown's July promise to raise five hundred men to put down the insurgents gained currency, and his comment about the need to shed a little blood was no secret. Ballinger and others heard stories that men were raising in every quarter to support the old government and that large bodies were on the march from St. Helena for Baton Rouge. Worse, he too heard of Indians and blacks arming to come against them.[23] At Bayou Sara stories said that Delassus, Folch, and Brown worked together with the people of St. Helena to prepare an attack on the convention.[24] Believing that Delassus planned to lay a trap for the convention leaders, Skipwith decided that the time for compromise was at an end.[25]

By the time of Delassus's dinner the rumors had gained unstoppable momentum. The committee probably heard of Delassus's appeals for more men. In such a small and relatively open village they had to know that Piernas brought a large amount of cash, for six thousand dollars was several years' pay for the small garrison, yet Delassus had not paid his men or his debts; the merchants of Baton Rouge would surely have known if he had. Was the cash really to strengthen the fort or pay more *soldados* when they arrived? Was it to pay Choctaw allies? No ordinary business of that tiny garrison called for so much silver. At the same time, the committee members surely learned that Delassus sent letters to Folch, though they could only speculate at the contents.[26] Then, while they voted, news arrived that Delassus had summoned Estevan's men to Baton Rouge. Clearly he expected to either repel an attack or make one, and all the other rumors left little doubt which it would be.

That same day John Leonard arrived from St. Helena. Shepherd Brown did not trust him now, but somehow Leonard learned that Brown was informing Delassus that he and his supporters would not wait for Folch. With the alcalde Michael Jones, he was raising as many loyal men as he could to come put down the convention and arrest the delegates. Leonard informed the committee immediately. Soon afterward he told a friend that "you will shudder My dear friend when I inform you that those truely loyal Subjects deputed by the people to prop up a rotten and corrupt government, were marked as the immediate objects of Destruction to be draged into slavery and their property to be sapped to fatten those who long [had] been fattening on the hard earnings of the honest community."[27] They had been betrayed.[28] In Baton Rouge Pierre-Joseph Favrot heard the same story, including the expectation that the leaders would be hanged and the rest imprisoned, and he was not surprised that the conventionalists had taken action before Folch could take them.[29]

The delegates never fooled themselves that Delassus cooperated willingly, but most assumed that he at least grudgingly acquiesced in their reforms and would be true to his word pending final decision from Havana. Both sides had been disingenuous, but the convention held the upper hand for three months with no serious challenge. Leonard's news suddenly and dramatically changed everything. Taking on a few dozen soldiers in a crumbling fort was one thing. They could bottle up Delassus and his men in the place and starve them out without a fight. Brown and several hundred men from St. Helena and Tangipahoa were a different matter, assuming Brown's boast of his support was accurate. It was not, but in the climate of rampant rumor and slow communications it was all too easy to believe, as were the threats of capture, imprisonment, and worse. They knew the fate of rebels in Spain's other colonies, and now they believed Delassus planned the same for them. "Death & proscription was the order of the day," Ballinger later told Toulmin. "A Black list was made out — which included all the members of the convention & all those who had been active in the Reformation."[30] Skipwith found that the convention and leading citizens shared this conviction.[31] Men act not on facts but on what they believe, and thanks to Leonard these men believed their lives and fortunes stood in imminent peril.

López attended Delassus's dinner but Hicky and Lilley did not, probably because they left Baton Rouge for the plantation Troy immediately on receiving Leonard's news.[32] Though López worked well with the convention, distrust lingered and the convention members may not have shared Leonard's news with López for fear he would tell Delassus. They did pass Leonard's news to Philemon Thomas, who attended the dinner so Delassus would not suspect anything. In the brief time available, Thomas, Hicky, and Lilley decided they must act quickly before Brown or Folch reached Baton Rouge. Hicky and Lilley would rally as many delegates as possible at St. Francisville so the convention could act officially in ordering Thomas to attack and take the fort. They further agreed that Thomas should march in two days.

That evening Thomas met with Ballinger and ordered him to ride through the night for Springfield on the Natalbany, forty miles east of Baton Rouge, to raise all the volunteers he could trust and get them some miles on the way to a rendezvous close to Baton Rouge. Thomas intended to go to St. Francisville to urge the delegates who gathered to call on the people to fight and to be present the instant they gave him any orders. He hoped the convention would order him to take the fort, but he told Ballinger frankly that with or without orders, he intended to march late on September 22, two nights hence, and capture the fort before Folch's rumored reinforcement arrived. Once in possession of the fort, Thomas hoped that he and whatever men came with him could hold out against Folch long enough for substantial numbers to rally to them.[33]

By the evening of September 21 only Rhea, Mills, Barrow, and John

H. Johnson had joined Hicky and Lilley at St. Francisville. That left them short of the two-thirds of the delegates necessary for a quorum, but parliamentary niceties were not on their minds. Since the committee represented the convention during the adjournment, and since Hicky and Lilley were two-thirds of the committee and thus a majority, and since Rhea was president of the convention, constitutionally they could act with some degree of justification. They faced three choices. They could do nothing and wait for themselves and their property to be seized. They could pack their families and their easily portable belongings and cross the line into Mississippi. Or they could stay and move against the Spaniards before they moved first.[34] Ballinger later said that "the Convention Trembled for the safety of themselves and the country, and numbers were preparing for flight — a few stood firm Determined to weather the Storm."[35]

There may have been no debate at all once Hicky and Lilley revealed Thomas's plans. The few in St. Francisville decided to act. Ballinger later said that "the Revolution here grew out of circumstances and many was forced into the measure for their own safety that never had thought of carrying things to that length."[36] They were, he said, "hurried into action by the Jealousies & incincerity of the Royalists."[37]

One of those presumed royalists, Benjamin Williams, arrived from St. Helena during the night, but as soon as he learned the matter at hand, he resigned his seat, pleading that his "local situation" did not permit him to attend any longer.[38] That situation, of course, was his sentiment in favor of Brown, or at least against a revolt. William Cooper certainly would not be coming, and Thomas and Spiller were still on their way, while Hawes, Morgan, Leonard, and López remained in Baton Rouge for the moment. That left the six, and fittingly, Feliciana, which had led the unrest for six years now, was the only district with its entire delegation present. Before dawn the next day the six delegates assembled at Rhea's order. Hastily cataloging Delassus's failings, they declared him unfit to govern and resolved to divest him of all authority, reserving his powers temporarily to themselves, and decreed that Thomas and the militia were to enforce the ordinance and take the fort, its stores, its artillery, and the public archives.

In the interests of time and urgency, they probably had already given Thomas his orders before they convened, but now they entered the order on the journal. Next they approved an address previously drafted to Governor Holmes. "We have been abandoned and betrayed by our Governor," they pleaded. Folch was coming and they stood determined to resist. They begged Holmes to send aid, promising that in a day or two they would have a declaration of independence in his hands to relieve the United States of any responsibility for their acts, yet beseeching Washington to take them into the Union. If Mississippi militia mobilized immediately, it would intimidate Tories who were thinking of enlisting with Brown and Cooper, while inspiring "honest tho' timid Americans." They added the hint that if American gunboats from Natchez appeared near Baton Rouge, "the Dons would be paralised." As soon as they finished, they adjourned, their confidence or optimism evident in the decision to reconvene in three days' time in Baton Rouge.[39]

That morning Thomas waited at Troy for his orders, and as soon as the delegates finished a draft, they ordered Major Isaac Johnson to ride with as many mounted men as he could raise for a rendezvous near Baton Rouge. With no apparent instructions or authorization from the committee or Thomas, Johnson had already decided he would need a flag for his column to follow. It is probable that his wife, Melissa, took his instructions and spent the day sewing a banner from blue cotton or wool, placing a large, white five-pointed star in the center.[40] The color of the flag may have symbolized something, or maybe it was simply the only fabric immediately at hand. The white star echoed the Stars and Stripes, and the single star stood for West Florida independent and on its own. While Melissa Johnson started work with needle and thread, Thomas rode hard to cover more than seventy miles to find Ballinger and his volunteers.[41] He reached the vicinity of Springfield sometime after noon to show Ballinger his orders, and Ballinger proudly presented to him a grenadier company of forty-four men, all of whom the commander said were "fit to fight a Battle for the freedom of the world."[42] Coincidentally, Ballinger armed some of them with guns brought from Washington County north of the line, where Burr's friends had sold them after Burr's plans exploded in 1807. Burr would never fight to free West Florida from Spain, but some of his rifles would.[43]

Thomas and Ballinger put the small company on the road immediately and marched without letup through the day and into the night, with almost forty miles to cover in no more than eighteen hours.[44] They went probably twenty-five miles by nightfall, putting them close to the Amite, but darkness made the road more difficult. Travelers there found it almost impossible to traverse any part of the country after dark, for the roads were no more than bridle paths. The woods on either side further darkened the rough roads to the point that getting lost was inevitable for the stranger and a constant hazard even for residents.[45] The moon waning in its last phase did not help either, yet by midnight they were only a few miles short of Baton Rouge, and in another hour they reached the rendezvous to find Major Johnson and twenty-one militia cavalry from Bayou Sara, along with a few private gentlemen who came along for the adventure. Thomas expected some men from St. Helena, and several had arrived on their own, though the remainder might come too late. In all they numbered about seventy-five men and officers, which, though three times the number of effective *soldados* in the fort, was not enough to be overconfident, considering that Delassus would have some protection from the fort's moldering walls and more than a dozen serviceable cannon. A great deal depended on surprising the Spaniards, which was Thomas's intention from the first.[46]

Yet by that time any hope of surprise should have evaporated. All day John Murdoch and others saw suspicious activity around St. Francisville — mounted men carrying rifles, residents giving weapons to riders who had none, and delegates riding in and out of town or huddled in whispered conversations. Murdoch sent two messengers to Delassus with the same warnings, which reached Delassus that afternoon, and several men in his garrison knew something was happening. Yet Delassus himself seemed strangely lethargic. He augmented the guard, but sent no picket guard out for early warning, and incredibly he left the fort's gate open all day and even after nightfall.[47] By now, several in his garrison were fed up with him. They all knew the discontent caused by the glacial course of justice and Crocker's corruption, just as they knew at least something about the several assemblies he had allowed to meet since June.[48] Delassus himself had only a few remaining confidants, chiefly Gilberto Leonard and a friend or two from New Orleans.[49] López was still reluctant to be the only Spaniard rebelling against Spain, and of course there was Crocker, of whom Favrot complained: "His boundless cupidity has caused the downfall of this place."[50]

The fort itself matched the morale of the garrison. Eulogio de Casas, the arsenal keeper, and chief of artillery Metzinger could boast of 112 bronze, brass, and iron cannon of all calibers and still some 14,000 rounds of various balls. Of course, many of the cannon were ancient or rusting, the softer brass guns blown out, while more of the guns lacked proper carriages to make them operable. The dwindling powder supply made even the sound ones only briefly serviceable. As for small arms, Casas counted enough paper-wrapped powder-and-ball musket cartridges for a thousand rounds per man, which sounded fine but for the fact that the garrison mustered only twenty-eight men and officers, and several of them were down with summer fevers in a badly equipped infirmary.[51] Everyone knew the fort's earthen walls had been eroding for years and that the wooden pickets atop the earthworks were rotted in places and ready to tumble.

Because the fort sat on a bluff overlooking the river, defenders often exaggerated its defensive advantages, but at the moment it rose not much more than twenty-five feet above the water line.[52] The Spaniards had long placed too much confidence in the fort's security from attack on that side. The road from St. Francisville approached from the north, descended a few yards to cross Bayou Gracie, and then climbed the opposite bank onto the plain in front of Baton Rouge. As travelers crossed the bayou they saw the Mississippi off to their right no more than two hundred yards distant. Except when the river flooded, a strip of bottomland ran back from the water's edge one hundred to three hundred yards to the foot of the bluff. Exactly thirty-one years earlier, on this same bottomland, although downriver from the fort, Spaniards under Bernardo de Gálvez had made their approach to launch the siege that led to a British surrender. Forgetting their own history, the Spaniards had since paid virtually no attention to the river side of the fort. Now the garrison's milk cows daily ambled through a gap in the palisade to the river to drink. Fort San Carlos had deteriorated into a tissue tiger. Its gate was open in the darkness, with an unguarded hole in its rear palisade, barely more than a score of able-bodied *soldados*, much of its artillery useless, and no advance guard posted to raise the alarm of a hostile approach. Delassus himself slept in his house in the village, as did Crocker and Leonard, while only a slightly augmented handful of men gathered to pass the night in the guardhouse under charge of Grand-Pré's son Lieutenant Luis de Grand Pré.

Thomas moved his consolidated command slowly forward in that same darkness. He hoped to take the place by stratagem rather than musketry, for over the years many of his men had become friends with the *soldados* of the garrison. He knew their weakness and reasoned that if he struck from two sides at once they would surrender without resistance. One of the few St. Helena men with him was Larry Moore, an illiterate Kentuckian from near Lake Maurepas who had seen the cows passing through the back wall of the fort. During the night march Moore spoke with Thomas and told him that he knew how to "get inter thet dinged ol' fort." If Johnson's cavalry left the road at Bayou Gracie and followed it to the river, they could move unseen over the bottomland at the foot of the bluff while the Spaniards were watching the plain in front of the gate on the opposite side. Then Johnson's men could move single file up the slope and through the gap in the pickets. "Ef them cows kin git in thar an' outen again," Moore told Thomas, "I knows my pony kin tote me in the same way, an' do h'it as easy as fallin' offen a log."[53]

Moore's quaintly expressed suggestion fit perfectly into Thomas's plans. When the column reached the bayou he sent Johnson's cavalry toward the river while he kept the rest on the road. Shortly after 3:00 A.M. they saw the fort in the dim moonlight, and as yet they had not been discovered. Lieutenant Grand Pré posted a sergeant, a corporal, and eight men as guard for the night, but only three sentinels were on duty at the moment and the rest were in the guardhouse. Two of Metzinger's artillerymen watched beside half a dozen loaded artillery pieces trained on the gate and the plain, though they failed to prepare the guns for firing. The other sixteen men and officers slept in their quarters; Delassus and the officers who had the keys to the magazine were asleep in town.

A few hours earlier another messenger from Murdoch got through, just before Thomas's column rendezvoused on the main road and cut off further communications. The rider found Estevan in the hospital and told him that talk in St. Francisville said the rebels meant to attack the fort before dawn. Estevan gave the message to Lieutenant Francisco Morejón, and he took it to Delassus, stopping on his way out of the fort to wake and upbraid a sleeping guard.[54] It was thirty minutes before Delassus dressed himself and walked the few hundred feet back to the fort, stopping on the way to wake Crocker. When he reached the fort, Delassus sent a guard to his house, where he kept the six thousand pesos left by Piernas. Only then did he meet with his awakened officers, but he seems to have done nothing more. Showing the aristocrat professional soldier's contempt for ragtag insurgents, the young Grand Pré dismissed the report of an attack, though he assembled the remaining *soldados* of his regiment and sent for a sergeant to come and take them to reinforce the men at the guardhouse. Incredibly, no one had closed the gate. Delassus left to see what was keeping Crocker, and he ordered his secretary to dress and get to the fort. Then the governor and Morejón began walking back to the gate.[55]

As Delassus woke Crocker the second time, Major Johnson and his horsemen finished their short climb up the face of the bluff and through the gap in the pickets, covered by darkness and a thin layer of predawn ground fog. Slowly and quietly they walked their horses to the river side of the parade ground where they formed in a ragged line, still undetected. Only then, somewhere close to four in the morning, did a sentinel hear one of the horses and turn around to see dim figures in the misty gloom.[56] He called out a challenge: "*¿Quién es?*" —"Who goes there?" When no reply came, he yelled, "Here they are now," across the parade ground, and another sentinel ran to awaken Grand Pré, who in turn dashed into the guardhouse to order out the *soldados* who had just joined the guard.

At almost this same moment, one of the few private citizens of Baton Rouge on the street at this time of morning saw Thomas and Ballinger's grenadiers marching toward the gate. When he asked what they were about, they spat out their disgust at the treachery of Delassus and Crocker's corruption and said they were going to take the fort.[57] As they approached the fort, Thomas told them not to fire unless fired upon. When they reached the gate he shouted in both French and English, "Ground your arms and you shall not be hurt," words clearly meant for Delassus since the native tongue of virtually everyone in the garrison other than Delassus was Spanish.[58] Then Thomas's infantry rushed through the open gate shouting "Hurrah! Washington!" — which to Spanish ears sounded like "Urrah! Whachinton!" — and called again for the guard to surrender.[59]

Across the parade ground, Luis de Grand Pré brought the rest of his men out of the guardhouse and formed them in line, then he drew his sword and walked toward Johnson's mounted men. Unaware in the darkness that Thomas had come in the gate, he apparently thought that these twenty-one horsemen were the only threat. He called out to them, "My friends, we are more numerous than you are; we don't want to hurt anyone." Boldly, if recklessly, he began beating at the flanks of the horses with his saber as he shouted at the insurgents to lay down their arms or retire. Only then did he hear the commotion as Thomas's men swarmed through the gate.

With his part of the guard facing Johnson, and the rest near the gate confronted by Thomas, Grand Pré knew they were outnumbered and threatened front and rear. "Carried away by his zeal," according to his father's friend Favrot, Grand Pré ordered his men to "Fire, fire!" His intent even then may have been to disable the horses and thus somewhat reduce the odds against him, but instead of a volley, his sleepy, unprepared, and frightened men in front of the guardhouse started firing individually. After their third shot, Thomas's men on the other side of the parade let fly a volley. One *soldado* fell dead on the spot, two fell with mortal wounds, and two more were injured.[60] Lying among the fallen was Lieutenant Luis de Grand Pré. Tragically, most of the volley had found him. He had two bullets in his arms, one in his thigh, another in his body, and a fifth and fatal ball in a kidney. Favrot saw him soon afterward "covered with blood." Now the mounted men began to use their pistols and sabers too as the Americans swarmed all over the parade. Ballinger was almost disappointed at what he called "a feeble Resistance from the Kings troops."[61] Many *soldados* threw down their muskets and surrendered, and a few managed to escape over the wall. Metzinger, wounded in the arm, made his way across the parade to the fallen Grand Pré, but not before a Floridian smashed his wrist with a pistol butt in the few moments of confusion.

It was over scarcely more than a minute after the firing of the first gun. Delassus heard the firing while on his way back to the fort, with Leonard and Crocker some two hundred feet behind. The governor broke into a run at the sound as, behind him, Crocker realized what was happening and what his fate might be at the hands of the insurgents. Thinking quickly he turned and ran around the fort to the bank where he and a few others found a skiff and began rowing across the river, though not without being seen by some of the garrison as they fled.[62]

Delassus entered the fort alone and was at first stunned by what he saw. "Alas, what is this?" Morejón heard him exclaim. Mounted men who had come across the parade grabbed Delassus at the gate and dragged him inside, while Morejón sank back into the darkness to make his escape. Confronted almost at once by men demanding that he hand over his sword, Delassus refused, and one of them knocked him to the ground with a musket butt. If Thomas had not at that moment intervened personally, the governor probably would have been beaten to death.[63]

Thomas began to assess the results, and it appeared that he had nineteen prisoners in addition to Delassus and Leonard. Not one of his own men had been wounded, as the Spaniards had probably never gotten off another shot after that first ragged effort at a volley and their artillery had never fired a round. Thomas had Gilberto Leonard accompany the wounded Metzinger and the dying Grand Pré to the hospital, and then he set his men to securing the fort.[64] Another party went to Delassus's residence, where it took the guard and searched the rooms by candlelight. The men found the locked box containing the six thousand pesos and cheered as they carried it back to the fort. Thomas himself confronted Eulogio de Casas and took the keys to the magazine.

It was still dark, but when the dawn came, Isaac Johnson found the ancient banner of Castile and León and dragged it across the dust and manure on the parade ground and through the streets of Baton Rouge. That banner would never fly over Fort San Carlos again. In its place, in the early-morning light, the volunteers shouted their hurrahs and cries of "Washington" and raised the lone star of West Florida.[65]

13

The Commonwealth of West Florida

A REVOLUTION, even a quick one, creates hearty appetites, especially on top of more than forty miles of marching. Thomas immediately spent his own funds to buy twenty-five barrels of corn for the soldiers and the animals, and he sent Manuel López to the Spaniards' storehouse to get beef for all the men.[1] As López issued rations, Thomas ordered a search of the fort. The rumor that Folch was on his way with five hundred men or more, including Choctaw and Negroes, meant the insurgents needed to know what they had that could be used in their defense. While some scoured the fort, others went into the village with Thomas's orders to take all firearms and other weapons from civilian hands. The guns might be needed to arm more volunteers, and Thomas also wanted to make sure they would not be used against him in any incipient backlash against the convention forces. Meanwhile, men looked for Crocker, not yet knowing that he had escaped. They confronted his wife, whom Crocker abandoned in his flight, and though she denied that he was in their home, the men pushed in and searched all the same, even looking for him under the mattress.[2]

Ballinger gleefully surveyed the abundance of provisions and arms found in the fort and noted even more happily that "this Country joined us almost en masse."[3] As word of the fort's fall spread, Ballinger and Thomas saw men start to come into Baton Rouge, at first singly, then in groups, then, by the end of the day, in whole companies. Faced with a growing army, and not even owning the pistols customary to his station, Colonel Thomas paid thirty dollars out of his own pocket to buy a brace of them from a local merchant.[4] Now equipped in keeping with his rank, he began organizing his increasing numbers while looking to see what could be done immediately to strengthen the fort in case Folch appeared. One of his officers reported 105 cannon great and small in the fort, over 30,000 rounds of ammunition, and 5,600 pounds of gunpowder, much of it useless; only eighteen carriages were in working order. Amazingly, the tiny garrison of fewer than thirty men had 1,135 muskets and bayonets with 25,000 cartridges, and a dozen pistols. Additionally there were a few barrels of rice and flour, and even a boat.[5]

The officer also found two cases of surgical instruments and a chest of medicine in the hospital, where volunteers took the casualties. With so few injured, the wounded Metzinger, who had first spread Shepherd Brown's comment about shedding a little blood, now wondered dolefully, "Is it possible that my blood is the only blood to be shed?"[6] Of course, one man lay dead and two others were dying; the other wounded would recover. Late that evening Father Lénnàn arrived to help attend to the wounded and dead.[7] No one could do anything for young Luis de Grand Pré. His condition gradually worsened through the day as he was tended by his brothers and his close friend Philogene Favrot. At 2:00 A.M., fewer than twenty-four hours after the skirmish, he died peacefully in Favrot's arms. He was just twenty-three, and no one missed the irony that the little revolution's worst casualty should be the son of the governor whose departure hastened this moment. The victors shared the sadness, for they felt only respect for the youth. After dawn they gave him a solemn funeral. *"Un soul trépas ternit votre victoire,"* Pierre-Joseph Favrot said in his eulogy: "A lone death held all your victory."[8]

As soon as the young lieutenant was buried, Thomas sent a report of the capture to Rhea, who had reached Baton Rouge along with the other delegates at St. Francisville. Thomas complimented the bravery and restraint of the volunteers. Indeed, they did show self-control, for the passions aroused by years of growing animosity, no doubt their ethnic contempt for the Spaniards, and the stories of betrayal could have led to serious bloodshed.[9] As evidence of the growing number of volunteers, López issued 560 pounds of meat that day, more than twice the ration of the day before, and by the end of the month the daily issue peaked at 660 pounds.[10] A more thorough search of

Delassus's home found a desk with $1,333 in gold of his own money, and the men turned that over to Thomas. Intent on keeping Delassus safe, Thomas confined him under guard in his own rooms pending the convention's determination of what to do with him.[11]

Some of the delegates already in town lodged at Valentine Foelkel's hotel along with General Thomas, Isaac Johnson, George de Passau, and others, and more continued to arrive.[12] The next morning the nine delegates present issued a resolution of thanks to the men who took the fort. Thomas's officers responded with an assurance that they recognized their subordination to the new civil authority, pleading that the convention not stop "till the work of Regeneration be complete."[13] The convention responded to the officers by walking into the fort and addressing the entire command drawn up on the parade. They complimented the volunteers on their bravery and patriotism, reminded them of Delassus's treachery and the justness of their response, and even expressed indirect sadness at the death of Grand Pré. In words meant for ears far beyond the fort's walls, they appealed for unity and harmony and asked that every district and settlement send immediately not only its own delegates, but as many others as it wished, without portfolio, so all could confer on how to frame permanent regulations to "secure the peace, liberty and prosperity of our country."[14]

The delegates sent an address to St. Helena and St. Ferdinand begging the people there to set aside the divisiveness promoted by Delassus, Brown, and Cooper and to come and meet with them to discuss the causes of their dissatisfaction. They were all brothers. They must not shed one another's blood. Amendments could be made to the new laws in order to unite them all "in the bond of Union, peace & good Government." Neither politics nor religion should divide them in their common pursuit of peace and prosperity.[15] With that message on its way, the convention adjourned to work on a declaration of independence.

Immediately after the attack, mail riders left with letters taking the news to New Orleans and Natchez. Writers of the letters spoke of Delassus's treachery, the suspicion that the United States was at the bottom of it all, and also of unverified reports of resistance sentiment among the communities in St. Helena and St. Ferdinand.[16] When the news hit the planters along the line, men took their guns and left for Baton Rouge in what they called "the American cause." That left their wives alone and unprotected, and hearing the rumors of Choctaw and blacks being led against them, some of the wives remembered the horrors of San Domingue and sent pleas to friends above the line to help them in their precarious situation. The next day, September 25, a friend of Governor Holmes warned that the spirit of revolt might not stop in West Florida, and if the slaves took arms, their now-peaceful country could become another San Domingue. If the convention decided to expel deserters, as had been rumored, they would wind up in Mississippi, and some wanted Holmes to send more militia to the line to apprehend these lawless men who had forfeited the protection of their own government.[17]

Holmes got his first hint of the attack late on September 24 when he received the convention's two-day-old notice of their betrayal and appeal for aid. Twenty-four hours later came confirmation. "The Parties in West Florida have resorted to force," he told Colonel Thomas Cushing. "How this business may terminate we cannot easily conjecture."[18] Walter Overton, a friend of both Reuben Kemper and Andrew Jackson, wrote to Old Hickory, as Jackson was known, of the eagerness of the army to assist in taking possession of territory that their lethargic government had purchased years before. He hoped Holmes would send in federal troops, "as we are panting for Exercise."[19]

The panting increased the next morning with the rumor that Folch was on the march with three hundred and fifty regulars and militia. "I expect the time not far distant, when your old warriors will have to come out and teach your children in arms, what you bought by experience," one officer wrote that day to an old Revolutionary War veteran. A petition from Pinckneyville sought protection, and Holmes sent a company of dragoons within twenty-four hours, with two more companies of infantry to follow.[20] That same day letters from Baton Rouge informed New Orleans of the fall of the fort, some suggesting that the U.S. flag flew over the fort, which mirrored expectations. It would be some days before stories got the right flag.[21]

The declaration of independence soon cleared any confusion. When the convention assembled at 9:00 A.M. on September 26, its first business was to consider a draft that had no doubt been composed over the previous couple of days. The convention members professed their good faith working with Delassus to enact reforms, but he had gone on to ignore or violate those measures. Betrayed, and with no hope of protection by Spain, they now had a duty to provide for their own security as a free and independent state, absolved from all allegiance to a government that no longer protected them. Consequently, they declared the several districts composing West Florida to be "a *free and independent state.*" Assuming the powers of a sovereign nation, they declared null any act by any tribunal not authorized by the convention and called on all peoples to acknowledge their independence and provide them aid according to the laws of nations. That said, and with a nod to Jefferson, they concluded pledging "our lives and fortunes" to the cause.

There were ten delegates present, since three were in St. Helena and Benjamin O. Williams had resigned. Still, they had a quorum under their own rules. When they voted, however, only nine assented to the declaration. Manuel López could not bring himself to make a complete break from Spain. Consequently, only nine signed the declaration, though López would continue serving ably and working hard in the business of the convention. When two of those absent arrived, they added their signatures.[22]

By an adjoined proclamation, they announced their new declaration to the world, promising a new constitution in time. For the moment they would retain the existing laws of justice and property under their ordinance, except that the convention now assumed the powers of the governor.[23] The delegates then adjourned and walked to the fort's parade ground to read the declaration to the assembled volunteers. Privately, Barrow expressed amazement that they had achieved so much with so little blood.[24]

That same day the convention sent copies of the declaration to both Holmes and Claiborne, to be forwarded to Madison, and expressed the hope that the United States would take them under its "immediate and special protection."[25] That made Skipwith think the declaration was unwise, for they had asked the governors to press for their annexation. If foreign powers recognized them as independent under their declaration, then subsequent acquisition by the United States looked like conquest, which Spain could use as a pretext for war.[26] Still, Skipwith arranged for the declaration and Thomas's report of the fall of the fort to be printed and distributed throughout the province and the United States. Soon enough the documents appeared in the New Orleans press, and from there made their way to eastern readers.[27]

Holmes got his copy of the declaration on September 29 or 30, and he promised to forward it to Madison.[28] He said nothing about sending soldiers or Mississippi militia, having resolved days earlier that it was his duty to avoid taking any part in the present contest. He did take precautions to protect Mississippians, and to that end he enjoined the convention to keep him advised of unfolding events.[29] He regarded seriously the possibility of Spain encouraging a servile insurrection, there being hundreds of slaves in upper Feliciana, and ordered his patrols on the line to notify him immediately of any hint of an uprising and to arrest all slaves found at large without passes from their owners.[30]

By this time John W. Leonard had reached Baton Rouge, taking his seat the morning of September 27, and reported treason. He had seen Shepherd Brown gathering planters loyal to Spain at Springfield, and building a fort on the Natalbany River. Knowing that Leonard was with the conventionalists now, Brown tried to capture him on the road for Baton Rouge, but Leonard evaded the snare.[31] Leonard may even have known that on the morning of September 26 Brown sent the sloop *Dolphin* with dispatches for Folch. If Brown had enough time and raised enough men, he could start a civil war that would make their infant republic easy prey for Folch or their own slaves. Perhaps because of Leonard's alarming news, the convention did nothing more that day than promote Thomas to brigadier general.[32] The rest of the day they gathered more reports on the situation at Springfield, while that same night Brown held a council of war among some of the local inhabitants at Springfield and determined to hold fast until Folch could arrive. He sent a promise to Folch of five hundred volunteers if he came with regulars to assert royal authority at Baton Rouge. Brown needed arms, ammunition, and provisions, and he warned that the convention forces gained strength daily while disarming those loyal to Spain. He doubted that he could sustain an attack now as his numbers were small, but he believed he could hold his fort by the river until Folch sent immediate aid by the *Dolphin*, though he warned that his situation was critical.[33]

In Baton Rouge people got only scattered rumors to add to Leonard's alarm, but the next day the recently resigned Williams joined them, choosing the convention over Brown, and he probably brought confirmation. The delegates ordered a thorough inventory of all public property in the fort and the village, clearly with a view to knowing all the resources at hand for defense. The next morning they ordered local planters to send slaves and tools for two days to repair the fort, and they put collecting the work force in the hands of Colonel William Kirkland, who had ridden with the Kempers in 1804. Then the officers in the fort announced that, after consultation with General Thomas, they would do whatever he advised to keep order and meet any threat.[34] Armed with that, the convention ordered Thomas to call for volunteers to put down the Brown uprising.[35]

The next day was a Sunday, but the emergency justified convening to address the crisis. They gave Thomas orders to arrest Brown and Cooper, by force if necessary, and provided a proclamation denouncing both:

> Deceived by a man of no Colour in Politics, by a Wretch who will abandon you at the hour of danger, by a man who accepted, meaning to betray, an appointment from the Convention of the highest trust & importance to the People, you will no longer suffer yourselves to be misled by the Cameleon, Brown; & much less by the Traitor from our own Bosom, whose Murderous cruelties, even at an age when the youth of his Beard might have taught the most criminal in lieu of the most innocent Captives, to expect mercy, will not allow him to remain quiet, — Cooper!

Thomas was also to take a copy of the declaration with him and invite people to subscribe to it. The delegates appealed for talk and compromise to bring the disaffected into the fold but warned that they would not treat with the forces of "anarchy & civil War."[36]

Robert Percy saw alarm in Baton Rouge over the opposition gathering in St. Helena, noting that every available supporter of the convention who could be spared from the plantations was under arms.[37] The turnout boosted the delegates' morale, and in its own way, Leonard's news had too. Brown posed a threat, but the fact that he was known to be writing to Folch in Pensacola meant that the Spaniard had not left his capital, and thus rumors of his marching with an army of *soldados*, Choctaw, and slaves were false. That was one threat gone, and as a result visitors found the convention in high spirits.[38]

On October 1 Thomas was ready. The volunteers in Baton Rouge had swelled to over 600 by now. He left 240 to garrison the fort and led 400 out that evening.[39] Just before he mounted to leave, Thomas told a bystander that he hoped West Florida would become a state in the Union and that they would soon add their star to the Stars and Stripes.[40] Townspeople watched as the volunteers marched from the fort and through the village on the road east, bound, said one, "to quell some disorderly persons over there."[41] A Natchez editor present hoped that Thomas and Brown might come to a peaceful settlement to avoid the anarchy with which they were threatened.[42] Someone paid four dollars to a local milliner to have a flag made for the expedition, and as they marched the lone star waved over them.[43] They moved at a far less frantic pace than Thomas's march to Baton Rouge, and on the morning of October 3 they crossed the Amite. Six miles beyond the river, Thomas halted the column and met with the alcalde Michael Jones, who many expected would act in concert with Brown and Cooper.

Jones had always been more loyal to Spain than most, perhaps because, as a Tory fugitive from the American Revolution, he felt more comfortable under a monarchy. He had helped put down the Kempers in 1804 and remained close to Delassus until his fall. For the past few days, he had tried to build a resistance, sometimes through intimidation by telling potential recruits that he had thirty Choctaw in war paint who would attack and plunder those who failed to join him. As a result, some families in the area simply fled, though others on their own gathered in hopes of dispersing Jones, who many regarded as nothing but a bandit.[44] Now he rather belligerently presented to Thomas his own plan for an association of the districts of West Florida, signed by himself and several others from St. Helena and St. Ferdinand, no doubt hoping that Thomas and his officers would sign as well and turn their backing to this new compact. Thomas refused even to negotiate, calling his bluff, and that evening Jones surrendered and signed the new declaration.

Jones's capitulation gave the expedition renewed vigor. That same evening Thomas sent Johnson with cavalry and infantry to make a forced march to Springfield, fewer than twenty miles off, hoping to take Brown and Cooper by surprise the next day. Brown had perhaps as many as two hundred and fifty men gathered at Bookter's Landing on the Natalbany, long the home of Brown's friend the troublesome one-time alcalde Alexander Bookter, who kept a tavern there.[45] Now the new village of Springfield was emerging on the spot, and Brown worked his people hard building an earthwork fort, which was known as both Fort Springfield and Fort Ferdinand. Rumor in the vicinity said they even ordered fifes and drums from New Orleans, along with powder and lead, but the fort was in no shape to withstand an attack when word came of Jones's surrender and the approach of convention forces of several hundred.[46] Outnumbered, Brown and Cooper evacuated Springfield during the night, and Johnson rode in unopposed not long after sunrise.

He may not have found the two traitors, but Johnson did find a number of inhabitants delighted to have protection from Brown and his people. They thought Brown had fled to New Orleans, and most of his followers had dispersed into the surrounding swamps and bayous.[47] Thomas soon sent detachments under the Kempers' old associate Colonel Frederick Kimball to sweep the areas along the Tangipahoa and Tchefuncte rivers, while the main body occupied Springfield on October 5, there to wait two days to see how many of the fugitives might be taken. Thomas displayed the declaration in the immediate vicinity and found most people eager to come into the fold. In fact, a new company of volunteers formed in Springfield and enlisted to serve the convention. On October 7 Thomas left a hundred and fifty men behind to continue gathering fugitives, who often just surrendered themselves, and put the bulk of the command on the road back to Baton Rouge via Brown's plantation and some of the Spanish settlements on Bayou Manchac.[48] One of the patrols left behind probably caught up to William Cooper and captured him, killing him later when he tried to escape.[49]

When the column arrived, on October 9, news of its actions had preceded it, and spirits ran high in the town and convention.[50] In fact, some believed that instead of returning from Springfield, Thomas marched to take Mobile.[51] Word of his success inspired a New Orleans man to proclaim that "I expect that the flame of revolution will spread to every part of the Floridas."[52] The next day two more companies of volunteers enlisted, raising the army to eight hundred or more, and the gathering power and popularity of the convention saw the collapse of virtually all remaining internal effort at resistance.[53] More and more came to Baton Rouge to take an oath of allegiance, and the day of Thomas's return, Shepherd Brown himself rode into town and surrendered. The convention immediately ordered Thomas to put Brown in close confinement pending trial.

Soon a rumor spread through the town that with the fort's jail already full of such men, the convention would release them instead of instituting treason trials, having no wish to start its nationhood by hanging political prisoners. A palpable relief settled over town and convention alike, and both returned to something like normal daily life. The repairs on the fort were complete and the people felt confident they could defend themselves against any foe. A Natchez man in town found everything tranquil.[54] When word of the successful expedition and the return of peace reached faraway Boston, an editor responded to the assertion that "General Thomas appears to be the Washington of West Florida" with a single word: *"Fudge!"* He dismissed the entire business of the past two weeks as "the little mimick Revolution of Florida."[55]

Jonathan Longstreth, a schoolteacher living at Lilley's place near the Plains, was not as dismissive as that New Englander. He responded to the general feeling of relief by composing a parody of the revolution thus far in biblical verse, perhaps to use with his students. Cumbersomely titled *The Book of the Chronicles of the Grand Sanhedrine of the Verdant Country Bordering on the Great Father of Rivers to the Westward & Extending Even unto the Tanchepaho as Thou Goest towards the Sunrising,* Longstreth's text gave the leading players sobriquets often based on appearance, temperament, or even simple puns on their names, such as "Charles the Gawlite" for the French-born Delassus and "John the Millwright" for John Mills. Poor Thomas Lilley became "Thomas the Lilley of the Vale." Shepherd Brown was "the

Brown Shepherd," but Longstreth saved the most biting nickname for Cooper, whom he called "William the Belialite," for the biblical king of Hell.[56]

The one demon Longstreth neglected to include was Raphael Crocker. When Folch learned a week after of the fall of the fort, he complained that Delassus had not behaved like a Spanish soldier.[57] Still, at least the governor had met his foe face-to-face, although he had gotten a crack on the head for his trouble. Crocker simply abandoned everything and everyone and ran, rowed across the Mississippi, reached an Acadian home where he rented a horse, and then rode several more miles to the home of his father-in-law in Iberville Parish. In company with an escaped corporal, he then made his way to New Orleans on September 24 to find several other fugitive Spaniards coming into the city.[58] He had left not only his wife in Baton Rouge but also whatever wealth he had accumulated. Now the man who had lived almost regally on the takings from his extortion could engage only a bare room with nothing but a bed and mattress.[59] Soon he lied to Maxent, telling him that instead of running at the first shots, he had actually rallied twenty soldados — almost more than the surviving garrison — outside the fort, planning to retake it before the Americans chased him away.[60] When Favrot heard the story, he grumbled that it was a rank "imposture."[61]

While Thomas was away, the convention stayed busy, quickly addressing money and land. It made provision to seek up to thirty thousand dollars in loans in New Orleans to cover the costs of government, and it repealed its earlier tax on slaves imported from the United States, realizing that it discouraged wealthier planters from coming to settle. At the same time it also provided that current residents could import without tax any slaves they already owned or leased.[62] When news of this reached Philadelphia, one editor felt outrage. "Here are pretty fellows," he said, "proclaiming liberty and independence, and among their first acts is to be found the encouragement of slavery."[63] They amended their land tax, assessing property based on quality. Then they declared as void all unsurveyed and untitled French and British land patents that the Spaniards had honored. Learning that Ira Kneeland had fled to Pensacola, taking with him all of his survey papers, they sequestered all his property pending an investigation.

Not forgetting another old enemy, they also ordered an inventory of Crocker's abandoned property.[64]

Thus far the delegates' conduct failed to excite observers. "The convention has, as yet, done very little, being very young in experience," one local man wrote on October 6. "They proceed with a great deal of diffidence and of course very slow," hinting that an abundance of lawyers may have slowed their proceedings.[65] However, they did more than some realized. The authorization for substantial loan debt, backed by appointing Hicky treasurer and refining tax policy, bid fair to get them on a sound financial footing. An authorization to raise two new companies of six months' regulars, to be commanded by Ballinger, provided a stable force to guard the fort and allowed the volunteers to go home for the moment.[66] On October 5 they appointed John H. Johnson as envoy to the United States, and three days later he rose to propose that with "the Spanish yoke being now thrown off, and a fair prospect of establishing our independence" before them, they should frame a constitution. Only Lilley objected, since such a step, like the declaration of independence, might be an obstacle to annexation by the United States. The convention delegated Johnson, Rhea, and Leonard to draft the document and report back with it as soon as possible.

On October 10, the final day of the session, they addressed a letter to Secretary of State Robert Smith setting forth their claims to independence and recognition from the United States. They were hardly subtle. If Madison did not embrace them, their weakness and exposed position would oblige them to look to some other government for succor. They wanted immediate admission as a state or territory, with permission to form their own government, or else to be united to Mississippi or, preferably, Orleans. Until they became a state they wanted to be governed by their existing laws, and they lost no time in focusing on the ever-present issue of land. Surely the United States would not contest their right to the unallocated land remaining in their little commonwealth, as the Union failure to press its own claims to the province since 1804 constituted a de facto relinquishment of any such claims. Hence all vacant land should belong to the people of West Florida "who have wrested the Government and country from Spain at the risk of their lives and fortunes." Sale of that land would build roads and canals in the new state and promote the prosperity of the nation as a whole. They also asked that Washington pardon all deserters living there and exempt them from further military service. In closing, they sought an immediate loan of a hundred thousand dollars, stating that they would not send their emissary Johnson to Washington until they received an expression of approval of their requests.[67]

The delegates addressed the letter to Smith via Governor Holmes, including a cover letter announcing that St. Helena was pacified and they had before them the most flattering prospect of support from all their inhabitants.[68] There was little left to do after that, and they adjourned, appointing a standing committee to act for the convention during its recess until November 5. In their last act, they agreed on the wording of an oath of allegiance to "the Commonwealth of West Florida."[69]

Within hours of the adjournment Pierre-Joseph Favrot received a letter from a friend in New Orleans reflecting on the new order. "It is left to us to find out to what class this drama's actors belong," he began. "I saw the birth of the French Revolution; I saw it growing for a number of years and I experienced its disastrous results to the extent that I was obliged to become an expatriate; therefore, every time the word revolution is mentioned, fear and terror take hold of my soul." Now he dismissed such sinister ideas. "We must hope that the honest inhabitants of your post and of all the Spanish possessions in America will feel the necessity to unite and work together in order to smother the seeds of trouble and dissent."[70] Had he been in Baton Rouge, he might have felt less sanguine, for even as delegates packed, the standing committee met to discuss new business with the original seed of "trouble and dissent."

Reuben Kemper was back.

14

Our Infant but Beloved Country

IT WAS A GRAND irony that, with West Florida in revolution, the Kempers of all people should miss the whole affair. Samuel ran his tavern in Alexandria, and Nathan raised his growing family in the Attakapas country. Reuben had left no trace in the region since buying Nathan's property at Pinckneyville and seems to have been content to work the *Go By* on the rivers. If he had known that Feliciana was about to erupt he could not have resisted being involved, but news traveled slowly and his work took him to remote places. A rumor circulated in New Orleans that Reuben first learned of the revolt only after it was over, while visiting Samuel, and that has the ring of probability. It would have been the end of September before the news could pass that far up the Mississippi and Red rivers, and another week before Reuben could barge back downstream, stop quickly at Pinckneyville, and then go on to Baton Rouge.

He probably saw the new lone star for the first time around October 8 or 9 and perhaps was there to see Thomas return from St. Helena. Kemper came on his own initiative, for no official sent for him. He knew many of the leaders. Some had been friends and some had not, for Mills, the Johnsons, and others helped put down his brothers' efforts in 1804. Still, most Americans regarded Reuben more highly than they did his siblings. His volunteering to ensure the peaceful turnover of Louisiana, his defiance of Murdoch, his long stand against what many regarded as corrupt justice, and perhaps even his whipping of the despised Kneeland lent him some stature. The Kemper name raised volunteers in 1804. Even if the convention did not send for him, bringing him into the cause now was still a powerful act, both in reality and symbolically.

He came at just the right moment too, for, no longer fearing an immediate threat from Folch or the malcontents west of the Amite, the convention turned from defense to offense. The very day that Thomas began the march back from Springfield, a man in Baton Rouge wondered "what will be the movements on the Pensacola I am as yet not able to say, as the government are at a loss what to do about it." Speculation in town was that a small force could not take Folch's capital, and raising a larger force now was not possible.[1] Just three days later, however, the delegates told Holmes they had little doubt of obtaining possession of the forts of Mobile and Pensacola soon.[2]

To date, distance and slow communications meant there had been no coordination between the convention and the plotters above Mobile and farther east. Kennedy's continued absence in Georgia and the exposure of Caller's plans left the Mobile Society essentially rudderless. As a result, no one in Baton Rouge knew what support or plans there might be for driving the Spaniards out. Yet if ever there was a time to strike, it was now, with the western four districts secured, Spain's colonial empire crumbling everywhere, and early assistance from the United States taken for granted. Since the convention was the only elected body vested with sovereignty, it took the initiative, and at such a moment the appearance of Kemper was providential. No one doubted his daring and resourcefulness. His imposing physical presence worked to his advantage, and his reputation for integrity was unmarred by his years of contention with John Smith and his failure as a merchant. What he did not have was experience enlisting or leading men, as he told Burr's subordinates in 1806. He might have been a subaltern in Clark's New Orleans volunteers, and the press reports in 1804 that confused him with Nathan referred to him as "captain" or "colonel." Nevertheless, within hours of the adjournment, the standing committee convened and commissioned Reuben a colonel of militia.

The next day they ordered him to go to the Mobile country to determine the numbers and locations of the peoples on the rivers flowing into the bay and enlist their support for the declaration and the convention. They also commissioned Joseph White a major to assist him and authorized Kemper to negotiate treaties and raise as many volunteers as he thought necessary to take Mobile. They gave Reuben a copy of the declaration as well as an address to the inhabitants and further authorized him to swear into the service any militia who came forward and to arm any volunteers he raised, giving him up to two thousand dollars to spend on the convention's credit.[3]

Kemper did not think twice about accepting his charge. "I was appointed by the Convention of West Florida to attempt a reconciliation of our conventional authoritys among the People of Mobille and its neghbouring country," he told his friend Andrew Jackson. "To this end (I done as you yourself under similar circumstances would have done) imbarked with Heart and soul devoted to the prosecution of the work of our infant but beloved Country."[4] He had to act quickly, for a new story emerged that the British were coming. A Pinckneyville man doubted it, but even if it was true, he said, "the temper of the conventionalists is too high to recede; and the men are too intrepid and full of resources, to be disconcerted by men of inferior metal and motives." Still, many feared that if the United States did not step in soon, Britain would, for many old British settlers still retained their attachments, and there seemed to be hundreds ready to join any party in opposition to the convention.[5]

Less than a week after Thomas left Springfield, people there were grumbling again, raising concerns that there was as much danger to be feared from the whites as from the Indians.[6] Then there was a small mutiny in the command Thomas left behind when several men refused to appear for a muster, and two had to be arrested after they threatened their captain and imperiously refused to sign the declaration.[7] It began to appear that Thomas might have to return to St. Helena to quell an incipient uprising, and if he did, one man predicted desperate bloodshed to come.[8]

False rumors said that Caller had already taken Mobile, leading to predictions that he might soon be the object of Spanish reprisals.[9] The Spaniards contended with the same wealth of misinformation. Folch was still trying to raise support from Michael Jones for Shepherd Brown more than a week after both were out of the picture, and definitive word of Brown's dispersal did not reach Mobile until October 15.[10] Ten days later another report placed armed rebels on the

Pearl River, and Perez made plans to evacuate his men and artillery aboard the *Dolphin*.[11] Meanwhile Fort Stoddert heard that Thomas's army was at Bookter's Landing en route to take Mobile, and people began fleeing the town for the protection of Perez's fort, some fearing that even that would not be safe. One man in the fort declared that Thomas "is brave and desperate and followed by men capable of anything." Stories inflated the convention forces to ten thousand militia, and one declared that Thomas actually sent Folch a challenge to meet him in personal combat.[12] In fact, neither was on the move, nor was Reuben Kemper, for problems in the fort at Baton Rouge suddenly took everyone's attention.

When the convention reorganized its militia, it commissioned new officers. One of them was Captain Stephen Winter, now to command a company of artillery. Winter was a fair-weather soldier, more interested in the trappings and prestige of rank than in patriotic service. He soon caused trouble over the cost of his uniform and, what he thought worse, the fact that Captain David Taylor Woodward Cook, a slightly senior officer, was placed over him. Winter felt slighted by Cook's appointment, thinking himself more knowledgeable, and he demanded permission to raise his own company, saying that if he did not get it he would resign.[13]

Winter's complaint about Cook may have been purely his own inflated ego talking, but he may have known of problems of another sort. The North Carolinian Cook had been a lieutenant in the Sixth U.S. Infantry in April of 1800, but the army discharged him honorably less than two months later.[14] In 1810 he moved to West Florida and bought land, probably in St. Helena.[15] He liked to play the fiddle, but he liked to drink even more, and somewhere in that mix lay the problem.[16] Being from St. Helena, he may not have felt all that attached to the new regime, though he joined the rest of the officers when they sent their September 25 pledge of support to the convention.[17] If the committee honored Winter's request to form his own company, Cook would have felt slighted, while more immediately he would have objected to the committee's October 15 order that no alcohol was to be sold to the garrison in the fort.[18] Of course that posed no problem for an officer like Cook unless he sold liquor to the soldiers.

The evening after the prohibition, the committee learned that Cook and two lieutenants planned a mutiny to take the fort and free Delassus and Brown, then somehow hand the place back to the Spaniards.[19] The committee acted quickly to prevent any outbreak and arrested Cook and his accomplices. It was probably never more than talk fueled by liquor, and perhaps some vestiges of sympathy with Brown. Three officers posed little threat to a fort garrisoned at the moment by 115 men under Ballinger. Two men had deserted in the past fortnight, but nothing suggested that the loyalty of the remainder was in question.[20] Besides, only a drunkard would suppose the fort could be turned over to Spaniards, the nearest being more than eighty miles away in Mobile. Coincidentally, just the day before learning of the plot — or perhaps because of learning of it — the committee made a special provision for the court-martial of any captain charged with an offense, reserving judgment and sentence to the convention.[21]

Rhea and the committee took the plot seriously enough to order additional repairs to the fort and to send thirteen cannon and half a ton of gunpowder to St. Francisville on October 21, as well as two hundred muskets.[22] It was probably a precautionary measure to get the arms and munitions out of the fort until there was no further threat of mutiny, for disaffection among some men ran deeper than many believed. Still, Haynie thought the fort would be secure "provided our enemies inside of it are taken proper care of."[23] Now they had to take care of three of those inside enemies. The committee had placed the power of trying and sentencing officers with the convention, but it was in recess at the moment, and thanks to Brown's delays the superior tribunal decreed by the ordinance had yet to convene. Now the committee commanded that the court commence a session on October 22, very probably to deal with Cook as well as other backlogged civil cases.[24]

That day a small crowd gathered outside the log house that was to serve as courthouse. Court day was a spectator event on the frontier, and inside, people had built a platform two feet high at the end of a room and placed on it three straw-bottomed chairs for the justices. Skipwith arrived punctually at 11:00 A.M. As befit a man of his reputation, he came in a four-horse coach and was dressed elegantly for the cheering crowd as he slowly walked through them, bowing as he strode through the door. He sat in the center chair and waited for the others to arrive. Soon Joseph Thomas appeared, having been appointed to represent St. Helena in Brown's place.[25] He stood in the doorway uncertain where to go until Skipwith beckoned him to sit beside him. There they sat waiting for Percy, and finally Skipwith suggested that they postpone any business until the next day and content themselves now with organizing the court and choosing a chief justice. Thomas agreed, suggesting Skipwith for the senior position, but the Virginian modestly proposed that they wait for Percy and then let him and Thomas make the decision.

Just then, after walking a mile from his home, Percy made his entrance; he was wearing an old and worn naval uniform, complete with feathered chapeau and a rusting sword.[26] Sweating from his walk and wiping his jowls with a red bandanna, he tapped his walking cane across the floor as he strode to his seat, whereupon Skipwith repeated his suggestion to first select a chief justice. True to form, Percy blustered, "Oh! If that is to be the question to be decided, that's ———— easily settled; I'm chief justice of *this* court, by ————." Skipwith did not argue, and then Percy called for the sheriff and asked if there were any prisoners in the jail. When told there were a few, Percy demanded that the first be brought forward as "I wish to try my hand upon him immediately."

The accused, quite possibly Captain Cook, came in, feebly attended by a young lawyer, whereupon Percy exploded that he would have nothing to do with lawyers and legal niceties. "If you are guilty," he told the accused, "which I have good reason to believe, I'll be ———— if you slip through these fingers." Skipwith and Thomas found it difficult to restrain Percy from this kind of summary justice at first, but in time the court began to operate as intended.[27] Captain Cook was fortunate if he did not have to come before a martinet like Percy. In the end he and the other two were simply cashiered and ordered to leave West Florida, though Cook, in fact, just went home to St. Helena and kept quiet.[28]

The emergency session of the convention gathered on October 24, but it only ratified Kemper's appointment and selected delegates from St. Ferdinand, which its inhabitants now called St. Tammany. Then the convention adjourned until the next morning, when it heard Leonard present his committee's draft of a constitution.[29] Barrow believed they were virtually unanimous in wanting the United States to take over. "Now I assure you is the moment," he told a friend. "The word liberty is an enchanting sound here," but still he detected divisions evidenced by the resistance mounted by Brown and Cooper.[30]

Leonard added anxiety to the cough and pain in his chest that Thursday morning before the gavel. For him it was a transcendent moment. Events and Delassus had forced this on them prematurely, he believed, but now they had to act "to Secure our lives and property to bust the Chains of Terany and establish freedom and Independence by adding a new and a brilliant Star to the greate Consillation which unites this happy Western World." Their new constitution would be republican, and with it to guide them, "our conquest will be followed up so far at least as to Secure our Independence."[31]

They debated and amended the constitution for three days, and then on Saturday morning adopted it unanimously. With only a few significant exceptions, the document they framed for "the State of Florida" followed the U.S. Constitution. It allocated one-year terms in the house of representatives to sixteen members from the several districts, including Mobile, in anticipation of Kemper's success, while a senate would hold one senator from each district. All free white males over twenty-one owning real property worth two hundred dollars or more could vote. Their chief executive would be a governor serving two years, to be elected first by the legislature and thereafter by the voters. The short incumbencies anticipated annexation by the United States. There was to be no cabinet, only an appointed secretary of state, and their supreme court was to have an unspecified number of justices for life.

Then they begin to vary dramatically from their model. Article four confirmed land to squatters, voided all French and British land patents whether subsequently recognized by Spain or not, and gave the legislature power to subdivide existing districts to create new ones. They prohibited a legislative emancipation without owners' permission and full compensation to them and implied that owners could not free their slaves without permission, particularly if the slaves were needed to satisfy creditors, since the freed slaves might then become a liability to the state. They also denied any power to prohibit settlers from bringing their slaves with them. Rather than abolishing the African slave trade, they reserved the power to open and close it at will. The constitution required owners to treat slaves humanely, threatening abusive masters with the seizure and sale of their slaves, and guaranteed trials to slaves charged with crimes. Then, as if they could find nowhere else to put it, a final section of this article mandated freedom of religion and separation of church and state.

A novel seventh article began with a paraphrase of Jefferson's Declaration of Independence. All free white men were equal, it said, and all power derived from the people. Then they borrowed verbatim the Bill of Rights, but with some special emphasis from their own experience, starting with a reaffirmation of freedom of religion. Recalling President John Adams's Sedition Act of 1798 to muzzle a hostile press, they explicitly guaranteed the right of journalists to examine the proceedings of the legislature or of any branch or officer of government, affirming that truth was its own evidence against charges of slander or sedition. Citizens had the right to bear arms in defense of themselves and the state, but there was to be no peacetime standing army. They added a novel guarantee of the right to emigrate from the state, and then affirmed that monopolies were contrary to a free state and ought not to be allowed. Regarding this article seven as their own bill of rights, they decreed that it was inviolable and immutable.

They called for an election of new delegates to take place on November 10, with the new legislature to convene at St. Francisville on November 19, at which time the powers of the current convention would expire. When the moment came to sign, they did it in random order, Johnson first, and Rhea last as president. Lilley laid aside his earlier reservations and signed along with the rest, but Manuel López, still unable to reconcile himself to their acts, did not appear at the session and would not be seen in the convention again.[32]

The document reflected parochial concerns, wider apprehensions over the growing opposition to slavery, and Republican reactions to the centralizing efforts of the Federalists. The Republicans may have concealed their sentiments in the early days of the convention, but now they produced a thoroughly Jeffersonian charter.[33] They met briefly on Sunday, knowing it was the last time the revolutionary body would sit, and conducted their final business, the appointment of a standing committee to consult with the military on the plan to take the forts at

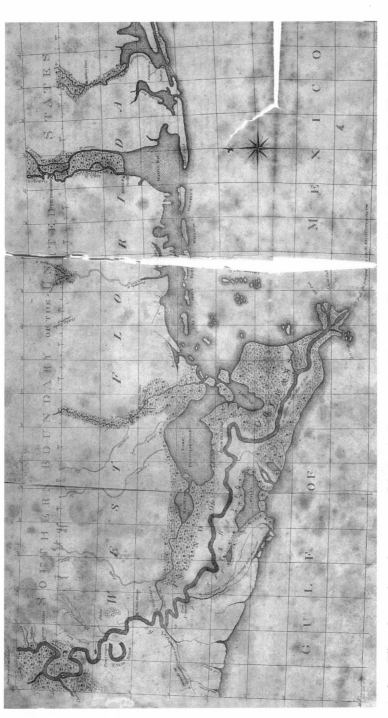

Andrew Ellicott's 1799 boundary survey of the border between the Mississippi Territory and Spanish West Florida. Ellicott's line runs eastward along the thirty-first parallel, from just below Fort Adams on the Mississippi River at left to the Escambia above Pensacola on the right. *Historic New Orleans Collection, accession no. 74-08-L.*

General Philemon Thomas, the crusty, semiliterate grocer and innkeeper who commanded the forces of the "revolution" in their one momentary battle.
Courtesy of the Collections of the Louisiana State Museum

John Smith of Ohio, whose partnership with Reuben Kemper at Bayou Sara indirectly inaugurated the unrest that resulted in the West Florida revolt.
Ohio Historical Society

Governor William C. C. Claiborne was Jefferson's and Madison's man on the scene, governing first Mississippi Territory, then Orleans Territory, and watching American interests in West Florida's developing unrest and revolt.
Courtesy of the Collections of the Louisiana State Museum

Governor David Holmes of Mississippi Territory worked closely with Claiborne in keeping the peace on the troublesome Ellicott line and then was instrumental in the assumption of power in West Florida.
Library of Congress

Kemper and Company began operations in a warehouse rented from David Bradford, whose estate, Laurel Grove (later renamed the Myrtles), may have been a temporary home for their retail establishment. *Wikimedia Commons*

The flag of the infant Republic of West Florida, seen again in Texas in 1836, and later as the Bonnie Blue Flag of the Confederacy in 1861.
Wikimedia Commons

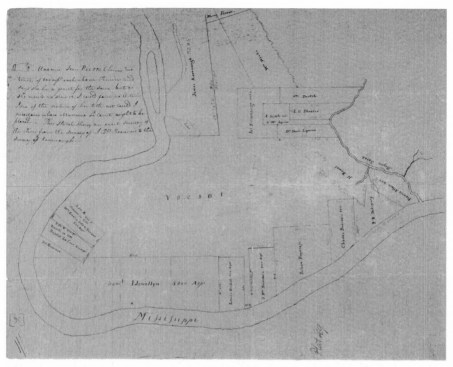

Pintado's survey of Reuben Kemper's neighborhood. The John Smith–Reuben Kemper property is unmarked, and was just to the right of Bayou Sara where it enters the Mississippi. Several of the Kempers' neighbors appear, both friends and foes in the West Florida troubles, such as Levi Sholer, James Kavanaugh, William Dortch, Henry Flowers, Julian Poydras, and others. *Library of Congress*

This 1804 map of the fort at Baton Rouge, illustrating the Spaniards' capture of the place many years before, shows the road at left from which Thomas's cavalry took off on the low ground along the river leading to the rear of the star-shaped fort marked *H*.

David Rumsey Map Collection, www.davidrumsey.com

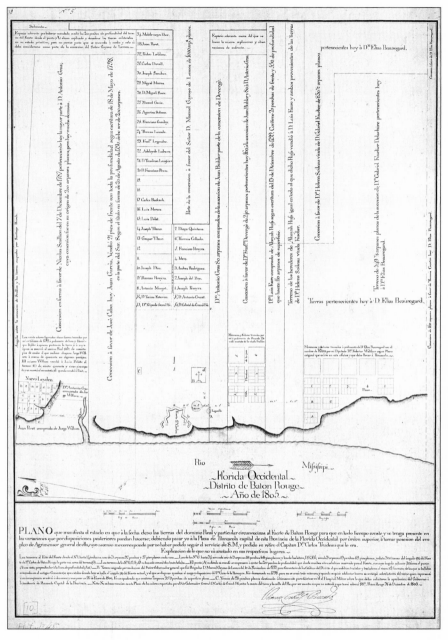

Pintado's map of Baton Rouge in 1805, when it was the center of the growing West Florida unrest during Carlos de Grand-Pré's governorship. Fort San Carlos is at the center left.
Library of Congress

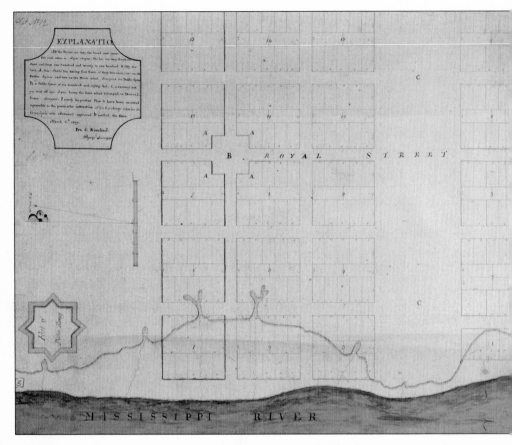

Pintado's deputy surveyor Ira C. Kneeland, his ears notched by the Kempers less than six months before, finished this plan of Baton Rouge on March 6, 1809. Grand-Pré had ordered it before his December 1808 departure, but Kneeland's recovery from the Kemper attack delayed its completion. *B* is the public square where the convention held its sessions with Delassus, and where the Lone Star first rose and last went down. Fort San Carlos is at lower left. The flatland along the river is clearly evident, as is the small ravine leading up the bluff by which the attackers entered the fort from the rear. *Library of Congress*

Mobile and Pensacola.[34] There was no questioning the importance of those places to the delegates. Before they left for home, they and others pledged $4,470 to finance the expedition.[35] The standing committee also committed to the cause the 6,000 pesos found in Delassus's room and the $1,333 in gold from his desk.[36]

Excitement spread in the community. "Wee are all anxiety in the town & vicinity about the contemplated expedition," Haynie told Ballinger. Everyone seemed eager to go. Some who were disappointed with Thomas's "timidity & want of firmness" in dealing with Brown and Cooper's rebels wanted to know who would command. Remembering the Kempers' actions in 1804 and their retribution on Kneeland, few feared excessive lenience with Reuben in command. Haynie thought they should stop first on the Amite and forcibly draft every able-bodied man at Michael Jones's settlement, since they had cost the country some expense and been the cause of some trouble but had not yet rendered any service. He also wanted to stop at Cooper's plantation to plunder anything of use to the expedition, and then "pay Mr. Brown the same compliment." Haynie himself had hoped to go, and jealous men in his district accused him of wanting to be a brigadier general in charge or even governor, "both of which accusations are d——d lies," he told Ballinger.[37]

The day after the adjournment the standing committee removed itself to St. Francisville, enjoining Ballinger before they left to protect the powder magazine from arson, warning him that after the Captain Cook episode the character of many of the men in the companies under his command suggested the necessity for strict discipline.[38] The mutiny still bred fears that Baton Rouge might not be safe. They wanted to be near the line for speedier communication with Holmes, as well as close to the assembly point for Kemper's expedition.

During the past fortnight little had been heard of Reuben. No doubt it took a few days for him and Major White to pack and arrange transportation. The convention gave him promissory notes totaling $25,500 to fund his mission and authorized him to borrow for anything he could not purchase with convention scrip.[39] He left no later than October 20, and probably traveled overland via Springfield and the Tangipahoa and Tchefuncte settlements. When White fell ill, Kemper continued alone.[40] He reached Fort Stoddert late on October 24, and his arrival attracted instant notice.[41] Within fewer than twenty-four hours men speculated that he had been sent by the conventionalists to divine the sentiment for revolt in Mobile. A man near Fort Stoddert warned James Innerarity that Kemper brought important *"secret"* papers explaining the intentions of the Floridians.[42]

Reuben boarded with his old friend Colonel Sparks and reported to Rhea a few days later that he found Sparks warm in their cause and eager to get Kemper's messages into Mobile to arouse support. Sparks believed there were only about fifty *soldados* in Perez's garrison and a few times that number of citizens who would stand by the Spaniards, though many in the town hoped for a change. The fort itself was run-down, the moat dry, and the defenders resorting to painted logs in the waterfront batteries to imitate cannon. Reuben learned that his old enemy James Horton and some others of his ilk entered Mobile recently, briefly panicking people with stories of the convention sending an army against them and of men from the Tombigbee preparing an attack. The Spaniards had spies out in every direction just in case.

Kemper intended to call on leading men in the community to sound their sentiment when they returned from court at Fort St. Stephens. He did not know the leaders of the Mobile Society, but he would meet them soon, and meanwhile Sparks assured him that if he raised the white star below the line, three days would produce enough volunteers to take Mobile. Kemper learned that instead of hundreds of reinforcements, Perez had only ten men, and he thought Perez might be willing to hand over Mobile and merge his command with the convention forces. If the committee sent him just one company of infantry as the basis for an army, he knew he could take the fort, especially since there was fever in Pensacola, and Folch's men would be too ill to reinforce Mobile.[43] Pensacola did have an epidemic, though what Kemper did not yet know was that at five o'clock on the very morning that he wrote to Rhea, the fever claimed the life of his old enemy Ira Kneeland.[44]

Kemper found leading citizens around the fort sympathetic, though many hoped the people of Mobile would embrace the new order without bloodshed. Reuben circulated the convention's proclamation inviting all to join them and threatening retaliation against those who stood in the way. A friend of Innerarity's warned that the force in

Mobile was not strong enough to resist this wave, for "The *Star of the West (such is the Flag of the conventionalists)* will attract myriads of *Boatmen* and *Sharp Shooting Kentuckians* whose object will not be so much the desire of lucre, as an *imaginary* glory and the novelty of the thing." He advised Innerarity to see if Perez would accept the assistance of U.S. forces in resisting Kemper, adding that from his knowledge of sentiment among the population of Mobile, internal foes were gathering so fast that loyalists must augment their numbers at once or be overwhelmed.[45]

Folch feared the same. Even before he learned of Baton Rouge's fall, he had asked for heavy reinforcements and two hundred thousand pesos to defend his province, but he got neither.[46] A few days after Kemper reached Fort Stoddert, Folch received a copy of the convention's declaration, which made it clear that they looked to Mobile to join them.[47] Men like Innerarity, a British subject doing business with the Spaniards, doubted that West Florida could sustain its independence, but the people there had to look to their own best interests, and the United States seemed a better prospect than Spain.[48] Then came news of Kemper meeting with planters just above the line and arousing old passions. Despite all its planning, the Mobile Society never had leadership to go beyond boast, but Spain knew from painful experience that Kempers did not stop at talk.

Neither did the committee of the convention. On October 29 they ordered half the military stores in the fort to be readied to equip the expedition to Mobile and Pensacola.[49] The next day they ordered the boat that had been captured with the fort, known as the King's Barge, to be repaired quickly to move supplies and munitions for the planned army, and they instructed the quartermaster to buy flour and bake a large quantity of "army bread," or hardtack.[50] By the end of the month the entire region knew that the convention planned to move to attack Mobile and Pensacola, and moderate men were worried that speculators had pushed the convention toward independence against the wishes of most of the settlers; despite genuine passions for liberty, it appeared to some that the underlying motive was venal. It disturbed some men that as holder of one of the larger Spanish grants, Justice Skipwith might now very well try land cases covering titles to sales from his own lands. One Mississippian believed that "good and worthy men have been obliged to stand forth in order to prevent bad men from involving the whole southern part of the continent."[51] Hours before learning of the new constitution, a man in Natchez wrote that the United States must give speedy attention to the situation of West Florida. It was weak and easy prey to a foreign power. Should one try to invade, Mississippians would not quietly watch the struggle. There was no question that the convention would joyfully accept any claim of sovereignty that the United States might assert.[52] Governor Holmes feared that what one man called the "throes and convulsions of the Floridians" might spread to Mississippi. "The storm seems to have gone by," he noted, "but none could tell for how long.[53]

A nephew of Claiborne quipped that every act of the West Floridians showed their "American characteristics" and that they were "full of 'cheek' and particularly cool."[54] Everyone understood that the final outcome of these acts depended less on what happened there than on decisions hundreds of miles to the northeast. Some in the East protested Washington's policy thus far of regarding the rebels as unlawful when the government should be fostering independence from Spain.[55] Madison trod a fine line, however, and the convention moved faster that summer than he liked. Holmes did not have his territorial militia ready yet, and the president feared that American deserters, British inhabitants, the few remaining French, fugitives from everyone's justice, and land speculators might form a coalition majority unwilling to accept annexation.

By October 19 he did not yet know of the fall of Baton Rouge, though recent advices spoke of the rapid disintegration. He told Jefferson that to occupy West Florida then risked offending Britain, Spain, and France and fomenting "not a triangular, but a quadrangular contest." Spain's crisis came home to their feelings and interests, he said, but a foreign war for a province they were likely to get by other means did not serve American interests.[56] Expansionist editors flayed the president for timidity, but Madison remained calmly unmoved.[57]

Then on October 22 a three-week-old letter from Holmes arrived on Madison's desk with a copy of the convention's declaration and its September 26 plea for aid and annexation. That put more pressure on the president; having declared itself independent, the regime in

Baton Rouge could try to ally itself with England if Madison did not move, and if it remained independent too long, it could muddy the American claim and invite foreign nations to meddle in any future takeover.[58] Within forty-eight hours Madison decided to take action. This was the ultimate end he desired; the seeds planted by Wykoff had simply germinated faster than anticipated.

By October 27 Madison completed a proclamation averring that West Florida had always been a part of the Louisiana Purchase and that America's failure to occupy it immediately was due to a willingness to negotiate the question peacefully. Spanish misrule had driven the province to crisis, and if he did not assert sovereignty now, the situation might lead to difficulty for the United States and Spain, threaten the peace of Mississippi and Orleans, and be seen as an abrogation of America's rightful claim. Consequently, Madison decreed possession and ordered Claiborne to take over in Baton Rouge and temporarily govern West Florida as part of Orleans. Madison neither recognized nor implied that West Florida was an independent entity with sovereignty.[59]

That same day, Secretary of State Smith ordered Claiborne to return to the Southwest via Natchez; to publish the proclamation in English, Spanish, and French; to distribute copies throughout the territory of West Florida; and then to use military assistance from Holmes to take possession of West Florida. If anyone attempted to resist, the commander of the regulars in Mississippi would provide the necessary strength to overcome them. However, Claiborne was not to act against any remaining Spanish force, no matter how small.[60] Better to gain peaceful possession of even part of West Florida than risk conflict with Spain to get it all. Robert Smith objected to Madison's final provision, thinking it humiliating to withhold full assertion of American claims, and he did not hide his disapproval. Madison would dismiss Smith within six months.[61]

Claiborne left for Natchez the very next day.[62] Meanwhile, Madison kept his act a secret for five weeks and would not present it until he gave his annual address when Congress reconvened on December 5, by which time Claiborne should be at Natchez, ready to move, supported by militia, regulars, and gunboats, for a quick and peaceful takeover. Madison might have preferred to consult with Congress before taking action, but even five weeks was a lot of time for unanticipated complications.

And the situation did get complicated. An essay by Judge Rodney may have reached Holmes and Madison in time to influence their thinking. A week or two after the convention's declaration, Rodney finished a paper he titled "The Exploration of and Title to East and West Florida, and Louisiana, the Spanish & French Colonies in America, the Louisiana Purchase, and the Rights of Deposit, etc." In it he concluded that West Florida had belonged to the United States all along. Spain may have held it for some years, but now Spain was in collapse everywhere, with no legitimate government in place in Madrid or Baton Rouge, and thus the United States was justified in taking possession. "It is not only Important to the Inhabitants of that district (who are mostly Americans) but is important to the back settlements, of the U.S. that they should have the free Navigation of the several rivers passing through that District to the Ocean," Rodney argued. But they were too weak to defend themselves, and that justified the United States' accepting the convention's September 28 invitation. Statute law prohibited the nation or its citizens from expeditions into foreign soil. The legitimate government of Spain was gone, and the United States was at liberty to assist colonies breaking away from Spain if solicited, said Rodney. "Nay the obligations of humanity towards mankind, requires that they should affoard such assistance and protection."

Americans were so disposed toward independence for Spain's New World possessions that if Washington agreed, "they would voluntarily affoard them any assistance that they may happen to stand in need of." Rodney saw that such sentiment could lead in a dangerous direction, however, and cautioned that "any assistance affoarded, should be regulated by, and under the direction of the government itself."[63] He knew the hazard of encouraging filibusters of the stripe of Burr and Wilkinson. What he did not know, of course, was that this was the very policy conceived by Jefferson, and now brought to fruition by his successor: encourage Americans to settle in Spanish territory and foment uprisings on their own, after which the United States could step in and declare annexation. In this Jeffersonian model for expansionism, West Florida looked to be the first success and a template for more to come.[64]

Now it all depended on the West Floridians and what happened in those five weeks. The same October 27 that the president finished his proclamation, the convention at Baton Rouge adopted its new constitution. By December 5 their new legislature would be elected and in session, and they would have a new governor.[65] With the taste of sovereignty in their mouths, would the revolutionaries be so willing to yield it, even to the United States? With Reuben Kemper that very day testing the sentiment at Fort Stoddert for an expedition against Mobile and Pensacola, in five weeks Madison might well be annexing a war with Spain.

15

The Star Will Rise and Shine

"THE IDEA OF an independent *state in West Florida, is preposterous,*" howled a New York editor soon after word of the new constitution reached the Atlantic seaboard.[1] Echoing the concerns of Lilley and Skipwith, a Philadelphia editor said the declaration of independence violated the rights of the United States, besides which nature had already ordained that Florida must one day be part of the United States.[2] Rodney added to his recent essay a letter to the *Natchez Aurora* on November 3, arguing that if Spain's colonies in America had the courage to assert their independence, then the United States had a duty to befriend them.[3] Most in West Florida thought the United States would intervene, but one Mississippian said Madison's "timid, temporizing disposition" would hardly allow him to protect America's own rights, let alone run afoul of Spain or Napoleon by interfering in West Florida.[4]

Ballinger confessed that they felt uncertain, especially with the prospect of a fight for Mobile. "Our Councils are much Divided," he admitted. Some wanted to prosecute the war vigorously, while others wanted to wait for the United States to step in, as a result of which he doubted that much military preparation would be undertaken until the new legislature convened. He knew the minds of the people and believed they preferred death to remaining under Spain, and if Madison did not act they would accept any other protection they could get. With no authority to do so as a mere militia officer, he appealed to Toulmin "to Drop some hints" with Madison, then disingenuously dropped one of his own about fictitious French overtures to West

Florida leaders, appealing to Toulmin to save the country "from the fangs of Joseph Napoleon."[5]

At that moment, some foreigners wanted salvation from the fangs of Reuben Kemper. Kemper advised Captain Perez on November 3 that he was there to negotiate an amicable adjustment. Given Spain's plight at home, a colony had a right to protect itself from despotism and adopt self-government. West Florida was now free, and he called on Perez to hand over his fort and join forces at the same grade and pay and to allow a referendum in Mobile to choose self-government with the convention. "If we have to resort to arms, the evils and horrors of war will *be laid to your door!*" he warned; "your answer will decide the fate of yourself and the destiny of your fellow citizens." It was the old Kemper bluster to be sure, but sensible, for bold bluff now might peacefully buy what would later cost time, money, and blood. He would await the decision at Fort Stoddert.[6]

After Sparks found a messenger for Kemper's letter, Reuben posted copies of the declaration and the call for the people of the eastern districts to elect delegates and state their terms for joining the convention.[7] Then he rode to McIntosh's Bluff on the Tombigbee to meet with the returned Joseph Kennedy, whose recent intelligence from Mobile indicated that Kemper's arrival had alarmed the Spaniards into extraordinary preparations for defense. Still, he told Reuben that he could soon have five companies of Mississippi militia, and if Baton Rouge sent four cannon and five hundred men, they could take both Mobile and Pensacola. Kennedy proposed that their forces unite on the bank of Saw Mill Creek midway between the line and Mobile, which meant that Kennedy would be leading American militia on an invasion of what might be foreign soil. He insisted that he and his officers should have the same rank that they currently held in Mississippi; patriotism required no compromise of ambition.[8] Persuaded that Perez would not yield peacefully, Kemper authorized Kennedy to raise his companies, though neither the convention nor Kemper had authority to enlist volunteers on Mississippi soil.[9] Trusting Kennedy's ability, Kemper decided that unless Mobile surrendered first, he would raise the convention flag on Sunday, November 25, at McCurtin's Bluff on the Tensaw River.[10] Then he rode up the Tombigbee to Fort St. Stephens to seek the support of the Choctaw agent Major John McKee, but McKee refused. Reuben insisted all the same that the convention stood committed to the independence of all the Floridas.

Harry Toulmin watched all of this anxiously, for he was deeply involved with the area. He had a cotton plantation nearby. His daughter Frances was married to Captain Edmund Pendleton Gaines of Fort St. Stephens.[11] Another daughter wed a son of General Wilkinson, and Toulmin's own son married the daughter of his persistent foe James Caller. The judge expected to remain in Mississippi for the rest of his life, and he tried sincerely to guard its interests while opposing filibusters such as Kennedy. In 1807 Toulmin arrested Aaron Burr and held him for a time at Fort Stoddert, and now, with Kemper in the vicinity and Kennedy returned, he was not about to relax vigilance. He wanted the Floridas to come under American governance, but only by legitimate means. Toulmin advised officers of the local militia to beware any attempt to revive the Mobile Society. He would be delighted to see Mobile's people evict the Spaniards, but they ought to do it on their own, he said. "We have no right to interfere."[12]

Late on November 5 Kemper returned to Fort Stoddert, where he met with Toulmin; Toulmin had been cordial thus far because he did not believe Reuben would go below the line but would simply encourage the people there to act on their own. Aware of the panic in Mobile caused by recent rumor, Toulmin thought Spain might evacuate without resistance, which meant that hostile action from above the line could move the Spaniards to change their minds. That made Kemper a potentially dangerous man.[13] To discourage him, Toulmin reported a recent reinforcement to Perez, adding that merchants in Mobile assured him that they were perfectly happy operating under Spanish rule.[14] All the next day Kemper got more rumors of the Spaniards strengthening their fort; he stayed up until 11:00 P.M. hoping for an answer from Perez, but none came. In fact, Perez sent Folch a copy of Kemper's demand that same day, having known of Reuben's arrival for a week, though at first he thought it was Nathan.[15] Finally Kemper gave up and advised Rhea that now it was up to them to do the best they could.

To do his best, Kemper bought gunpowder, lead for bullets, salt, corn, and a keelboat for transportation. He appealed to Rhea to send pork, flour, and whiskey, suggesting that Randolph at Pinckneyville could help, and asked for cash and blank commissions for the officers in the regiment he would raise. "Prompt and Inerjetik measures must be adopted," he told Rhea. It might take two or three months, but they could seize all of Florida except St. Augustine on the Atlantic coast, which would fall by itself in time. He urged that they bend every effort to win the allegiance of the people below the line. Knowing that Toulmin was opposed to their efforts, and that as postmaster Toulmin had access to all mail, Kemper sent all of his correspondence by secret messenger.[16]

While Mississippians might posture and threaten, especially with Kennedy now stirring them up, Toulmin doubted they would act on their own.[17] Then came a rumor that the convention was sending up to three thousand men, followed by news that Colonel Thomas Cushing was bringing three companies from his Second U.S. Infantry and five gunboats from Natchez to Fort Stoddert.[18] When the gunboats finally left on November 16, people wondered about the exact intentions of Kemper, the convention, and Madison, and a story spread briefly that the Floridians would declare war on the United States, forcing Madison to send soldiers and incorporate West Florida into the Union by arms.[19]

Certainly it looked as if the United States was not going to let Kemper and Kennedy start a war, and recurrent reports of British interest in Mobile and Pensacola only put more pressure on both American authorities and Kemper. A letter from the settlers on the Pascagoula River about fifty miles west of Fort Stoddert cheered Reuben on November 15. Hearing a false report that Kemper had already taken a Spanish outpost at the mouth of the Pascagoula, Captain Sterling Duprée and thirty-four others notified him that they had elected civil officers to pass laws consonant with those of the convention and would send officers to meet with him.[20] The news encouraged Kemper. "I am a stranger in the Country and must obtain such information and Counsil as I can," Reuben replied to Duprée. He enclosed copies of the declaration and the convention's address and spoke hopefully of the time when "the Star will Rise and shine" at Mobile. He also sent Major William Hargraves to help Duprée raise volunteers, seize any

Spanish supplies they found, and take the locals' oaths to the declaration. Kemper ordered that no harm be done to any who refused to swear the oath, but advised that any who opposed them should be arrested and their property protected from reprisals.[21]

Reuben dropped the pretense of cordiality with Toulmin after learning that the judge had criticized him in a letter to Rhea. On November 14 Kemper had what he called "a long War talk" with the judge, telling him he was a fool and warning that there might be a demand for satisfaction if Toulmin's letters did any injury to his reputation. They parted on distinctly unfriendly terms. When Kemper told Sparks, the colonel dismissed Toulmin, saying thousands would join Reuben.[22] "Kemper talks in high style," Toulmin told Innerarity the next day, but he believed Reuben was being misled by Kennedy and others.[23] As if to prove Toulmin right, Kemper sent another demand to Captain Perez, who declined to reply and alerted Folch that Kemper and Kennedy plotted to attack his garrison.[24] By now spies in Mobile reported the Spaniards were more confident, and the citizens cautious about a change.

Kemper still planned to raise his flag on November 25, and Kennedy assured him that men would step forward. "We are most Cordually Received by every one," Reuben advised Rhea the evening of November 16, and if Toulmin did not interfere, they ought to succeed. He circulated the convention address to the French community near Mobile and planned to send a spy to Pensacola, from which he learned at last of Kneeland's death. If they were going to strike, he told Rhea, they must do it soon and be assured that Rhea and the committee would support them.[25] Two days later Duprée said he and Hargraves would soon be ready to cooperate against Mobile.[26] Meanwhile Kemper went to the confluence of the Alabama and Tombigbee, trying, as he put it, to "revolutionize" the settlers in the area. He expected that volunteers would rally to him despite Toulmin's efforts, but he did not change his plan to raise the star on the east bank of the Alabama, regardless of how many came to join him. "We have the Colours made and ready to Hoiste," he told Rhea with six days to go. "We must make the trial."[27]

In St. Francisville, the standing committee strove to make that trial successful. They assembled on November 2 at the St. Francisville Hotel in a rented meeting room and immediately ordered two cannon emplaced to protect the town.[28] Observers differed on the state of affairs. Some regretted what they saw happening, while Judge Rodney thought that the people of Florida west of the Pearl River were "Enjoying Independence."[29] The November 10 election of representatives and senators passed quietly, and two days later the committee started in earnest raising the Mobile army, despite the objection of Fulwar Skipwith.[30] While he admired "so zealous, so active, & so brave an agent, as Mr. Kemper," Skipwith thought the whole plan hazardous, especially since as yet West Florida had not received any sign of interest or support from the United States.[31] At first the committee waited to hear the results of Kemper's feelers to Perez, but receipt of Reuben's dispatches from the first week of the month made clear that Perez was not going to go quietly.

The committee issued a call for 618 infantry and cavalry to be ready to march the instant they received the order. It first approached old Colonel Kimball to command the column, but he declined. The departure of the Natchez gunboats for Mobile made it clear to Kimball that Madison intended to take over, and he saw no sense to incurring the expense of a campaign when it seemed certain the United States was going to enforce its claim.[32] The committee put Kirkland in command instead, seconded by Ballinger, and authorized a draft if sufficient men did not volunteer. Conscription, if it had to be resorted to, would be the convention's first exercise of arbitrary authority over its citizens, but the provision aroused scarcely a peep of protest.[33] As a Mississippian observed a few days later, "the people of Florida have now gone too far ever to submit to any king."

When the new legislature convened on November 19, visitors found a state of calm in St. Francisville.[34] It was certainly a quiet beginning, for it took two days to assemble a quorum in the house of representatives and three days to assemble the senate's. There were familiar faces here, such as Philemon Thomas, Champ Terry, Rhea, Barrow, John H. Johnson, and Williams, along with new men, such as James Neilson, Dudley Avery, and Llewellyn Griffith, who rode with the cavalry that had taken the fort. At ten in the morning on November 22 they convened to elect their governor and settled unanimously on Skipwith.[35] To some the selection might seem odd, for others, such as Hicky and

Lilley, had played far greater roles in the revolt and convention. The key to Skipwith's selection lay in his friendships. He was close to Jefferson, Madison, and other Republicans, and the legislature counted on that influence to speed West Florida into the United States, as Skipwith himself understood. He accepted only because he saw a danger of confusion at that critical hour and hoped that with good men at his side he could maintain justice and order until the United States took over. If Madison did not step in, then Skipwith expected to resist all efforts by Spain to reassert itself and would form an alliance with England.[36]

During the following week a seeming lethargy set in. For several days the senate again failed to make a quorum, while the house did little more than create an additional committee to study the development of a navy. Then at eleven in the morning on November 29 they gathered in joint session to see Skipwith take his oath of office.[37] In his inaugural address, he spoke of the urgency of these first hours in the birth of their infant republic, and in quick order reminded them of all they had to do to organize their armed forces, establish their justice system, apportion representation more equally, and enact taxes that would be equitable for all classes of citizens. Their cause was too glorious to be disgraced by fear or by submission. They would prevail, and soon they would be welcomed into the United States. "The blood which flows in our veins, like the tributary streams which sustain the father of waters, encircling our delightful country, will return, if not impeded, to the heart of our parent country."[38] To Federalists in the East, Skipwith's address seemed to confirm suspicions of the involvement of expansionists in Washington, while the so-called declaration of independence was nothing but a contrivance to give Madison an excuse to invade.[39] One damned the convention as a violent minority representing little more than Feliciana but intimidating the rest "by terror and outrages."[40]

West Florida's course now lay more in Reuben Kemper's hands than the new governor's. He got more supplies, including twenty barrels of flour that he actually spirited through Mobile, and by November 21 sent Kennedy away to complete his own efforts to arouse volunteers while advising Duprée to arm and equip his men by purchase or loan.[41] Folch had arrived in Mobile by this time, and he started a canny backlash by promising to end the duties on American goods as soon as he had confirmation that Kemper's expedition was canceled. If not, then he would meet force with force, but he wanted to save bloodshed "*between men who will probably soon become citizens of the same community.*" The hint was hardly subtle, and Folch knew Innerarity would share it with Toulmin, as he did. Thinking it the key to peace, Innerarity rushed it to the judge, hoping he did so in time to prevent Kemper's volunteers from crossing the line.[42]

Even though Reuben kept his November 25 rendezvous a secret, everyone seemed to know that something was coming soon. Toulmin warned Madison on November 22 that something rash would be done, fearing that Kemper and Kennedy were having considerable success in the Tombigbee settlement by implying that after victory there would be plunder and 640 acres of land for every volunteer. The St. Stephens settlement resisted such blandishments, and the people on the Tensaw River seemed undecided. William Buford, a local justice who actively promoted the Mobile scheme on the Tensaw, promised Toulmin that he would oppose it, but the judge remained skeptical, knowing the local policy "of preparing for all events, by taking both sides."

Toulmin believed Kemper was exceeding his powers, since the commissions he was issuing to Mississippians were intended only for Americans enlisting below the line. As for Reuben's threat of a duel, the judge believed that Kemper's bluster was based on a false expectation of success. "I ought, however, to speak of this gentleman with considerable caution," he told Madison. "He has no doubt been led away by men with whom I am better acquainted than he is." Toulmin doubted that more than a hundred men would come forward, not enough to take the fort, though they might burn and sack the town. Duprée was supposed to be moving with sixty men to take the Spanish post at the mouth of the Pascagoula, and Toulmin certainly knew of the November 25 rendezvous at McCurtin's Bluff on the east bank of the Tensaw. He hoped the people of Mobile would forestall violence by petitioning the United States to take possession. Folch, being a man of sense, would deal with that calmly and without bloodshed.[43] Toulmin also believed Kemper had fallen under Kennedy's spell, and that both were swayed more by ambition for personal popularity and power than by any public consideration. Folch's hint about abandoning Mobile before long anyhow ought to be persuasive to honest men, he thought, and with that in mind, Toulmin decided to go to the rendezvous at McCurtin's Bluff himself to present Folch's offer to those there assembled. He knew he would be at considerable risk, but the hope that common sense might prevail urged him on.[44]

Kemper was all activity in those last few days. He had the temerity to send a copy of the convention's address to Pintado in Pensacola, asking his old foe to show it to the people and to Folch and report their reaction. When he learned that Folch was actually in Mobile, Reuben sent a message to town to sound opinion and spread word that he now believed his government was sending a thousand men. The arrival of one of "the boys in the house in 1804" spurred him to ask after Samuel and Nathan, as apparently he thought they might be coming. He still planned to raise the convention flag at dawn that coming Sunday. He hoped for a respectable turnout, he told Rhea. "I am in high spirits."[45]

Kemper's messenger returned from Pensacola to report that affairs there did not look good for the Spaniards, who read the departure of Cushing and the gunboats for Fort Stoddert not as a move to stop Kemper but as a move to take the rest of the province. The garrison was demoralized after months without pay, and some of its officers spread rumors that two thousand Americans were coming to sack Mobile and then Pensacola. Folch reportedly arrested the civil officials who delayed the pay, then dispersed the troublesome officers to other garrisons.[46] The dissidents were disgusted at not knowing to whom they owed allegiance: Spain, Bonaparte, Washington, or the West Florida government.[47] One of Carlos de Grand-Pré's sons served in the garrison despite his having just had his hand amputated after a cannon accident, and he frankly told Kemper's agent that the fever that killed Kneeland a few weeks before was still prevalent, and Pensacola could mount but slight opposition. They were expecting eight hundred more *soldados* from Havana, but Havana had too often promised much and delivered little. Meanwhile, on November 24 Kemper's informants in Mobile told him that the citizen militia refused now to rally to the fort unless Folch arrested them.[48] Kennedy told him that more than eighty men were coming from above

Fort Stoddert and that he was sending more gunpowder and supplies.[49] "Our Cockade is mounting freely more so than I could have
expected from the circumstance of Judge Toulmans Villianous exer-
tions," Kemper wrote Rhea November 24. "He is a base Devil filled
with deception & Blading [bleeding] Rascality."[50]

In the camp at McCurtin's Bluff only sixty or seventy men appeared
that first day as Kennedy and Kemper raised the lone star of West
Florida and symbolically renamed the place Bunker Hill; this was
hardly what Kemper had expected. One of the men, a physician from
above the line, said he came to join a revolution in progress because it
sought to gain human rights and "the gifts of nature."[51] Another less
principled volunteer was William Buford, who, after promising Toulmin that he would oppose the expedition, now appeared in the camp.
Last-minute problems kept the "base Devil" himself from appearing,
but he sent two soldiers with letters to Kemper and Kennedy relating
Folch's hints and promises, and Kemper promptly arrested them.[52] He
also arrested a justice of the peace carrying another letter from Toulmin, and Kemper opened it, then handed it to Buford, who altered the
wording and read it to those assembled there to make it appear that
Toulmin actually endorsed their efforts.[53] The volunteers were in high
spirits thanks to Kennedy's whiskey, and that set a pattern for liquor's
role in keeping the men together.[54]

Back at Fort Stoddert Toulmin doubted that Reuben would raise
much of an army. "I know the country much better than Kemper,"
he said the day after the rendezvous. Still, he feared that enough volunteers had appeared to encourage Reuben to continue. He wished
them success at making Florida a republic but hoped he could convince them, if only they would listen to reason instead of their own
ambitions, that "outrage and plunder will not lead to republicanism,
or to peace, or to honour."[55] Now Toulmin sent his son-in-law Gaines
to see Folch, hoping to get from him in writing his promise to halt
the duties if the United States stopped the expedition. Folch obliged,
reiterating his belief that negotiations then pending would hand over
Mobile anyhow and mendaciously implying that Havana had sent an
offer to cede Florida to the Americans. But the judge feared nothing
could stop Kemper. "We are in the utmost confusion," he lamented on
November 27. "Every effort to stop them has been used in vain."[56]

Over the next day or two Kemper operated what he called a "moving camp," traveling about and inviting the inhabitants to come under his protection.[57] The invitation seemed more like intimidation to one settler who complained that they forced him to declare himself for or against their enterprise, while the leaders breathed out vengeance against all who opposed them. They especially condemned Toulmin, and Reuben still maintained that he daily expected a thousand men from Baton Rouge and a boatload of provisions.[58] Given that Kemper had heard virtually nothing from the convention, it began to seem more and more like bluff. Meanwhile he had arrested two U.S. soldiers, and now he notified Sparks that he had them and announced that his people at Bunker Hill met under "the protection of the Star."[59] Sparks demanded their release and asked Kemper and Kennedy to return to Fort Stoddert to meet with him. Reasonably expecting that he and Kennedy might now be arrested above the line, Kemper sent back the two soldiers, pretending that he mistook them for deserters, and then remarked that while he would be happy to receive any communications interesting to their two governments, he could not at the moment leave his command.[60] Toulmin did not expect them to come, nor did he believe that any impression would be made on men who had gone so far.[61]

In fact, the actions of the leaders and their men started to make an impression that did not reflect well on the new state of West Florida. Duprée and his men had been plundering on the Pascagoula for weeks, forcing people to take the convention oath and stealing livestock, slaves, and money. Duprée himself with seven of his men forced their way into a widow's home one night and stole a slave woman and her children. At the river landing they commandeered private schooners and loaded them with plunder, including half a dozen slaves, and when locals resisted, Duprée's men reportedly killed two and dispersed the rest. Duprée himself took over a private home for his headquarters, flying the convention flag overhead; he plundered the house even to the bolts and door locks and other iron hardware when he left with the schooners to return upriver to his home.[62] By late November people not actively sympathizing with Duprée felt in constant danger from his band, and they appealed to Skipwith to either stop the raiders or provide protection.[63] The depredations recalled fears of an earlier plan to oust Spain, a Mississippian complaining on November 28 that Kemper and Kennedy were annoying them "with another *Burr* project."[64]

By this time some of the delegates in St. Francisville believed that Kemper had already taken Mobile the day of the rendezvous, but that did not stop their buildup of materiel.[65] They amassed thousands of rounds of artillery and musket ammunition, a quarter ton of gunpowder, and had already bought a schooner in New Orleans for their navy. Skipwith's naval agent found that officers and seamen of experience were eager to enlist, and merchants seemed happy to extend credit to the new government.[66] Of course Kemper had not taken Mobile, but the situation grew more critical each day.[67] Kemper sent Folch a letter on November 29 presenting the compliments of the new government and proposing a thirty-day armistice to negotiate a peaceful turnover of Mobile, but Folch, like Perez, would never correspond with an agent of a rebellious junta. He wrote another in a long series of complaints to Havana saying that, without men and money, it was hopeless to hold on longer. Delivering an ultimatum of his own, Folch said that if he did not receive support by the end of the year, he would give up Mobile, Pensacola, and all.[68]

Innerarity saw the signs of approaching collapse in Mobile. "The Reins of Government are held with a loose & careless hand & the public distress & discontent are every where conspicuous," he told his employer, John Forbes, in Pensacola. Late pay, tardy justice, corruption, and venality all hastened the rot, and he added that "the Star of the West for such is the flag of the people of Baton Rouge, has shed its baleful influence as far as Tombigbie & Tensaw."

Some Americans fled Mobile and tried to reach Pensacola for safety, but Kemper and his men stopped travelers and attempted to intimidate them into enlisting. Spain no longer had the will or the muscle to dispute the American claim to territory west of the Perdido.[69] By now rumor exaggerated the force supposedly coming under Kirkland to eight thousand men.[70] No one yet knew that Governor Claiborne was just miles away from Washington, Mississippi, and within days of promulgating Madison's proclamation to take over West Florida on

December 5. Even then, word of it could not reach Fort Stoddert until some days afterward, more than enough time for the crisis to erupt.

If all this gathering madness was to be stopped short of war, something had to be done. Judge Toulmin and Vicente Folch were about to act, and this time they hoped it would be Reuben Kemper on the defensive.

16

Vive la West Floriday

HAVANA DID not make Folch's job any easier. Folch had proposed that his superiors open talks on settling the Orleans-Texas border, which would make stopping Kemper in the United States' own best interest during ensuing negotiations. Havana never even replied, so now he had to try another tactic.[1] First he needed time, though, so on December 2 he addressed a letter to Madison in which he stated that if he was not reinforced by the end of the month, he would hand over the province under an equitable capitulation. He blamed his own government for abandoning him but could not refrain from grumbling about Kemper and his superiors. "The inhabitants of Baton Rouge may figure to themselves many motives," he said, "but they cannot produce even a single one which can make tolerable the tyrannical, illegal, and unjust obstinacy with which they insist, that the other districts of the province should subject themselves to their will." He begged Madison to force Kemper to withdraw and tell him that if he threatened Mobile and Pensacola, the United States would join with Spanish troops in repelling him.[2]

It would take three weeks for the letter to reach Washington, but Folch knew when he sent it by John McKee that the Choctaw agent would share the content with Toulmin and Sparks first, and it would be generally known soon and work to pressure authorities to stop the expedition.[3] Just three days later people in Fort Stoddert felt a palpable relief that Mobile and Pensacola might be theirs without a fight if they could control Kemper and Kennedy, who still waited for the Baton Rouge column and men under Caller from the Tombigbee. One man at the fort complained now that these *"choice spirits"* chiefly occupied themselves by robbing locals of their hogs and chickens. Emboldened, Toulmin made his first offensive move and issued a warrant to arrest Buford, hoping that would slow recruiting and perhaps make Kemper desist.[4] They had been terrorizing the inhabitants, many of whom had come above the line for safety, Toulmin told the president. Caller had arrived boasting of a hundred volunteers coming, and he declared that he trusted Reuben Kemper to get Mobile more than he trusted Madison. Caller's men supposedly threatened to assassinate any official who tried to prosecute them, but while Toulmin went ahead with the Buford warrant and issued another for Duprée, no one could be found to serve the documents, probably out of fear.

Toulmin knew that he placed himself in danger by opposing Caller and Kemper but felt he had no alternative but to call them to account. Convictions seemed unlikely, for impaneling a jury would be a challenge, especially since many had swallowed a rumor that Washington encouraged the troubles in the Floridas to gain possession. Toulmin would have been startled to learn that Madison and Claiborne had employed Wykoff to do just that.[5] Meanwhile he confessed himself still at a loss as to Kemper's real objective, and even wondered if the real goal was to foment insurrection in Mississippi in order to join it with West Florida under the St. Francisville government. Feeling threatened and alone, Toulmin freely admitted that "my situation is critical."[6]

For his part, Kemper still felt confident, if restive at waiting for Kirkland's column. After the flag raising, an onlooker at a distance speculated that something more than a "speck of war" might lay ahead.[7] New men arrived singly or in pairs so as not to arouse suspicion when they crossed the line.[8] On December 1, Kemper camped near the tiny village of White House on the eastern shore of the Tensaw River, barely four miles from the Spanish fort, and Kennedy managed to get a flatboat to him with provisions. When a small mounted company joined, Kemper sent some of them out under Dr. Thomas G. Holmes to find more provisions and weapons.[9] Reuben proudly reported to Rhea that his men made "a fine show in the mellow autumn sunlight, and with consciousness of right in their breasts, and that the eye of God was upon them."[10]

The next day, Kemper moved the camp to a plantation near the bank of Minette Bay, little more than a mile from the fort but still close enough to the Tensaw for him to communicate with friends above the line. They lived off the contents of the planter's storehouse and barn until the boatload of provisions from the legislature finally arrived.[11] Kemper had defiantly told St. Francisville to send the boat past Fort Stoddert and "let them stop it if they dare," but its pilot prudently took a circuitous route from New Orleans that bypassed the fort.[12] Then on December 3, a man named Henry de la Francia appeared in camp to see Kemper. He said he wanted to sell three hundred muskets with bayonets, twenty kegs of powder, a ton of musket balls, another ton of lead bars, and a barrel of musket flints that were all on a nearby oyster boat. Francia said Perez had turned the munitions over to him to take to Pensacola, but Francia saw a chance to profit personally by selling his cargo to Reuben. It was a bonanza for Kemper, and two days later he negotiated a purchase for $11,850, due in one year at 10 percent interest. Having no cash, Kemper gave Francia his personal security for the debt, and Francia arranged for secret turnover of the munitions.[13] Reuben already had four small cannon and two horse artillery guns, so this addition to his arsenal left him needing only men for the muskets.[14]

It all seemed to be going well, if slowly, but then it began to turn. "Mobilians" living in the district affirmed that they wanted to become American citizens but did not want to be conquered by the St. Francisville government, or by what one of them called "any banditti whom they may excite to do the business for them." Kemper had predicted that enough people below the line would enlist for their expedition to succeed, but in fact few came forward, the rest either still loyal to or afraid of Spain, and almost all of the volunteers were in fact from Mississippi.[15] Then weather and the boredom of waiting for action began to tell on the men. They had no tents, and cold daily rains dampened spirits and left nerves raw. Some men began to leave, and an argument between Dr. Holmes and another physician volunteer escalated into a fight that sent the latter back above the line with a pistol ball in his chest, only to be arrested by Toulmin.[16] Kennedy's speeches failed to sustain morale, and Kemper allowed too liberal access to the whiskey barrel.[17] Kennedy got a furlough on December 6 to return to the United States to seek more assistance, but when he stopped in Fort

Stoddert, Toulmin arrested him for violation of the military expedition statutes, dismissing Kennedy's claim that his move to the camp was a change of residence, which made him a citizen of West Florida and not subject to American law.[18] The judge would stop Kemper if he had to arrest his men one at a time.

Folch was striking back too. The weather foiled two efforts to disperse Kemper's camp.[19] Still, Reuben concluded that he was too exposed on Minette Bay. He was down to just twenty-four men and the mounted company, and on December 7 he ordered Major Hargraves to put the unmounted men on the boat and row them across Mobile Bay to the Mobile River, to make camp on the west bank a dozen miles upstream at Saw Mill Creek. Kemper planned to lead the mounted men above the line to cross the Tombigbee at Abram Hollinger's Ferry, less than two miles from Fort Stoddert, then ride down to join Hargraves.[20] The whole movement would take several days, and Hargraves would almost certainly reach Saw Mill Creek first.

Had Kemper known of Toulmin's arrest of Kennedy he might not have passed so close to Fort Stoddert, since he had refused earlier requests that he and Kennedy come to the fort. When Toulmin learned on December 8 that the mounted party had reached Hollinger's Ferry, he got Sparks to send a message asking Reuben to come to the fort to see Folch's letters suggesting a handover of Mobile by the end of the month.[21] The lure worked, and on Sunday evening, December 9, Kemper rode to the fort along with Caller, who fought boredom by staying drunk. Toulmin immediately served warrants on both of them. After the formalities of arrest, Toulmin released Kemper and Caller to Sparks, who took them to his home. Kemper repeated the old story that five hundred or more were on their way from Baton Rouge, but he also knew of Folch's offer, and he asked Sparks to send a messenger to Folch requesting that he take no offensive action pending Madison's response. Of course, Kemper hoped to stall Folch until Kirkland arrived.

Toulmin told Sparks that allowing Kemper to communicate through an American officer would be to acknowledge him as representing a legitimate sovereignty and amount to recognition of West Florida independence. If Kirkland arrived and settled the issue with Folch on his own, Toulmin could do nothing about that, but at least he could keep the United States out of it. The judge dismissed Kemper's suggestion as nothing but an "artful device to obtain some colour of an acknowledgment of the new government."[22] When Sparks sent letters from Kemper to Folch and Innerarity all the same, Toulmin stopped the courier and concluded that the colonel was credulous where Kemper was concerned, and politically out of his depth.[23]

Over the next three days Toulmin questioned Kemper and others. The once-boastful Caller now tried cravenly to obscure his involvement by saying he went below the line only as an observer. "As to Kemper nothing can be clearer," the judge wrote Madison, "tho' he feels perfectly at ease under the idea that he is a citizen of Florida." Reuben maintained that the men who volunteered to join him came of their own volition, and that his enterprise was laudable and honorable. He even claimed disingenuously that he had no expedition in mind when he arrived in late October, but merely chanced to associate around Fort Stoddert with men who later looked to him for leadership when he went below the line. Toulmin had Buford under arrest by this time, as well as another captain who threatened the judge with death but then escaped.[24]

During the second day of testimony, appalling news arrived. Hargraves and the two dozen men at Saw Mill Creek had been attacked. They had made camp there on the evening of December 8, expecting to be joined in a day or so by Kemper's mounted party and men from Pascagoula under Duprée.[25] With little to do while waiting, and a lot of whiskey and more than one fiddler, they commenced what Dr. Holmes called "a frolic." If they also continued their habit of foraging from the storehouses of men who refused to join them, then it is no wonder that one such local went to tell Folch of their presence and of how easily they could be taken by surprise.[26] At about sundown on December 9 Folch put eighty *soldados* and another twenty Mobile militia in pirogues and sent them up the Mobile. With a full moon to light their journey, they covered the twelve miles to the Saw Mill Creek vicinity and got there well before midnight. At about eleven o'clock they approached Hargraves's camp, got past the sentinels if any were posted, and followed the sound of fiddles and singing for the last few hundred yards.

With no warning they opened fire and kept firing. Completely surprised, the Americans ran in all directions. Four fell dead on the spot, and another three went down with wounds. Hargraves tried to rally a defense, killing two Spaniards and wounding two others, but the attackers easily forced their surrender. Perhaps ten men got away. The second "battle" in the life of West Florida lasted no longer than the first. The Spaniards burned one building and took the slaves of the poor planter whose property Hargraves used as a campground, then loaded their prisoners in their own boat along with all their military supplies and returned to Mobile. Folch intended to launch an attack the next day at Minette Bay, not yet knowing that Kemper and the mounted men had left.[27]

Some of the fugitives made their way to join Duprée, while the rest ran above the line, where Toulmin promptly issued arrest warrants.[28] Meanwhile Toulmin continued the hearings of Kemper, Kennedy, and others already under arrest. Having released Kennedy on bail pending trial, he knew he would have to do the same with the rest, but he worried that if Kirkland's column should arrive after Kemper was freed, the reinforced enterprise might go ahead.[29] On December 13 as Kemper finished giving testimony, word reached Fort Stoddert that instead of marching to join Kemper, Duprée had been plundering the settlement at the mouth of the Pascagoula. There were also stories of rival groups within Duprée's command fighting among themselves over booty.[30]

The news must have disheartened Kemper. Duprée was not coming, Hargraves's command was erased, and his own mounted contingent was leaderless and disintegrating below the line. If he retained any lingering hope for his expedition after Caller's brother James arrived and bailed out both of them that afternoon, it should have vanished that evening. James Caller brought with him a dispatch from Governor Holmes and copies of Madison's proclamation, the first news anyone in Fort Stoddert had had of the takeover of West Florida. Toulmin saw Reuben immediately after the proclamation arrived and thought he looked mortified at the news.[31] Yet, if anything, the situation seemed even more charged to take Mobile. Caller also brought Holmes's order for Sparks to call up Caller's Sixth Regiment if he needed militia.[32] Sparks immediately fell under this Caller's influence just as he had Kemper's, and Caller persuaded him to issue the call, making no effort to conceal his indignation at Toulmin's attempts to stop Kemper. They also learned that Skipwith was governor and that Claiborne was on his way to take over the four districts.

Toulmin worried all the more when he saw Caller, Sparks, and Kemper spend the next several days in almost constant confidential conversation. Caller gave Reuben a commission in the Mississippi militia, which he could do since Kemper was a resident of Pinckneyville. Toulmin felt alarmed at the open and undisguised patronage given to Kemper, for he remained as uncertain of Reuben's personal motives as ever, since he still claimed to be a citizen of West Florida and recommenced raising Mississippian volunteers for Kirkland's anticipated column. "As to Kemper himself," the judge wrote Madison, "whether he really expected to establish his extravagant pretensions or merely wished, by associating his men with the militia, to hold up the idea of a connection between him and the federal government, and to pave the way for his personal influence and for the advancement of his followers under the new order of things to be established by govr. Claiborne, I do not know." Toulmin even wondered if Kemper had schemed to establish West Florida's independence from the United States so he could hand it over to the British or the French. Reuben's promising every recruit 640 acres below the line confirmed Toulmin's belief that land hunger lay at the root of the revolution. As for Kemper, after this turn of his affairs, he taunted Toulmin that the white star of Florida would fly over the fort at Mobile before the Stars and Stripes did.[33]

The president's proclamation caused joy in Fort Stoddert generally. Mistaking Holmes's militia order for authority to call for Mobile's surrender, Sparks sent a demand to Folch the next morning; Folch refused it, and that rather pleased some. They might yet have an opportunity for a fight, a friend of Rhea's wrote the following day, "& the cowardly Dons deserve a little harassing for their base & infamous manour." Survivors' exaggerated stories of the Spaniards' butchering some and mistreating others in the attack on Hargraves generated cries for retribution, which were only amplified when reports from Mobile told of the prisoners' being starved and put in public stocks and left outside exposed to the weather. One of Kemper's lieutenants then in Fort Stoddert declared that "I hope we may be revenged."[34] More families in the Mobile area left for their own safety, fearing that "Kemper & Co." might attack them in vengeance for Hargraves's men.[35]

Kemper did send agents into the Tensaw and St. Stephens country seeking volunteers, and soon he had his new plans set. On the morning of December 17, unwilling to wait for the Mississippi militia, he left Fort Stoddert with a small company, and at the line he sent them on to join the remnant of his mounted command. He turned his own horse southwest for Pascagoula, hoping to find Duprée's men and have them in place to meet Kirkland's approach. Of course, the open question was if Kirkland would be coming, and when. The silence from St. Francisville exasperated Kemper. The night before he left, he complained to Rhea that he still had no knowledge of his leaders' intentions. Madison's proclamation may have opened the door for him to try for Mobile again, but it also muddied things, since he could not be sure of the terms on which West Florida was annexed and whether his commission and instructions remained valid. He needed to know if he should continue to move on Mobile. The fact that he wrote to Rhea showed how much in the dark he was, for Rhea's presidency of the convention had ended eight weeks earlier. Rhea was not even on the standing committee, and since the new legislature had already assembled, he was just the senator for the Feliciana District. Kemper should have been writing to Governor Skipwith.[36] Still, he left town that morning encouraged by men who looked forward to his taking Mobile before the United States did so he could welcome American forces with "open arms & joining the one Star with the many."[37]

What no one there knew was that Reuben Kemper was trying to communicate with a government that no longer existed. Two weeks earlier, on December 3, Skipwith had issued a general address rehearsing the old litany of grievances with Spain and congratulating the people on breaking the chains that Spain had fastened upon them. Prosperity and good government lay just ahead, along with a few sacrifices, meaning the taking of Mobile and Pensacola. Still, Spain could pose no great force against them, therefore "let it not be said, that our numbers are too few, and our physical force too inconsiderable."[38]

Skipwith tried to get on with the everyday business of government, such as filling his vacancy on the supreme court and commissioning privateers out of New Orleans to prey on Spanish shipping.[39] However, the seemingly endless preparations to get Kirkland's militia on the road absorbed most of his attention. Hicky had hoped the expedition might be ready to move by December 5, but the work of outfitting and preparing went on with agonizing slowness. To the supplies already forwarded to St. Francisville were added tents and tools and haversacks for up to a thousand men.[40] Details from the existing companies in Baton Rouge were sent first, to act as a nucleus for the new army, then, on December 4, Skipwith ordered all but twenty-five militiamen at Baton Rouge to rendezvous with Kirkland on Redwood Creek a dozen miles east of St. Francisville by December 8; they were to take any clothing they needed from civilians in the town.[41]

One of the volunteers on the Redwood Creek passed the time by composing a marching song to use should they ever leave their staging area. He called it "Vive La":

> *Vive la* the new convention.
> *Vive la* the rights of man.
> *Vive la* West Floriday.
> The new convention is the plan.

It boasted of Thomas driving the Spaniards from the fort and of the St. Helena campaign against Jones and Brown, predicting that, free from king and tyranny, West Florida should be respected among the nations. Then it spoke of the immediate future:

> We can drink and not get drunk.
> We can fight and not be slain.
> We can go to Pensacola
> And can be welcomed back again.[42]

But instead of taking the road for Mobile and Pensacola, the "West Floriday" army just waited on the Redwood.

In addition to some routine business, the legislature busied itself with the Mobile expedition. The two houses' first legislation was a December 3 authorization for the campaign, and otherwise they passed but little legislation not directly related to the expedition. Tempers began to flare at the glacial pace of getting Kirkland launched, and some resented the mundane business tying them to their chairs when they would rather have been in the field. There were indecorous eruptions, and more than one delegate challenged another, but intermediaries managed to settle all difficulties without resorting to the dueling field. Still, when the house of representatives voted to reconvene at Baton Rouge after its adjournment, John H. Johnson, so much at the heart of everything since the early meetings at his plantation, resigned in a huff over the loss of value his St. Francisville property would suffer by the legislature's move.[43]

Then the shocking news hit. Madison's proclamation had remained a well-kept secret, but two days before Claiborne arrived in Natchez, on December 1, rumor said he was coming to take control of the territory west of the Perdido.[44] Claiborne immediately had a local printer make dozens of copies of Madison's proclamation, and he met with Governor Holmes and planned a careful and effective takeover. Claiborne would leave Natchez for Point Coupée on December 4, followed the next day by several hundred soldiers on gunboats, while Holmes would ride across the line to St. Francisville to meet with the legislature in session, capitalizing on the goodwill he enjoyed there. Then Claiborne would join him and determine whether to go on to Baton Rouge or, if they anticipated resistance, call on the militia. Meanwhile Commodore John Shaw was to leave Natchez the morning of December 6 with more gunboats, and two days later Colonel Zebulon Pike and nine hundred men were to march from Mississippi to West Florida.[45] Claiborne resolved to avoid bloodshed if possible, but he and Holmes realized that some, especially the speculating element, would resent losing their newfound independence.[46] The day before he left Claiborne sent a hundred copies of the proclamation to Fort Stoddert, and Holmes sent Colonel Caller his orders to mobilize the militia.[47]

The governors decided not to send advance word to Skipwith of their coming or their mission, for treating him as anything other than a private citizen risked embarrassing complications. Still, Claiborne wanted to avoid any chance of a clash. He knew many of the members of the old convention wanted the United States to take over, but he believed that some would acquiesce only if the United States assumed West Florida's debts and if the Morales grants to speculators were recognized. He resolved not to make terms, however. Madison had promised to protect their liberty, property, and religion, Claiborne declared on December 2, and that was all they could reasonably desire.[48] Two days later he left Natchez with a small escort, and the following day people saw detachments of artillery and the U.S. Second Infantry boarding transports and gunboats at Natchez and assumed they were going to occupy West Florida. No one anticipated resistance. Judge Rodney had recently found the sentiment below the line more in favor of Madison's taking possession of West Florida than the citizens' organizing a revolution at their own risk, and he believed that Claiborne's coming would be universally popular.[49] Some worried about the garrison at Baton Rouge, for rumor said many men there were deserters who might fight rather than surrender unless granted immunity; Rodney wondered whether the deserters would be made hostages if Skipwith's government resisted Claiborne.[50]

Claiborne's mission was not going to make Governor Skipwith happy. He had no inkling of it until December 5, when he heard reports of men riding through Feliciana distributing the proclamation. Claiborne had sent planter William King to Baton Rouge with copies and orders to talk with leading citizens; after that he was to cross the river to Wykoff's house and then come with Wykoff to meet Claiborne at Point Coupée.[51] The governor sent another agent, Audley L. Osborn, to St. Francisville with more copies and instructions to call on the legislature and sound their sentiments. Both were to determine if Claiborne was likely to encounter any opposition and to learn the strength and position of West Florida's militia as well as the current state of Kemper's expedition. Claiborne's agents were to say only that he had left Natchez and would be in Baton Rouge shortly and that he brought no militia with him, though he had soldiers close at hand if needed. They were to say that the proclamation contained all the information needed as to the United States' intentions.[52] Claiborne did not yet know the content of Skipwith's recent addresses to the legislature and the people, hence he could not guess if the governor was likely to resist, but before leaving Fort Adams he wrote Secretary Smith that he did not believe that force would be necessary. All the same, his having the means at hand to deal with resistance might ensure a peaceful takeover.[53]

Claiborne's agents met a mixed reception at their destinations. When King walked into Baton Rouge he posted a few copies of the proclamation and managed to read it to a group of citizens, but then civil officials arrested him, suspecting he was an agent sent by Folch to lull the people into relaxing their preparations against Mobile. When the commandant ordered King to the fort's jail, he pointed to the white-star flag flying overhead and said it would take a good deal of blood to pull it down.[54] In St. Francisville, Holmes actually arrived before Osborn; he rode into town at noon on December 5 and dismounted in front of the St. Francisville Hotel, where he found several of the legislators talking during a midday recess. Word of the proclamation had already spread, and some said they felt slighted at not having been officially informed. Holmes said he came to prevent unpleasantness. They were American citizens now and nothing could injure them more than resistance. Since West Florida had always belonged to the United States, Madison could not treat them as an independent sovereignty, nor could he countenance any stipulations they might make, as they had not the power to make them.

The legislators raised concerns over land claims and their public debt, and Holmes tried to address these, also assuring them that American deserters would probably be pardoned, unaware that Madison had issued such a pardon exactly one month earlier.[55] Some of the delegates protested that the proclamation seemed to leave the door open to negotiations with Spain that might see West Florida reverted to that nation in exchange for some other territory; that would be fatal to them as rebels, but Holmes assured them the United States would never surrender the province. He spent almost the whole day talking with the legislators, addressing their questions and objections, and in the main they appeared to be mollified. A man passing through town saw that most people welcomed the takeover and were ready to take a new oath of allegiance.

There remained one very important citizen to hear from. One of the legislators said Holmes should see Governor Skipwith, but Holmes replied that he recognized no such governor.[56] Late that afternoon Skipwith sent a message asking Holmes to call. Holmes politely declined, stating that West Florida officials had no lawful standing, although he would be happy to speak with him as a private citizen. Soon enough Skipwith called at Holmes's hotel, but the conversation was tense and inconclusive. Skipwith protested that Madison's conduct confounded him.[57] Holmes treated him with kindness and consideration but still advised full compliance with Claiborne's instructions, adding that Claiborne was not authorized to accept stipulations.[58] Skipwith insisted that he had always wanted American annexation, but he objected to the manner of it. Still, he hinted that he might accept an unconditional turnover, and at that he left. That evening, a dragoon company came in from the Redwood Creek rendezvous; Holmes spoke with them and believed he won them over, a good start at quashing the Mobile expedition.[59]

Swallowing his anger after talking with Holmes, Skipwith composed a letter to Madison that evening before he left for Baton Rouge. Writing as if he had not seen Claiborne or the proclamation, he said he had always expected West Florida to join the United States. His people still wanted a union consistent with their honor and interests and would agree to anything reasonable, whether it be territorial status, conjoining to another territory such as Orleans, or statehood. However, he could not agree that they already belonged to the Union. Rather, he sought a loan to finance the Mobile and Pensacola campaigns, promising success with Madison's help, and then asked the president to appoint local commissioners to meet with the legislature to negotiate how West Florida should enter the Union.[60] It was clearly a tactic to keep Claiborne from completing his mission. That done, Skipwith and several legislators left for Baton Rouge, whether to organize a turnover or resistance none could say.[61]

The next day the legislature saw Skipwith's letter and a statement of what he knew of William King's activities.[62] The reaction was an angry response framed as a reply to Skipwith's recent November 29 address to the assembly. They saw West Florida about to be swallowed by the overwhelming power of "a neighbouring Nation on whose professions of regard for justice and the laws of Nations, we had relied with implicit confidence." They protested Madison's calling on them to consider themselves subjects of the Orleans Territory until their statesmen and foreign ministers decided to whom they belonged. Their cause was too glorious to be disgraced by fear or submission, and an unconditional surrender was intolerable. They would accept an honorable union with Orleans, but only if done by their constitution, not Madison's. They approved Skipwith's letter, and if Madison tried to take West Florida without guaranteeing their rights or left them liable to be negotiated back to Spain, they pledged themselves ready to make "a proper resistance to the usurpation of a Nation who in violating every principle of justice and of their own Constitution, as well as of the natural ties of consanguinity which unite us with them, compel us to consider them as we do the rest of Mankind enemies in war in peace friends." It was less a declaration of resistance than a statement of hurt pride covering some real concerns. Eleven members of the legislature signed; the rest simply did not come to the session.[63]

By this time Holmes had left for Point Coupée, and soon afterward Osborn arrived and met with several of the members; he must have found them calmed a bit, for he concluded that there would be no opposition, except perhaps for Skipwith, Philemon Thomas, and a few lesser officers. However, there could be resistance in Baton Rouge. At the moment, the garrison in the fort would be no match for the force coming downriver, but another seventy men and more artillery would be there in a day or so, and this very day Osborn learned that orders had gone out to the Mobile column to return to Baton Rouge.[64] That would add another six hundred infantry and cavalry, giving West Florida nearly eight hundred men and more than thirty working cannon in the fort, which could make a very creditable resistance indeed. For those hesitant about Claiborne's taking over, Osborn found the great sticking point to be the same as it was for Skipwith. The people of West Florida wanted to be treated as citizens of an independent nation and to negotiate the terms of their annexation before they submitted.[65]

As soon as they finished meeting with Osborn, the senate members passed a resolution calling on the governor to send an agent to determine Claiborne's instructions and authority. Then both houses immediately adjourned, planning to reconvene in Baton Rouge two days later.[66] With the order recalling the Mobile column, it looked like a concentration of civil and military forces gathering for a last stand.[67] When he received the resolution, Skipwith appointed the recently resigned John H. Johnson to meet with Claiborne and told him to propose that Claiborne delay taking possession until Madison replied to Skipwith, which of course would take nearly two months if the president responded at all.[68]

Holmes and Claiborne met again the following morning, December 7, at Point Coupée. Johnson came with Holmes; when he met Claiborne, he said that he personally welcomed Madison's proclamation, but then he presented a letter from Skipwith demanding explanations for the legislature. Claiborne explained that Skipwith was not the governor of a legitimate state, and therefore he could not receive official correspondence from him. However, Claiborne told Johnson to inform his people that he entertained only friendly feelings toward them. Johnson's response was a verbal message from Skipwith and not what Claiborne had hoped to hear. The governor had retired to the fort at Baton Rouge, and he and the assembly would sooner fight and die under the star of Florida than submit. Before he would surrender the country unconditionally, he would "surround the Flag Staff and die in its defense."[69] When asked, Johnson repeated what he had said but then added that he himself was devoted to the United States. He urged Claiborne to come to St. Francisville immediately, promising that the two armed companies and many citizens there were eager to recognize him as governor. Johnson's statement, combined with Osborn's report, convinced Claiborne to go at once. Even if Skipwith and some legislators intended to resist, a peaceful takeover of Feliciana would isolate and morally weaken any opposition in Baton Rouge.[70]

They rowed across the river to Bayou Sara, where the promised citizens and militia escorted them to the village. When Claiborne reached the center of town he saw the lone star flying and asked the militia to form a square around the flagstaff. He walked to the center and had a local man read Madison's proclamation. Then he told those assembled that he came as the president's emissary, bringing protection of their rights of person and property and religion, and that he proudly assumed their governorship. Claiborne ordered the white-star flag brought down and did not comment as militia and citizens alike cheered its last descent. Then he turned over a Stars and Stripes he had brought with him and had it run up the staff to similar cheers.[71]

Frederick Kimball watched the ceremony, and that evening wrote to a friend that "the american colours is flying in St Francisville," and the people of the village seemed satisfied except for a few aristocrats who held appointments under the old regime and feared they might not fare well under the new one. He could not help feeling a bit wistful.

"We had all things going on bravely a governor and Senate and house of Representatives and an army just marching for Mobeal," Kimball said with pride. He had expected an American takeover, and looking back on the recent disorder in the legislature, he concluded that it was fortunate that Claiborne had come or they might have disintegrated in confusion. He still half expected that angry confrontations in the legislature's last session might yet lead to duels.[72]

Claiborne spent the rest of the day at administrative tasks, setting up county offices and the like, and that evening the two governors agreed that Holmes should go to Baton Rouge the next day while Claiborne would wait there until the gunboats and soldiers arrived and then go downriver with them.[73] He did not know what to expect when he arrived. He hoped to dissuade Skipwith from any rash or imprudent actions and believed the turnover could be accomplished peacefully, but if there was a sign of resistance, he resolved to order his troops to take the fort.[74]

Holmes left in the morning with some of the Bayou Sara cavalry as an escort. On the road he learned of King's arrest and that some soldiers in the fort said they would not surrender without conditions, which he guessed meant they were deserters. Holmes slowed his travel to give time for anxieties to cool, and he did not approach the town until the following day, December 9. He sent two men ahead to the fort to see if he would be allowed to approach unmolested; when they did not return he moved to within two hundred yards of the fort, where he heard an order to halt. Finally a signal came that he and his escort could enter the town, where he found the legislature in session once more and in a state of considerable confusion.[75] They had reconvened the day before in joint session at Skipwith's request, adopted two resolutions, and then adjourned. The first resolution ordered the immediate parole of Delassus and Shepherd Brown. Skipwith did not want Claiborne to take them, probably because Madison's view meant that West Florida had never had the lawful right to hold them, making their captors liable for civil or criminal action.

The second resolution reaffirmed the sovereignty of West Florida and announced the threat of invasion by "a neighboring power," requesting the governor to ready the armed forces for defense pending a fuller understanding of Claiborne's purposes. The next day the two houses convened once more and did all but nothing, the sole work of the senate being passage of an act compensating their secretary and doorkeeper for paper and firewood used during the recent session and for the work of one of their slaves in making their fires. They did not bother to adjourn officially or set a time to reconvene. They knew they would never meet again.[76]

For Skipwith now, almost everything was a final act. In his last official correspondence, he wrote to his naval agents in New Orleans to inform them that the government was suspending operation.[77] That evening he met again with Holmes, this time after more mature reflection. He would not resist, he said, but he could not speak for the soldiers in the fort, some of whom were desperately afraid.[78] He wrote another letter to Madison, once more protesting Claiborne's conduct and accusing him of trying to make the people of West Florida distrust their own government. The "patriot Americans of this Country were in a state of guard & defiance, or both the Tomahawk and dagger, from the number of Indians, Slaves, & Assassins among & around us, might have been raised against our bosoms," he said. All the same he acknowledged that he had taken the governorship only to promote peace and to see West Florida go to the United States, he hoped as part of the Orleans Territory.[79]

The next morning Skipwith came to Holmes's room and asked him to walk to the fort, where Holmes announced that although he had no authority to negotiate anything, he believed that deserters would be pardoned if they offered no resistance now. Colonel Ballinger found that acceptable and agreed to hand over the fort to Claiborne and his U.S. troops when they arrived. Holmes was just leaving the fort when word came to town that the gunboats had been sighted two miles upriver. Immediately he rode to the scene to find the soldiers coming ashore, and he told Claiborne the good news.[80]

Back in Natchez some had feared that if Claiborne presented himself at Baton Rouge, he might be arrested by Skipwith's forces, who spoke as if determined to defend their independence.[81] Even now a rumor headed east that Holmes had actually been arrested.[82] Claiborne's party approached cautiously but did not enter the town, and soon Hicky came out bearing a letter from Skipwith. Concealing his anger and humiliation, Skipwith expressed pleasure that they were all to be American citizens, even if the circumstances did not accord with his own sense of honor or justice. Satisfied that surrendering West Florida to the United States was the only means by which the latter could have full and lawful title to the former, and still maintaining the pretense that there was a genuine issue of sovereignty involved, he announced his willingness to turn over the territory. Still, he could not resist adding that his act was "produced by your entering among us with an armed force, which the people of this Country are unable to resist." He insisted that Claiborne show no disrespect to their flag. Because he could never give an order that might result in shedding a drop of American blood, he had instructed the garrison not to disgrace their flag by resisting. If Claiborne insisted that it come down, the garrison would retire without resistance. Still concerned about the deserters, he asked for their safety.[83]

Claiborne requested that the fort be evacuated at two thirty that afternoon and that the soldiers march out and stack their arms. He agreed that when they struck their flag, they might pay it suitable honors, and he promised not to molest deserters. Claiborne realized that much of the opposition had been aroused by the proclamation itself; his introducing it via agents, rather than by sending it to Skipwith and the legislature first, did not accord respect to their government. He sensed the frustration at the sudden end of the Mobile expedition and the dashed hopes for land after conquest. Claiborne even felt sympathetic toward Skipwith, and he forgave him his recent intemperate language.[84]

Skipwith received Claiborne's reply and went to some of the leading members of the adjourned legislature and presented it to them. They agreed that Claiborne had met most of their immediate concerns and that there was no alternative, but still and to the last they observed the parliamentary niceties and consented to allow the U.S. troops to occupy the fort and all territory in their hands. At the appointed hour the troops marched out of the fort with drums beating and colors flying. They paid one last salute to the white-star flag, lowered it, laid down their arms, and disbanded.[85] With that, the seventy-nine-day republic quietly expired.

17

The Whole of the Mississippi
Is Now American

REUBEN KEMPER was neither a thug nor a murderer, and by the standards of the frontier he was a humane and honorable man. The prevailing rumors that he wanted vengeance for the attack on Hargraves surely had some truth. His implacable resentment and visceral loathing for Spaniards were — or soon would be — legendary. However, at that moment, if Kemper wanted to murder anyone it was likely one or all of the leaders of the convention for leaving him in the dark.

Reuben had not gone on to meet Duprée after all when he left Fort Stoddert on December 17. Instead he stayed close by, hoping to hear something from St. Francisville, Baton Rouge, or Kirkland and the Mobile column. He was still waiting three days later, and by then the "Mobile Regiment," as he called it, numbered close to a hundred and fifty men and officers, with Kennedy back in command as colonel.[1] Reuben, Kennedy, and the Callers took out their frustration by haranguing the men about Toulmin's villainy, and many of the men signed a memorial to Congress petitioning for the judge's impeachment.[2] On December 20 Kemper returned to Fort Stoddert to check for dispatches, and when he found none he exploded. "God knows the cause," he wrote Rhea that afternoon. "I should believe that a confidential agent was intitled to some respect but not a word has been Received by me and I am left altogether in the dark." The neglect was unpardonable.[3] Part of the reason for the silence was that one of his letters miscarried when a courier sent to Rhea fell into Folch's hands and was soon on his way to join Hargraves in prison, but of course the main reason was that Kemper's government had been defunct for almost two weeks.[4]

Reuben spent the night with Sparks, an amiable old officer who Kemper's men thought was sympathetic to their views.[5] But now Sparks was worried. He expected that Reuben would drop his own plans upon learning that the United States had claimed Mobile and everything east to the Perdido, but when Kemper kept looking for orders from Skipwith or the legislature, Sparks suspected that he pursued a personal agendum beyond patriotic service to the government of West Florida. When Kemper voiced his frustration at receiving no orders but nonetheless rode out the next morning to rejoin his company, Sparks gave in to the circulating rumors of a vengeance raid, concluding that Reuben's object was "to *commit depredations on the Inhabitants,* and probably *deluge it in blood,* as a revenge."[6]

Tired of waiting for the militia, Reuben left early on December 21 with thirty or more mounted men, determined, as Toulmin believed, to try his luck with a few men of his own. Sparks mistook Kemper's intentions, but after nightfall someone told Toulmin that Reuben intended to ride on Mobile the next evening to capture the garrison's commandant at an outpost some distance from the fort. With the hostage, Kemper supposedly expected to force the fort to surrender, a repeat of his brothers' scheme to use a hostage Grand-Pré to force the surrender of the fort at Baton Rouge. Toulmin immediately took the story to Sparks and Gaines. Sparks was doubtful at first, saying that he still thought Kemper might have some U.S. sanction now that he was an officer in the Mississippi militia, but Toulmin dismissed that as a common trick much overplayed by then.[7] Sparks finally ordered Gaines to interpose fifty men between Kemper and Mobile. At the same time, hoping to avoid a confrontation and without Toulmin's knowledge, Sparks sent a message to Kemper alerting him to Gaines's mission and advising him to come back to Fort Stoddert rather than risk bloodshed. Sparks also instructed Gaines to ask again for the handover of Mobile, though he was not sure Folch would comply. At least Gaines might prevent violence by Kemper's Mobile regiment and perhaps avert an international incident.[8]

Reuben's position was far more precarious than even he realized, and it fully justified his frustration. He was still acting on general instructions from a government that no longer existed to commit a hostile act that the United States would condemn. Worse, if he attacked the Spaniards — and even if he did not — he might come into conflict with Gaines, putting him at war with two nations at once. As an American citizen and an officer in the Mississippi militia, he could be guilty of insurrection, while as a citizen and an officer of a defunct government, he could be regarded as a foreign invader by both the United States and Spain. At this moment he was virtually all that remained of the government of West Florida. He knew of Madison's proclamation, but as yet he knew nothing of the takeover at Baton Rouge, the demise of governor and legislature, or the recall of Kirkland and the column supposedly coming to join him. Even now he could still start a small war.

On the evening of December 21 Sparks wrote to inform Claiborne of his orders to Gaines, and though it would take two weeks for Claiborne's reply to arrive, the governor approved, though he doubted that Gaines could intimidate Kemper into abandoning his plan. Still, Claiborne would send explicit orders directly to Gaines that he was to stop Kemper by force if he attempted to attack the Spaniards.[9] Of course, by the time Claiborne's letters reached their addressees, the situation on the scene would have resolved itself. In Mobile, Captain Perez knew that Kirkland's expedition had been canceled but little or nothing of Kemper's movements.[10] On the evening of December 22, when Reuben should have been moving on Mobile, he got Sparks's warning. Gaines had moved quickly and was already between Kemper and Mobile, meaning Reuben would have to go through him first to strike Perez. Kemper had never contemplated taking on U.S. Army regulars, and now there was no question of going any farther. Leaving his men where they were, he rode back to Fort Stoddert that night without being challenged. No sooner did he arrive than Judge Toulmin served yet another warrant for his arrest, probably on the same charges as before and now with the added infraction of his violating Madison's order that Spaniards in the territory were not to be molested.[11]

For the next several days Reuben could only watch from afar as the game was in Gaines's hands. He notified Perez that he had orders to occupy Mobile, and the Spaniard tried to delay by pleading he had not yet seen a verified copy of Madison's proclamation. Perez proposed that Gaines remain in place while he sought instructions from

Folch, but some of the Americans strayed anyhow, and on December 30 Perez warned that if he saw any more of them approaching his fort he would open fire. Fearful citizens began to evacuate once more, afraid that Kemper and Kennedy still might come to loot.[12] Poor Sparks scarcely knew what to do, for his reading of the proclamation and Claiborne's instructions left him uncertain of what was expected of him. Meanwhile, James Caller insisted that the Mississippi militia was almost ready to march. Finally, on December 24, Sparks formally called out Caller's regiment, and six days later Caller said he had three to four hundred militia and two pieces of artillery ready. Sparks decided that a show of force would settle the issue without bloodshed, and so on the same day of Perez's warning to Gaines, Sparks sent Gaines notice that on January 3, well after Folch's December 31 deadline for evacuation, he would join Gaines with the regiment and they would take town and fort.

When Sparks's message arrived in Gaines's camp a mile above Mobile, Toulmin happened to be there, having brought supplies to his son-in-law. The last thing the judge wanted was the hothead Caller and his undisciplined militia plundering the town, for only about fifty of the men coming were experienced regulars who could be depended upon. Toulmin knew that Colonel Cushing, with the gunboats and artillery, had arrived at the Petit Bois island just twenty miles from the entrance to Mobile Bay. At once he hired a boat, and he sailed all day on December 31 to find Cushing, who was shocked at Sparks's plans. Cushing immediately wrote a countermand to Sparks's order, and the next day, January 1, 1811, Toulmin took it back up the bay to Fort Stoddert.[13] He arrived very late and with barely twenty-four hours left before the campaign's launch. He gave Sparks a copy of Cushing's orders to assume command, the countermand, and an order for the militia to disband and go home. Caller exploded. He formed his regiment and used the forum to denounce Toulmin, who stepped forward to respond. Caller shouted him down, calling him "traitor, liar, dam—d saltwater son of a b——h, British emissary," and more.[14]

A few days before, on December 29, when Reuben learned that Gaines was coming to stop him, he ordered Kennedy to disband the Mobile regiment.[15] Rather unconvincingly, he argued, or had Kennedy argue, that with Mobile soon to be taken by Gaines they had accomplished their object, and now they all should be loyal to the United States.[16] As soon as he saw Caller's regiment disbanded, Toulmin began examining Kemper and Kennedy, and he continued to do so until January 4. When he offered them release on bail, both said they wanted to be questioned first, and the judge suspected that Kemper had lost heart after so long with no word from Skipwith, the legislature, or Kirkland. Toulmin believed that Reuben was glad of an excuse to give up.[17]

The day before the testimony concluded, Cushing reached Fort Stoddert, and perhaps just in time. Caller was attempting to stir up the residents against Toulmin, and when the judge released Kemper and Kennedy on bail, they joined in the outcry.[18] The three of them denounced the judge, burned him in effigy, and raised talk of calling for his impeachment and removal, meanwhile still threatening vengeance against the Spaniards for the deaths of Kemper's men.[19] Toulmin complained that the ringleaders and their friends were treating him harshly because he had slighted their patriotism and stopped them when they thought the prize was within their grasp. His supporters, however, believed that without Toulmin, Mobile would have suffered the same fate as the effigies. The brave judge "thus saved us once more from the firebrands of the Tombigbie."[20]

Two hundred miles west at Baton Rouge the firebrands never had a chance to cause concern. As soon as the lone star came down the staff in Baton Rouge, the Stars and Stripes was run up, and Claiborne assumed control.[21] Afterward, Skipwith and Claiborne met cordially, though the former complained that after he had sent Wykoff to incite the people to rise against Spain, Madison had refused to recognize their legitimacy. Skipwith accused the president and Claiborne of intentionally leading them on, just as Madison had gotten the people of West Florida to do his work for him. "Who can now doubt but that they were secretly urging us on to fight their battles placing us between them & the wall," he later grumbled, only to "strip us of our conquests & appropriate the fruits of our victories to themselves." The whole affair raised the theoretical possibility that Congress might treat the leaders of the rebellion and the republic as no better than

Burr and his filibusters, though Madison was not about to do that after acquiring the long-sought province without spilling an ounce of American blood or spending a penny from its treasury.[22]

With the ceremonies done, it was time for the inevitable paper-work, and Claiborne immediately dove into inventories of military stores and records of minor civil and militia appointments. He dealt with those concerned that new courts might review cases of assault and false imprisonment that had occurred before December 10. If that happened, officers feared liability for prosecution by everyone they had arrested, imprisoned, or took property from under the conven-tion. Claiborne concluded he had to avoid the legal mire and leave it to the legislature of whatever territory absorbed West Florida.[23] Mean-while, business correspondence still arrived for Skipwith and the de-funct legislature, particularly from the hapless naval agents in New Orleans.[24] When the agents had finally learned of the "unforeseen at-tack of our Natural friend or the impolitical attack of the Government of the U. St.," their credit dried up and they could not pay their ex-penses except with West Florida's state paper, which a few places still accepted in hopes of the United States' honoring it later.[25]

In fact, the business of closing down the old government lasted until December 13.[26] As late as Christmas Day, the proprietor of St. Francisville Hotel still accepted West Florida scrip in payment for meals provided while the legislature met.[27]

A week after the takeover everything appeared to be proceeding smoothly. Only then did Claiborne receive Secretary of State Smith's November 15 letter in response to the convention's October 10 memo-rial seeking annexation and setting out its terms. Recent events had made much of the content immaterial now, and as far as the conven-tion's desire to reserve the vacant lands for the benefit of current or future West Floridians, Smith said the territory's residents should not expect the United States to surrender for the West Floridians' exclu-sive benefit land that had been purchased from the common treas-ury for the benefit of all. The land would become a part of the public domain.[28]

Claiborne met with the man he called "the Ajax of the late Revolu-tion," Philemon Thomas, and found that he welcomed the American takeover. Leading citizens from the old convention and legislature expressed concern over their official debt, expecting that it would be assumed by Madison's government since that government was now the beneficiary. Claiborne found a small dissatisfied party — the speculators, the old Tories, and the adventurers — who preferred a state of revolution. "A more heterogeneous mass of good and evil was never before met with in the same extent of Territory," he concluded at the end of that first week. "Good men commenced & directed the late Revolution; but had not the Government of the United States interfered, bad men would very soon have acquired an ascendancy." The inevitable office seekers beset him as soon as he organized the four districts into an equal number of parishes (soon to be called the Florida Parishes) for amalgamation into the Orleans Territory. Claiborne understood local politics, and he predicted that every appointment he made would add twenty to the list of his enemies. Running West Florida as well as Orleans would be a huge task, and he hoped Congress would soon make it all one state.[29]

Claiborne also faced international concerns. Skipwith and the legislature had recalled the Mobile expedition, which had never gotten beyond the Amite in any case, so there was no risk of its causing any unfortunate incidents. Still, on December 20 he sent Folch the president's proclamation, advising him that the West Floridians' acting as an independent state in territory that belonged to the United States required the president to assert his authority. Madison now assumed control of all the territory from the Mississippi to the Perdido and advised that any Spanish military forces crossing that territory going to or from Pensacola would be committing an act of war.[30]

Skipwith's hurt pride reasserted itself. When Claiborne offered him an appointment as justice of the peace, he declined. "The sudden fall of the State of Florida has evidently affected him," Claiborne wrote on Christmas Eve, "and I suspect he still thinks, that the local authorities as established here by the people, ought to have been consulted."[31] Skipwith emphasized that assumption when he visited Claiborne the day after Christmas bringing his legislature's last defiant resolution disapproving of the conduct of the United States and calling it the act of a big power bullying a weak one. Claiborne warned Secretary Smith of the dissatisfied party; he still feared that if they tried to make trouble, the speculators would willingly join them, though he could not say whether a protest would be by political means or something more direct. Claiborne dismissed the rumors that Skipwith had been among the worst of the speculators. Nevertheless, he confessed that he feared the dissatisfaction there was more deeply rooted than he had at first supposed.[32] Skipwith reciprocated the governor's courtesy and generally approved his new appointments, but he could not keep from grumbling at Claiborne's descent upon them with what he characterized as "the rapidity of Wild Pidgeons." He also objected that Claiborne had not waited just two weeks to allow time for Kemper to take Mobile.[33]

Claiborne continued reorganizing the old districts into the new parishes of Feliciana, East Baton Rouge, St. Helena, and St. Tammany, leaving the residue of the occupied territory to be arranged into more parishes later. He appointed parish judges and amalgamated the local militia into the Orleans territorial forces.[34] The governor met occasionally with Delassus, who had risked crossing the river in hopes of retrieving his property, and Claiborne saw Delassus's mortification at the loss of the fort. The Frenchman feared Spain would charge him with criminal neglect or even treason and wanted to remain in American territory for his own safety.[35] If Claiborne felt sympathy for Delassus, he felt even more for the family of the slain Grand Pré. To honor the brave if impetuous young officer, Claiborne appointed his younger brother a midshipman and assigned him to one of the gunboats.[36]

It heartened Claiborne to find that the people in the area seemed to have little interest in the bogus Morales titles. Many in fact urged that the new regime not confirm them, and the governor learned that the real speculators, most of them in New Orleans, so feared the loss of their claims that they had sent messengers to Pensacola trying to get authorities there to backdate their titles to prior to the Louisiana Purchase so there could be no question of legitimacy.[37] The concern ran deeper than Claiborne at first realized. Within a fortnight of the takeover, inhabitants sent an entreaty to Mississippi's delegate in Congress stating their fear that because of speculation, the United States might annul all Spanish grants dated after the Louisiana Purchase. The citizens were not to blame if the United States had abandoned them to Spain for seven years, one protested. Spain disallowed the large speculators' claims, they said, and the Americans should do likewise, but the majority of people were small grant holders who paid for their surveys and, relying on the soundness of their claims, had settled and improved the land. Almost none of them held more than five thousand arpents, and most lived on much less.[38] Claiborne sympathized and in time so did Washington, which recognized all but the Morales grants.

All the while Claiborne faced Mobile and Folch. The governor did not like the man and expected him to rail loudly over the loss of the western districts. "I know well the man & shall be disappointed, if he does not hold a menacing and insulting language," he told Smith. The governor was eager to be given the authority to oust Folch from Mobile as well.[39] Two days after Christmas, Claiborne again suggested that Folch hand Mobile to Captain Gaines, though he doubted the Spaniard would yield peacefully. Still, Claiborne wanted no use of force should Folch refuse, especially since, stymied in their efforts to get Mobile, some men in Baton Rouge now made noises about wanting to mount an expedition to take Pensacola instead.[40] The recent rebellion in West Florida attracted too many of these adventurers, he told Smith on December 28, and he could not risk any action that might precipitate a popular mobilization he could not control.[41] In fact, when he took over at Baton Rouge, he heard a rumor that Kemper had already taken Mobile and Pensacola both.[42] Even then, orders were on their way from Washington to quash the Mobile expedition and make certain there were no more unfortunate incidents like the attack on Hargraves and his men.[43] Claiborne dealt carefully with people angered over Mobile. Old Kimball grumbled that the West Floridians had bested Spain in every contest, and if Madison had only waited a few more weeks they would have taken every Spanish post east of the Mississippi.[44] Skipwith never ceased complaining that "a few weeks more would have made us masters of the whole Country."[45]

As the year closed they all felt a bit exhausted from the excitement and uncertainty, the tension and frustration. Would they get Mobile without a fight or not? Would Pensacola follow? What would happen to West Florida? Would it be joined with Orleans or Mississippi, or would it be made an independent territory, or even a state? Some of the old convention nursed resentments, the speculators panicked, and many legitimate planters remained uneasy. The now-defunct legislature owed thousands in debts that the United States might not honor, Kemper and Kennedy sat in a jail cell, and Folch and Perez felt isolated and forgotten. It was a messy and complex end to such a short-lived republic, and about the only certainty was that the lone white star had set for good. In the East, Madison's critics decried the takeover. "Claiborne & his myrmidons are at hand," said a Baltimore editor, "and will not long leave them any choice, after they have been made instrumental in reducing their fellow subjects to what they call *independence*."[46]

The day after Christmas, Ballinger wrote to President Madison to assure him that the West Floridians' constitution gave sufficient evidence of their republicanism and love for the United States. "If the course pursued was not the least exceptionable that human intelligence might have conceived," he said, still "it was such as the spirit of the times our peculiar situation, and our views of the subject appeared to Warrant."[47] No one denied the worth of the prize. Once he felt Baton Rouge was secure from any public outbreak or resistance, Claiborne sent most of his soldiers back to Fort Adams. One of the returning officers felt no doubt over the importance of recent events. "Though we should proceed no farther, our acquisition must be considered as valuable — *the whole of the Mississippi is now American*," he told a friend. "The commerce of western America will no longer be subjected to the imposition of a petty military despot (the vassal of a foreign government) but will glide securely on to Orleans, the great emporium of the west."[48]

18

The Star of Florida Is Not Set

WHILE CLAIBORNE built a new administration, the debate began over where the province ought to fit on the political map. Should it be added to an existing territory, established as an independent territory, or even go directly to statehood? Judge Rodney opposed annexing it to Orleans, for that would give control of all the rivers in the region, from the Mississippi to the Perdido, to one territory, guaranteeing disproportionate prosperity to Orleans. He thought Congress should attach it to Mississippi and then divide that territory by a line running north from the middle of the Gulf coast to the Tennessee River, so that all three territories would have river outlets to the sea. That is basically what eventually happened, cleaving the Alabama Territory from Mississippi.[1]

Some in Mobile agreed. They had no natural connection with New Orleans, they argued. They shared no common interests and would be in commercial competition with each other soon. Their future tied them to the peoples and produce of Pascagoula and Pensacola. If the Mobile region should be annexed to Orleans—assuming the Spaniards left—"she will feel us as a tumor wasting her body and whose progress she will endeavor to retard." Mobile Bay and the rivers flowing into it would become commercial rivals to the great Mississippi, making it unjust for the commerce of this region to be subject to the self-interested legislation of government from New Orleans. Judge Toulmin agreed, but he thought that after recent events, the people of the Mobile area preferred the rule of New Orleans to the rule of a local administration that might be dominated by the ruffians of the Tombigbee, what some called "our neighbours the Bigbians."[2]

Claiborne had opposed Orleans statehood only a couple of years before, but by the dawn of 1811 he had changed his mind, and West Florida had influenced his thinking. He saw the divided opinion in his own territory. The American faction wanted West Florida because adding its ten thousand overwhelmingly American inhabitants weakened the existing French Creole majority; for these same reasons, those Creoles wanted West Florida joined with Mississippi.[3] Farther to the north and east, a controversy centered on slavery and its role in the balance of power between North and South began to drive the political debate. Opposition to making West Florida either a territory or a state on its own grew; people feared upsetting the current equity between slave and non-slave states.[4] Some did not want West Florida at all, regarding its seizure as a shabby sort of gratitude to Spain for its help during the Revolution. In an early rumble of what later came to be called the slave-power conspiracy, opponents charged that Madison acted "to fill the pockets of a few southern nabobs and land speculators — To feed ambition — and satiate avarice — To add another *Southern* state to the Union."[5]

Spain objected to Washington adding West Florida to anything. When Madison made his proclamation public in his annual message on December 5, the Spanish chargé d'affaires in Washington immediately voiced his government's outrage. If, as the president stated, he occupied the province subject to negotiation, then why not negotiate with Spain, which governed it, rather than with a band of desperados who were little better than speculators? Instead of aiding Spain in fighting for its liberty, Madison, he charged, with an act of open hostility had taken advantage of Europe's turmoil to rob Spain of its possession. Britain was allied with Spain against Napoleon, and he warned that England might come to the aid of its ally.[6]

Madison and his secretary of state Smith knew well the shifting diplomatic ground, and they tried to assure Britain of the basis on which they took West Florida. In recent years, relations with the mother country had steadily deteriorated, but Madison saw Britain's preoccupation with Napoleon and felt secure for the moment. England's support for Ferdinand served its own ends, and it gained nothing by involvement in a transatlantic conflict to support the colonial claims of a helpless ally. In peacetime it might have been different, but once again Madison read the situation correctly. Spain was too weak to hold on to West Florida, and Britain was too distracted to interfere. While the lions fought over a whole carcass, a clever fox could steal a leg.

On December 18 the U.S. Senate heard a bill to incorporate West Florida into Orleans, but heavy debate stalled it until January 3, when the president said that more immediate measures were required. He sent copies of Folch's letters to show that the Spaniards were willing to leave Mobile, and he proposed declaring that the United States would not allow bordering Spanish territory to go to another nation, making West Florida one of the seeds of the later Monroe Doctrine. He sought authorization to take the rest of the province. Congress quickly produced a secret declaration that the nation's safety could not allow the province to pass to another power, and they authorized the president to occupy the territory pending future negotiation, which begged the question of what negotiation might achieve when they had declared no other nation should have it. On January 15 they authorized the president to occupy West Florida and East Florida, using the armed forces as necessary, and appropriated a hundred thousand dollars for the purpose. They also empowered him to establish temporary government in the territory until Congress made other arrangements.[7]

Throughout, Madison carefully omitted informing Congress of his instructions to encourage an uprising, but Skipwith's grumbling had to have reached eastern ears. Two weeks after Congress passed its authorization, a man returned from Baton Rouge to reveal to the press what was common knowledge in West Florida. Madison's promise to cover Wykoff's expenses, he argued, meant that Wykoff was on government business and that the convention believed it had official sanction.[8] Federalist editors trumpeted this proof of "the perfidious arts by which the revolution in West Florida was produced, and the disgraceful and disgusting hypocrisy which has been employed in that transaction."[9]

While Congress debated the title to a province, Claiborne dealt with individual farms and plantations. Holders of Grand-Pré's grants that were made after the Louisiana Purchase were suddenly apprehensive about their titles, now that the United States was enforcing its assertion that West Florida was part of the Purchase. Did that mean that Spanish grants after 1803 were invalid? Madison eventually recognized the validity of all such titles, even though it compromised his own argument that Spain had no right to grant them. Almost as pressing was the question of the West Florida republic's debts, in part because the sudden demise of the government battered the local economy. The legislature had substantial contracts out when Claiborne took over, and it owed more than twenty thousand dollars for goods and loans to individuals in Baton Rouge alone.[10] Congress had said nothing so far about assuming debt, though it was always one of the conditions the Floridians proposed. For the time being, people holding accounts against West Florida had to wait.

Claiborne had to administer more than West Florida, and he returned to New Orleans after New Year's, but not without seeing behind him some bitter prejudice against those who had not supported the rebellion. Some convention men pressed him to heed their prejudices when making his appointments, and he made enemies when he refused.[11] From a distance Toulmin thought Claiborne's appointments wise, since his choices seemed to build confidence among the American population and curtail the excesses of the Baton Rouge party with their pretended federal authority.[12] Finding anyone qualified for appointment sometimes presented a problem. Claiborne created two new parishes, Biloxi and Pascagoula, covering the territory between the Pearl and Pascagoula, and he sent an agent to raise the flag, appoint local justices of the peace, and warn Sterling Duprée that the United States would prosecute all malefactors.[13] Claiborne's man tried to persuade Duprée to return plundered property, but when it came to appointing magistrates, the agent found the people living in primitive circumstances and not a single literate man of the three hundred and fifty at Pascagoula to make justice of the peace.[14]

In Baton Rouge some grumbled that Madison would have allowed Claiborne to use force against them but not to drive Folch from Mobile.[15] Then on January 6 Claiborne got word of 1,500 *soldados* and 50,000 pesos en route to Folch from Havana.[16] Aware that it might be only the latest in months of rumors, Claiborne nonetheless sent a reminder to Folch that the United States must now consider any such move hostile.[17] Claiborne might have been less concerned had he known that even then Folch was writing to Someruelos complaining that West Florida was more trouble than it was worth. Given that the United States would inevitably take it all someday, they should abandon it now.[18]

Without warning, a new crisis claimed everyone's attention and bought Folch more time. No one had expected the example of West Florida's rebellion to be followed by others in their midst, but on January 8, 1811, less than a month after the lone-star flag went down, a free mulatto named Charles Deslondes led a slave revolt on a plantation about sixty miles downriver from Baton Rouge. He began a march toward New Orleans, with runaways joining him on the road, and soon at least two hundred in his "army" were burning crops and houses. The next day they attacked a planter and killed his son with an ax. When the news reached New Orleans, Claiborne ordered the regulars to go out and cut off the rebels' route to the city.[19] Two days later, about eighty local planters found the rebels at Destrehan plantation, about twenty-five miles from the city, defiantly standing beneath their own improvised flag. The planters attacked and overran them, killing perhaps forty and driving the rest into nearby woods. Before long another fourteen or more were cornered and killed, and many more captured.[20] By the night of January 12 Deslondes and all the leaders were in custody, with only a few fugitives at large.[21]

"We must make a great example," said the father of the slain man.[22] At least twenty-nine captives were shot or hanged, and of the two hundred to five hundred slaves involved, ninety-nine lost their lives, with only two whites slain. It was the largest slave insurrection in American history. Claiborne blamed it on the baleful influence of free blacks who brought with them the poison of the San Domingue revolt, yet surely what happened at Baton Rouge fewer than three months earlier had played a role.[23] In case more slaves were at large, he kept up patrols in the Florida Parishes through the end of January.[24]

It took a few weeks for Baton Rouge to return to relative quiet, and yet with annoying regularity, anger and resentment flared. The nation's Federalist press accused Skipwith of being a leading speculator along with Daniel Clark, despite the fact that all Skipwith owned was Montesano and a large grant west of the Mississippi on which he actually owed twenty-five thousand dollars, and pummeled him for his French attachments after his years in Paris. Even now he was selling plots from his Baton Rouge land to meet expenses.[25] The Philadelphia papers charged that "the disorder and insubordination of the people during the *short reign* of gov. Skipwith [were] beyond belief," while "the poor man appears to have taken much to heart the instability of human greatness."[26] In fact, at that moment Skipwith was warning Washington to guard against the French Creoles in the region should Napoleon attempt to retake Orleans or Louisiana. "I would as soon suspect the Jews of raising the standard of rebellion at the approach of the Messiah," he said on January 14, "as that Frenchmen would oppose the Imperial Eagle, when resting on the shoulders of 20,000 French Grenadeers."[27] Elsewhere people objected to Claiborne's changing their administrative divisions from districts to parishes before they knew their fate among the territories, yet they chafed at the delay in allowing them to choose representatives for whatever territorial legislature might eventually embrace them.[28]

Then, on January 27, the coming of a hero distracted everyone's attention. Reuben Kemper rode into town that day met by cannon salutes and mobbed by people. "Never did I witness a more lively expression of joy," said a man in town. That evening people put on a grand illumination of torches and besieged Kemper with dinner invitations. He told them of the situation at Fort Stoddert and Mobile as of when he had left, a week before, and asserted his belief that despite Cushing's gunboats and Folch's promise to leave, the Spaniards would hold out until the Americans used force. If Claiborne ordered Cushing to attack, Reuben believed Folch would leave. Revealing one of his concerns thereafter, he said that reports from Mobile stated that Hargraves and his men were being well treated.[29]

Reuben was in the eastern press again now, part of the political ball bouncing between Madison and the Federalists, though Kemper seemed to have irritated everyone. Recollections of his name from five years earlier returned. "The outrages of the Kempers a few years ago are not forgotten," remarked a Philadelphia Federalist editor, going on to say that "that family has on the recent occasion displayed its accustomed contempt for the laws of society."[30] Administration papers called Reuben an opportunistic adventurer, a speculator, and a filibuster, and several editors condemned the whole family together as revolutionaries who wanted to take West Florida for themselves.[31]

Kemper would have been delighted for anyone to take the rest of West Florida. Before he left Fort Stoddert on January 20, he, Caller, and Kennedy held what Toulmin derisively called "high courts of impeachment," condemning the judge for interfering with Kemper as West Florida's agent, and Reuben's departure seemed to relieve the inhabitants of Mobile from fears of violence against themselves.[32] When Kemper left, Cushing had his flotilla anchored opposite Mobile and his infantry bivouacked nearby, but they made no move and waited for Folch to leave voluntarily.[33] However, the close connections between Kemper and Kennedy, and between leading citizens in Mississippi and within its militia, convinced the Spaniards that the United States countenanced the West Florida revolt. This only complicated negotiations with Folch, whose situation had changed dramatically by this time.[34] John McKee reached Washington on January 14 with Folch's December 2 letter about handing over Mobile at almost the same moment that Folch complained of the treachery and greed of Madison's proclamation, which he thought almost a declaration of war.[35]

McKee met several times with Madison and James Monroe, who was soon to replace Smith as secretary of state.[36] Madison quickly secured permission from Congress to accept the offer, and on January 26 he sent McKee and George Matthews back to Mobile authorized to receive the handover of Mobile and even of Florida east of the Perdido should Folch offer it. Madison agreed to assume all reasonable expenses of the evacuation and those owed by Spain to the inhabitants, and he guaranteed Spanish land-grant titles. If his agents saw any sign of a foreign power moving to occupy the territory before Folch handed it over, Cushing was to take Mobile immediately by force, and in any case Claiborne was to send soldiers to garrison the place.[37] Then on February 27 Folch shocked them all when he announced that the deal was off. The arrival of substantial cash and the promise of more assistance relieved his financial embarrassments. Meanwhile, Madison and Claiborne had stopped both Kemper and Kirkland, and thus the Americans themselves had removed the threat to his garrison. Now Folch's orders required him to hold what remained of West Florida to the last extremity.[38]

The old convention forces felt outraged. Madison had kept them from easily taking Mobile when they could have, and now Folch had outwitted Madison, and Mobile might hold out indefinitely or cost a bloody fight to seize. Stories spread of Sparks and Cushing's being arrested for disobedience, betokening ineptitude or cross-purposes.[39] Locals complained of confusion prevailing in the country, and this seemed to confirm it.[40] Philemon Thomas warned Claiborne of discontent over militia appointments, and reports said Duprée's men were still committing depredations on the Pascagoula.[41] Early in March Toulmin heard of men on the Pascagoula plotting to seize the rest of Spanish Florida if the United States did not, while a friend in Baton Rouge saw a lot of murmuring and discontent as some now regretted giving themselves to the United States. A few spoke of taking Mobile if Washington did not act.[42]

Meanwhile, Reuben Kemper went home to Pinckneyville after his welcome in St. Francisville and then traveled to Fort Adams and probably Natchez by late February when the first word of turmoil at Mobile reached him.[43] Whether he went on personal business — which he had neglected for more than four months now — or to contribute to the spirit of discontent, he was close to the scene as once more St. Francisville erupted in unrest.

Several grievances coalesced in the first week of March 1811. Madison's proclamation attached the area to the Orleans Territory, and the parishes had elected representatives to the territorial legislature in New Orleans, but then on February 20 Madison signed an enabling act for a new state that excluded West Florida from its boundaries. Would the representatives be accepted if they were not to be part of the state? That led to talk that they would be attached to Mississippi instead, a popular idea with men above the line, but virtually all in Feliciana saw their interests more aligned with Orleans.[44] The uncertainty bred resentment, and some wondered if they would be cast loose as a territory on their own. "If we do I am sure the Americans must wish to make a hell for us," Kimball groused, "as they are like to make us Devils."[45] Further outrage erupted in Baton Rouge when the military evicted some people from homes near the fort, maintaining that it was public land; the usual exaggeration swelled the evictions to one-third of the town's population.[46] The open question of the West Florida regime's debts left many embarrassed for money, and a further irritant was what a judge in St. Francisville saw as the rigorous manner in which American law had brought some people "to the Grindstone."[47] In particular, the sporting element in town objected to being prosecuted for running gambling and bawdy houses.[48] The grumbling grew louder, fueled no doubt at those establishments, and for several days unknown persons directed vandalism and pranks at the local authorities.

On Sunday morning, March 10, people in town awoke to see the old lone-star flag tied to the top of the sixty-foot flagpole. No one felt like climbing it to remove the banner, but as the day wore on, the more sober citizens feared that it would be seen as a sign of resistance to the United States. Some wanted to cut down the pole, but others argued that it was public property. An officer arrived from Baton Rouge and, calling the flag an insult to the nation, ordered it cut down immediately. When civic leaders approached the pole, others shouted again that it was public property, whereupon the officer, Hampton, declared that if the townspeople did not take down the flag, he would have soldiers do it on the morrow; at that, they cut down the staff.

Someone got away with the offending banner, and the following day at three o'clock in the afternoon, a few veterans of Thomas's army put the flag in a small coffin, marched it around the stump of the flagpole, and then lowered it into a grave to the accompaniment of three musket volleys. Someone even wrote an epitaph. Within minutes a new irritation arrived: word was received that the Orleans legislature had refused admission to the Florida Parishes' representatives. Passions swept through the village, and the next day men talked of taking their grievance directly to Madison.[49] Meanwhile during the night someone had opened the new grave and retrieved the flag, leaving the judge concerned that some of his fellow citizens "determined not to be at peace." How this matter would end, he could not conjecture.[50] Three days later a mob attacked the home of the judge who was prosecuting the gambling houses and broke all of his windows and doors.[51]

Claiborne attributed the behavior in St. Francisville to the citizens' fear of separation from Orleans, deploring it as the conduct of a few thoughtless young men. Raising the old West Florida flag could complicate his wish to see the parishes included with Orleans at statehood.[52] It was not a good time for Skipwith to make noise again.[53]

East Baton Rouge Parish elected him a delegate to the territorial legislature, which he declined, but in April he published the address he would have given if he had taken his seat, nothing but all his old complaints calculated to arouse feeling.[54] The fourth estate could not have chosen a more ill-timed moment for its inaugural appearance, but that same week James M. Bradford established the parish's first newspaper, the *Time-Piece*, in St. Francisville. His first editorials spoke of hopes for the future and lingering fears of being handed back to Spain. Washington would not do anything that did not respect the rights of West Floridians, Bradford declared, but if it did, he predicted that the people of the province would take arms and fight for their rights.[55]

Then the case of Hargraves and the other prisoners added to the discontent. When Kemper left Fort Stoddert on January 20, he thought it possible they would soon be released.[56] Instead Folch sent them to the Morro Castle prison in Havana.[57] On March 9 Claiborne sent a plea for clemency, pointing out that the captured officers and men in Baton Rouge had been released long since.[58] He hoped that if Havana freed the prisoners it would dampen the restiveness in Baton Rouge and on the Tombigbee. Should the Spaniards execute Hargraves and the others, it would be all but impossible to control his people.[59] Claiborne maintained his efforts for the next several weeks, but Someruelos would have none of it.[60] They were all guilty of promoting insurrection and would be dealt with accordingly.[61] For the moment Claiborne could do nothing more, but a letter from Hargraves reached him in late April saying that the prisoners were well treated. The governor feared they might be in the Morro for a long time.[62]

At least the controversy over the Florida delegates came to a good end. Baton Rouge chose Ballinger in Skipwith's place, and he, Philemon Thomas, Larry Moore, and two others presented their credentials in New Orleans. French Creole members, led by white-haired Jean Blanque and Joseph Ruffignac, who was noted for a bulbous nose almost as purple as the wine that made it, opposed their admission. The legislature allowed the delegation to make its case for inclusion; Thomas did most of the talking while Moore sat beside a fireplace. As debate between Thomas and Blanque became particularly heated and Ruffignac approached the fireplace, Moore grabbed a hot poker from the flames and called to Thomas, "You take that white-headed French scoundrel, and I'll take blue-nose." Moore drove Ruffignac back to the wall with the poker, yelling, "Take the question, General Thomas! We come here to be admitted, and d — me if we won't be, or this goes through your bread-basket, I tell you, Mr. Raphy Blue-nose!"[63]

Despite Moore's colorful outburst, in April the legislature reversed itself and seated the delegates.[64] Meanwhile, on March 5 Congress admitted Orleans Territory into the Union, though it was weeks before news reached Claiborne, who was anxious to call a convention to frame a constitution and apply for statehood. He felt uneasy that West Florida might be separated from Orleans and his fears were realized when he finally saw the legislation.[65] A few weeks later Bayou Sara proposed petitioning for West Florida to be reunited with Orleans as it sought statehood, though any action on that would wait months before a resolution.[66] Seeing West Florida omitted, Kimball grumbled that he had no idea what Washington intended for them "unless Congress intends to make Devils of us." He did not try to control his mounting disgust:

> I wish I had had command of the fort when Claiborne arrived and that I had known as much as I do now. I certainly would have Blown him out of the River and then he must take his own Course Either to Heaven or hell. Certain I am no such deception would of taken him to Heaven there fore to hell he must a gone.[67]

The troublemakers Kemper, Kennedy, and the Callers remained a problem. Toulmin expected to start their trials on March 4, but he doubted he could even get indictments from a sympathetic local jury despite having enough testimony from the principals to make a small book.[68] An indictment was even more unlikely with William Buford as foreman of the grand jury. On the appointed day Reuben Kemper did not appear, and Kennedy entered the courtroom armed, leading Toulmin to believe Kennedy came to assassinate him. Instead of indictments of Kemper, Kennedy, and others, the grand jury returned a bill of impeachment against Toulmin, drafted by Kennedy, and sent it to Congress.[69] James Caller began attacking Toulmin in mendacious letters to the eastern press, and soon Toulmin was writing published letters in his own defense.[70] Kennedy boldly applied to Claiborne for a judgeship, making him just one of what Innerarity told McKee was "a great scramble for the loaves and fishes that this poor sand-bank and quagmire may eventually produce."[71]

The aftermath of the Mobile expedition became even more tangled and messy. Cushing was ordered to appear at a court-martial growing out of the now ancient prosecution of General Wilkinson. When Cushing refused to leave his post he was arrested to face a court-martial of his own.[72] Then Sparks faced charges for his action in demanding Mobile's surrender without explicit orders.[73] Courts cleared both officers, but Caller rejoiced at the command vacuum created by their departure.[74] He even crowed to Governor Holmes over the lack of leadership at Fort Stoddert with the colonels gone and Toulmin perhaps about to face impeachment. Failing to read Holmes, Caller boasted that his militia was ready to move on Mobile if Holmes but issued the call.[75]

More sensitive than most to the confused atmosphere, Toulmin traveled to Baton Rouge at the beginning of May to read the sentiment among the people. He returned to Fort Stoddert rather heartened. For a start, the country was settling, so much so that he found good road all the way and a house to stay in every night but one. In the countryside he found the residents with a prevailing gladness at being a part of the United States, even if their status was as yet ill-defined. The people he met even discountenanced the failed Mobile expeditions and professed to know little of Kemper and respect him less.[76] Still, he saw resentment at being left out of Orleans Territory. The *Time-Piece* condemned Congress for making West Florida essentially a colony of a colony. Even Spain had never done that to them, and defiantly Bradford proclaimed that "The STAR of Florida is not set."[77] Bayou Sara considered sending a mission to Congress with their grievance, and as one planter complained, the conduct of the United States toward them thus far had been ill calculated to win their loyalty. First annexed to Orleans, they were left out when Congress allowed it to frame a territorial government, while the presence of the Spaniards at Mobile and Pensacola had made it worse. "*Forcing us to submit,* and at the same time permitting a few Spaniards to hold a valuable part of the province," complained a planter, "are things that make the people murmur with a *loud voice.*"[78]

At least one Spaniard was gone by then, for Someruelos had re-called Folch and replaced him with Maxent. It marked no change in policy but rather a final loss of confidence in Folch. He had seriously underestimated Grand-Pré, yet it is difficult to see what he could have done to make the situation in the remainder of Spanish West Florida any better. If anything, his successful finessing of Madison over Mo-bile stopped the Kemper expedition cold at a time when it stood a good chance of success. Now Mobile seemed destined to remain in Maxent's hands indefinitely.[79] In a few weeks another incident almost provoked conflict when Maxent turned back an ammunition vessel bound for Fort Stoddert, and gunboats came to its support. People in Mobile thought the small armada intended to attack the town, and again women and children fled and Maxent's garrison prepared for action. The commander of the gunboats intended only to protect the ammunition vessel as it sailed past the fort, and Maxent prudently decided not to interfere with the ship, thus averting violence once more.[80] Maxent soon met with Claiborne in Pensacola to discuss a solution for vessels passing through Mobile Bay to the Tombigbee and to Alabama settlements and forts.[81]

Claiborne returned from Pensacola with Mobile still in Spanish hands, and the dashed expectations proved almost too much for Reu-ben Kemper, who happened to be in New Orleans at the time. If the United States did not soon take Mobile, he declared, he would raise five hundred of the old conventionalists and take it himself.[82] It was not the most prudent thing for him to say at that particular moment, since another grand jury in Fort Stoddert was scheduled to consider an indictment against him and others for their earlier Mobile ven-tures. Kemper may have been tough and sometimes impetuous, but he was also methodical, a man of integrity by regional standards, and far from unsubtle. A few weeks earlier, knowing that he faced a grand jury, he got out a copy of his lengthy 1807 account of his involvement with Burr's supporters and his trip to Washington. It was written as a deposition for one of the courts-martial in the Burr affair, and now it was needed in yet another. Kemper provided a copy to the press, and in late May it appeared in print. The timing could hardly be co-incidental that with a grand jury about to consider whether Kemper had treasonous designs on Mobile, Kemper's account of his repudiation of Burr's similar schemes had just come before readers' eyes.[83] On August 17 when the U.S. district court met at Fort Stoddert to consider indictments against Kemper and others, the grand jury declined to find any bill of indictment.[84]

Court business in Feliciana seemed equally inconclusive and was made worse by men venting their frustration at the political limbo on one another. "It is the hardest times here ever Experienced," Kimball groused in June. "Some men will think nothing of sueing their Neighbour for Three or four bits and Run them to Six or Eight dollars cost." Few justices other than parish judge Rhea seemed willing to act, and the only judge in the whole parish hearing criminal cases was a man reputed to have fled Virginia to avoid starvation. "It Requires money to obtain justice," Kimball went on. His legal expenses mounted alarmingly in a civil suit over land, yet he resolved in spite of cost to pursue it with a determination "to make a spoon or spoil the horn."[85]

Despite their mounting anger at the United States, several communities gathered on July 4 to honor the anniversary of the Declaration of Independence. In St. Francisville an orator began speaking of the days of 1776 and Jefferson and Benjamin Franklin but then made a parallel to 1810 and Hicky and Rhea.[86] Similar celebrations elsewhere went harmoniously but could not hide the undercurrent of disaffection.[87] Claiborne thought a few men worked to inflame resentment and convert the undecided into opponents of the United States, though they made little impression.[88] As usual the chief troublemakers were in Feliciana, most notably James M. Bradford in the pages of his *Time-Piece*. Claiborne credited the editor with genius but no judgment, for week after week Bradford abused Congress for its treatment of the orphaned Florida Parishes.[89] With a convention to frame a constitution for the new territory coming, their delegates would be voiceless, leaving Kimball grumbling that they were at a greater loss than ever before.[90]

The planters of Feliciana decided to send Ballinger to Congress to petition for the inclusion of the Florida Parishes in the Orleans Territory.[91] First, though, they met on September 26 to celebrate the anniversary of their own declaration of independence, making Claiborne fear that agitators like Bradford might try to frame inflammatory resolutions to send with Ballinger. Fortunately Judge Rhea remained a reasonable and dispassionate voice for moderation and did his best to calm the dissidents.[92]

Meanwhile West Floridians tried to go about other business. Hicky, Mather, Wykoff, and others began to build a public market in Baton Rouge.[93] A grand jury chaired by William Buford returned an impeachment indictment against Toulmin.[94] But the all-pervasive concern over their political status left energy for little else. The exclusion from Orleans widened a divide between men of the eastern and western parishes. On November 20, 411 citizens of the Tombigbee region sent a memorial to Congress asking not to be included in Orleans, for if they were, "we will be subjected to all the inconveniences and miseries resulting from a difference of people, language, manners, customs, and politics." They did not want to be pawns in American efforts to counter the French Creoles, for natural immigration would accomplish that in time. The distance, difficulty, and expense of traveling more than a hundred and fifty miles to New Orleans would impede business and government. Since West Florida was too small to be a state in its own right, they argued that their best hope for the future lay in being attached to Mississippi, with which they shared the same language, blood, and customs.[95]

Mississippi's delegate George Poindexter presented it in Congress, to the alarm of those hoping to see the Florida Parishes joined with Orleans.[96] But in New Orleans things started looking more favorable, and by late November Claiborne thought he saw a clear majority of the delegates in his convention in favor of all or part of West Florida being annexed to Orleans; a fortnight later he had no doubt that they wanted Feliciana at least.[97] Encouraged, Skipwith and Rhea called a meeting of citizens in Feliciana on December 14 and drafted resolutions to send to Ballinger, who was finally on his delayed mission to Washington.[98] A few days later Claiborne advised a gathering at the Plains on wording for an address to Congress seeking inclusion with Orleans.[99]

Ballinger reached Washington the day after Christmas and presented Madison a petition asking that Feliciana at least should be affixed to Orleans. Admitting that some might prefer association with Mississippi, Ballinger argued that the bulk of the inhabitants had similar laws and business and family attachments as Orleans. They wanted the United States to evict remaining Spaniards from West Florida; they wanted the Morales titles repudiated, but the Grand-Pré grants upheld. In a novel instance of putting Washington at the root of West Florida's problems, Ballinger argued that if the United States had asserted its right to West Florida at the outset in 1804 and evicted the Spaniards then, these Grand-Pré grants would not exist, thus the least Washington could do was to recognize them now. His petition again sought debt assumption, for if Congress did not assume the debt and if the Grand-Pré grants were not recognized, the people would face a double hardship of losing their land and not having money to buy it again. That would "palsy the Energies of the Country, Stifle its patriotism and sink it into its original nothingness," Ballinger argued.[100] Claiborne personally directed more petitions to sympathetic congressmen, and when the convention completed a constitution, on January 22, 1812, it followed with a memorial urging that the Florida Parishes as far as the Perdido be joined with the future state.[101]

After that the Floridians could do little but wait. The House of Representatives, which was also considering Mississippi's application for statehood, received the constitution on March 5 and for several days debated whether West Florida was originally a part of the Purchase and whether it should be attached to Orleans or Mississippi, left by itself, or even divided in two, as Toulmin had suggested months before. Poindexter proposed that the parishes be split along the Pearl, everything west going to Orleans, everything east to Mississippi. A proviso to that effect passed in the debate on Mississippi's application, and on March 16 the House approved a bill putting Mississippi on the road to statehood. If Orleans got any of West Florida, it would be only the parishes west of the Pearl. Two days later the House took up the bill to admit Orleans as the State of Louisiana. The bill that passed on March 20 did not include the Florida Parishes, but it anticipated subsequent legislation to that effect by providing that they be allowed equal rights and representation in Louisiana's legislature and treated as if already a part of the state. The Senate deleted all of the West Florida provisions from the House bill, partially in response to the memorials still coming from inhabitants, and simplified things by a proviso dictating that if the legislature of the new state asked, the Florida Parishes could be annexed and treated as if part of the original state. The House approved the revision without amendment, and on April 8 Madison signed Louisiana into statehood, effective the last day of the month. Meanwhile the Senate postponed Mississippi's application.[102]

It took four weeks for the decision to reach the new state of Louisiana and the Florida Parishes; Claiborne anxiously waited to hear the result.[103] On April 22 he learned of the division of West Florida along the Pearl, and twelve days later he finally received notification of admission and the proviso for including the Florida Parishes, though their people could not vote in the election to choose the legislature that would subsequently petition Congress to include them in the new state. Action was needed, and soon, for the economic decline caused by the failure to satisfy debts from the eleven weeks of quasi-independence had led to a number of foreclosures on property, which vultures in Feliciana bought at bargain prices.[104] When the new superior court convened in New Orleans immediately after April 30 and statehood, one of its first rulings decreed that Skipwith's Montesano was lawfully in the Orleans Territory. If that was so, then West Florida had been a part of the Louisiana Purchase from the outset, and its debts were Washington's.[105] In a related decision, the court decreed that Louisiana had been dismembered temporarily after 1803, but the territory between the Mississippi and the Pearl below the line was and always had been part of the Purchase.[106]

The Florida Parishes took no part in the stormy election that summer, the first hard conflict between the American and French Creole factions. On a technicality, the French maintained Claiborne's ineligibility to seek the governorship of Louisiana, since he still governed the Florida Parishes. Claiborne countered by resigning that governorship to the secretary of Orleans Thomas Bolling Robertson, who thus became for a matter of weeks governor over the Florida Parishes. On July 10 ballots showed that Claiborne had won.[107]

When the new legislature sat on July 27, a major part of Governor Claiborne's first message was the importance of petitioning Congress to include the Florida Parishes. The body had already acted on the proviso, and Claiborne signed a joint resolution August 4, the new legislature's first real act. Three weeks later they authorized representation in the general assembly, and on August 25 Claiborne happily sent copies of the new constitution and legislative apportionment documents to the parishes.[108] That fall the four parishes held elections for their first representatives, and when the legislature reconvened on November 23, 1812, the new delegates were there.

Some of the names were familiar, such as Philemon Thomas and Philip Hicky, but more were new, men not prominent in the short-lived rebellion and the republic that followed. Rhea, Lilley, John H. Johnson, Kimball, and more were not there, and neither, of course, were the troublesome Kempers. Revolutions have a way of leaving behind their leaders as the quest for stability seeks calmer heads, but soon an entirely different sort of service would take them back to the days of September of 1810 when they had needed the steady Thomases and the impetuous Kempers. If statehood brought promise, it also brought responsibility, and on June 18, 1812, when Congress passed a declaration of war on Britain and its ally Spain, the citizens of the Florida Parishes found themselves in the anomalous position of being perhaps the only Americans at war who had had no representation in Congress's decision. The remnant of the infant republic that began in conflict with Spain now had to demonstrate its patriotism by taking up arms yet again.

19

The Old Hero

THE FLORIDA Parishes watched the second war with Britain from afar. Troubles already fermenting with the Creek Indians in the Tombigbee region were another matter, and there armed and ugly conflict erupted in 1813 to 1814. Mississippi militia participated, but the men of the old districts that were now part of Louisiana did not. Tennessee sent volunteers under Colonel Andrew Jackson to put down the conflict, and it was the making of Jackson, who ended the Creek War a general and a national hero. In the process, he took half of future Alabama and much of southern Georgia. From that triumph he moved on to assemble the forces that repulsed Britain's approach to New Orleans on January 8, 1815, in the most improbable and lopsided victory in the history of American arms.

The irrepressible General Wilkinson had taken Mobile in April of 1813, since Spain was allied with Britain. Three years after the war Jackson turned his attention to Florida east of the Perdido. Since 1812, a succession of ill-led attempts to emulate the West Florida revolt had failed to wrest East Florida from the Spaniards; by 1818 they retained only weak, token garrisons at Pensacola, St. Augustine, and a few other points. Using troubles with the Creek and Seminoles as a pretext, Jackson invaded and took virtually all of it but St. Augustine, which the Spaniards finally evacuated after the Adams-Onís Treaty of 1819 settled all of Florida in American hands at last.

In the end virtually all of Spanish Florida except for West Florida fell to military force. In 1810 the Florida Parishes were more heavily settled and developed than any other part of Spanish Florida, and more prosperous. Thanks to Natchez and New Orleans, parish inhabitants enjoyed a proximity to trade and ideas and information that few other places, even in the United States, boasted. Those people also shared a continuity of blood and culture as offspring of the Revolution. They had brought to it American preoccupation with law and order and the perception of individual rights, and they had expected those to fit into a province governed by a minority with a far different political and civil culture, all at a time when growing American sentiment for expansion collided with the impotence of Spain's dwindling empire. By 1810 Spain stood in the way of West Floridians' realizing the prosperity they presumed was their American birthright. It was not entirely about land, or Spanish corruption, or latent patriotism. It was about all of those things, and more.

Revolt represented their last hope of stability, of preserving an environment in which they could grow and prosper in domestic peace, secure in the belief that civil and criminal justice would be fair and swift, and that political authority recognized their rights. They had watched too many of the blocks of their society fall in recent years: the removal of Grand-Pré, the decline in land values, the breakdown of civil remedies in court, a growth in crime, a rise in corruption, the halting of immigration and land grants, and a moratorium on surveys and confirmation of existing grants. By the fall of 1810 little remained in their small world to depend upon, while the United States looked secure and promised almost all of what Delassus and Spain no longer delivered.

Beneath the surface of their expedient but straightforward loyalty to Spain lay always the assumption that Spain would reciprocate by ensuring an environment in which they could grow and prosper. When that environment evaporated, so did their loyalty, and when resistance emerged, first in the chaotic efforts of the Kempers and then with the Troy meetings and the convention, what began as a minority movement gradually gained adherents. The convention and its ordinances promised to fill the vacuum. Theirs was a revolution of last resort.[1] Grand-Pré's old friend Favrot said ten weeks after the revolt that this was "a revolution which was not prompted by the inhabitants' hostility toward the government." Rather, these events happened "when justice and the interests of the people are entrusted to mercenary characters."[2]

All the nation watched at a distance of a month's delay, and its response reflected events in the East in the battle between Republican and Federalist, North and South. Often reactions were derisory, like that of the Boston editor who referred to it as "the little mimick Revolution of Florida."[3] Yet most realized that substantive issues underlay modest events. West Florida gave the Union unchallenged control of the Mississippi all the way to New Orleans, with incalculable strategic and economic advantages. Occupation of the Florida Parishes denied a Mississippi foothold to other empire builders, particularly Britain and France. It also brought ten thousand people of largely American birth under the Stars and Stripes and added hundreds of thousands of acres of new public land for exploitation. This opened the door for a considerable expansion of slavery to work those new lands, which tossed West Florida right into the center of the slavery debate. These may have been small events in a small place, but this was no "mimick" of a revolution, and its repercussions would be felt for the next half century.

It rarely takes long for men to crave their earlier days, and on February 1, 1820, less than a decade after the rebellion, a St. Francisville man lamented that "we have anxiously looked for a faithful history of the revolution," but none was yet forthcoming. "Many of the most active and conspicuous actors in that revolution, are now no more," he said, "and yet a few years and the small number of survivors will be swept away." No doubt his anxiety was prompted by the passing within the previous sixteen months of Percy, Leonard, John Hunter Johnson, and Lilley. He wanted to memorialize "the noble effort made by a few faithful inhabitants, to rescue their country from danger, and preserve to themselves and their children, something like freedom—from sinking into oblivion." He appealed to the people for recollections or public papers for a history he intended to write, but if his work was begun, it was never completed.[4]

Sadly, many of the papers he needed were lost forever when the ship carrying Spanish West Florida's archives to Havana in 1818 sank in a storm.[5] Claiborne showed little interest in the official archives of the West Florida convention or legislature. Philip Hicky took many papers home with him, where they remained for generations in his family; other papers dispersed elsewhere.[6] Consequently, with no one having access to the raw materials, no history was written. Years later, in 1845, Skipwith's kinsman Henry Skipwith dabbled in bits and pieces of the story.[7] Like so many others, however, he showed more interest in the ancient pretensions that the United States should compensate the Florida Parishes for the land acquired in the annexation. As late as 1882 Skipwith still argued that while West Florida's sovereignty logically ended when the Stars and Stripes replaced the lone star, "it was not, in our opinion, quite so logical that a stranger who happened to be a guest in the house of the decedent at the time of his dissolution should inherit every acre of his broad domain at the expense of his rightful heirs."[8]

The only history the Spaniards wrote just preserved their embarrassment in courts-martial and recriminations. Almost all of the men who lost the fort were released not long afterward; only Delassus was held until December. He settled briefly at Point Coupée and sent a friend to retrieve his remaining possessions from his house in Baton Rouge, but the man found only a bureau, a knife, and a pair of carbines.[9] As Delassus had feared, his superiors commenced an investigation in March of 1811 and spent three months taking hundreds of pages of testimony. The resulting "Copia del Sumario sobre el modo como fue soprendido el Fuerto de Baton Rouge" was in its way a history of the fall of Baton Rouge.[10] The inquisitors focused on Raphael Crocker, though in the end they apportioned blame among Crocker, Metzinger, and Delassus, with posthumous criticism of Grand-Pré for his part in the poor condition of the fort. Only Crocker, the most culpable of all, came to defend himself. It was 1814 before final verdicts came down: six months' suspension for Crocker, a year for Metzinger, and death for Delassus.

The disgraced colonel made good on his determination to remain in America. He lived in New Orleans briefly, where he married the daughter of his friend Gilberto Leonard in March of 1811, and the couple soon moved upriver to St. Louis, Missouri.[11] He spent years trying to recover the money that was lost when the fort fell, as well as his other claims, his case actually reaching the Supreme Court in 1835. In the end all he was awarded was the $1,333 taken from his bureau and American citizenship, and he lived out his days in New Orleans.[12] Metzinger simply vanished, and so did Crocker, to no one's disappointment. Pintado, the best of Delassus's officers, left for Havana in 1817, where he died a dozen years later. In 1836, just months after his brother James Bowie's death at the Alamo, Rezin Bowie purchased all of Pintado's surveys from his widow and brought them back to Louisiana, where they became the basis for settling title claims for the next century.[13]

Of the kidnappers of the Kempers in 1805, Kneeland was dead before Claiborne took over.[14] Abram Horton disappeared after fleeing to West Florida, and William Barker remained in Feliciana. Twelve years after Alston's death, in 1809, his sister Lucretia, the wife of the alcalde James Pirrie, hired an itinerant painter to tutor their daughter Eliza, bringing John James Audubon to their Feliciana plantation, Oakley. Shepherd Brown returned to St. Helena, and when the British invaded he marched with the parish volunteers. After the war he moved to Baltimore, where he died on January 7, 1818, leaving behind fifty-six squares of lots in the town, and hundreds of arpents of cypress land on the Mississippi, from which his speculation never profited.[15]

On the other side of the revolt, Edward Randolph remained in Pinckneyville in the mercantile business and died on November 26, 1821, leaving a widow and several sons.[16] Dr. Martin Haynie scarcely outlived his revolution, dying in St. Francisville in 1816.[17] The pompous and irascible Captain Robert Percy took no further part in public affairs and died November 9, 1819, at the age of fifty-seven. Dr. Thomas G. Holmes, who evaded the surprise attack that captured Major Hargraves, made a far more harrowing escape on August 30, 1813, during the Creek Indian War. He and about five hundred and fifty others occupied the stockade at Fort Mims, only a few miles east of Fort Stoddert, when a surprise attack by the Creek killed more than five hundred. Surrounded and with the stockade on fire, Holmes used an ax to hack his way through the pickets, escaping with a few others.

Samuel Kemper gave up on West Florida before the climax came, but he did not yield his conviction that it was America's destiny to rule the continent, and in his fashion he continued the family's conflict with Spain. After his brief visit to help Reuben chastise Kneeland in the fall of 1808, Presley Kemper went back to Ohio, where he served as a wagon master during the war with Britain. He had many years and many children ahead of him. After moving to the Attakapas country, Nathan and his family continued to grow as well, with five sons and six daughters. He left his rebellious ways in Pinckneyville apparently, for soon after Louisiana became a state, he won a seat in its house of representatives. Early in January of 1815, when General Jackson's orders to concentrate all militia and defend New Orleans arrived, Kemper and others appealed to keep theirs in place so they could guard their vulnerable coastline from British landings and at the same time protect themselves from their growing slave population. After the Point Coupée outbreak, there were fears of slave uprisings even in peacetime, but with the call for militia to Jackson's army, there would not be enough men to mount slave patrols to "Keep the Blacks in order."[18] After the war Nathan continued planting in St. Mary's, though he still owned and leased part of his old grant in Feliciana, and he kept up with accomplices from the 1804 raids, such as Colonel William Kirkland.[19] A success as a planter, in 1825 he produced twenty-five hogsheads of raw sugar with only four field hands, meriting notice in the New Orleans press.[20] Seven years later, on January 29, 1832, he died in St. Mary's.[21]

The men of the old convention met varying fates, but most remained in the Florida Parishes. John Mills returned to St. Francisville desperately ill, dying soon after reaching his home, Propinquity.[22] John W. Leonard returned to his nine-thousand-acre St. Helena plantation, where he died on November 1, 1818.[23] John H. Johnson served in the Louisiana senate, and in 1814 to 1815 wrote his observations of the British and American forces for the readers of the *Time-Piece*.[24] He died at Troy in March of 1819. Thomas Lilley outlived his brief republic by only a decade, dying at his home near the Plains in 1820. By the time of William Barrow's death at his Highland plantation, on November 9, 1823, he had become one of the largest slave owners in the state. John Rhea lived on in East Feliciana Parish until May 7, 1843, when he died at the age of eighty. Manuel López, the only Spaniard in the revolt, remained in Baton Rouge for a decade and then slipped out of sight, and several other leaders also fell into obscurity.

Philip Hicky loyally worked on the estate of his friend Grand-Pré well into the war with Britain.[25] He defeated Skipwith to become East Baton Rouge Parish's first state senator and also built the first sugar mill in the parish when cane emerged to compete with cotton. On January 7, 1815, his first crop of ground sorghum was actually awaiting shipment to New Orleans when volunteers from Kentucky and Tennessee marched past to join Andrew Jackson's army and commandeered his barges.[26] When he died at his estate, Mount Hope, on October 1, 1859, aged eighty-two, he was the last native-born citizen of Louisiana to have lived through the successive regimes of Great Britain, Spain, France, and the United States.[27]

Philemon Thomas became sheriff of his parish after the war, then won a seat in the legislature, and in 1822 he moved to the state senate, where he led the movement to relocate the capital to Baton Rouge. Somewhat ironically he lost a race for the governorship in 1828 to Pierre Derbigny, the brother-in-law of Delassus, but then won a seat in Congress in 1830. He was genuinely nonpartisan in his politics, supporting Jackson against South Carolina's nullification and secession talk in 1832 yet opposing Old Hickory by backing the National Bank. In 1840 he presided over Louisiana's Whig convention, then he returned to the legislature. The *Baton Rouge Gazette* called him "one of the few relics of the Revolution that time has spared to gladden the spirit of our generation." Thomas was eighty-eight when he died, on November 18, 1847, an expansionist to the end, and friends gave him a grand funeral in the American cemetery near the site of the fort he had taken in 1810.[28] One friend declared, "He was a man universally esteemed in all the relations of life, public and domestic."[29]

Fulwar Skipwith became registrar of the land office at Baton Rouge for a time, then took a seat in the state senate, only to volunteer at age fifty-two for the New Orleans city guard when the British approached. After the war he turned down the consulship to Paris and later, in 1818, lost a bid for Congress. Thereafter he held minor local offices, at the same time seeking, unsuccessfully, to collect more than sixty-five thousand dollars in back salary and expenses from his earlier service as consul and chargé.[30] In old age he spent evenings by his fire reminiscing to his nephew Henry, drinking juleps and picking seed from a basket of cotton at his side as he smoked his meerschaum and talked of men and politics. At the end of every evening, he rose and, ever formal and dignified, walked backward to the door, bowed to his nephew, and retired.[31] He died on January 7, 1839, nearly bankrupt.[32]

After surviving the unsuccessful attempt at impeachment, Harry Toulmin continued his efforts to maintain peace on his frontier as outbreaks of violence with the Creek Indians led to war in 1813. He recognized error on both sides, which made him unpopular with a number of his old antagonists. When Mississippi Territory finally achieved statehood, at the end of 1817, Congress split off the new Alabama Territory, and in 1819 he sat in its constitutional convention and took a seat in the new legislature. Four years later he died at his plantation, at the age of fifty-seven.

The war years broke David Holmes's health, leaving him so ill by 1815 that he took a year's leave of absence. On his return he presided over the 1817 convention that framed a constitution and applied for Mississippi statehood, and then he won the election to be the first governor of the state of Mississippi. He later spent five years in Washington as one of the state's senators before winning the governorship once again. He resigned after only six months due to failing health and returned to his old home in Winchester, Virginia, where he died on August 20, 1832, at the age of sixty-three.[33] Only Claiborne did as much as he to ensure peace with Spain during the years before the annexation of West Florida, and Holmes's subtle efforts during the turnover contributed much to the peaceful outcome.

Claiborne, of course, was Jefferson and Madison's man-of-all-trades throughout, and neither ever had a more effective servant. Constantly at odds with the French Creoles, the speculators and adventurers, Casa Calvo and Folch, and several of West Florida's leaders, not least of whom was Fulwar Skipwith, he nonetheless kept the peace and pressed each president's policies forcefully. With Holmes, he pursued a subtle, nonconfrontational, and ultimately successful approach to the takeover of West Florida, and thereafter remained sensitive to all factions as he rebuilt the political structure of the Florida Parishes. Nor did he abandon those parishes when other forces threatened to omit them from the future state of Louisiana. As governor of Louisiana, Claiborne saw the state through the British invasion of 1814 through 1815. In 1817 the legislature elected him to the U.S. Senate, but he died before he could take his seat, on November 23. Ironically, he was buried in the same cemetery as his foe Daniel Clark, who had died in 1813 after his political career collapsed.

Forty years after the capture of Baton Rouge, only five veterans remained: Hicky, James Flower of St. Francisville, Benjamin Collins of Point Coupée, Charles Johnson of West Baton Rouge, across the river from the capital, and Dr. Cornelius French.[34] Flower and Johnson were the next to go, and then Collins died on June 18, 1860, at the age of seventy-eight. The Virginian had ridden with Llewellyn Griffith's cavalry in the attack on Baton Rouge, and he later commanded the fort and occasionally acted as secretary to the standing committee of the convention. He was a friend of Reuben Kemper and remained so in spite of his having to seize Reuben's property in 1819 when he was sheriff of Feliciana Parish.[35]

That seizure was evidence that Reuben's fortunes at Bayou Sara were no better after the revolution than before. Kemper never returned to the barge business.[36] He had neglected his personal affairs, and he had matters to put in order.[37] Besides, the coming of the steamboat signaled the end of man-propelled barge transport, and Kemper rather welcomed it. When the *New Orleans*, the first steamboat to pass down the Mississippi, reached New Orleans on January 10, 1812, he took a keen interest in it, and told an associate that "I am happy to find that the steam boat is so well addapted to the trade of the Mississippi." When Smith's counsel told Kemper that he was "prepared to blow us out of the water" in the suit, Reuben joked to his new attorney Edward Livingston of New Orleans that they ought to advise the *New Orleans'* captain to have his vessel on the river at Bayou Sara on court day since "I hope to be as well prepared as posable."[38]

Kemper bought five hundred acres at Bayou Sara and a family of six slaves to work the ground, but when he learned that Samuel had joined more than a hundred others at Natchitoches for a filibustering campaign to drive the Spaniards from Texas, Reuben went to lend a hand.[39] Samuel still ran the Kemper Tavern in Alexandria on the Red River, and Reuben ran the tavern while his brother went on the expedition led by Colonel Augustus Magee and the young Spaniard Samuel had met at dinner in 1806, Bernardo Gutiérrez de Lara.[40] They crossed into Texas in August of 1812, took Nacogdoches, and their numbers swelled to three hundred or more. When Magee died, on February 6, 1813, Samuel assumed command and achieved considerable success, but it turned ugly when Gutiérrez allowed subordinates to murder prisoners captured with the garrison at San Antonio de Béxar on March 29. Disgusted, Kemper resigned and returned to Alexandria.[41]

After a few days Reuben left for Bayou Sara to meet his attorneys to prepare for the victory over Smith "that I have ever been entitled to."[42] More than a year passed without a court date for his suit.[43] With the case in the doldrums, he bought another 240 acres at Bayou Sara, but passing time made him careless.[44] Washington had set a deadline of October 18, 1814, for holders of Spanish claims to file for confirmation of title, and Kemper let the date slip past him. The very next day, happening to be in St. Helena, he filed both his purchase of the Grand-Pré grant from Duplantier in 1800 and Nathan's 1804 grant.[45] Two weeks later, back in Pinckneyville, he transferred the land that Nathan won from Horton to the minor sons of Randolph, who were already living on it rent free because of Reuben's affection for their late father.[46]

Within days Reuben learned that Samuel had died, on November 4, aged just thirty-eight.[47] Samuel had lived mostly in the shadow of his older brothers, his questionable actions in 1805 being mostly attributed to Reuben. His one moment of notoriety in his own right came with his return from the Gutiérrez-Magee expedition, when Alexandria and St. Francisville acclaimed him as "the invincible hero of Labahia and St. Antonio."[48] Like his brothers before him, he had become an apostle of manifest destiny.

Reuben had little time for mourning, for within weeks of Samuel's death a British army threatened New Orleans. Reuben had earlier enlisted in a battalion of Mississippi cavalry, but he then raised his own company and was once again Colonel Kemper.[49] When Jackson arrived to defend New Orleans, Kemper answered his call. On January 2, 1815, Jackson held a line on the Mississippi east of the city that allowed him to concentrate his fire on the enemy as long as the British found no way around his left flank posted on a swamp. He sent Kemper on a dangerous reconnaissance to confirm the safety of that flank, and the next night Jackson ordered Kemper to go out again with a few volunteers to scout the British positions. At one point Reuben left his men and went on alone, meeting a British patrol that opened fire as he ran to warn his comrades, who scattered. The British set the prairie grass along the bayou ablaze to force the Americans into the open, and Kemper and part of his command only reached safety the following morning, but his information helped Jackson plan his defense in some confidence.

The great battle of January 8 was a stunning victory, and when the British began their evacuation on the nineteenth, Jackson sent Kemper and his company after them. Reuben's report of a strong enemy rear guard persuaded Jackson to call off the pursuit.[50] Later, on February 18, while Kemper's company was stationed at the Mons Boré plantation two miles west of the city, his attorney Livingston arrived from Fort Bowyer, off Mobile. He brought the news that the Treaty of Ghent had been signed on December 24, ending the war, and it was Colonel Reuben Kemper who forwarded the happy news to Jackson and New Orleans.[51] One outcome of the campaign was the development of a friendship between Kemper and Old Hickory, based on mutual respect and certainly some similarity of character and temperament. That is what gave Reuben the opportunity to enlist Jackson, now the nation's greatest living hero, to aid him in a private quest.

In the fall of 1815, even after five years had passed, Kemper had not lost sight of his obligation to Hargraves and his fellow prisoners, which he told Jackson "has cost me many sleepless hours."[52] After several weeks in irons in Pensacola, the captives had been taken to the Morro Castle prison in Havana, where for five years they worked in a chain gang. Reuben worried especially about Hargraves, who was nearly seventy. "Heavens what a spectacle to behold he must now be with his Frosty beard fifteen or twenty inches long starved and naked accompanied by a few fine young Americans of respectable parentage," Reuben wrote Jackson. The government had taken some steps to free them, but with no effect, so Secretary of State Monroe told Kemper to propose a means to secure a release and he would adopt it. Reuben suggested sending an agent to Havana to work for their release and nothing else.[53] Monroe agreed and authorized Kemper himself to make the trip. After getting a passport in Washington on January 3, 1816, he left for Cuba.[54] Given his reputation in Spain, Kemper took considerable risk going to Havana, but the State Department provided protection.[55] Happily, the mission succeeded.[56] Within a few months, Spain released the men, and all returned to their homes.[57]

On his visits to Washington, Kemper pressed Congress to pay the debt incurred by the West Florida convention.[58] Ballinger failed in 1811, and the coming of war halted further efforts. Congress passed an act on April 18, 1814, to liquidate the debt, and in December of 1815, Monroe engaged Reuben to collect all of the claims along with supporting evidence.[59] Reuben Kemper spent the rest of his life working on them, some of them his own, and amassed a considerable amount of paperwork.[60] In July of 1816 he returned to Washington to submit his first results to Monroe, and thereafter he made frequent trips to the capital.[61] On one trip in 1817 he stayed with his older brother Colonel John Kemper and found that he was lionized a bit even in the East.[62] Attorney General William Wirt entertained him as an honored guest one evening, and another young man present was "forcibly struck" by Kemper's "towering, Achilles-like form, and majestic aspect and demeanor."[63]

While working on the claims, Kemper never lost sight of the Smith suit, but seemingly the courts did.[64] John Smith had moved back to Feliciana in the spring of 1810 but took no role in the ensuing revolt, though he remained loyal to his old friends from the Grand-Pré days.[65] The collapse of his political career mirrored that of his personal fortunes and left him a broken man. Hardship and poverty drove him back to his original calling, and he spent the rest of his years an ardent Baptist preacher. When it came to that old suit, however, he was just as dogged as Kemper. In February of 1818, after five years, the judge of the district court for Feliciana finally ordered the relevant papers in the case to be sent from Point Coupée.[66] The file had assumed substantial proportions, with documents in English, Spanish, and even French, and many of the official Spanish papers had been lost.[67] With vital witnesses dead and others moved away, Kemper's always fragile case weakened even more. At the spring term of the Feliciana Parish court, he lost.[68] A year later, when he could not pay the judgment decreed by the court, his old friend Sheriff Collins had no choice but to seize part of his property at the mouth of Bayou Sara to sell at auction.[69] Reuben soon lost his remaining half claim to the rest of the contested Feliciana property in another suit.[70] Attorneys' fees left John Smith with little gain, and still impoverished and in failing health, he continued his hardscrabble ministry. On July 30, 1824, he died in St. Francisville after falling ill on the way home from preaching.[71]

Apparently, as it had Samuel before him, the defeat soured Kemper on West Florida, and he moved to Alexandria in 1819.[72] His final obsession was the debt due to creditors of the convention. The 1814 legislation had agreed to reimburse all claims up to a total of $62,356, but those Kemper collected, including his own, soon exceeded that amount.[73] The process of evaluating each claim proved time-consuming, and Kemper often had to hunt for more documents or testimony.[74] He stayed with the task diligently, and in 1820 the first batch of claims was settled, including most of Reuben's own.[75] The U.S. Treasury gave the awards to Kemper to distribute, which took time, leading Philemon Thomas to complain that "he has got all the people's money, which he keeps," though he did not accuse Reuben of mischief.[76] Knowledge that Kemper was slow in paying gave rise to a false rumor that he kept ten thousand dollars that belonged to Hicky.[77]

On his visits to Washington Kemper saw Louisiana's growing importance in national affairs. "Louisiana is begining to be thought an object among men of enterprise here to locate a property in and must grow more and more," he told Livingston.[78] Reuben himself relocated to Bayou Billy in the area known as Calcasieu on the outskirts of Alexandria with his family of slaves, and he became a small-scale planter.[79] The Kemper name carried such weight in Rapides that he immediately became a political force, especially thanks to his close ties to Jackson, whom Reuben sometimes advised on men and affairs.[80] In the 1822 congressional election, the brother of the Democrat incumbent Josiah Stoddard Johnston believed that Reuben's support meant victory, calling Kemper "indefatigable when he interests himself in the service of another."[81] Local hopefuls for political appointments in Washington sought his endorsement.[82] Men in trouble came to Kemper when they had nowhere else to turn, and Johnston's brother remarked that one unfortunate fellow "would have been ruined but for Kempers energy and attention."[83] Sensitive to changing political winds, Kemper cared little for what remained of Jefferson's old Republican Party, remaining loyal to expansionist Democrats such as Jackson and Johnston.[84]

Then Kemper's political influence and the Florida debt suddenly merged. When he had bought those Spanish arms from Henry de la Françia in 1810, he had given his personal note as security. After disbanding his men he handed the weapons to U.S. authorities, and most of them eventually went to Jackson's defense of New Orleans.[85] West Florida did not pay Françia before the republic's demise, which left Reuben liable. He kept the ailing and impoverished Françia in his Bayou Sara house for several years and sold some of his own Pinckneyville property to give the man more than four thousand dollars while also covering his expenses. In January of 1817 Françia authorized Reuben to collect the claim on his behalf, but it remained unpaid two years later when Françia died on a keelboat at Baton Rouge.[86]

The problem was that the arms had not been Françia's to sell, and that would remain the problem with the claim. It was rejected in 1821, and so Françia's son Joseph filed suit against Kemper.[87] A state court in Alexandria awarded the son a hefty judgment against Kemper, and for the next year Reuben sought a solution to the mess.[88] Josiah Johnston pressed Reuben's case in the Senate; Congressman Livingston worked for him in the House of Representatives; and Jackson, also a senator now, gave his assistance. Reuben appealed to Jackson and Monroe to "relive me from evident distruction" and sent a steady stream of correspondence to Washington in his mounting anxiety.[89] He enlisted Louisiana's governor Henry Johnson as well.[90]

Then came the 1826 race for the local congressional seat. Kemper's friends hoped to beat incumbent William Brent, who had defeated Josiah Johnston two years before. The best available candidate was a shady frontier character hardly less fabled than Reuben himself, James Bowie. He was just thirty years old but already had a reputation from his days smuggling slaves into Louisiana with Pierre and Jean Laffite, the notorious filibusters and privateers. Now Bowie was much better known as the author of innumerable forged Spanish grants in the most ambitious land-fraud scheme in the nation's history.[91] Bowie was close to another shadowy figure, Charles Mulhollan, the executor of Henry de la Françia's estate, who for some years lived next to Françia.

In May of 1826 Bowie called on Kemper to inform him that through Mulhollan, Bowie had purchased the claim from Joseph de la Françia, which entitled him to the court's award against Kemper, and he had França's power of attorney to collect the debt. Reuben suspected that some "unfair contrivance" had been used to acquire the claim and begged friends in Washington to redouble efforts to settle the claim so that he could satisfy Bowie.[92] There was an unmistakable hint of coercion in Bowie's approach. The Reuben of old would never have found him intimidating, and at fifty-six Reuben was not an elderly man, but he had lived the hard life of the frontier. His health may have been declining by this time, and his rough-and-tumble days were past. Bowie probably used the França judgment as leverage to get what he really wanted from Kemper, which was his endorsement. He might have gotten it anyhow, since Kemper wanted to defeat Brent. Certainly by October Reuben was telling people that "Jim Bowie of Rapides is the only man in the District who can turn Brent out."[93] Democrats wrote in disgust that "Bowie & the Kempers have formed an alliance which if not holy will be sufficiently violent."[94]

All that changed in December. Washington continued to reject the França debt.[95] When Bowie visited Kemper on December 12 and learned that he had bought a worthless claim, Bowie exploded in a rage. What he only then discovered was that months earlier Reuben had agreed to sign over to Joseph de la França forty thousand dollars' worth of his own approved claims. There was no question of their validity, and when Congress appropriated the funds, the França matter would be settled, though Reuben would be the loser. When he calmed, Bowie promised to do nothing further in the matter. "I have my doubts of his sincerity," Kemper wrote Johnston.[96] Bowie left the meeting in a foul mood, and a day or two later in Alexandria got into a vicious brawl that ended with a bullet in his chest and one of his teeth in his antagonist's wrist. Nine months later he engaged in a frontier melee on a sandbar near Natchez that left one enemy dead by Bowie's knife, and Bowie himself dangerously wounded. Such acts were the stuff of frontier lore, but they dashed his chance for a seat in Congress, though he never gave up on the França claim.[97]

In January of 1827, just weeks after he met with Bowie, Reuben Kemper went to Natchez on business. His affairs often took him there and to New Orleans, sometimes on the steamboat *Feliciana*, though that may have been as close as he ever came to setting foot in the old province.[98] He also visited Pinckneyville to see old friends and to help settle first Randolph's estate, and then his widow's, the loss of whom he thought "irreparable."[99] Old faces were disappearing. Soon enough his would be gone too.

In Natchez he suddenly fell ill. No epidemic gripped the town at the moment. Perhaps it was just the ravages of an active life filled with losses and disappointments. Still, there was much more for him to look back upon with satisfaction during the hours confined to his sickbed. Nathan still lived and had two new grandsons.[100] Andrew Jackson looked certain to win the presidency in 1828. Louisiana, including the old West Florida, had fast become one of the most prosperous states in the Union. Feliciana and St. Francisville had grown into garden spots of the Mississippi, the plantations and stately mansions of millionaires confirming Reuben's faith in their future.

On a grander scale, he had witnessed Spain's continuing disintegration at home and abroad. Independence movements commenced in several South American colonies in 1810. Paraguay and Uruguay both gained freedom from Spain in 1811. A junta in Argentina struggled for eight years until 1818 brought independence, while Venezuela spent a full decade in revolt before it succeeded, in 1821. By that time Colombia had gained independence in 1820, followed by Ecuador in 1822, Bolivia in 1824, and Peru in 1825. Chile's junta stood for freedom just a week before Philemon Thomas's army took Baton Rouge, and Chile finally ejected the last of the *soldados* just months before Reuben came to Natchez for the last time. Revolt had commenced in Mexico exactly one week before the fall of Baton Rouge, and in 1821 Spain gave up, yielding not only Mexico, but Texas, the Southwest, and California. Reuben Kemper had been a part of the first mainland revolt in Spain's New World empire to evict the Spaniards successfully, and now he could know that all that remained of that empire were the islands of Cuba and Puerto Rico. He had helped to realize Jefferson's original conception of the Louisiana Purchase territory, and in his wake America was following its destiny across the continent.

The fall of Napoleon returned Europe to peace, and Britain's concurrent failure to subdue the United States — Reuben Kemper once more lending a hand — freed the new nation to begin transforming itself into a continental power. First Texas won its independence in 1836 and was admitted to statehood in 1845. Then the United States took California and the Southwest — the New Mexico Territory — in 1846 to 1848. From 1860 to 1861, eleven slave states seceded from the Union; six of them — more than half — had been absorbed from Spain: Alabama, Mississippi, Texas, Arkansas, Florida, and Louisiana. Without that half a million square miles of cotton and sugar land so conducive to the spread of slave labor, the remaining slave states could never have challenged federal authority in 1861. When that challenge failed, in 1865, the victorious Union emerged as the dominant power in the hemisphere. Fittingly, it closed out a century that had begun with the acquisition of Louisiana and West Florida with a brief summer's war in 1898 in which Spain lost the last of its American possessions, Cuba and Puerto Rico. The halting and uncertain dance with Spain for land had taken America from confusion and cross-purposes, through unanticipated success, to near self-immolation, and then on to a leading place among the great nations. Coincidentally, the peace treaty ending the Spanish-American War was signed on December 10, 1898, exactly eighty-eight years after the lone star of West Florida went down for the last time in Baton Rouge.

Reuben Kemper could hardly know the country's future, but by January 28 he knew that his own was almost over. So did friends in Natchez, some of whom sat with him in his final hours. Reuben's last visitors noted the calm with which he faced the end. Colonel John McCarty of Virginia, a noted duelist and one-time Federalist in the Virginia legislature, happened to be in Natchez and visited his dying friend. When he left, he declared that when Kemper died "the race of the old Romans would be extinct."

Reuben remained conscious almost to the last, the dark morning hours of January 29, five years to the day before Nathan's death. Friends performing their last offices knew that Kemper never identified with a church despite his Baptist upbringing and lifelong profession of faith, so they appealed to the city's clergy, regardless of denomination, to attend the casket to the grave and there perform the final rites of their orders. At 2:30 that same afternoon the Natchez Fencibles formed to escort the coffin to the edge of town and the cemetery, with Kemper's friends and the clergy in the procession. At the graveside the Rev. George Potts performed the funeral service, and as they lowered the casket into the earth the Fencibles gave it military honors and a musket salute.

Captain Gilbert Russell of the Third U.S. Infantry wrote an obituary for the Natchez press. "His life has been an eventful one," he said, citing Kemper's services in West Florida and at New Orleans under Jackson. In an oblique reference to the França arms, Russell added that "at his own expense he armed and equipped the patriots of Florida, and led them to victory." He had been a benefactor to the distressed, as evidenced by his charity to França. "Virtue found in him a steadfast friend — vice a determined foe." Acknowledging Kemper's intellect and wide range of interests, Russell added that "with an irresistible resolution and firmness of purpose, he steadfastly pursued those objects in the attainment of which he believed himself right." His efforts to free Hargraves, secure payment of the Florida claims, and settle the França matter established that. "In everything he did he expressed the utmost candor," said Russell. "In his opposition he was implacable, yet magnanimous — in his attachments sincere and ardent." Obituaries are studies in positive overstatement, but Russell's words well mirrored Kemper's life.

In a private letter to Potts just hours after Reuben's death, Russell said more. "The deceased was an extraordinary man," he wrote.[101] It took several days for the news to make its way up the Red River to Rapides and Alexandria. When it came, a friend of Reuben sent word at once to Senator Johnston in Washington that "the old hero" was gone.[102] Words like *extraordinary* and *hero* came to mind thirty-three years later at Benjamin Collins's death, when a New Orleans editor mused on the generation of the West Florida rebellion and republic. "This was one of the most gallant and daring exploits of American valor and enterprise, and the historians of our Republic have failed in nothing so much as in the due and proper tribute to its brilliancy and importance," he wrote. "It is not much to the credit of the nation and the people, that so little gratitude has been evinced to those patriotic Americans who, at so great a risk, solved so vexatious a problem, and who, after dispossessing the Spaniards, were themselves superseded, somewhat rudely and harshly, by the United States Government in a few weeks after the conquest."[103] His reference to the United States was more than just nostalgic rhetoric, for at the moment Collins was laid in his grave, the Union faced a crisis like none before.

North and South, free states and slave states, sat on the verge of being torn apart, not by the issues that had driven West Florida to rebel but very much from byproducts of that revolt. The Florida Parishes were the Union's first uncompensated land acquisition from another power, obtained via Jefferson's and Madison's policy of passive expansion. Texas followed, and in 1845 expansionists declared that America had a "manifest destiny" to possess the continent from sea to sea. Rapid growth and settlement required more land, but as territories became states there arose a question of balance of power. The determining factor in that balance was slavery. An industrializing North did not need it, but an expanding agricultural South required slaves to work the cane and cotton that powered its economy. The balance depended on the South's ability to expand westward, creating new territories and more new slave states to maintain parity in Congress with the North.

In 1860 it came down to whether or not slavery could expand west of the Mississippi. If it could, the balance might be preserved. If not, then a growing majority of free states carried an implicit threat to slavery where it already existed, risking political, financial, and social ruin for the South. Forty years of debates and compromises only postponed the crisis, and in 1860 a new Republican Party was pledged to halt the expansion of slavery. Collins's death on June 18 came the very day that the Democratic Party met in Baltimore and disintegrated, fatally divided over slavery expansion. The split virtually guaranteed Abraham Lincoln's election in November, and radical Southerners declared that rather than live under a Republican regime, they would leave the Union by secession and perhaps form a new confederation of slave states.

The West Florida rebellion of half a century before did not cause secession or the Civil War that followed, which would have come with or without the events of the fall of 1810. It did, however, inaugurate a push for more land to plant that led from Baton Rouge to Mobile and Pensacola, and then westward to Texas and beyond to the Pacific. Planting meant slaves, slaves meant wealth and power, and in republics power inevitably produces conflict between those who have it and those who want it.

Incidentally, that editor misspoke in calling Benjamin Collins the last of the rebellion generation. Probably a few septuagenarians and even perhaps an octogenarian or two still lived in 1860, men who had answered a muster in 1810 for a few days and then sunk back into obscurity. The leaders were all gone, though, and only one man who held any position of importance yet remained. Dr. Cornelius R. French of New Jersey lived in Baton Rouge and had turned seventy-five when Collins died. He had performed surgical and medical services for the soldiers in the fort, and it was perhaps fitting that the last of them alive should be one of the physicians who, like Haynie, stood so much at the center of the agitation.[104] When French died at Baton Rouge on June 28, 1863, the local press spoke of "taking a last farewell of 'the days that are no more.'"[105] He had lived to see a Mississippi convention vote for secession on January 9, 1861, followed by Louisiana secession on January 26, and he died as Union and Confederate forces were fighting at Donaldsonville, barely twenty-five miles below Baton Rouge. No one noted the irony that the last survivor of a revolution bound up in fears of France was himself named French.

Southerners in 1861 clearly thought about symbols of resistance and revolution and remembered that in 1810 a flag of rebellion flew over West Florida. Someone made and had ready a large blue flag with a single white star in the center, the lone-star flag of West Florida. Others had turned to it before. When the Texans achieved their independence from Spain in 1836 in a virtual reprise of the West Florida revolt on a vast scale, they adopted the lone star as their flag. So it seemed natural that as the cannon fired and the people cheered the announcement of Mississippi's secession, a man ran into the convention hall waving the Star of Florida. An Irish comedian named Harry McCarthy happened to witness the moment and that night wrote a song he called "The Bonnie Blue Flag," which became a Confederate anthem. On January 26 Mississippi incorporated the old lone star into its new state flag the very day that Louisiana followed it into secession, thirty-four years exactly since Reuben Kemper had seen his last sunset.

Kemper's old comrade Dr. French was still there early in February of 1861 when Louisiana adopted its own new flag: thirteen red, white, and blue stripes for the old Union and a solid red field in the upper left corner. In its middle they placed the single star of West Florida.

And French lived to see the old lone star, now as the Bonnie Blue, go off to war once more as young Southerners, including some from the Florida Parishes, followed his old banner of rebellion into a new revolution.

ACKNOWLEDGMENTS

NOTES

BIBLIOGRAPHY

INDEX

ACKNOWLEDGMENTS

HAPPY DEBTS of gratitude always accumulate in writing a work of this kind, and many friends have provided much appreciated assistance. Foremost must be Mary Herbert Price and Vonnie Zullo, whose extensive help with research in Louisiana, Mississippi, and Washington made the task of bringing all of the necessary material together vastly less challenging. Ann Lipscomb-Webster, friend and colleague at Mississippi's outstanding Department of Archives and History, was wonderful in locating obscure Spanish documents in its collections. Friends Aaron Crawford and Ervin Jordan helpfully located resources in Tennessee and Virginia, and special thanks go to William K. Bolt of the Andrew Jackson Papers project for help in finding Reuben Kemper's correspondence with Old Hickory. Samuel C. Hyde Jr., director of the Center for Southeast Louisiana Studies at Southeastern Louisiana University at Hammond, frequently offered assistance. Several other friends provided helpful tips and advice, among them John Coski, Else Jensine, Pam Keyes, Thomas Lowry, Sylvia Frank Rodrigue, Tracy Roe, and Elizabeth "Budge" Weidman. The Interlibrary Loan staff at Virginia Tech's Newman Library were quick and effective in locating an onerous number of volumes and microfilm, and my graduate assistant Jeremy Whitlock did much footwork. A special debt is due to Andrew McMichael, author of the excellent *Atlantic Loyalties: Americans in Spanish West Florida, 1785–1810*, for giving this manuscript a careful and most helpful reading. Finally, two very patient women deserve special thanks: first, my editor Jenna Johnson at Houghton Mifflin Harcourt, who waited a long time for this book; and second, Sandra Davis, to whom the wait must have seemed even longer.

NOTES

Abbreviations

Facsimiles	Archivo General de Indias, Papeles de Cuba, Facsimiles from Spanish Archives, Library of Congress.
HSP	Historical Society of Pennsylvania, Philadelphia.
LC	Library of Congress, Washington, DC.
Letter Books	Rowland, Dunbar. *Official Letter Books of W.C.C. Claiborne, 1801–1816.* 6 vols. Jackson: Mississippi Department of Archives and History, 1917.
LSU	Louisiana State University, Baton Rouge.
MDAH	Mississippi Department of Archives and History, Jackson.
NA	National Archives, Washington, DC.
"Official Records"	Padgett, James A., ed. "Official Records of the West Florida Revolution and Republic." *Louisiana Historical Quarterly* 21 (July 1938): 685–805.
Parker, *Calendar*	Parker, David W. *Calendar of Papers in Washington Archives Relating to the Territories of the United States (to 1873).* Washington, DC: Carnegie Institution, 1911.
PdeC	Papeles Procedentes de la Isla de Cuba, Archives of the Indies, Madrid, Spain, Microfilm copies at Hill Library, Louisiana State University, Baton Rouge.
Robertson	Robertson, James A. *List of Documents in Spanish Archives Relating to the History of the United States, which have been Printed or of which Transcripts are Preserved in American Libraries.* Washington: Carnegie Institution, 1910.
Spanish Papers	Mississippi Provincial Archives, Spanish Domination, 8 September 1802 to December 1806, Archives of the Indies, Seville, Cuban Papers, Mississippi Department of Archives and History, Jackson.

Sumario   "Copia del Sumario sobre el modo como fue soprendido el Fuerto de Baton Rouge," 1811, *legajo* 163B, PdeC.

Territorial Papers, Mississippi

        Carter, Clarence Edwin, comp. *The Territorial Papers of the United States*. Vol. 5, *The Territory of Mississippi 1798–1809*. Washington, DC: Government Printing Office, 1937.

        ————. *The Territorial Papers of the United States*. Vol. 6, *The Territory of Mississippi 1809–1817*. Washington, DC: Government Printing Office, 1938.

Territorial Papers, Orleans

        Carter, Clarence Edwin, comp. *The Territorial Papers of the United States*. Vol. 9, *The Territory of Orleans 1803–1812*. Washington, DC: Government Printing Office, 1940.

UVA   University of Virginia, Charlottesville.

WFP   Archives of the Spanish Government of West Florida, 1782–1816, 19th Judicial District Court, Baton Rouge, LA.

1. Realm of Happiness

1. Willis Miller Kemper and Harry Linn Wright, *Genealogy of the Kemper Family in the United States, Descendants of John Kemper of Virginia* (Chicago: George K. Hazlitt and Co., 1899), 64. Statements of the Kemper brothers' physical size are many and exaggerated; none of them apparently came from anyone who actually saw or knew them. Perhaps the earliest is Alexander Walker, who wrote in the 1850s that Reuben was "of gigantic frame" (Alexander Walker, *The Life of Andrew Jackson* [Philadelphia: Davis, Porter and Coates, 1866], 285). Although Henry L. Favrot of Baton Rouge was born after all the brothers were dead, he could have spoken with people who knew them, and in 1896 he described Reuben, Nathan, and Samuel as "three celebrated giants of pioneer Mississippi" (Henry L. Favrot, "The West Florida Revolution and Incidents Growing Out of It," *Publications of the Louisiana Historical Society* 1, part 3 [1896]: 40). Stanley Clisby Arthur probably built on Favrot's statement and also interviewed some Kemper descendants in the 1930s, though of course none of them would have ever met their ancestors. Arthur claimed that all of the Kemper brothers were "over 6 feet, 200 lbs or more," and he further described Reuben in particular as being six feet six inches tall and "active as a cat" (*The Story of the Kemper Brothers* [St. Francisville, LA: St. Francisville *Democrat*, 1933], 3, 11). However, Reuben Kemper's height and coloring are conclusively detailed in his 1816 passport application, presumably from someone's direct observation or by his own statement (passport application of Reuben Kemper, January 3, 1816, Register of Passport Applications, December 21, 1810, to October 7, 1817, General Records of the Department of State, Record Group 59, National Archives, Washington, DC, 17).

2. Kemper and Wright, *Kemper Family*, 66–67. The date of Peter Kemper's family move to Cincinnati is uncertain, but writing in 1820, Reuben Kemper stated that he was living in Cincinnati in 1793. Reuben Kemper to Richard M. Johnson, February 23, 1820, Documents in Relation to the Claim of James Johnson for Transportation on the Missouri and Mississippi Rivers, March 1, 1821, House Document 110, Serial Set Vol. 55, Session Vol. 8 (Washington, 1821), 72.

3. Kemper and Wright, *Kemper Family*, 64.

4. Charles Frederic Goss, *Cincinnati, the Queen City, 1788–1912* (Chicago: S. J. Clark Co., 1912), 471–72.

5. Favrot, "Incidents," 22.

6. Kemper to Johnson, February 23, 1820, Documents in Relation to the Claim of James Johnson; Benjamin Van Cleve, "Memoirs of Benjamin Van Cleve," *Quarterly Publication of the Historical and Philosophical Society of Ohio* 17 (January–June 1922): 59.

7. Robert W. Wilhelmy, "Senator John Smith and the Aaron Burr Conspiracy," *Cincinnati Historical Society Bulletin* 28 (Spring 1970): 39–40; M. Avis Pitcher, "John Smith, First Senator from Ohio and His Connections with Aaron Burr," *Ohio History* 45 (January 1936): 68–70.

8. Reuben Kemper in account with John Smith, August 20, 1803, Reuben Kemper in account with John Smith, 1799, Kemper in account with John Smith, 1798, John Smith–Reuben Kemper Papers, Hill Library, Louisiana State University, Baton Rouge (hereinafter cited as LSU).

9. Account of Goods Purchased by Reuben Kemper, Archives of the Spanish Government of West Florida, 1782–1816, 19th Judicial District Court, Baton Rouge, 19, 6–7. Hereafter cited as WFP.

10. Kemper in account with Smith, 1799, Smith-Kemper Papers.

11. Memorandum, August 19, 1803, ibid.

12. Receipt of John Clay to John Smith, October 29, 1799, ibid.

13. The house belonged to David Bradford, a man who had a colorful background. In 1794 he promoted discontent over taxes among western Pennsylvanians; this eventually led to the so-called Whiskey Rebellion, with federal officers beaten, mails robbed, and loose companies of rebels arming themselves to resist. Bradford fled when President George Washington sent militia to quell the uprising, and he made his way to Bayou Sara, where he obtained a land grant and built the house he would rent to Smith. By 1797, he had moved to a much grander mansion, which he called the Myrtles, in the village of St. Francisville, a mile back from the bayou; the house still stands today.

14. Stanley Clisby Arthur, *The Story of the West Florida Rebellion* (Baton Rouge: Claitor's Publishing, 1975; reprint of 1935 edition), 6.

15. Louise Butler, "West Feliciana — a Glimpse of Its History," *Louisiana Historical Quarterly* 7 (January 1924): 97–98.

16. Arthur, *West Florida*, 18–20; Papers in re the Will of Anne Lejeune, June 1803, WFP, 7, 117ff.

17. Andrew McMichael, *Atlantic Loyalties: Americans in Spanish West Florida, 1785–1810* (Athens: University of Georgia Press, 2008), 28–29.
18. A General list of the First Quarter of New Feliciana, July 4, 1798, Vicente Pintado Papers, Library of Congress, Washington, DC (hereinafter cited as LC).
19. Powell A. Casey, "Military Roads in the Florida Parishes of Louisiana," *Louisiana History* 15 (Summer 1974): 232–33n.
20. A good general description of the region is in Butler, "West Feliciana," 93–94.
21. Andrew McMichael, "The Kemper 'Rebellion': Filibustering and Resident Anglo American Loyalty in Spanish West Florida," *Louisiana History* 43 (Spring 2002): 140–41.
22. Samuel C. Hyde Jr., *Pistols and Politics: The Dilemma of Democracy in Louisiana's Florida Parishes, 1810–1899* (Baton Rouge: Louisiana State University Press, 1996), 18–19.
23. Thomas D. Clark and John D. W. Guice, *Frontiers in Conflict: The Old Southwest, 1795–1830* (Albuquerque: University of New Mexico Press, 1989), 17.
24. Isaac Johnson to Pintado, October 1, 1799, Pintado Papers, LC.
25. *New York Gazette and General Advertiser*, January 15, 1811.
26. L. N. McAlister, "Pensacola During the Second Spanish Period," *Florida Historical Quarterly* 37 (January–April 1959): 306.
27. Deposition of John Smith, April 17, 1800, WFP, 4, 170.
28. Partnership agreement, June 14, 1799, account transcript, 1798–1799, Smith-Kemper Papers. The partnership document is also on file in WFP, 19, 5–6.
29. It is uncertain just when Nathan Kemper appeared in Feliciana. He may have come downriver with Reuben and Smith, or he may have followed them. He first appears on the record as a debtor to the firm in the inventory of the property of Reuben Kemper and Company, September 10–12, 1800, WFP, 4, 280–87.
30. Deposition of Isaac Johnson, October 11, 1802, WFP, 5, 385–86; Papers in re will of Anne Lejeune, June 1803, 7, 117ff; Arthur, *West Florida*, 32; *New York Public Advertiser*, December 8, 1810.
31. Inventory of the property of Reuben Kemper and Company, September 10–12, 1800, WFP, 4, 280–87; Inventory of accounts of Reuben Kemper and Company, September 26, 1800, 289–92; Inventory of open accounts of Reuben Kemper and John Smith, September 26, 1800, 292–99.
32. Account transcript, 1798–1799, Smith-Kemper Papers.
33. Sale of a negress from Father Charles Burke to Reuben Kemper and Company, January 27, 1800, WFP, 4, 94–95.
34. Armand Duplantier to Reuben Kemper and Company, March 25, 1800, WFP, 19, 3–5.
35. Kemper in account with Smith and Kemper, 1800–1801, Smith-Kemper Papers.
36. Petition of John Smith, April 24, 1800, WFP, 4, 169. It is not clear just when Smith notified Kemper of intent to dissolve the partnership. The fact that the

order for an inventory of goods and accounts went out on July 27, almost exactly three months after Smith's April 24 petition, suggests that the firm continued in operation until that date.

37. Inventory of accounts of Reuben Kemper and Company, September 26, 1800, WFP, 4, 289–92, Inventory of open accounts of Reuben Kemper and John Smith, September 26, 1800, 292–99.

38. Ibid., 292–99.

39. Conveyance, April 19, 1802, Smith to Kempers, ibid., 7, 76–78.

40. Just what Smith had the Kempers doing is murky. It has been suggested that they managed a farm for him, but there is no evidence that Smith was as yet a planter, and no population censuses show him or the Kempers as having slaves sufficient to be planters on a scale requiring two managers.

41. Inventory and auction sale of the property of Benjamin Scott, September 15, 1801, WFP, 5, 82–83; Reuben Kemper to Richard M. Johnson, February 23, 1820, Documents in Relation to the Claim of James Johnson for Transportation on the Missouri and Mississippi Rivers; Kemper and Wright, *Kemper Family*, 84.

42. Succession of Antonio Rodriguez, January 22, 1803, WFP, 7, 108.

43. Reuben Kemper complaint, June 30, 1802, WFP, 5, 346.

44. *Hagers-Town (MD) Gazette*, December 18, 1810.

45. James A. Padgett, ed., "The West Florida Revolution of 1810, as Told in the Letters of John Rhea, Fulwar Skipwith, Reuben Kemper, and Others," *Louisiana Historical Quarterly* 21 (January 1938): 77.

46. Reuben Kemper v. James Wilkins, n.d. [1803], Adams County, Mississippi Territory, Minutes of the County Court, 2, 1802–1804, 158, Mississippi Department of Archives and History, Jackson (hereinafter MDAH).

47. Kemper in account with Smith and Kemper, 1800–1801, Smith-Kemper Papers.

48. *New York Daily Advertiser*, February 15, 1803; *Augusta (ME) Kennebec Gazette*, March 3, 1803. The call for war came from Senator Samuel White of Delaware.

49. Robert Livingston to James Madison, May 28, 1802, *State Papers and Correspondence Bearing upon the Purchase of the Territory of Louisiana* (Washington, DC: Government Printing Office, 1903), 29, Madison to Livingston, May 1, 1802, 24.

50. Livingston to Madison, April 24, 1802, ibid., 23, Madison to Charles Pinckney, July 26, 1802, 33.

51. James Monroe journal, May 1803, ibid., 171.

52. Jefferson to Madison, August 25, 1803, ibid., 236.

53. John Sibley to Claiborne, October 10, 1803, Clarence Edwin Carter, comp., *The Territorial Papers of the United States*, vol. 9, *The Territory of Orleans 1803–1812* (Washington, DC: Government Printing Office, 1940), 72 (hereinafter *Territorial Papers, Orleans*).

54. Don Carlos de Grand-Pré to Vicente Folch, July 19, 1804, *legajo* 106, Papeles Procedentes de la Isla de Cuba, Archives of the Indies, Madrid, Spain, micro-

film copies at Hill Library, Louisiana State University, Baton Rouge (hereinafter cited as PdeC).

55. Kemper to Alexander Stirling, n.d., May–June 1804, in Grand-Pré to Folch, June 20, 1804, Mississippi Provincial Archives, Spanish Domination, 8 September 1802 to December 1806, Archives of the Indies, Seville, Cuban Papers, MDAH, James A. Robertson #4979 in *List of Documents in Spanish Archives Relating to the History of the United States, Which Have Been Printed or of Which Transcripts Are Preserved in American Libraries* (Washington, DC: Carnegie Institution, 1910), hereinafter cited as Spanish Papers, Robertson.

56. Grand-Pré to Casa Calvo, July 19, 1804, Spanish Papers, Robertson #4982.

57. *Mississippi Herald and Natchez Gazette*, November 16, 1804.

58. Draft of agreement, February 22, 1806, attached to Reuben Kemper to James Brown, April 7, 1806, James Brown Papers, LC; Reuben Kemper in account with John Smith, August 20, 1803, Miscellaneous accounts transcript, Receipt of John Clay to John Smith, October 29, 1799, Smith-Kemper Papers; Carlos de Grand-Pré to Marqués de Casa Calvo, July 19, 1804, Spanish Papers, Robertson #4982. The arbiters concluded that Kemper owed Smith $10,533. The arbiters also decreed that Maria and the land belonged to Smith, meaning that Smith owed Kemper a credit for his half of their current value, which they put at $4,726 and which showed what a wise purchase that tract at Bayou Sara had been. Still, the math in the agreement was faulty, for it stated that Kemper owed $5,756 instead of $5,807, an error of $51.

59. Power of Attorney, August 20, 1803, WFP, 6, 244–45. John Smith to John Murdoch, September 14, 1807, ibid., 12, 102, makes specific reference to "the decision of the arbitrators sanctioned by the tribunal."

60. Kneeland first appears in the historical record doing work for Pintado in October of 1801 (Kneeland to Pintado, October 24, 1801, Pintado Papers, LC). Kneeland's friendship with Smith is attested to when Smith listed Kneeland as a character witness when involved in the Burr episode (*Spooner's Vermont Journal*, February 8, 1808). Kemper's only open statement about his reason for hating Kneeland was made on September 23, 1808; he and his brothers attacked Kneeland, and Reuben shouted at him about his "unworthy arbitration" in the John Smith affair; see Declaration of Ira C. Kneeland, October 24, 1808, *legajo* 1566, Archivo General de Indias, Papeles de Cuba, Facsimiles from Spanish Archives, LC (hereinafter cited as Facsimiles). The connection of Kneeland with timber poaching is pure surmise, based on the fact that in 1807, when Kneeland tried to get possession of that same land through purchase or donation, he stated that "the timber is an object to me" (Kneeland to Pintado, March 24, 1807, Pintado Papers).

61. Reuben Kemper to Richard M. Johnson, February 23, 1820, Documents in Relation to the Claim of James Johnson for Transportation on the Missouri and Mississippi Rivers.

62. Gilbert C. Russell to Rev. Dr. Potts, January 29, 1827, J.F.C. Claiborne, *Mississippi As a Province, Territory, and State, with Biographical Notices of Eminent Citizens* (Jackson, MS: Powers and Barksdale, 1880), 311n.

63. Grand-Pré to Casa Calvo, July 19, 1804, Spanish Papers, Robertson #4982.
64. Kemper and Wright, *Kemper Family*, 119.
65. Grand-Pré to Pintado, October 22, 1803, Pintado Papers, LC.
66. Deposition of Nathan Kemper, November 15, 1803, WFP, 7, 78, Power of Attorney, John Murdoch to Chew and Rolf, November 22, 1803, 40.
67. Thomas Jefferson to Albert Gallatin, October 29, 1803, cited in Roger G. Kennedy, *Mr. Jefferson's Lost Cause: Land, Farmers, Slavery and the Louisiana Purchase* (New York: Oxford University Press, 2003), 194–95. Kennedy is a quirky and not entirely reliable source.
68. Claiborne to Daniel Clark, November 18, 1803, Dunbar Rowland, ed., *Official Letter Books of W.C.C. Claiborne, 1801–1816* (Jackson: Mississippi Department of Archives and History, 1917), 1, 288 (hereinafter cited as *Letter Books*).
69. Clark to Claiborne, November 22, 1803, *Territorial Papers, Orleans*, 118; Charles Gayarré, *History of Louisiana: The French Domination* (New York: William J. Widdleton, 1866), 607; John W. Monette, *History of the Discovery and Settlement of the Valley of the Mississippi* (New York: Harper and Brothers, 1848), I, 561. Citing Monette, McMichael, *Atlantic Loyalties*, pages 60–61, says that Kemper in fact was elected colonel of this company, but this is a misreading of the source.
70. Gayarré, *History of Louisiana*, 607.
71. Woodson Wren letter, November 5, 1846, quoted in *Tennessee Old and New: Sesquicentennial Edition, 1796–1946* (Nashville: Tennessee Historical Commission, 1946), 357–58; Arthur Preston Whitaker, *The Mississippi Question 1795–1803, a Study in Trade, Politics, and Diplomacy* (New York: D. Appleton-Century, 1934), 250–52.
72. Claiborne to Madison, April 3, 1802, *Letter Books*, 1, 69.
73. Ira Kneeland Survey Book, October 1, 1802, Grand-Pré to Pintado, December 22, 1802, Pintado Papers, LC.
74. Bolling to Pintado, March 10, 1804, ibid.
75. Patrick Marrin to Pintado, October 25, 1803, ibid.
76. Marrin to Pintado, November 24, 1803, ibid.
77. Christopher Bolling to Pintado, n.d., ibid.; William Dunbar to Pintado, September 23, 1802, William Linter to Pintado, September 19, 1802; Clarence Edwin Carter, comp., *The Territorial Papers of the United States*, vol. 5, *The Territory of Mississippi 1798–1809* (Washington, DC: Government Printing Office, 1937), 312–13 (hereinafter *Territorial Papers, Mississippi*).
78. Bolling to Pintado, December 10, 1803, John Johnson to Pintado, January 12, 1804, Alexander Bookter to Pintado, January 29, 1804, Patrick Marrin to Pintado, February 11, 1804, Pintado Papers, LC.
79. Grand-Pré to Pintado, October 22, 1802, ibid.
80. Patrick Tegart to Pintado, November 30, 1803, Marrin to Pintado, December 11, 1803, ibid.
81. Agreement, January 12, 1804, Notarial Record A, 415, Clerk of Court, West Feliciana Parish Courthouse, St. Francisville, LA.

82. Reuben Kemper to Richard M. Johnson, February 23, 1820, Documents in Relation to the Claim of James Johnson for Transportation on the Missouri and Mississippi Rivers, 72.

83. Claiborne to Jefferson, February 25, 1804, *Territorial Papers, Orleans*, 191, John Ballinger to James Monroe, December 26, 1811, ibid., 965.

84. Claiborne to Madison, April 9, 1804, *Letter Books*, 2, 88.

85. Claiborne and Wilkinson to Pierre Laussat, March 26, 1804, *Territorial Papers, Orleans*, 216–17.

86. Madison to Livingston, March 31, 1804, *State Papers and Correspondence Bearing upon the Purchase of the Territory of Louisiana*, 275–77.

87. John Sibley to Claiborne, October 10, 1803, *Territorial Papers, Orleans*, 72.

88. Fortescue Cuming, *Sketches of a Tour to the Western Country* (Pittsburgh: Cramer, Spear and Eicheuam, 1810), 311–12; Timothy Flint, *Recollections of the Last Ten Years in the Valley of the Mississippi* (Carbondale: Southern Illinois University Press, 1968; reprint of 1926 edition edited by George R. Brooks), 215–16.

89. Flint, *Recollections*, 215–16.

90. Plan of Fort of Baton Rouge, 1804, in Georges Henri Victor Collot, *A Journey in North America* (Paris, 1826), LC.

91. Map of Florida Occidental, Distrito de Baton Rouge, Año de 1805, Pintado Papers, LC.

92. Cuming, *Sketches*, 312.

93. Claiborne to Madison, March 26, 1805, *Territorial Papers, Mississippi*, 425.

94. John Watkins Report, February 2, 1804, *Letter Books*, 2, 7.

95. Derek N. Kerr, *Petty Felony, Slave Defiance, and Frontier Villainy: Crime and Criminal Justice in Spanish Louisiana, 1770–1803* (New York: Garland Publishing, 1993), 11–14.

96. Ibid., 25–26.

97. Ibid., 28–29.

98. In April of 1803 Frederick Kimball of Bayou Sara, another friend of Kemper, maintained a dispute with his neighbors the merchants Rhea and Cochrane. He set a fire on his property to clear some land and then apparently left it untended. A wind arose and the fire spread and soon crossed over to Rhea and Cochrane's property and engulfed a cotton mill and other outbuildings, missing only the main house and their warehouse. A considerable quantity of cotton went up in flames, in all doing twelve hundred pesos in damage. It turned out that Kimball had been a constant irritant to Rhea and Cochrane ever since they had employed his enemy Kneeland to do a survey for them. When the partners bought a cotton gin and some land from Kimball and then hired Kneeland to run their store and the gin for a time, Kimball said he did not want Kneeland on land that had been his and demanded that they dismiss him. They refused, and thereafter Kimball became so threatening that Kneeland feared for his life and got the governor to make Kimball post a bond for a year not to disturb him. Deposition of William Brent, September 29,

1803, WFP, 8, 203–4; 7, 200; *Mississippi Herald and Natchez Gazette,* November 16, 1804, quoted in McMichael, *Atlantic Loyalties,* 197n.

99. Kerr, *Petty Felony,* 197–98. Kerr is not always persuasive as far as West Florida is concerned, not having examined the local records in depth, and he concentrates far more on criminal than civil law. As an example of the so-called Black Legend about Spanish justice, J. W. Carrighan in 1851 stated that the will of the governor was law, and his decisions were often regarded by the American settlers as arbitrary and unjust. "It was on account of a judgment of this character rendered against Reuben Kemper, that a revolt took place in 1804." Carrighan was no doubt repeating common assumption in Louisiana at the time. "Historical and Statistical Sketches of Louisiana," *DeBow's Review of the Southern and Western States* 11, New Series 4 (September 1851), 255. Expansionism has long been excused by claims of lazy, bumbling, corrupt, cruel rule by Spanish colonial administrators, who are also depicted as Catholic and fanatical. The reality is far different, as a study of almost every Spanish colonial administration in North America would attest. Seen in this light, the Kempers, rather than being products of Spanish injustice, appear as independent agents acting for their own interests and cloaking themselves in American colors. McMichael, "Kemper 'Rebellion,'" pages 133–35, offers a good brief analysis of the conventional historiography of Spain in West Florida, citing more in-depth sources.

100. Claiborne to Jefferson, August 24, 1803, *Territorial Papers, Mississippi,* 6, 20–21.

101. Illegible to Pintado, December 28, 1800, Decree, February 23, 1801, Pintado Papers, LC.

102. McMichael, *Atlantic Loyalties,* 131. See for instance the case of Luther Smith for assault on a Dr. Williamson in October 1802, Deposition of Thomas Clayton, October 1802, WFP, 5, 386. In February 1802, Reuben Kemper discovered a corpse in a road, and the possibility existed that he had met his death by violent means (Richard Duvall to John Murdoch, February 18, 1802, ibid.).

103. McMichael, *Atlantic Loyalties,* 132.

104. Richard Duvall to Grand-Pré, August 28, 1803, Duvall to Pintado, September 1, 1803, October 2, 1803, Pintado Papers, LC.

105. Grand-Pré to Pintado, April 6, 1801, ibid.

106. McMichael, *Atlantic Loyalties,* 50.

107. Flint, *Recollections,* 229–30.

108. *Letter Books,* 1, 65, Claiborne to Henry Dearborn, June 30, 1802, 134–35.

109. Ephraim Kirby to Jefferson, April 20, 1804, *Territorial Papers, Mississippi,* 5, 318.

110. Kirby to Jefferson, May 1, 1804, ibid., 324–25.

111. L. N. McAlister, "Pensacola During the Second Spanish Period," *Florida Historical Quarterly* 37 (January–April 1959): 300–1, 307–10; William Coker and G. Douglas Inglis, *The Spanish Census of Pensacola, 1784–1820: A Genealogical Guide to Spanish Pensacola* (Pensacola: Perdido Bay Press, 1980), 89–90.

112. Claiborne to Cato West, April 21, 1804, *Letter Books*, 2, 109–10.
113. Claiborne to Granger, June 17, 1804, ibid., 212–13.
114. Gideon Granger to Claiborne, April 12, 1804, ibid., 206.
115. Claiborne to Thomas Jefferson, May 29, 1804, ibid., 176.
116. Richard Claiborne to Jefferson, February 16, 1804, *Territorial Papers, Mississippi*, 5, 307.
117. Characterization of New Orleans Residents, July 1, 1804, *Territorial Papers, Orleans*, 255.

2. Kemper & His Madly Deluded Party

1. Arthur, *Story of the Kemper Brothers*, pages 4–6, erroneously says that Nathan was the oldest brother and that he was the one who was Smith's agent. Arthur goes on to say that, unhappy with him, Smith fired Nathan and ordered him to leave Bayou Sara; when Nathan refused, Smith went to Grand-Pré. Arthur is not always to be trusted as a source.
2. John Mears to Pintado, July 8, 1804, Pintado Papers, LC.
3. Duvall to Pintado, September 1, 1803, ibid.
4. John H. Johnson to Pintado, June 5, 1804, ibid.; statements by Johnson, Murdoch, and Grand-Pré, April 1804, WFP, 8, 142, 144–45.
5. Sale agreement, April 1804, WFP, 8, 165.
6. Pintado to Stirling, June 13, 1804, Pintado Papers, LC. McMichael, *Atlantic Loyalties*, page 85, says Smith applied for the order in June, citing Isaac Joslin Cox in *The West Florida Controversy, 1798–1813* (Baltimore: Johns Hopkins Press, 1918), 152. McMichael also cites a letter of John Moore to Pintado, June 11, 1804, in the Pintado Papers, but this appears to be a miscitation, for no such letter is to be found in the Pintado Papers, nor is there any other letter containing this information. Cox actually does not say when Smith sought or received the eviction order, only that the attempt to carry it out was made in June. McMichael says that Smith's suit in 1804 listed Nathan and Samuel Kemper, but he provides no source for this assertion, and none has been found by this author (which is not to say that McMichael is incorrect).
7. Joseph Groves, *The Alstons and Allstons of North Carolina* (Atlanta: Franklin Printing and Publishing, 1901), 199–206; sale of slaves from the estates of John Turnbull, April 25, 1800, WFP, 4, 172.
8. Grand-Pré to Folch, June 20, 1804, Spanish Papers, Robertson #4979; Pintado to Stirling, June 13, 1804, Stirling to Pintado, June 13, 1804, Pintado Papers, LC.
9. *Salem (MA) Gazette*, August 28, 1804.
10. Study of the 1810 and 1820 censuses for Louisiana and Mississippi provides approximate ages for about half of the party, though it is not always possible to match names of those in 1804 with later census listings.
11. Stirling to Pintado, June 15, 1804, in Grand-Pré to Folch, June 20, 1804, Spanish Papers, Robertson #4979.

12. John O'Connor to Pintado, July 2, 1804, Pintado Papers, LC. Others known to be with the Kempers were James Sullivan, George Garnhart, Ransom O'Neil, James Cooper, Frederic Miller, Richard Law, Henry Still, William Whittaker, William Westbury, Nathan Bradford, and Henry Bradford.

13. *Walpole (NH) Political Observatory*, October 6, 1804; *Philadelphia United States Gazette*, October 8, 1804.

14. Kemper to Stirling, n.d. [June 1804], Grand-Pré to Folch, June 20, 1804, Spanish Papers, Robertson #4979.

15. Claiborne to Casa Calvo, September 10, 1804, *legajo* 179, PdeC.

16. Reuben Kemper to John Rhea, November 23, 1810, Padgett, "West Florida Revolution," 120; John Mills to Pintado, June 16, 1804, Pintado Papers, LC.

17. John Mills to Pintado, June 16, 1804, Pintado Papers.

18. Stirling to Pintado, June 18, 1804, ibid.

19. Alexander Stirling to Champney [Champness] Terry, June 18, 1804, ibid. McMichael, *Atlantic Loyalties*, page 195, note 45, inadvertently cites this letter as John Smith to Pintado, June 18, 1804. The address side is marked "by John Smith," meaning it was sent in Smith's care, not written by him, and it is quite certainly addressed to Terry.

20. John Mills to Pintado, 10:00 A.M., June 19, 1804, Pintado Papers, LC.

21. Stirling to Pintado, June 20, 1804, in Grand-Pré to Folch, June 20, 1804, Spanish Papers, Robertson #4979.

22. Grand-Pré to Folch, June 20, 1804, ibid.; June 21, 1804, ibid., #4981.

23. Grand-Pré to Pintado, June 21, 1804, Pintado Papers, LC; Grand-Pré to Casa Calvo, July 19, 1804, Spanish Papers, Robertson #4982.

24. John Mills to Pintado, June 23, 1804, 10:00 A.M., Pintado Papers, LC.

25. No actual copy of an amnesty offer has been found, but it seems to be referred to in Grand-Pré to Casa Calvo, August 28, 1804, Spanish Papers, Robertson #4996. Cox, *West Florida*, page 154, states that the Kempers refused such an offer, but cites no source.

26. Grand-Pré to Pintado, June 25, 1804, Pintado Papers, LC.

27. Stirling to Pintado, June 28, 1804, ibid.

28. Grand-Pré to Pintado, June 26, 27, 1804, ibid.

29. Grand-Pré to Pintado, June 28, 1804, ibid.

30. Pintado to Grand-Pré, July 2, 1804, O'Connor to Pintado, July 2, 1804, ibid.

31. Alston to O'Connor, July 2, 1804, O'Connor to Pintado, July 3, 1804, ibid.

32. O'Connor to Pintado, July 6, 1804, ibid.

33. Julien Poydras to Pintado, n.d. [July 1804], ibid.; Claiborne to Poydras, August 6, 1804, *Letter Books*, 2, 293–94.

34. Alexander Stirling to Pintado, 2:00 P.M., June 27, 1804, Pintado Papers, LC.

35. Stirling to John Rhea, June 30, 1804, ibid. It is not certain that Stirling was the author of this letter, but he seems to be the only person who fits the context.

36. Inventory of property taken belonging to the rebel party, June 30, July 6, 1804, Pintado Papers, LC; Philip Alston Gray to Grand-Pré, July 21, 1804, WFP, 10, 42.

37. Inventory of property found under guard at the mouth of the Bayou Sara belonging to the Kempers and others, June 30, 1804, Pintado Papers, LC.

38. John Rhea to Pintado, July 1, 1804, Receipt, July 1804, Terry to Pintado, July 2, 1804, ibid. The other prisoners were James Coutch, William McConkey, John Beck, Obadiah Nicholls, David Moore, and Henry and Frederick Miller.

39. Proclamation, July 2, 1804, Pintado to Grand-Pré, July 8, 1804, ibid.

40. Rhea to Pintado, July 2, 1804, ibid.

41. Pintado to Grand-Pré, July 7, 1804, ibid.

42. *Salem (MA) Gazette*, August 28, 1804.

43. Claiborne to Jefferson, June 26, 1804, *Letter Books*, 2, 221.

44. Claiborne to the Marqués de Casa Calvo, July 24, 1804, ibid., 265–66.

45. Claiborne to Madison, June 27, 1804, ibid., 228–29.

46. John Mears to Pintado, July 8, 1804, Pintado Papers, LC.

47. *Salem (MA) Gazette*, August 28, 1804.

48. O'Connor to Pintado, July 5, 1804, Rhea to Pintado, July 2, 1804, Pintado Papers, LC.

49. Grand-Pré to Casa Calvo, July 19, 1804, Spanish Papers, Robertson #4982; *Salem (MA) Gazette*, August 28, 1804.

50. Pintado to Grand-Pré, July 15, 1804, Pintado Papers, LC.

51. Murdoch to Pintado, July 8, 1804, ibid.

52. Solomon Alston to Pintado, July 8, 1804, ibid.

53. *Salem (MA) Gazette*, August 28, 1804.

54. O'Connor to Pintado, July 3 and 5, 1804, Pintado Papers, LC.

55. Grand-Pré to Casa Calvo, July 19, 1804, Spanish Papers, Robertson #4982.

56. O'Connor to Grand-Pré, July 17, 1804, Pintado Papers, LC.

57. Grand-Pré to Pintado, July 17, 1804, *legajo* 185, PdeC.

58. Pintado to Grand-Pré, July 18, in Grand-Pré to Casa Calvo, July 21, 1804, Spanish Papers, Robertson #4984.

59. Sale of Land by John O'Connor, July 23, 1800, WFP, 4, 261–62; mortgage, March 2, 1804, ibid., 8, 83.

60. Grand-Pré to Folch, July 18 and 21, 1804, *legajo* 185, PdeC.

61. Grand-Pré to Casa Calvo, July 19 and 21, 1804, Spanish Papers, Robertson #4982, 4984.

62. Claiborne to Julien Poydras, August 6, 1804, *Letter Books*, 2, 293–94.

63. Claiborne to Casa Calvo, August 27, 1804, ibid., 309–10; Grand-Pré to Folch, July 21, 1804, *legajo* 185, PdeC. Claiborne stated in his letter that he gave Reuben some advice and had hoped it would calm affairs in West Florida, but he did not specify what that advice was. Since this meeting between them occurred at virtually the same time as Claiborne's pardon offer via his father, it seems reasonable from the context to connect the two events.

64. Grand-Pré to Folch, July 21, 1804, *legajo* 185, PdeC.

65. Claiborne to Julien Poydras, August 6, 1804, *Letter Books*, 2, 293–94.

66. O'Connor to Pintado, July 21, 1804, Pintado Papers, LC; O'Connor to Stirling July 20, in Grand-Pré to Casa Calvo, July 21, 1804, Spanish Papers, Robertson

#4984. O'Connor actually reported that the party rode back to Mississippi on the "Sligo road," which is now U.S. Highway 61 to Woodville.

67. Reuben was in New Orleans at least from June 27 through August 27. On December 4, 1806, in giving testimony in *R. Kemper v. A. & J. Horton,* Nathan stated that Reuben was "unacquainted he believes with his Operation." William Baskerville Hamilton, *Anglo-American Law on the Frontier: Thomas Rodney & His Territorial Cases* (Durham, NC: Duke University Press, 1953), 247.

68. Casa Calvo to Claiborne, August 11, 1804, *Letter Books,* 2, 309. Casa Calvo's complaint speaks of *letters,* in the plural.

69. Ron V. Jackson, comp., Accelerated Indexing Systems, online database, *Mississippi Census, 1805–90.* McMichael, "The Kemper 'Rebellion,'" page 155, says Randolph was a Revolutionary War hero, citing Cox, *West Florida,* pages 155–56. The citation from Cox actually appears only on page 155 and says nothing of the Revolution, and Cox himself cites the *Charleston (SC) Courier* for September 2, 1804. In one of Cox's frequent errors in citation, the issue is actually that of September 25, and it makes no mention at all of Randolph or his origins. Cox also mistakenly calls Randolph Edmund rather than Edward. As for his being a Revolutionary War veteran, Randolph was only ten years old when that war concluded, in 1783.

70. Will of Patience Radford, February 16, 1804, WFP, 8, 75–76; Ancestry.com, online database, *Mississippi State and Territorial Census Collection, 1792–1866.*

71. Power of Attorney of Edward Randolph, May 9, 1804, WFP, 8, 191; *Boston Independent Chronicle,* October 21, 1805; Thomas Hutchins to ?, April 22, 1805, *Letter Books,* 3, 44–45.

72. Reuben Kemper to George, William, and Edward Randolph, November 7, 1814, Wilkinson County Land Deed Record A, 386–88, Chancery Court Records, Wilkinson County Courthouse, Woodville, MS.

73. Thomas Hutchins to unknown, April 22, 1805, *Letter Books,* 3, 44–45.

74. *Natchez Mississippi Herald and Natchez Gazette,* September 9, 1805, cited in McMichael, *Atlantic Loyalties,* 196, note 67.

75. Guice and Clark, *Frontiers in Conflict,* page 47, speculate that in fact the Kempers were tools of John Smith and Randolph (who they mistakenly state came from Virginia), arguing that both wanted to stir unrest. Smith seems an unlikely candidate for that, given his good relations with the Spaniards at this time, but he might already have had similar designs as Aaron Burr's in mind. Grand-Pré, in his August 19, 1804, letter to Casa Calvo, Spanish Papers, Robertson #4992, said he believed Daniel Clark and Randolph instigated the raid.

76. Thomas Hutchins to unknown, April 22, 1805, *Letter Books,* 3, 44–45. Hutchins appeared in his letter to speak of "Conrad Randolph" but was actually speaking of Edward, and this is probably just an editorial misreading of the manuscript document.

77. Virtually everyone has assumed that Randolph authored the declaration, though no contemporary record has been found to confirm that assumption.

The closest is Grand-Pré to Casa Calvo, August 19, 1804, Spanish Papers, Robertson #4992, in which Grand-Pré states that people in Feliciana believed Randolph had something to do with it. In 1918, Cox (*West Florida*, 155) averred that the declaration was "supposedly the work of Edmund [*sic*] Randolph," though his only cited source is the *Charleston (SC) Courier* of September 2, 1804, which he misdated and which makes no mention of Randolph or anyone else as author. Arthur, *Kemper Brothers*, page 6, follows Cox, as does McMichael, *Atlantic Loyalties*, page 91. While all the Kempers were literate, Reuben was the only one sufficiently comfortable with the pen to have authored the declaration. However, he was in New Orleans throughout this period and quite possibly was not even aware of his brothers' plans. Randolph, older and apparently better educated than Nathan or Samuel, therefore seems a natural choice.

78. *Washington (DC) Federalist*, September 15, 1804. The proclamation was published in at least a dozen newspapers, all based on its August 14 appearance in the *Natchez Mississippi Herald and Natchez Gazette*, with some minor variations in wording.

79. William Horace Brown, *The Glory Seekers* (Chicago: A. C. McClurg, 1906), 165–66, 178. Brown claims that some sources said the Kempers had Spanish land grants in the Baton Rouge District that they knew would be more valuable if the United States took over. Other than the thousand-arpent grant to Nathan, there is no indication that the Kempers ever owned anything other than the Bayou Sara plot next to Smith's. Brown is very anti-Kemper and iconoclastic in general, referring to him as "the buccaneer Reuben Kemper" and, in another instance, as "a profane braggart, a whiskey-guzzling, marauding, law-defying ruffian of the border."

3. The Late Insurrection at Baton Rouge

1. Isaac Sharp Deposition, September 2[7], 1804, WFP, 8, 268, Jessie Kirkland Deposition, September 25, 1804, 266.

2. Cuming, *Sketches*, 304–5.

3. Anonymous letter, August 7, 1804, *Natchez Mississippi Herald and Natchez Gazette*, August 14, 1804, quoted in *Harrisburg (PA) Oracle of Dauphin*, September 15, 1804. Cox, *West Florida*, page 156, and McMichael, *Atlantic Loyalties*, page 91, both state that the field on the flag was blue, but the only eyewitness description is the letter above cited written that same August 7 by the unnamed traveler who met the riders at the line, and he clearly states that the field was yellow. Grand-Pré apparently gave an identical description of the flag to Casa Calvo, as evidenced in a letter of Casa Calvo to Claiborne, August 11, 1804, *Letter Books*, 2, 309.

4. George Cavanaugh Deposition, September 26, 1804, WFP, 8, 263.

5. Jessie Kirkland Deposition, September 25, 1804, ibid., 264. Others with the band included William Westbury, Jonathan Clark, George Garnhart, George

Cavanaugh, Edwin Falks, John Moore, Isaac Sharp, Levi Sholar, James Bell, Samuel Perry, Mathew Douchet, David Beek, Jessie Kirkland, and three men known only as Hughes, Morgan, and Kelly.

6. Sales of Sundry Merchandise by Mr. John Hunter Johnson for account of John Smith from the 17 April 1800 to the 26 July 1808, ibid., 12, 160.

7. Jessie Kirkland Deposition, September 25, 1804, ibid., 8, 262.

8. Thomas Rodney to Caesar Rodney, October 20, 1804, Simon Gratz, ed., "Thomas Rodney," *Pennsylvania Magazine of History and Biography* 44 (no. 1, 1920): 60–61.

9. George Cavanaugh Deposition, September 26, 1804, WFP, 8, 253, 263, 269, 270.

10. George Garnhart Deposition, September 27, 1804, ibid., 254, 263, 265.

11. Levi Sholar Deposition, September 27, 1804, ibid., 254, 256.

12. Isaac Sharp Deposition, September 2[7], 1804, ibid., 254, 255, 258, 263, 267.

13. George Garnhart Deposition, September 27, 1804, ibid., 266.

14. Jonathan Clark Deposition, September 27, 1804, ibid., 267.

15. Levi Sholar Deposition, September 27, 1804, ibid., 254, 266.

16. Jonathan Clark Deposition, September 27, 1804, ibid., 263.

17. Jessie Kirkland Deposition, September 25, 1804, ibid., 266.

18. *Washington (DC) National Intelligencer*, June 8, 1804.

19. Cuming, *Sketches*, 304–5.

20. Henry Garnhart Deposition, September 26, 1804, WFP, 8, 260. Carrighan, "Historical and Statistical Sketches of Louisiana," page 255, states that O'Connor's express got through and warned Grand-Pré, but this was written almost half a century after the fact and is gainsaid by the contemporaneous evidence that the warning actually came from John Mears.

21. George Garnhart Deposition, September 27, 1804, WFP, 8, 261, makes it clear that Pintado was taken first after O'Connor, and then Stirling.

22. Proclamation, August 4, 1804, Grand-Pré to Pintado, August 1, 1804, Pintado Papers, LC.

23. Decree, May 1, 1804, ibid.; George Garnhart Deposition, September 27, 1804, WFP, 8, 257, Jessie Kirkland Deposition, September 25, 1804, 257, 261.

24. Jessie Kirkland Deposition, September 25, 1804, WFP, 8, 253, 258, 260, George Garnhart Deposition, September 27, 1804, 257.

25. George Garnhart Deposition, September 27, 1804, ibid., 261.

26. Grand-Pré to Casa Calvo, August 8, 1804, Spanish Papers, Robertson #4988.

27. Grand-Pré to Folch, August 3, 1804, *legajo* 106, PdeC.

28. Grand-Pré to Casa Calvo, August 8, 1804, Spanish Papers, Robertson #4988.

29. *New York Weekly Museum*, October 6, 1804.

30. Grand-Pré to Casa Calvo, August 8, 1804, Spanish Papers, Robertson #4988.

31. Proclamation, August 7, 1804, *legajo* 179, PdeC.

32. George Cavanaugh Deposition, September 26, 1804, WFP, 8, 260, Levi Sholar Deposition, September 27, 1804, 260, Jonathan Clark Deposition, September 27, 1804, 261, Henry Garnhart Deposition, September 26, 1804, 260.

33. George Cavanaugh Deposition, September 26, 1804, ibid., 257.
34. Jessie Kirkland Deposition, September 25, 1804, ibid., 257, 267, Henry Garnhart Deposition, September 26, 1804, 257.
35. Jonathan Clark Deposition, September 27, 1804, ibid., 264.
36. Levi Sholar Deposition, September 27, 1804, ibid., 262, George Cavanaugh Deposition, September 26, 1804, 261.
37. Levi Sholar Deposition, September 27, 1804, ibid., 263, George Garnhart Deposition, September 27, 1804, 266, Henry Garnhart Deposition, September 26, 1804, 263, Jessie Kirkland Deposition, September 25, 1804, 266.
38. *Walpole (NH) Political Observatory*, September 29, 1804.
39. None of the published transcripts of the declaration carry the names of any signatories.
40. Henry Garnhart Deposition, September 26, 1804, WFP, 8, 258, George Cavanaugh Deposition, September 26, 1804, 258; *Otsego (NY) Herald*, September 27, 1804.
41. George Cavanaugh Deposition, September 26, 1804, WFP, 8, 266.
42. Isaac Sharp Deposition, September 2[7], 1804, ibid., 261; *Walpole (NH) Political Observatory*, September 29, 1804.
43. Letter from Natchez, August 8, 1804, *Norwich (CT) Courier*, September 12, 1804.
44. Charles Howard to Pierre-Joseph Favrot, September 11, 1804, Wilbur E. Meneray, ed., *The Favrot Family Papers: A Documentary Chronicle of Early Louisiana* (New Orleans: Howard Tilton Memorial Library, 1997), vol. 4, 162.
45. Deposition of Mrs. Mary Routh Johnson, October 27, 1806, WFP, 11, 255–56.
46. Grand-Pré to Casa Calvo, August 17, 1804, Spanish Papers, Robertson #4991.
47. Grand-Pré to Casa Calvo, August 17, 1804, ibid.; Grand-Pré to Folch, August 17, 1804, *legajo* 106, PdeC.
48. Grand-Pré to Casa Calvo, August 19, 28, 1804, Spanish Papers, Robertson #4992, #4998.
49. *New York Weekly Museum*, October 6, 1804.
50. Fulton and Duplantier to Thomas Dowson, August 21, 1804, Spanish Papers, Robertson #4994, Dowson to Fulton and Duplantier, August 21, 1804, #4995, Dowson to Fulton and Duplantier, August 22, 1804, #4996.
51. Casa Calvo to Morales, August 2, 11, 13, 1804, Morales to Casa Calvo, August 13, 15, 1804, Pedro Olivier to Miguel Toler, August 19, 1804, *legajo* 595, PdeC.
52. Grand-Pré to Folch or Casa Calvo, August 20, 1804, *legajo* 179, PdeC. Grand-Pré's letter is a scribal copy and actually appears to refer to Edward McCabe, but the context, with mention of the store at Tunica, makes it clear that he was speaking of Randolph, and the copyist simply misread his original.
53. Casa Calvo to Claiborne, August 11, 1804, *Letter Books*, 2, 309.
54. Claiborne to Casa Calvo, August 27, 1804, ibid., 309–10.
55. Claiborne to West, August 29, 1804, ibid., 311, Claiborne to Poydras, August 30, 1804, 313.
56. Claiborne to Madison, August 30, 1804, ibid., 312.

57. The Natchez editor apparently sent his exchange copies downriver to New Orleans, then via packet ship to Washington and New York. If the copies had been sent by rider northeast on the Natchez Trace, the reports of the Kemper episode would have appeared in the Nashville papers first rather than in the New York and Alexandria papers, and the news would have been published two to three weeks sooner.

58. The earliest appearances of the manifesto appear to be in the *New-York Herald*, September 15, 1804, and the *Washington Federalist* of the same date.

59. McMichael, *Atlantic Loyalties*, 57.

60. *Frederick-town (MD) Hornet*, October 2, 1804.

61. Editorial of October 23, 1804.

62. *Charleston (SC) City Gazette*, March 2, 1805.

63. This evaluation of press coverage is based on a survey of all articles on the Kemper affair in newspapers, indexed on the site www.genealogybank.com. This site chiefly carries newspapers in the collections of the American Antiquarian Society, Worcester, Massachusetts; there are no doubt numerous other journals in existence that carried coverage as well, though there seems no reason to suppose that their coverage was any different, since they all depended on extracts from the Natchez press. The actual number of articles on the Kemper affair to be found on the site are July: 0; August: 15; September: 78; October: 29; November: 6; and December: 8.

64. *Charleston (SC) Courier*, October 8, 1804.

65. *Walpole (NH) Political Observatory*, October 6, 1804; *Philadelphia United States Gazette*, October 8, 1804.

66. *Richmond and Manchester Advertiser*, September 26, 1804.

67. Casa Calvo to Claiborne, September 13, 1804, *Letter Books*, 2, 331.

68. Claiborne to Casa Calvo, September 13, 1804, ibid., 330.

69. Rodney to Caesar Rodney, October 20, 1804, Gratz, "Rodney," 60–61.

70. Rodney to Caesar Rodney, October 13, 1804, ibid., 58–59.

71. Grand-Pré to Casa Calvo, August 28, 1804, Spanish Papers, Robertson #4998.

72. *Richmond Enquirer*, December 1, 1804.

73. Grand-Pré to Folch or Casa Calvo, August 20, 1804, *legajo* 179, PdeC.

74. *Richmond Enquirer*, December 1, 1804.

75. *Hartford Connecticut Courant*, December 5, 1804.

76. *Philadelphia Aurora General Advertiser*, November 24, 1804; *Peacham (VT) Green Mountain Patriot*, December 18, 1804.

77. *Peacham (VT) Green Mountain Patriot*, December 18, 1804.

78. *Providence (RI) Phenix*, September 29, 1804.

79. *New York Weekly Museum*, October 6, 1804.

80. *Charleston (SC) Courier*, October 8, 1804.

81. *New York Mercantile Advertiser*, September 25, 1804.

82. Claiborne to Jefferson, October 27, 1804, *Territorial Papers, Orleans*, 315.

83. Pedro Cevallos to Casa Calvo, January 14, 1805, *legajo* 176B, PdeC.

84. Claiborne to Madison, December 11, 1804, *Letter Books*, 2, 25.

85. McMichael, "Kemper 'Rebellion,'" 135.
86. Ibid., page 160, is an excellent analysis of the reasons so few rallied to the Kempers.

4. Birds of a Feather

1. Claiborne to Granger, June 17, 1804, *Letter Books*, 2, 212–13.
2. *Washington (DC) National Intelligencer*, December 25, 1804.
3. Kirby to Jefferson, May 1, 1804, *Territorial Papers, Mississippi*, 5, 324–25.
4. John Callier to Jefferson, December 17, 1804, ibid., 368–69. The name is found spelled as both *Caller* and *Callier*, but the brothers themselves spelled it as it appears in the text. Cox, *West Florida*, page 169, confuses the brothers for each other, as do other authors.
5. Casa Calvo to Carlos Howard, October 8, 1804, *legajo* 55, PdeC.
6. Albert James Pickett, *History of Alabama and Incidentally of Georgia and Mississippi, from the Earliest Period* (Birmingham, AL: Birmingham Book and Magazine Co., 1962; reprint of 1851 edition), 474–75.
7. Folch to Casa Calvo, July 17, 1804, Folch to Ignacio Balderas, September 4, 1804, *legajo* 55, PdeC.
8. Letter from Baton Rouge, October 8, 1804, *Hagers-Town (MD) Herald*, November 30, 1804; *Richmond Enquirer*, December 1, 1804.
9. Bond of George Cavanaugh, September 26, 1804, WFP, 8, 271–74; Petition of friends of Levi Sholar, July 11, 1805, 10, 43–44. Similar bonds were sworn out for Clark, Kirkland, Sholar, and both Garnharts.
10. Claiborne to Madison, December 11, 1804, *Letter Books*, 2, 25.
11. Pintado to Grand-Pré, n.d. [1805?], WFP, 10, 26–27. No business of any kind is recorded in the West Florida Papers from August 6 to August 27, 1804.
12. Philip A. Gray to Grand-Pré, May 15, 1805, WFP, 10, 41–42; Philip A. Gray v. Kemper Brothers, 11, 206; Gray to Grand-Pré, April 15, 1806, 206.
13. Letter from Baton Rouge, October 16, 1804, *Richmond Enquirer*, December 1, 1804.
14. Claiborne to Madison, April 21, 1805, *Territorial Papers, Orleans*, 438.
15. Thomas Rodney to unknown, October 20, 1804, *Richmond Argus*, December 1, 1804.
16. Claiborne to Madison, October 22, 1804, *Letter Books*, 2, 372.
17. Claiborne to Madison, October 24, 1805, ibid., 3, 211–12.
18. *Pittsfield (MA) Sun*, February 25, 1805.
19. Toulmin to Madison, July 6, 1805, *New York American Citizen*, December 16, 1805.
20. *New York Spectator*, November 30, 1805.
21. *Alexandria (VA) Advertiser*, December 13, 1805.
22. Toulmin to Madison, October 11, 1805, *New England Palladium*, December 24, 1805.
23. Toulmin to Lattimore, December 6, 1805, *Territorial Papers, Mississippi*, 5, 431.
24. Claiborne to Folch, October 31, 1805, *Letter Books*, 3, 221.

25. Toulmin to William Lattimore, December 6, 1805, *Territorial Papers, Mississippi*, 5, 437.

26. Claiborne to Madison, October 5, 1804, *Letter Books*, 2, 347–48.

27. *New York Commercial Advertiser*, December 13, 1804.

28. Claiborne to Madison, October 28, 1804, *Letter Books*, 2, 347.

29. Petition to Governor Claiborne, November 9, 1804, *Territorial Papers, Orleans*, 326.

30. Rodney to Caesar Rodney, October 31, 1804, Gratz, "Rodney," 66.

31. Claiborne to Madison, November 23, 1804, *Letter Books*, 3, 14–16; Claiborne to Casa Calvo, November 18, 1804, 17–19.

32. Madison to Claiborne, January 5, 1805, *Territorial Papers, Orleans*, 364.

33. McMichael, "Kemper 'Rebellion,'" 135.

34. *Sag Harbor (NY) Suffolk Gazette*, December 31, 1804.

35. Madison to Claiborne, November 10, 1804, *Territorial Papers, Orleans*, 332–33.

36. Characterization of New Orleans Residents, July 1, 1804, ibid., 255.

37. Isaac Briggs to Jefferson, February 9, 1805, *Territorial Papers, Mississippi*, 5, 382, Briggs to Jefferson, May 18, 1805, 404.

38. Madison to Claiborne, March 18, 1805, *Territorial Papers, Orleans*, 419.

39. Claiborne to Madison, March 26, 1805, ibid., 425.

40. C. C. Robin, *Voyages dans l'Intérieur de la Louisiane* (Gretna, LA: Firebird Press, 2000; reprint, trans. by Stuart O. Landry Jr.), 223.

41. McMichael, *Atlantic Loyalties*, 65.

42. Ibid., 146–48.

43. Claiborne to Casa Calvo, August 3, 1805, *Letter Books*, 3, 146; Claiborne to Madison, August 5, 1805, 151; Claiborne to Casa Calvo, August 9, 1805, 161; Claiborne to Madison, August 20, 1805, 178–79.

44. Pintado to Bolling, March 11, 1805, Pintado Papers, LC.

45. Anonymous to Pintado, May 3, 1805, ibid.

46. McMichael, *Atlantic Loyalties*, 146–48.

47. McMichael, "Kemper 'Rebellion,'" 139.

48. Luther Smith to Grand-Pré, March 9, 1805, Statement, February 21, 1805, Pintado Papers, LC.

49. McMichael, *Atlantic Loyalties*, 65, 97.

50. John Mills to Stirling, March 28, 1805, WFP, 8, 60–62, Mills to Grand-Pré April 14, 1805, 65–66; Grand-Pré order to Stirling, May 9, 1805, 66. In this, as in most such cases, the WFP contains nothing to reveal the ultimate outcome of the charges.

51. Cuming, *Sketches*, 303, 308.

52. Mississippi Territorial Tax Rolls, Series 510, Wilkinson County, 1805, MDAH; 1805 Wilkinson County, Mississippi, Census, Ancestry.com, *Mississippi State and Territorial Census Collection, 1792–1866*. Nathan and Samuel are on the census but Reuben is not. Reuben appears as a landowner on the tax roll, Nathan as a tenant, and Samuel as a person with no fixed abode. The dates of the two enumerations are unstated and may account for the anomaly of Reuben's

being on the one but not the other. If he bought his property after the census but before the tax enumeration, he would have missed the first one; another possibility is that he may simply have been absent on business when the census was taken and so did not appear, since the census lists heads of households but not property owners. The tax list shows Samuel with no property at all, while the census shows him having three slaves, an unexplained anomaly. Arthur, *Kemper Brothers*, page 9, mistakenly says it was Samuel who opened the tavern.

53. Armand Duplantier sale, April 20, 1805, WFP, 9, 308; Reuben Kemper to James Brown, April 7, 1806, James Brown Papers, LC.

54. The best recent examination of the Burr conspiracy will be found in Milton Lomask, *Aaron Burr: The Conspiracy and Years of Exile, 1805–1836* (New York: Farrar, Straus and Giroux, 1982), 3ff.

55. *New York Republican Watch-Tower*, September 19, 1804.

56. *Portland (ME) Jenks' Portland Gazette*, October 1, 1804.

57. Lomask, *Aaron Burr*, 52–53.

58. Ancestry.com, *Mississippi State and Territorial Census Collection*.

59. Claiborne to Madison, November 5, 1804, *Territorial Papers, Orleans*, 320.

60. John Rhea to ?, September 7, 1803, WFP, 4, 139–40.

61. [Thomas Hutchins] to ?, April 22, 1805, *Letter Books*, 3, 44–45.

62. Casa Calvo to Claiborne, May 6, 1805, ibid., 44.

63. Claiborne to Casa Calvo, May 8, 1805, ibid., 45–46.

64. Claiborne to Williams, May 8, 1805, ibid., 47.

65. Claiborne to Madison, May 10, 1805, ibid., 52–53.

66. *Charleston (SC) City Gazette*, July 13, 1805.

67. *New-York Herald*, June 29, 1805.

68. Claiborne to Madison, August 27, 1805, *Letter Books*, 3, 183.

69. *New Orleans Gazette*, June 28, 1805.

70. Claiborne to Madison, August 6, 1805, *Territorial Papers, Orleans*, 489.

71. Reuben Kemper to James Brown, April 7, 1806, Brown Papers, LC.

72. Thomas Holden Statement, September 7, 1805, with Robert Williams to Madison, September 14, 1805, *Washington (DC) Universal Gazette*, December 19, 1805.

73. William Flanagan Statement, September 7, 1805, with Robert Williams to Madison, September 14, 1805, *Washington (DC) Universal Gazette*, December 19, 1805.

74. Claiborne to Madison, August 27, 1805, *Letter Books*, 3, 183.

5. You Have Ruined Our Country

1. Hamilton, *Territorial Cases*, 247. The selection of Horton as ringleader is solely deductive and comes from the fact that he is apparently the only participant in the beatings and kidnappings whom Reuben and Nathan afterward brought to court, even though they knew the identities of several others.

2. Wilkinson County Census 1805, Ancestry.com, *Mississippi State and Territorial Census Collection, 1792–1866.*

3. Thomas Estevan to Pintado, April 16, 1810 (misfiled as 1802), Pintado Papers, LC.

4. Hamilton, *Territorial Cases,* 246; Statement of Minor Butler, September 26, 1805, certificate of information on the assaults on the Kemper Brothers, February 9, 1806, Spanish Papers, Robertson #5060.

5. Wilkinson County Census 1805, Ancestry.com, *Mississippi State and Territorial Census Collection, 1792–1866.*

6. Pintado to Bolling, July 19, 1805, Bolling to Pintado, August 17, 1805, Pintado Papers, LC; *Territorial Papers, Mississippi,* 5, 312–13.

7. Deposition of John Say, September 20, 1808, WFP, 16, 133.

8. Land sale, October 24, 1805, ibid., 11, 164–65.

9. Dunbar Rowland, *Mississippi, Comprising Sketches of Counties, Towns, Events, Institutions, and Persons, Arranged in Cyclopedic Form* (Atlanta: Southern Historical Publishing Association, 1907), 1, 996.

10. Arthur, *Kemper Brothers,* page 9, states that Grand-Pré actually offered a reward for the apprehension of the Kempers at this time, but there seems to be no evidence. Pickett, *Alabama,* pages 484–85, stated in 1851 that Grand-Pré decided to seize the Kempers and sent "a company of kidnappers." The attorney general of Mississippi Territory alleged on December 2, 1805, that the Hortons were paid by Grande-Pré. Hamilton, *Territorial Cases,* 318.

11. Kemper to Brown, April 7, 1806, Brown Papers, LC; Pickett, *Alabama,* 484–86. In his letter Kemper says there were five slaves in the party, but the year before in his deposition immediately after the event he had spoken of seven. Pickett cites "Historical MS. Notes in the possession of E. T. Wood, of Mobile," for his account, as well as the depositions as published in the American State Papers.

12. Statement of Ira C. Kneeland, September 26, 1805, Certificate of information on the assaults on the Kemper Brothers, February 9, 1806, attached to Grand-Pré to Folch, December 23, 1805, Spanish Papers, Robertson #5060.

13. The placement of Samuel at the tavern and Nathan and Reuben elsewhere is derived from the testimony of the brothers and other witnesses, and it seems the only scenario that fits the sources.

14. This account is constructed from the statements of John Atkinson, Henry Garnhart, Richard Richardson, and John Whittaker, September 3, 1805, Reuben Kemper, September 5, 1805, and Nathan Kemper, September 5, 1805, all attached to Robert Williams to Madison, September 14, 1805, *Washington (DC) Universal Gazette,* December 19, 1805; Pickett, *Alabama,* 484–86; Hamilton, *Territorial Cases,* 246–47. Also important is a narrative based on interviews with one or more of the Kempers, dated September 5, at Fort Adams, originally appearing in the *Natchez Mississippi Herald* of September 13, 1805, and reprinted in the *New York Spectator,* October 25, 1805, and elsewhere.

15. Robin, *Voyages*, 118.
16. This account is constructed from the statements of Samuel Kemper, September 5, 1805, William Westberry, September 3, 1805, James Latta, September 3, 1805, and Arthur Cobb, September 3, 1805, attached to Williams to Madison, September 14, 1805, *Washington (DC) Universal Gazette*, December 19, 1805; *Natchez Mississippi Herald*, September 13, 1805, reprinted in the *New York Spectator*, October 25, 1805.
17. This account is compiled from the statements of Adam Bingaman, William Barker, Reuben Kemper, Samuel Kemper, and Nathan Kemper, all of date September 5, 1805, attached to Robert Williams to Madison, September 14, 1805, *Washington (DC) Universal Gazette*, December 19, 1805; *Natchez Mississippi Herald*, September 13, 1805, reprinted in the *New York Spectator*, October 25, 1805; Hamilton, *Territorial Cases*, 246.
18. This account is based on the statements of Solomon Alston, Ira Kneeland, Minor Butler, September 26, 1805, Elrid Barker, September 28, 1805, Briton Barker, Clement Stewart, Samson Chandler, Denis Bradley, September 29, 1805, George Rowe, Robert Russell, October 1, 1805, John Ratliff, Adam Bingaman, William Barker, October 24, 1805, in Certificate of information on the assaults on the Kemper Brothers, February 9, 1806, attached to Grand-Pré to Folch, December 23, 1805, Spanish Papers, Robertson #5060.
19. This account is compiled from the Statements of Adam Bingaman, William Barker, Reuben Kemper, Samuel Kemper, and Nathan Kemper, all of date September 5, 1805, attached to Robert Williams to Madison, September 14, 1805, *Washington (DC) Universal Gazette*, December 19, 1805; *Natchez Mississippi Herald*, September 13, 1805, reprinted in the *New York Spectator*, October 25, 1805.
20. *Boston Independent Chronicle*, October 21, 1805; Statement of Minor Butler, September 26, 1805, in Certificate of information on the assaults on the Kemper Brothers, February 9, 1806, attached to Grand-Pré to Folch, December 23, 1805, Spanish Papers, Robertson #5060. The source says nothing about ransacking, but it seems logical that they did so, because otherwise there was no reason to evict Randolph's employee. The source also says that Randolph's store was at Bayou Sara, whereas it was actually at Tunica Landing.
21. Besides Barker they were Adam Bingaman, Charles Stewart, John Ratliff, George Rowe, and John Morris.
22. *New York Spectator*, October 25, 1805. This account is based on the statements of John Ratliff, Adam Bingaman, John Morris, William Barker, October 24, 1805, George Rowe, December 7, 1805, Certificate of information on the assaults on the Kemper Brothers, February 9, 1806, attached to Grand-Pré to Folch, December 23, 1805, Spanish Papers, Robertson #5060.
23. William Wilson to Robert Williams, September 6, 1805, *Rutland (VT) Herald*, January 4, 1806. This account is constructed from the statements of Samuel, Nathan, and Reuben Kemper, William Barker, and Adam Bingaman, all of date September 5, 1805, attached to Robert Williams to Madison, September 14, 1805, *Washington (DC) Universal Gazette*, December 19, 1805; *Natchez*

Mississippi Herald, September 13, 1805, reprinted in the *New York Spectator,* October 25, 1805, and statement of John Ratliff, October 24, 1805, Certificate of information on the assaults on the Kemper Brothers, February 9, 1806, attached to Grand-Pré to Folch, December 23, 1805, Spanish Papers, Robertson #5060.

24. William Wilson to Robert Williams, September 6, 1805; *Rutland (VT) Herald,* January 4, 1806.

25. Claiborne to William Wilson, September 9, 1805, *Letter Books,* 3, 185.

26. Robert Williams to Madison, September 14, 1805, *Washington (DC) Universal Gazette,* December 19, 1805; William Wilson to Robert Williams, September 6, 1805, *Rutland (VT) Herald,* January 4, 1806.

27. Statements of Arthur Cobb, William Westberry, James Latta, John Atkinson, Henry Garnhart, Richard Richardson, John Whittaker, September 3, 1805, attached to Robert Williams to Madison, September 14, 1805, *Washington (DC) Universal Gazette,* December 19, 1805.

28. *Natchez Mississippi Herald,* September 6, 1805, quoted in *Boston Democrat,* October 16, 1805.

29. This account has possible anomalies. As republished in eastern papers, it is supposedly a letter from Fort Adams dated September 5. As of that date, however, the Kempers were still at Point Coupée and would not reach Fort Adams until September 20, meaning the writer could not have met with them at Fort Adams by that date. The content of the letter makes it certain that Samuel Kemper, at least, spoke directly with the writer at Point Coupée. However, the writer also discusses reaction in Pinckneyville. A further anomaly is that the writer speaks of the kidnapping taking place the previous Thursday night, whereas September 2 was a Monday. It seems most likely that the *Herald,* in setting type for the first appearance of the story on September 13, carelessly conflated Thursday, September 5, when the letter was written, with the actual day of the attack. It is just barely possible that the writer could speak with the Kempers at Point Coupée during the day on September 3 and then travel to Fort Adams in time to write his letter on the fifth.

30. Williams to Ellis, September 9, 1805, in Walter S. Franklin and Walter Lowrie, eds., *American State Papers: Foreign Relations* (Washington, DC: Gales and Seaton, 1832), 2, 687.

31. *Natchez Mississippi Herald,* September 13, 1805, reprinted in the *New York Spectator,* October 25, 1805.

32. Williams to Grand-Pré, September 6, 1805, in *American State Papers: Foreign Relations,* 2, 686.

33. Grand-Pré to Williams, September 9, 1805, ibid., 687–88. It is interesting, though not necessarily significant, that the WFP for this period are completely silent on the attack on the Kempers.

34. Williams to Sparks, September 23, 1805, ibid., 688.

35. Thomas Rodney to Williams, September 30, 1805, ibid., 689.

36. Williams to Grand-Pré, September 30, 1805, ibid., 688.

37. Certificate of information on the assaults on the Kemper Brothers, February

9, 1806, attached to Grand-Pré to Folch, December 23, 1805, Spanish Papers, Robertson #5060.

38. John Graham to Claiborne, September 16, 1805, *Territorial Papers, Orleans*, 505.

39. Claiborne to Williams, October 10, 1805, *Letter Books*, 3, 194–95.

40. Claiborne to Dearborn, September 11, 1805, ibid., 188.

41. *Newburyport (MA) Herald*, November 19, 1805.

42. *New York Northern Post*, November 14, 1805.

43. *Boston Repertory*, November 22, 1805; Claiborne to Madison, October 30, 1805, in David W. Parker, ed., *Calendar of Papers in Washington Archives Relating to the Territories of the United States (to 1873)* (Washington, DC: Carnegie Institution, 1911), document #7293.

44. David Hart White, *Vicente Folch, Governor in Spanish Florida, 1787–1811* (Washington, DC: University Press of America, 1981), 82; Claiborne to Folch, October 31, 1805, *Letter Books*, 3, 221.

45. *Alexandria (VA) Advertiser*, November 19, 1805.

46. The number of newspapers carrying the various accounts of the Kemper affair, as found on the Genealogybank.com database, are September: 0; October: 37; November: 20; December: 31; January 1806: 3; February: 1; March: 0; April: 4. Since this only represents the journals in the collections of the American Antiquarian Society, and many newspapers appeared in America at the time that are either not represented in this collection or have disappeared entirely, these numbers should be adjusted upward by probably at least a factor of 2.

47. *Suffolk (NY) Gazette*, November 4, 1805.

48. *New York Daily Advertiser*, October 18, 1805; *Doylestown (PA) Pennsylvania Correspondent*, November 11, 1805.

49. *Richmond Enquirer*, April 18, 1806.

50. James D. Richardson, comp., *A Compilation of the Messages and Papers of the Presidents, 1789–1897* (Washington, DC: Bureau of National Literature, 1900–1904), 1, 384.

51. *Springfield (MA) Hampshire Federalist*, February 11, 1806.

52. Casa Yrujo to Madison, December 6, 1805, *Baltimore Sun*, February 22, 1806.

53. *New York Northern Post*, November 14, 1805.

54. *Alexandria (VA) Advertiser*, November 19, 1805; Hamilton, *Territorial Cases*, 293n. No record of a criminal trial of these two has been found, and the newspaper report of it could be in error, though it is evident that the Hortons were not present in Pinckneyville when Rodney considered whether or not the slaves involved could be tried.

55. Rodney to T. Gammel, October 2, 1805, Gratz, "Rodney," no. 2, 187–89.

56. Pickett, *Alabama*, page 507, gives an account of the Kempers' revenge that was apparently derived from manuscript notes provided in 1851 or earlier by E. T. Wood of Mobile. It details acts against Barker, Horton, Kneeland, and Alston, starting with the Kempers jumping Barker as he strode out of the courthouse in Fort Adams, then dragging him away to some cover where they beat and whipped him. The passage of almost half a century had considerably

embellished the story, building sometimes upon the barest of facts. The cases of Horton, Kneeland, and Alston will be dealt with hereafter in the appropriate places. Suffice it to say that an assault on Barker at Fort Adams would have been a punishable crime in violation of the bond posted by the Kempers, while Barker, like his companions, was escorted under guard to the line, and therefore the Kempers would have had no opportunity to get at him.

57. Robert Williams to Jefferson, December 21, 1804, *Territorial Papers, Mississippi*, 5, 369.
58. Petition to Congress, October 3, 1805, ibid., 422–23.
59. Reuben Kemper's passport application on January 3, 1816, specifically mentions the scars on his chin and face as distinguishing features. Register of Passport Applications, December 21, 1810–October 7, 1817, General Records of the Department of State, Record Group 59, National Archives, Washington, DC, 17.
60. Sale Josiah Taylor to John Smith, October 24, 1805, WFP, 9, 310.
61. J. F. Watson to G. W. Morgan, August 20, 1807, *Cincinnati Liberty Hall and Cincinnati Mercury*, July 16, 1808.
62. Gilbert C. Russell to Rev. Dr. Potts, January 29, 1827, Claiborne, *Mississippi*, 311n.
63. Alexander Walker, *The Life of Andrew Jackson* (Philadelphia: Davis, Porter and Coates, 1866), 285. Though published in 1866, this was written in the 1850s.
64. Pickett, *Alabama*, 484–86. Pickett cites "Historical MS. Notes in the possession of E. T. Wood, of Mobile," for his account.
65. Favrot, "West Florida," 40.

6. Live Hogs, Bees-Wax, Coffee, Etc.

1. Junta de Guerra to Grand-Pré, January 29, 1806, *legajo* 55, PdeC.
2. Claiborne to Madison, August 26, 1805, *Alexandria (VA) Advertiser*, December 13, 1805; Isaac Briggs to Albert Gallatin, March 3, 1806, *Territorial Papers, Mississippi*, 5, 453.
3. Clark and Guice, *Frontiers in Conflict*, 49.
4. William Lattimore to John Quincy Adams, April 11, 1806, *Territorial Papers, Mississippi*, 5, 455–56.
5. Postmaster General to Toulmin, April 25, 1806, ibid., 461–63.
6. Power of Attorney of John Smith, September 9, 1805, WFP, 14, 203, Revocation of Power of Attorney to James Murdoch, 204, Smith to Meeker, Williamson and Patton, April 7, 1806, 207.
7. Draft of Agreement between John Smith and Reuben Kemper, February 22, 1806, with Kemper to Brown, April 7, 1806, Brown Papers, LC.
8. Reuben Kemper to James Brown, April 7, 1806, Brown Papers, LC.
9. Ibid.
10. Deposition of John Murdoch, June 16, 1808, WFP, 14, 344–45.
11. Contract between John Ellis and Christopher Stewart, October 25, 1807, ibid.,

13, 125–26, Statement of Christopher Strong, February 19, 1808, 127–28, Partition of slaves, May 29, 1809, 15, 155.

12. Deposition of Clifford Jones, June 17, 1808, ibid., 14, 347–48.

13. Kemper to Brown, April 7, 1806, Brown Papers, LC.

14. Deposition of Clifford Jones, June 17, 1808, WFP, 14, 347–48. Jones said he thought it was Samuel Kemper who landed at Bayou Sara, but Samuel was already in New Orleans at this time.

15. Examination of John Ellis continued, August 29, 1808, ibid., 14, 353.

16. Reuben Kemper to John Ellis, March 7, 1806, ibid., 337.

17. Examination of Major John Ellis, August 17, 1808, ibid., 350–51, Deposition of John Murdoch, June 16, 1808, 344–45, Deposition of Clifford Jones, June 17, 1808, 347–48.

18. *Walpole (NH) Political Observatory*, April 3, 1807.

19. Claiborne to Jefferson, August 30, 1804, *Territorial Papers, Orleans*, 284.

20. Reuben Kemper's deposition described him only as "a good Mexican, who I, from Samuel's description of the man, believed to be young —."

21. This account of one of the dinner meetings is based on depositions by William A. Murray and Francis Small, in *Philadelphia Weekly Aurora*, March 26, 1811; *Walpole (NH) Political Observatory*, April 3, 1807.

22. Except where otherwise cited, this account of Reuben's visit to New Orleans is taken from Deposition of Reuben Kemper, August 8, 1807, in *Carlisle (PA) Gazette*, May 31, 1811. This deposition was first published in the *Baltimore Whig* on an unknown date, probably May 1811.

23. *New-York Herald*, March 11, 1809.

24. *New York Commercial Advertiser*, May 10, 1806. This is the earliest eastern appearance found for this letter, though it may have been in the Baltimore press some days earlier.

25. Kemper to Brown, April 7, 1806, Brown Papers, LC.

26. *Portsmouth (NH) United States Oracle and Portsmouth Advertiser*, March 26, 1803.

27. Baker lived six dwellings away from Butler in Pinckneyville per Wilkinson County Census 1805, Ancestry.com, *Mississippi State and Territorial Census Collection, 1792–1866*.

28. *Brattleborough (VT) Reporter*, July 12, 1806.

29. Reuben makes no mention of Samuel's being with him on the trip, but in one instance does speak of "our arrival" at Nashville. John Smith to Meeker et al., September 1, 1806, from Cincinnati, WFP, 14, page 214, says "the Kempers are here and therefore they cannot make much noise down there," which shows that one of Reuben's brothers was with him, and Samuel would be the logical one.

30. Anthony Merry to Lord Mulgrave, November 25, 1805, Foreign Office, General Correspondence from Political and Other Departments, General Correspondence before 1906, United States of America, Series II, FO 5/45, National Archives, Kew, Richmond, Surrey, England.

31. Claiborne to Grand-Pré, April 8, 1806, *Letter Books*, 3, 287.

32. Claiborne to Madison, June 26, 1806, ibid., 346–47.
33. Juan Morales in Pensacola, license to Armand Duplantier in Baton Rouge, July 5, 1806, Favrot Family Papers, Tulane University, New Orleans.
34. Reuben Kemper Deposition, August 8, 1807, *Carlisle (PA) Gazette*, May 31, 1811.
35. Paul Leicester Ford, comp., *The Writings of Thomas Jefferson* (New York: G. P. Putnam, 1897), 8, 473–74 and n.
36. Smith to Meeker et al., September 1, 1806, WFP, 14, page 214, makes it clear that the Kempers had arrived by that date. Burr did not reach Cincinnati until three days later. Reuben's recollection of chronology at this point in his 1807 deposition is off by a few days, implying that Burr had left Cincinnati before the Kempers arrived.
37. Smith to Meeker, Williamson, and Patton, June 30, 1806, ibid., 212.
38. Smith to Meeker, Williamson, and Patton, September 1, 1806, ibid., 214.
39. Contract between John Smith and Henry Dearborn, June 6–7, 1806, ibid., 209–10, Smith to Meeker, Williamson, and Patton, September 1, 1806, 214.
40. Reuben Kemper Deposition, August 8, 1807, *Carlisle (PA) Gazette*, May 31, 1811.

7. A Second Edition of the Kemper Attempt

1. *Frankfort (KY) Western World*, November 8, 1806.
2. Rodney to Caesar Rodney, November 21, 1806, Gratz, "Rodney," no. 4, 292.
3. Claiborne to Madison, November 25, 1806, *Territorial Papers, Orleans*, 688–89; Proclamation, November 27, 1806, Ford, *Writings*, 8, 481.
4. Statement, December 3, 1806, *Letter Books*, 4, 39, Claiborne to John Shaw, January 1, 1807, 74.
5. *Territorial Papers, Orleans*, 694–95; Thomas Perkins Abernathy, "Aaron Burr in Mississippi," *Journal of Southern History* 15 (February 1949): 9.
6. Claiborne to Dominic Hall, January 2, 1807, *Letter Books*, 4, 78–79.
7. Wilkinson to Claiborne, January 14, 1807, ibid., 95; *Burlington Vermont Centinel*, March 25, 1807, *Rutland (VT) Herald*, May 2, 1807.
8. Claiborne to Williams, February 10, 1807, *Letter Books*, 4, 119–21.
9. *Richmond Enquirer*, March 17, 1807.
10. *Lexington (KY) Reporter*, May 7, 1808.
11. Reuben Kemper Deposition, August 8, 1807, *Carlisle (PA) Gazette*, May 31, 1811; *Richmond Enquirer*, March 17, 1807. Kemper's deposition ends with the Floyd-Ralston visit.
12. *Lexington (KY) Reporter*, May 7, 1808.
13. Rodney to Caesar Rodney, February 1807, Gratz, "Rodney," no. 4, 300.
14. John Smith to Jefferson, February 2, 1807, *Territorial Papers, Mississippi*, 5, 510.
15. Claiborne to Williams, February 10, 1807, *Letter Books*, 4, 119–21.
16. White, *Folch*, 86.
17. *New York Spy*, April 21, 1807.
18. Williams to Jefferson, March 14, 1807, ibid., 528–29.

19. José Collins to Pintado, August 12, 1806, Pintado Papers, LC.
20. Rodney to Caesar Rodney, April 14, 1806, Gratz, "Rodney," no. 3, 279.
21. *Amherst (NH) Farmer's Cabinet*, May 20, 1806.
22. Rodney to Caesar Rodney, September 6, 1806, Gratz, "Rodney," no. 4, 290.
23. Kneeland to Pintado, October 12, 1806, Pintado Papers, LC.
24. Wilkinson to Secretary of War, September 8, 1806, James Wilkinson, *Memoirs of My Own Times* (Philadelphia: Abraham Small, 1816), 2, appendix 60, no pagination.
25. Kneeland to Pintado, October 12, 1806, Pintado Papers, LC.
26. Thomas W. Maury to Albert Gallatin, December 26, 1806, *Territorial Papers, Mississippi*, 5, 492.
27. Henry Dearborn to Thomas Swaine, November 8, 1806, ibid., 485.
28. Edmund P. Gaines to Henry Dearborn, January 19, 1807, ibid., 5, 495.
29. Frank L. Owsley Jr. and Gene A. Smith, *Filibusters and Expansionists: Jeffersonian Manifest Destiny, 1800–1821* (Tuscaloosa: University of Alabama Press, 1997), 62.
30. Cowles Mead to Madison, June 27, 1806, *Territorial Papers, Mississippi*, 5, 466–67, Madison to Meade, August 14, 1806, 477.
31. John Smith to Jefferson, February 2, 1807, ibid., 510; Hamilton, *Territorial Cases*, 249.
32. Ibid.; Reuben Kemper to George, William, and Edward Randolph, November 7, 1814, Wilkinson County Land Deed Record A, 386–88, Chancery Court Records, Wilkinson County Courthouse, Woodville, MS. Nathan's suit, tried as *Territory v. Hortons*, came to trial in May 1807. The above deed states that this property was awarded to Nathan to satisfy the court award. Hamilton, *Territorial Cases*, 253, 305–306.
33. Smith to Meeker et al., August 3, 1807, from Pinckneyville, WFP, 14, 221.
34. Deposition of John Smith, January 18, 1808, *Spooner's Vermont Journal*, February 8, 1808; Wilhelmy, "John Smith," 52–53.
35. Wilhelmy, "John Smith," 54, 57–58.
36. *Carlisle (PA) Gazette*, May 31, 1811.
37. Kneeland to Pintado, July 2, August 25, 1806, Pintado Papers, LC.
38. Appointment, February 1, 1806, Kneeland to Pintado, August 26, 1806, ibid.
39. Pintado to Kneeland, January 8, 1807, ibid.
40. Kneeland to Pintado, October 12, 1806, ibid.
41. Kneeland to Pintado, August 25, 1806, ibid.
42. Pintado to Kneeland, February 14, 1807, ibid.
43. Pintado to Kneeland, December 5, 1806, ibid.; Folch to Maxent, August 4, 1807, *legajo* 55, PdeC.
44. Kneeland to Nicholas Highland, August 15, 1807, Natchez Trace Collection, Center for American History, UT.
45. Kneeland to Pintado, December 23, 1806, Pintado Papers, LC.
46. Kneeland to Pintado, n.d., ibid.
47. Kneeland to Pintado, January 2, 1807, Appointment of Kneeland, February 1, 1806, ibid.

48. Kneeland to Pintado, March 24, 1807, August 10, 1808, ibid.

49. Daniel Clark, "Remarks on the Population, Culture, and Products of Louisiana," *Literary Magazine and American Register* 7 (1807): 45–57.

50. Thomas Rodney to Caesar Rodney, June 29, 1807, Gratz, "Rodney" (no. 1, 1921): 40.

51. The story of Jefferson's efforts to gain West Florida is ably laid out in Clifford Egan, "The United States, France, and West Florida, 1803–1807," *Florida Historical Quarterly* 47 (January 1969): 227–52 passim.

52. McMichael, *Divided Loyalties*, 163n.

53. Kneeland to Pintado July 26, 1808, Pintado Papers, LC.

54. John Smith to John Murdoch, September 14, 1807, WFP, 12, 101–2, Power of Attorney to A. D. Abrams, August 22, 1807, 96–97, James Williamson and Charles Patton to Grand-Pré, March 2, 1808, 14, 222–24.

55. John Murdoch to Ambrose Dudley Smith, February 11, 1808, ibid., 13, 20–21, Duplantier power of attorney to Thomas Estevan, March 8, 1808, 14, 226–27.

56. *New Orleans Louisiana Courier*, March 25, 1808.

57. Ambrose D. Smith to Grand-Pré, February 26, 1808, WFP, 13, 31, Ambrose D. Smith to Matilda Blair, February 12, 1808, 24.

58. Marriage contract, June 2, 1802, ibid., 19, 19ff, Fulwar Skipwith to Charles de Hault Delassus, July 10, 1810, 18, 34ff.

59. Kneeland to Pintado, August 10, 1808, Pintado Papers, LC.

60. WFP, 12, 205ff.

61. William Bell v. James McMullen, August 29, 1807, ibid., 210.

62. Abernathy, "Burr," 16–17.

63. Folch to Claiborne, June 15, 1807, document #7462, Parker, *Calendar*, 370.

64. Contract between John Ellis and Christopher Stewart, October 25, 1807, WFP, 13, 125–26.

65. James McElroy Deposition, June 17, 1808, ibid., 14, 346; Deposition of John Murdoch, June 16, 1808, 344–45; Examination of Major John Ellis, August 17, 1808, 352; Christopher S. Stewart Deposition, June 16, 1808, 341–42; Declaration of Matilda Stewart, June 16, 1808, 339–40.

66. McMichael, *Atlantic Loyalties*, 102–26; Examination of Major John Ellis, August 17, 1808, WFP, 14, 352, Examination of John Ellis continued, August 29, 1808, 353; George de Passau Power of Attorney, April 5, 1809, 13, 47.

67. Deposition of John Ellis, 1808, WFP, 13, 206; Declaration of John Holmes, June 8, 1808, 14, 338–39; Deposition of Matilda Stewart, June 7, 1808, 333, Declaration of Matilda Stewart, June 16, 1808, 339–40; Declaration of Christopher Stewart, June 7, 1808, 332; Christopher S. Stewart Deposition, June 16, 1808, 341–42.

68. Christian Schultz, *Travels on an Inland Voyage* (New York: Isaac Riley, 1810), 160.

69. Deposition of John Murdoch, June 16, 1808, WFP, 14, 344–45. In his deposition, as translated from the original Spanish, Murdoch refers to a "Randall" in Pinckneyville, but he must have meant Randolph.

70. James McElroy Deposition, June 17, 1808, ibid., 14, 346; Deposition of Clifford

Jones, June 17, 1808, 347–48; Deposition of Hercules O'Connor, June 17, 1808, 348–49; Examination of John Ellis continued, August 29, 1808, 353; Deposition of James Chauveau, July 1, 1808, 349–50; John Horton Deposition, June 16, 1808, 343–44.

71. James McElroy Deposition, June 17, 1808, ibid., 346.

72. "Descendants of Alexander Stirling," March 16, 2002, http://www.clanstirling .org/Main/families/USA/pdf/alexanderstirlinglouisana.pdf; Bryan McDermott to Grand-Pré, June 11, 1808, WFP, 14, 334–35; Deposition of Bryan McDermott, September 22, 1808, 356; James Pirrie to Grand-Pré, June 15, 1808, 336–37.

73. Deposition of Benjamin Richardson, State v. Patrick Vaughan, June 30, 1808, WFP, 13, 273–74, Deposition of Richardson, September 27, 1808, 274, Deposition of Joseph Moffat, June 30, 1808, 175–76, Deposition of Samuel Smart, June 30, 1808, 274–75, Deposition of Patrick Vaughan, September 11, 1808, 277–78.

74. *Boston New England Palladium*, July 29, 1808; *Petersburg (VA) Intelligencer*, August 9, 1808.

75. Grand-Pré to Claiborne, August 3, 1808, Document #7513, Parker, *Calendar*, 372, August 24, 1808, Document #7514, 373, Claiborne to Grand-Pré, August 6, 1808, Document #7515, 373; Claiborne to Grand-Pré, August 31, 1808, *Letter Books*, 4, 197, Claiborne to Madison, August 31, 1808, 201, Claiborne to Grand-Pré, November 13, 1808, 248–49.

76. Summary Proceedings Against Deserters, August 2, 1808, WFP, 13, 251–57.

77. Deposition of Ira C. Kneeland, August 26, 1806, ibid., 11, 226.

8. Our Tribunal Cannot Be Men of Business

1. Pintado to Kneeland, December 5, 1806, Pintado Papers, LC.

2. Kneeland to Pintado, March 24, 1807, ibid.

3. Kneeland to Pintado, December 12, 1807, ibid.

4. Ellis and Stewart mortgage to John Murdoch and Ira Kneeland, January 28, 1808, WFP, 13, 10–10A.

5. Christopher Stewart to Grand-Pré, September 6, 1808, ibid., 14, 358, Deposition of slave Cupid, September 6, 1808, 359, Examination of John Ellis continued September 22, 1808, 357, Deposition of John Ellis, 1808, 13, 206.

6. John Ellis and Christopher Stewart to Grand-Pré, December 6, 1808, ibid., 13, 354–55, Ellis to Grand-Pré, November 21, 1808, 356.

7. The date of Samuel's departure is uncertain. He appears on the 1810 Louisiana Census for Rapides and was not present with his brothers on the September 23, 1808, attack on Kneeland, so it seems reasonable to assume that he had moved prior to that time. Pickett, *Alabama*, page 507, states that "Reuben caught another of these wretches named Horton, and chastised him as long as the latter could receive it, and live." This information is credited to "MS. Notes in the possession of Mr. E. T. Wood, of Mobile." The Wood story ap-

parently conflates the whipping of Kneeland with Horton, for no evidence survives of any physical assault on Horton.

8. David Holmes to Robert Smith, October 22, 1809, *Territorial Papers, Mississippi*, 6, 23.

9. William D. McCain, "The Administrations of David Holmes, Governor of the Mississippi Territory, 1809–1817," *Journal of Mississippi History* 29 (November 1967): 328–30, 335. McCain's article is almost all there is in print in the way of a David Holmes biography, but he cites several theses and dissertations that offer somewhat more information.

10. Holmes to Joseph Johnson, September 21, 1808, *Territorial Papers, Mississippi*, 6, 18; Holmes to William Connell, September 21, 1808, 19–20.

11. Hamilton, *Territorial Cases*, 318. Henry Flowers testified to seeing six men, including the Kempers. Declaration of Henry Flowers, October 24, 1808, Archivo General de Indias, Papeles de Cuba, *legajo* 1566, Facsimiles from Spanish Archives, LC (hereinafter cited as Facsimiles). The version of this that appeared in Pickett, *Alabama*, page 507, has Samuel present but not Nathan and says each gave Kneeland a hundred lashes, then cut off his ears with a "dull knife," saving the ears for exhibition in a pickling jar at their tavern.

12. Declaration of Ira C. Kneeland, October 24, 1808, *legajo* 1566, Facsimiles.

13. Declaration of Henry Flowers, October 24, 1808, ibid.

14. Declaration of Samuel Flowers, October 24, 1808, Declaration of Juan Croker, October 24, 1808, ibid.

15. Declaration of Elijah Adams, October 24, 1808, Declaration of Patience Kimball, October 24, 1808, Declaration of Michael Williams, October 24, 1808, ibid.

16. Grand-Pré to Williams [Holmes], November 11, 1808, ibid.

17. Folch to Marqués de Someruelos, January 24, 1809, ibid.

18. Kneeland to Marqués de Pintado, December 10, 1808, Pintado Papers, LC.

19. Arthur, *Kemper Brothers*, page 11, said in 1933 that Kemper family tradition maintained that the ear story was true but that the brothers had not used a dull knife, and it also denied the ears being kept in spirits. The family — who in 1933 would have to have been descendants of Nathan, since neither Reuben nor Samuel married or had children — said the intent was to "ear-mark" Kneeland, which certainly agrees with Kneeland's own description of the act. And the family did maintain that a slice from each ear was kept in the tavern in Pinckneyville.

20. Grand-Pré to Folch, October 19, 1808, Spanish Papers, Robertson #5159.

21. Claiborne to Robert Smith, March 19, 1809, *Letter Books*, 4, 332–33.

22. Clark and Guice, *Frontiers in Conflict*, 52–53.

23. Francisco Casa y Luengo to Pierre-Joseph Favrot, January 29, 1809, Pierre-Joseph Favrot Correspondence, Tulane; Elie Beauregard to Mr. Marion, October [December] 19, 1808, WFP, 16, 346–47.

24. Address of residents of Feliciana to Grand-Pré, 1808, *legajo* 185, PdeC; Representation to Grand-Pré, October 19, 1808, Spanish Papers, Robertson #5158.

25. Marriage contract of Samuel Fulton and Hélène de Grand-Pré, December 6, 1808, WFP, 12, 380–84.

26. Sale of lots of Carlos de Grand-Pré to Pierre Favrot, December 23, 1808, ibid., 388; Will of Carlos de Grand-Pré, December 28, 1808, ibid., 16, 219.

27. Discourse of Grand-Pré, November 15, 1808, *legajo* 185, PdeC.

28. Thomas Lilley Appointment, June 2, 1806, WFP, 10, 10, William Addison to Thomas Lilley, May 25, 1799, 3, 68–69, Report of inspection of bridge, January 3, 1799, 4.

29. Journal of Events in the Assembly of Alcaldes and Syndics, December 7, 1808, attached to Assembly to Someruelos, December 9, 1808, Lilley to Grand-Pré, December 12, 1808, *legajo* 185, PdeC.

30. Lilley to Grand-Pré, December 12, 1808, with enclosures, ibid.

31. Grand-Pré to Lilley, December 17, 1808, ibid.

32. Estevan to Murdoch, December 20, 1808, ibid.

33. Herries to Grand-Pré, December 27, 1808, ibid.

34. Marriage contract of Samuel Fulton and Hélène de Grand-Pré, December 6, 1808, WFP, 12, 380–84. Carlos de Grand-Pré hyphenated his surname, but his son Luis de Grand Pré did not.

35. Pierre-Joseph Favrot to Someruelos, January 8, 1811, Pierre-Joseph Favrot Correspondence, Tulane.

36. Claiborne to Madison, February 10, 1805, *Territorial Papers, Orleans*, 391.

37. Schultz, *Travels*, 160.

38. Slave sale Francisco Miranda to Juan Perez, December 30, 1808, WFP, 12, 392–93; Delassus to Folch, February 4, 1809, *legajo* 1567, Facsimiles.

39. J. W. Carrighan, "Statistical and Historical Sketches of Louisiana," *DeBow's Review of the Southern and Western States* 11, New Series 4 (December 1851): 612–13. John S. Kendall, "Documents Concerning the West Florida Revolution, 1810," *Louisiana Historical Quarterly* 17 (January 1934), page 82, says Hicky was born in 1778. No certain date can be fixed.

40. *New York Public Advertiser*, December 8, 1810; Cuming, *Sketches*, 307; John R. Bedford to James Madison, July 4, 1810, *Papers of James Madison: Presidential Series*, 2, 399–400.

41. Henry Eugene Sterkx and Brooks Thompson, "Philemon Thomas and the West Florida Revolution," *Florida Historical Quarterly* 39 (April 1961): 378–79; *Hagers-Town (MD) Gazette*, December 18, 1810; LeRoy E. Willie, comp., *History of Spanish West Florida and the Rebellion of 1810 and Philemon Thomas, Patriot* (Baton Rouge: General Philemon Thomas Chapter, Sons of the American Revolution, 1991), 1. Thomas first appears in the WFP in June of 1806 when he signed as surety for Lilley; see Thomas Lilley Appointment, June 2, 1806, WFP, 10, 10.

42. Favrot, "Incidents," 28; Arthur, *West Florida*, 92.

43. William Henry Sparks, *The Memories of Fifty Years* (Philadelphia: E. Claxton and Co., 1870), 417; *Hagers-Town (MD) Gazette*, December 18, 1810.

44. Auction Sale of Property of Samuel Steer and Mary Lintot, April 26, 1808, WFP, 14, 122.

45. Cuming, *Sketches*, 312–13.

46. Gilbert Leonard to Wilkinson, April 1, 1797, Wilkinson, *Memoirs*, 2, appendix 23, n.p.

47. *Hagers-Town (MD) Gazette*, December 18, 1810; *New Orleans Louisiana Gazette*, February 23, 1818; David A. Bice, *The Original Lone Star Republic: Scoundrels, Statesmen, and Schemers of the 1810 West Florida Rebellion* (Clanton, AL: Heritage Publishing, 2004), 92–94; Arthur, *West Florida*, 42.

48. *New York Spectator*, October 23, 1805.

49. Walter S. Franklin and Walter Lowrie, eds., *American State Papers: Public Lands* (Washington: Duff Green, 1834), 3, 40, 43, 57, 61.

50. Solomon Alston Estate Document, April 27, 1809, LSU; Groves, *Alstons*, 209.

51. Arthur, *Kemper Brothers*, 11.

52. The 1851 account in Pickett, *Alabama*, page 507, based on the manuscript notes of Wood, says Alston died of edema contracted while hiding from the Kempers for many nights in a row in an open boat on a bayou. Even if Alston had lain in a cramped position all night, causing his legs to swell, the edema would have disappeared the next day, and repeated instances would not lead to a life-threatening condition. An extreme and improbable explanation offered by Dr. Thomas Lowry is that Alston could have gotten strep throat as a result of exposure, and that, followed by glomerulonephritis (Bright's disease), could cause edema and lead to death.

   If Alston had fatal edema, it also could have arisen from other, less complex causes. Tuberculosis is one explanation for his demise, especially since Alston lived for a few weeks after making out his will. Another possibility is congestive heart failure, which is caused by hypertension or heart disease; the heart is not able to pump efficiently, leading to edema in the legs and, eventually, death. It is a fairly common phenomenon, though today it is treatable.

   Quite probably his death had nothing to do with the Kempers, but the relatively sudden and perhaps at the time unexplained death of Alston was easily attached in legend to the Kempers. During most of February of 1809 Reuben Kemper was on the Mississippi taking a cargo of sugar to New Orleans, and he was still in that city at least as late as February 23, rather than in Feliciana hounding Alston to such a degree that the man believed he was mortally ill five weeks later. River protest, February 23, 1809, Notary John Lynd, 4, 512–13, New Orleans Notarial Archives.

53. Estate of Governor Grand-Pré to Samuel Fulton (as executor), February 1810, the Estate of the late Gov'r Charles De Grand-Pré with Philip Hicky, April 1810, Receipt of Gilbert Leonard, n.d., Carlos de Grand-Pré Succession Papers, LSU. It was a substantial estate, and Hicky was still faithfully working on it a year after the 1810 revolt.

54. Kneeland to Pintado, July 9, 1809, Pintado Papers, LC.

55. Pierre-Joseph Favrot to Someruelos, January 8, 1811, Pierre-Joseph Favrot Correspondence, Tulane.

56. Kneeland to Pintado, June 8, 1809, Pintado Papers, LC.

57. Kneeland to Pintado, May 10, 1809, ibid.

58. Adair, quoted in Robert Taylor, "Prelude to Manifest Destiny: The United States and West Florida, 1810–1811," *Gulf Coast Historical Review* 7 (Spring 1992): 48.

59. Claiborne to Smith, April 21, 1809, *Letter Books*, 4, 344–45.

60. Marriage contract, June 2, 1802, WFP, 19, 19ff; Skipwith to John Graham, January 14, 1811, Padgett, "West Florida Revolution," 170; Henry Bartholomew Cox, *The Parisian American: Fulwar Skipwith of Virginia* (Washington, DC: Mount Vernon Publishing Co., 1964), 1–2, 6, 9, 15, 22–23, 27, 121, 123. Cox is all but silent on the years 1810 through 1812, when Skipwith was involved with the West Florida episode.

61. Kendall, "Documents," 87–88.

62. *Hagers-Town (MD) Gazette*, December 18, 1810.

63. Skipwith to John Graham, January 14, 1811, Padgett, "West Florida Revolution," 170.

64. Abram Horton to Someruelos, August 17, 1809, Thomas Estevan to Pintado, April 16, 1810, Lénnàn to Pintado, April 13, 1810, Pintado Papers, LC. Horton's letter does not state when he lost his land to Nathan, but at least it indicates that it must have been in the summer of 1809.

65. Reuben Kemper to George, William, and Edward Randolph, November 7, 1814, Wilkinson County Land Deed Record A, 386–88, Chancery Court Records, Wilkinson County Courthouse, Woodville, MS. This deed does not indicate when the sale took place, but the 1810 Louisiana census shows Nathan living in Attakapas, so presumably the transfer took place in 1809 or early 1810.

66. *Alexandria Louisiana Planter*, May 15, 1810.

67. River protest, February 23, 1809, Notary John Lynd, 4, 512–13, New Orleans Notarial Archives.

68. *Washington (DC) National Intelligencer*, June 3, 1808.

69. *Newburyport (MA) Statesman*, January 19, 1809.

9. The Spirit of Independence

1. Meeting of the officials and report of the happenings at the beginning of the revolution, August 21, 1810, WFP, 18, 78–84.

2. Samuel Fulton et al. to Grand-Pré [Delassus], January 11, 1809, Spanish Papers, Robertson #5161.

3. Those others were John Rhea, Robert Percy, James Pirrie, Richard Duvall, Francis Herrault, William Herries, and Samuel Llewellyn.

4. Report of an Industrial Council, January 25, 1809, ibid.; Relation to Delassus, January 11, 1809, Address of Delassus to Convention of alcaldes and Syndics, n.d., Delassus to Folch, February 4, 1809, *legajo* 2356, Facsimiles.

5. Auction Sale of the Property of Valentine Thomas Dalton, October 7, 1807, WFP, 12, 306–9; Estimation of the Costs in the Proceedings of the Succession of Valentine Thomas Dalton, October 11, 1807, 310.

6. His first name appears in variant spellings as *Rafael,* and his last as *Croker* and *Croquer.*

7. Land sale, October 21, 1809, WFP, 15, 213.

8. Fees in case against George de Passau, November 6, 1806, ibid., 11, 273–74; Costs in Proceedings, July 15, 1808, 13, 188–89.

9. Statements of Hamanse Domingo Manuel Villanueva, Andres Martinez, Eulogio de Casas, "Copia del Sumario sobre el modo como fue soprendido el Fuerto de Baton Rouge," 1811, *legajo* 163B, PdeC. This translates to "Copy of the Summary about the way the fall of the Fort of Baton Rouge came to pass." Hereinafter cited as Sumario.

10. Favrot to Someruelos, January 8, 1811, Pierre-Joseph Favrot Correspondence, Tulane.

11. Ibid.

12. Lewis Stirling to Pintado, June 19, 1810, Pintado Papers, LC.

13. Favrot to Someruelos, January 8, 1811, Pierre-Joseph Favrot Correspondence, Tulane.

14. José de la Peña Statement, Sumario.

15. Favrot to Someruelos, January 8, 1811, Pierre-Joseph Favrot Correspondence, Tulane.

16. Raphael Crocker statement, August 13, 1812, Sumario; Crocker to Folch, September 24, 1810, *legajo* 63, PdeC.

17. Statements of Martinez, Michael Harrold, José de la Peña, Sumario.

18. *Providence Rhode Island American, and General Advertiser,* June 8, 1810.

19. Folch to Someruelos, August 4, 1809, *legajo* 1567, Facsimiles.

20. Claiborne to Smith, August 9, 1809, *Letter Books,* 4, 403.

21. John Ballinger to Monroe, December 26, 1811, *Territorial Papers, Orleans,* 965.

22. Holmes to Smith, May 30, 1810, Document #4365, Parker, *Calendar,* 221.

23. McMichael, *Atlantic Loyalties,* pages 146–48, shows a study of 325 land sales from 1791 to 1810 from the WFP.

24. WFP, 18, 113A.

25. McDermott to Pintado, February 8, 1810, Pintado Papers, LC.

26. Kneeland to Pintado, April 7, 1810, ibid.

27. Kneeland to Pintado, June 14, 1810, Pintado to McDermott, May 20, 1810, ibid.

28. Pintado to Kneeland, April 25, 1810, ibid.

29. Deposition of Henry Garnhart, April 29, 1810, WFP, 17, 313–14; Deposition of Levi Sholar, April 29, 1810, ibid., 314; George and James Cavanaugh to Delassus, May 12, 1810, ibid., 305ff.

30. Samuel Fulton to Madison, April 20, 1810, *Madison Papers,* 2, 320–21. Robert Taylor, "Prelude to Manifest Destiny: The United States and West Florida, 1810–1811," *Gulf Coast Historical Review* 7 (Spring 1992), page 48, interprets Fulton's letter as a veiled offer to turn over his Spanish militia if Madison chose to take West Florida, but there is nothing in the letter that even hints at this.

31. *New York Public Advertiser,* December 8, 1810; Cuming, *Sketches,* 307; John R. Bedford to James Madison, July 4, 1810, *Madison Papers,* 2, 399–400; Sale of Land, Thomas Green to William Barrow, November 23, 1801, WFP, 5, 119.

32. William Barrow to John R. Bedford, June 4, 1810, *Madison Papers,* 2, 400.

33. *Madison Papers,* 2, 306–10.

34. Persons Recommended by Governor Claiborne for Members of the Legislative Council of the Orleans Territory, August 1804, *Territorial Papers, Orleans,* 278.

35. Claiborne to William Wykoff, June 14, 1810, *Letter Books,* 5, 31–33.

36. Smith to William Wykoff, June 20, 1810, *Territorial Papers, Orleans,* 883–84.

37. Smith to Madison, February 8, 1810, *American State Papers, Foreign Relations,* 3, 341.

38. Joseph P. Kennedy to Cayetano Perez, July 19, 1810, Kennedy to Zenon Orso, June 7, 1810, copy with Perez to Maxent, June 20, 1810, Vicente Folch, Governor of West Florida, and Juan Ventura Morales, Intendant of West Florida 1810, Scribe's copies of Correspondence, University of Virginia, Tracy W. McGregor Library of American History, Special Collections, Charlottesville (hereinafter cited as Correspondence of Folch and Morales, UVA). Kennedy's letter also appears in a variant later translation in "West Florida and Its Attempt on Mobile, 1810–1811," *American Historical Review* 2 (July 1897): 700.

39. Perez to Maxent, June 20, 1810, Correspondence of Folch and Morales, UVA.

40. Maximilian de St. Maxent to Richard Sparks, June 25, 1810, *Territorial Papers, Mississippi,* 6, 77.

41. Sparks to Perez, n.d. but June–July 1810, Correspondence of Folch and Morales, UVA.

42. Statement of Raphael Crocker, August 13, 1812, Sumario; Crocker to Folch, September 24, 1810, *legajo* 63, PdeC. Crocker maintained that all the trouble started with these physician gatherings, which hardly seems likely since none of them later appeared particularly prominently in the meetings that led to the convention. However, since one of the early acts of that convention was the creation of a medical society to promote professional knowledge, that most likely reflects a desire for a more formalized extension of the informal meetings they were already having, lending at least modest corroboration to Crocker's claim.

43. Statement of Estevan, Sumario.

44. Arthur, *West Florida,* page 31, says that the discussions in these meetings were kept secret thanks to the participants being Freemasons honoring pledges of confidentiality. In all the primary literature on the West Florida business, there does not seem to be even one reference to anything Masonic. Arthur did not usually just invent things, though he often misread evidence and accepted far-fetched statements as fact if they were in print. Probably this Masonic connection was some local lore prevalent in the 1930s, when he was writing.

45. Delassus to Convention, July 30, 1810, James A. Padgett, ed., "Official Records

of the West Florida Revolution and Republic," *Louisiana Historical Quarterly* 21 (July 1938): 696 (hereinafter cited as "Official Records").

46. Nothing actually confirms June 16 as the date of this meeting, but virtually all of the meetings in this period were scheduled on Saturdays, and this is the latest date the meeting could have been held and still have an account of it appear two days later in the New Orleans press. Any earlier and Estevan would have notified Delassus of it prior to when he did.

47. *New Orleans Louisiana Gazette*, June 18, 1810, and *New-York Commercial Advertiser*, August 22, 1810.

48. John W. Leonard to Edward Duffel, October 24, 1810, Walter Prichard, "An Original Letter on the West Florida Revolution of 1810," *Louisiana Historical Quarterly* 18 (April 1935): 360–61.

49. *New Orleans Louisiana Gazette*, June 18, 1810, and *New-York Commercial Advertiser*, August 22, 1810.

50. The newspaper accounts mistakenly say the meeting was to be held at Richard Duvall's home.

51. *New Orleans Louisiana Gazette*, June 18, 1810, and *New-York Commercial Advertiser*, August 22, 1810.

52. Arthur, *West Florida*, 34. No contemporary source has been found for this colorful quote but, as stated before, Arthur did not invent quotations, though he was sometimes inaccurate in their transcription.

53. *New Orleans Louisiana Gazette*, June 18, 1810, and *New-York Commercial Advertiser*, August 22, 1810.

54. Pierre-Joseph Favrot to Someruelos, January 8, 1811, Pierre-Joseph Favrot Correspondence, Tulane.

55. Delassus to Maxent, June 22, 1810, Correspondence of Folch and Morales, UVA.

56. *New Orleans Louisiana Gazette*, June 27 and 30, 1810.

57. Holmes to Smith, June 20, 1810, General Records of the Department of State, Record Group 59, National Archives, Washington, DC (hereinafter cited as NA).

58. Delassus to Maxent, June 20, 22, 1810, Correspondence of Folch and Morales, UVA; Delassus to Maxent, May 26, 1810, Maxent to Someruelos, July 30, 1810, *legajo* 1574, Facsimiles.

59. Holmes to Smith, June 20, 1810, RG 59, NA. Nothing seems to indicate the precise date of Delassus's order, and no copy of it has been found. Estevan in his June 18 letter to Delassus (quoted in Delassus to Maxent, June 20, 1810, Correspondence of Folch and Morales, UVA) refers to the good effect that a recent letter or decree from Delassus had on the people of Bayou Sara, which almost certainly refers to the eviction notice. That suggests that Estevan must have had it in hand no later than his June 16 or 17 visit from Johnson and the others. The only contemporary reference implying a date is a June 24 letter from Point Coupée in the *New York Columbian*, August 30, 1810, which refers to the expulsion taking place two weeks earlier — which would be June

10 — but that reference could be approximate. Thus June 10 seems a reasonable date, but it could well be in error by a day or two.

60. Cox, *West Florida*, pages 337–38, somewhat confuses the chronology of these events, implying that Johnson called on Estevan before rather than after the June 16 meeting.

61. Delassus to Maxent, June 20, 1810, Correspondence of Folch and Morales, UVA.

62. Delassus to Estevan, June 25, 1810, *legajo* 185, PdeC; Delassus to Convention, July 30, 1810, "Official Records," 696.

63. Jonathan Longstreth, *The Book of the Chronicles of the Grand Sanhedrine*, 1810, Philip Hicky and Family Papers, LSU.

64. Meeting of the officials and report of the happenings at the beginning of the revolution, August 21, 1810, WFP, 18, 78–84.

65. R. Fowler to Hicky, July 8, 1810, Hicky and Family Papers.

66. Skipwith to Delassus, July 10, 1810, WFP, 18, 34ff.

67. *Washington (DC) National Intelligencer*, August 17, 1810; *New York Columbian*, August 30, 1810.

68. Cox, *West Florida*, pages 340–41, confuses this June 23 meeting with another held July 1.

69. *Washington (DC) National Intelligencer*, August 17, 1810; *New York Columbian*, August 30, 1810.

70. *Norwich (CT) Courier*, September 5, 1810.

71. Barrow to Bedford, August 5, 1810, *Madison Papers*, 2, 509.

72. *Bridgeport (CT) Gazette*, August 15, 1810.

73. "To the Inhabitants of the district of New Feliciana," July 1, 1810, Hicky and Family Papers, LSU.

74. John H. Johnson, William Barrow, John Mills, and John Rhea to Hicky, George Mather, Richard Duvall, and Thomas Lilley, July 3, 1810, Hicky and Family Papers, LSU.

75. Leonard to Duffel, October 24, 1810, Prichard, "Original Letter," 360–61.

76. *New Orleans Louisiana Gazette*, July 2, 1810.

77. John R. Bedford to Madison, July 4, 1810, James Madison Papers, LC.

78. *Kennebunk (ME) Weekly Visitor*, August 18, 1810.

79. *Raleigh (NC) Star*, August 9, 1810.

80. *New Orleans Louisiana Gazette*, July 10, 1810.

81. Thomas B. Robertson to Smith, July 6, 1810, *Territorial Papers, Orleans*, 888.

82. *Norwich (CT) Courier*, September 5, 1810.

83. Holmes to Smith, July 11, 1810, RG 59, NA.

84. Skipwith to John Graham, January 14, 1811, Padgett, "West Florida Revolution," 165.

10. A New Order of Things

1. Meeting of the officials and report of the happenings at the beginning of the revolution, August 21, 1810, WFP, 18, 79.

2. Hicky et al. to Shepherd Brown, July 6, 1810, Hicky and Family Papers, LSU.

3. Petition to Delassus, July 6, 1810, *legajo* 185, PdeC.

4. Delassus to delegates, July 6, 1810, ibid.; Delassus to Hicky, Lilley, and López, n.d. [July 6, 1810 misidentified as July 30 in Parker #4377 p. 222], Pintado Papers, LC.

5. *Concord New Hampshire Patriot*, December 18, 1810.

6. Ibid.

7. *New York Public Advertiser*, December 8, 1810. They met at the home of Thomas Egan. Attending were Hicky, Mather, Lilley, Davenport, Duvall, Joseph Sharp, William Norris, and López.

8. Hicky et al. to Shepherd Brown, July 6, 1810, Hicky and Family Papers, LSU.

9. Delassus to Committee, July 30, 1810, "Official Records," 697.

10. R. Fowler to Hicky, July 8, 1810, Hicky and Family Papers, LSU.

11. Arthur, *West Florida*, page 42, says the meeting occurred at Fulton's home. Though as usual Arthur gave no authority for saying this, the absence of any evidence to the contrary suggests that he was probably right, though he misdated the meeting to July 8. The Fowler letter to Hicky cited above specifically refers to Saturday, July 14, as the meeting date, and that is more likely, given that securing Delassus's permission on July 6 hardly left time to get a call for attendance circulated, while July 14 still gave the appointed delegates eleven days to prepare for the July 25 assembly.

12. John Mills to Hicky, July 14, 1810, Hicky and Family Papers, LSU.

13. Arthur, *West Florida*, 42; Brown to Estevan, March 10, 1810, WFP, 18, 178.

14. Brown to Delassus, July 10, 1810, *legajo* 185, PdeC.

15. Delassus to Brown, July 13, 1810, ibid.

16. Brown to Delassus, July 23, 1810, ibid.

17. *New York Public Advertiser*, December 8, 1810; Leonard to Duffel, October 24, 1810, Prichard, "Original Letter," 355–56.

18. *Philadelphia Weekly Aurora*, November 13, 1810.

19. Skipwith to John Graham, January 14, 1811, Padgett, "West Florida Revolution," 165.

20. Madison to Robert Smith, July 17, 1810, *Madison Papers*, 2, 419.

21. Ibid., 312–13.

22. No surviving sources establish just who drafted the constitution. Arthur, *West Florida*, pages 43 and 45, states that "most of the evidence at hand seems to prove" that the document "was wholly written by Edward Randolph." Arthur's use of *most* and *seems* makes his conclusion equivocal at best, and, as usual, he provides none of the evidence leading him to his conclusion. Arthur probably based this on Randolph's authorship of the Kempers' 1804 manifesto, but the two documents show no similarity in wording. The fact that the draft was in circulation early enough to appear in a Natchez newspaper on July 17 means that it was done before the delegates from St. Helena and Tangipahoa could have reached the vicinity, limiting authorship to men from

Baton Rouge and Feliciana, and it was almost certainly before Feliciana delegates were chosen, on or about July 14. Of course, it did not have to be delegates who prepared the document, and this seems most likely, even though the author(s) was almost certainly chosen as a delegate. Given that the July 17 editorial accompanying the document stated only that it "is said to have been well received in the neighbourhood of Baton Rouge," while commenting at some length on sentiment in Feliciana, it seems clear that the document originated and got more circulation in the latter. Feliciana was also the most direct source of communication with Natchez. This all points to the author as one of the Bayou Sara men who were always ahead of everyone else: John H. Johnson, Rhea, Mills, or Barrow, or some combination of them.

23. As with the authorship of the constitution, there is no evidence to demonstrate when it was completed. It is a lengthy document that would have taken some time to set in type before its publication in Natchez on July 17. Allowing one day for that and two days for it to get from Bayou Sara to Natchez, that makes July 14 the latest probable date of completion. If the statement that it had been circulated in Feliciana and near Baton Rouge is true, then completion should be pushed back another few days to allow time for it to get to leading men for comment and approbation.

24. *New Haven Connecticut Journal*, August 23, 1810.

25. Ibid.

26. *Raleigh (NC) Star*, August 23, 1810.

27. Inventory of the Estate of John Christian Buhler, January 10, 1794, WFP, 2, 3, 3, 97; Cuming, *Sketches*, 309. It was also known as Buhler's or Buller's Plains, after local planter John Christian Buhler, and some also called it St. John's or Duvall's Plains.

28. Barrow to Bedford, September 11, 1810, *Madison Papers*, 3, 5.

29. *Hagers-Town (MD) Gazette*, December 18, 1810; *Washington (DC) Monitor*, May 24, 1808; *Washington (DC) Expositor*, April 23, 1808.

30. John Ballinger to Toulmin, November 3, 1810, Madison Papers, LC.

31. *Hagers-Town (MD) Gazette*, December 18, 1810.

32. Ibid.

33. Power of Attorney, December 20, 1809, WFP, 18, 132.

34. Barrow to Bedford, September 11, 1810, *Madison Papers*, 3, 5.

35. William Cooper to Folch, September 12, 1810, *legajo* 1568, Facsimiles.

36. Barrow to Bedford, September 11, 1810, *Madison Papers*, 3, 5.

37. Holmes to Smith, July 31, 1810, *Territorial Papers*, Orleans, 890; Eulogio de Casas statement, April 9, 1811, Sumario.

38. "Official Records," 688–89.

39. Ibid., 689–91. The chronology of this official journal of the proceedings is at variance in some respects with the transcript that appeared in the *Washington (DC) Universal Gazette* on September 27, 1810, and also in the Proceedings of convention at St. John's Plains, July 26–27, 1810, *legajo* 185, PdeC.

40. The journal of these proceedings records only motions and resolutions. It is certain that considerable debate and exposition preceded each resolution, so

it should not be assumed that those not moving or seconding motions stayed silent throughout the proceedings.

41. Favrot, "West Florida," 41–42.
42. *New York Columbian,* September 4, 1810.
43. Holmes to Smith, July 31, 1810, *Territorial Papers, Orleans,* 890.
44. *Frederick (MD) Hornet, or Republican Advocate,* September 19, 1810.
45. "Official Records," 691–95.
46. *Natchez Weekly Chronicle,* August 6, 1810.
47. *Boston Columbian Centinel,* September 5, 1810.
48. *Baltimore Federal Republican,* August 23, 1810.
49. Sparks to William Eustis, July 12, 1810, *Territorial Papers, Mississippi,* 6, 79–82.
50. Toulmin to Madison, July 28, 1810, ibid., 85–90.
51. Kennedy to Cayetano Perez, July 19, 1810, Correspondence of Folch and Morales, UVA. This also appears in "West Florida and Its Attempt on Mobile, 1810–1811," 700–1.
52. Folch to Morales, July 28, 1810, Correspondence of Folch and Morales, UVA.
53. Toulmin to Madison, July 28, 1810, *Territorial Papers, Mississippi,* 6, 85–90.
54. Holmes to James Caller, July 31, 1810, ibid., 92–93.
55. Holmes to Smith, July 31, 1810, *Territorial Papers, Orleans,* 890; Holmes to Caller, August 28, 1810, *Territorial Papers, Mississippi,* 6, 103.
56. *Richmond Enquirer,* August 20, 1810; McCain, "Holmes," 336.

11. Thus Has Terminated the Revolution

1. Kendall, "Documents," 477. Delassus wrote in Spanish. He had access to translators, but leaving the translation to the delegates reinforced the fact that Spain still ruled and determined the language of official documents; it also used the delegates' time rather than his own. Even though López could have done the translation, the committee held it for more than a week, perhaps distrustful of their only Spaniard, though the letter contained nothing confidential. Finally they gave it to William Herries to translate on August 11, allowing him just two days to do the job, which he took on immediately, though his only reason for still being at the Plains was that he was too ill to ride.
2. Delassus to the Convention, July 30, 1810, "Official Records," 696–99. A copy of this in the original Spanish is in *legajo* 185, PdeC.
3. John Mills to Delassus, August 3, 1810, West Florida Rebellion Papers, LSU. The Spanish original of this is in *legajo* 185, PdeC.
4. *Windsor Spooner's Vermont Journal,* September 24, 1810.
5. Kendall, "Documents," 477.
6. Holmes to Smith, August 8, 1810, *Territorial Papers, Orleans,* 891–92.
7. From July 25, 1810, until September 18, only nineteen notarial acts are entered. WFP, 18, 302–33.

8. *Richmond Enquirer,* August 20, 1810.

9. Meeting of the officials and report of the happenings at the beginning of the revolution, August 21, 1810, WFP, 18, 79.

10. Inhabitants of St. Francisville to their Representatives at St. John's Plains, August 13, 1810, West Florida Rebellion Papers, LSU.

11. Ancestry.com, *Louisiana Marriages to 1850; Easton (MD) Eastern Shore Republican Star of General Advertiser,* September 14, 1802; Martin L. Haynie to John Ballinger, October 25, 1810, Southern Historical Collection, University of North Carolina, Chapel Hill (hereinafter SHC, UNC).

12. Martin L. Haynie to John Ballinger, October 25, 1810, SHC, UNC.

13. "Official Records," 699.

14. Estevan to Delassus, August 14, 1810, *legajo* 185, PdeC; Report of the Events of August 14, 1810, WFP, 18, 81.

15. A Friend of the People, "Anonymous Proclamation to the Inhabitants of Florida and others Exhorting them to Rise against the Government of Spain to become Citizens of the United States," n.d. [August 13, 1810], Spanish Papers, Robertson #5172. A copy of the broadside is also in *legajo* 185, PdeC.

16. Estevan to Delassus, August 14, 1810, *legajo* 185, PdeC.

17. *Morristown (NJ) Palladium of Liberty,* October 2, 1810.

18. Johnson to Holmes, August 14, 1810, quoted in Arthur, *West Florida,* 59–60.

19. Rhea et al. to Delassus, August 15, 1810, "Official Records," 700–2.

20. Report of the Events of August 14, 1810, WFP, 18, 81–82.

21. *New York Columbian,* October 2, 1810.

22. Report of the Events of August 14, 1810, WFP, 18, 81–82.

23. Morales to Someruelos, August 18, 1810, Correspondence of Folch and Morales, UVA.

24. Sumario.

25. Brown to Delassus, August 19, 1810, *legajo* 185, PdeC.

26. Robertson to Smith, August 26, 1810, *Territorial Papers, Orleans,* 896.

27. Also attending was New Orleans notary Cristobal de Armas, a lot owner in Baton Rouge who was also a lieutenant in the American city's provincial militia and thus rather out of place at a confidential meeting of Spanish officers.

28. Meeting of the officials and report of the happenings at the beginning of the revolution, August 21, 1810, WFP, 18, 79–82.

29. Sumario.

30. Report of the Events of August 14, 1810, WFP, 18, 83.

31. This ordinance was printed in one hundred copies, but as of 1935 only one remaining copy was known to exist, which Arthur reproduced in full in *West Florida,* 69–88. Since no original has been found, there has been no choice but to trust that Arthur accurately reprinted it.

32. "Official Records," 702–5.

33. Ibid., 705–6.

34. Receipt of L. V. Foelkel, September 29, 1810, ibid., 800–1.

35. Report of the Events of August 14, 1810, WFP, 18, 83.

36. Estevan to Delassus, August 20, 1810, *legajo* 185, PdeC.

37. Henry L. Favrot, "Some of the Causes and Conditions that Brought about the West Florida Revolution in 1810," *Publications of the Louisiana Historical Society* 1 (part 2, 1895): 45.

38. "Official Records," page 708, shows Thomas named as colonel, but Delassus's August 25 response makes it clear that by the time the suggested appointment reached him, Thomas had been "promoted" to brigadier.

39. "Official Records," 706–10.

40. *Sag Harbor (NY) Suffolk Gazette*, October 13, 1810; *New York Evening Post*, September 29, 1810.

41. Convention to Delassus, August 25, 1810, West Florida Rebellion Papers, LSU.

42. "Official Records," 710–12.

43. Report of the Events of August 14, 1810, WFP, 18, 81; *Raleigh (NC) Star*, October 4, 1810.

44. Delassus to Committee, August 25, 1810, Kendall, "Documents," 483.

45. Report of the Events of August 14, 1810, WFP, 18, 83; Inventory of the contents of a Small Chest the property of Ira Kneeland, October 3, 1811, Pintado Papers, LC.

46. "Official Records," 713–16; Leonard to Duffel, October 24, 1810, Prichard, "Original Letter," 361. The original of this letter is in the Southern Historical Collection, University of North Carolina, Chapel Hill.

47. Arthur, *West Florida*, 62.

48. Convention to the Inhabitants of the District of Baton Rouge, August 29, 1810, Kendall, "Documents," pages 484–85, is clearly a rejected draft of the August 29 address.

49. Undated address of convention to the people of Baton Rouge, Kendall, "Documents," 475–76. The context of this document makes it certain that it was issued August 29 or 30.

50. *Morristown (NJ) Palladium of Liberty*, October 23, 1810.

51. Robertson to Smith, August 26, 1810, *Territorial Papers, Orleans*, 896.

52. Leonard to Duffel, October 24, 1810, Prichard, "Original Letter," 361.

53. Barrow to Bedford, September 11, 1810, *Madison Papers*, 3, 5.

54. *Richmond Enquirer*, October 5, 1810.

55. *Richmond Virginia Patriot*, October 19, 1810.

56. *Morristown (NJ) Palladium of Liberty*, October 23, 1810.

57. Holmes to Smith, September 12, 1810, *Territorial Papers, Mississippi*, 6, 116.

58. Skipwith to Graham, January 14, 1811, Padgett, "West Florida Revolution," 170.

59. Bedford to Madison, August 26, 1810, *Madison Papers*, 2, 508–9.

60. Ballinger to Toulmin, November 3, 1810, Madison Papers, LC.

61. William Cooper to Folch, September 12, 1810, *legajo* 1568, Facsimiles.

62. Murdoch to Pintado, September 13, 1810, Pintado Papers, LC.

63. Affidavit of Jean Baptiste Metzinger, October 15, 1810, West Florida Rebellion Papers, LSU.

64. *Frederick (MD) Hornet, or Republican Advocate*, September 19, 1810.

65. Pierre-Joseph Favrot to Someruelos, January 8, 1811, Pierre-Joseph Favrot Correspondence, Tulane.

12. A Battle for the Freedom of the World

1. Resolution, September 4, 1810, Philip Hicky and Family Papers, LSU.
2. Charles M. Audibert to Skipwith, September 4, 1810, Padgett, "West Florida Revolution," 87–88.
3. Paul Lachance, "Repercussions of the Haitian Revolution in Louisiana," David Geggus, ed., *The Impact of the Haitian Revolution in the Atlantic World* (Columbia: University of South Carolina Press, 2001), 222.
4. Delassus to Hicky, Lilley, and López, September 12, 1810, *legajo* 185, PdeC. Kendall, "Documents," page 486, published this document as a proclamation, which it clearly is not.
5. Hicky, Lilley, and López to Delassus, September 13, 1810, Proclamation September 14, 1810, *legajo* 185, PdeC; Delassus to Hicky et al., September 14, 1810, Hicky and Family Papers, LSU.
6. Folch to Someruelos, August 27, 1810, *legajo* 1568, Facsimiles.
7. William Eustis to Wade Hampton, August 29, 1810, *Territorial Papers, Mississippi*, 6, 101.
8. Holmes to Robert Smith, February 2, 1811, Executive Council Proceedings, Mississippi Territory, MDAH; Holmes to Folch, September 4, 1810, *Territorial Papers, Mississippi*, 6, 104–5.
9. Holmes to Toulmin, September 8, 1810, *Territorial Papers, Mississippi*, 6, 113, Holmes to Sparks, September 9, 1810, 115, Holmes to Caller, James Carson, James Patton, September 8, 1810, 113–14, Holmes to Caller, Carson, and Patton, September 16, 1810, 119, Holmes to Toulmin, September 28, 1810, 120–21.
10. William Cooper to Folch, September 12, 1810, *legajo* 1568, Facsimiles.
11. John Murdoch to Pintado, September 13, 1810, Pintado Papers, LC.
12. John Scott to George de Passau, August 23, 1810, WFP, 18, 310.
13. Juan Metzinger to Estevan Dalcour, Power of Attorney, September 15, 1810, ibid., 18, 332.
14. Cristobal de Armas to Pintado, September 16, 1810, Pintado Papers, LC.
15. Manuel López to Pintado, September 17, 18, 1810, ibid.; Receipt, September 18, 1810, WFP, 18, 333.
16. Statement from Bayou Sara circa December 11–12, 1810, published in *New Orleans Louisiana Gazette*, December 1810, quoted in Arthur, *West Florida*, 144.
17. Ibid.
18. Delassus to Folch, September 18, 1810, *legajo* 185, PdeC.
19. *Concord New Hampshire Patriot*, December 18, 1810.
20. Cox, *West Florida*, page 393, says this order was done "through the influence of the convention." Arthur, *West Florida*, page 100, paraphrasing Cox as he does so often, restates this to say that Estevan got "written orders from the convention." However, Francisco Galban, one of the four soldiers at Bayou

Sara with Estevan, stated that the order came from Delassus (Statement of Francisco Galban, Sumario). Other statements in the Sumario led Cox to think the committee had some influence on the order, which seems unlikely. First, the convention was in recess, so if it had any involvement, it was through the standing committee. Second, nothing in the recently adopted ordinance gave the convention or its committee any authority whatever over military movements. The order had to come from Delassus, as Galban stated, which leaves two choices. Either Delassus ordered the men in on his own initiative, or he was influenced to do so by the committee. If both sides were expecting an eruption soon, then it only makes sense for Delassus to have summoned Estevan as a reinforcement, for surely the committee would not try to increase the strength in the fort if it expected that it might soon be attacked.

21. Statement of Marcos Aguilina, Sumario.
22. Skipwith to his Constituents, April 1, 1811, Padgett, "West Florida Revolution," 174–75.
23. Ballinger to Toulmin, November 3, 1810, Madison Papers, LC.
24. Statement from Bayou Sara circa December 11–12, 1810, *New Orleans Louisiana Gazette*, quoted in Arthur, *West Florida*, 144.
25. Skipwith to Graham, January 14, 1811, ibid., 170.
26. Statement from Bayou Sara circa December 11–12, 1810, *New Orleans Louisiana Gazette*, quoted in Arthur, *West Florida*, 144.
27. Leonard to Duffel, October 24, 1810, Prichard, "Original Letter," 361.
28. James M. Turner Oration Delivered at St. Francisville, July 4, 1811, Padgett, "West Florida Revolution," 188. Turner is the only source to indicate that Leonard informed the committee of Brown's correspondence to Delassus, and the information dates from just nine months after the fact. The earliest — and only firsthand — contemporary mention of captured correspondence being the catalyst is in, of all things, the lampoon written by Jonathan Longstreth, who taught school in Lilley's house at the Plains and thus had an opportunity to hear of it. His *Book of the Chronicles of the Grand Sanhedrine* is undated, but internal content suggests that it was composed very soon after September 23, 1810. It refers to Brown, Cooper, and Jones raising their force and sending the letter to Delassus promising to capture and deliver all of the convention delegates. The original is in the Philip Hicky and Family Papers, LSU, and a generally accurate transcription is in Arthur, *West Florida*, 125–27. The earliest published assertion of a captured letter appears in Favrot, "West Florida," 45–46, written in 1895. Favrot gives no source for the statement, but Cox used him as an authority in 1918, and so did Arthur. Of course, if a letter was intercepted it would not now be in the Spanish archives, and the original could well have been lost or destroyed while in the convention's archives. The last known correspondence between Brown and Delassus was weeks earlier, and no copy of any letter to Brown in mid-September is known to exist.
29. Favrot to Someruelos, January 8, 1811, Pierre-Joseph Favrot Correspondence, Tulane.

30. Ballinger to Toulmin, November 3, 1810, Madison Papers, LC.
31. Skipwith to his Constituents, April 1, 1811, Padgett, "West Florida Revolution," 174–75.
32. Statement from Bayou Sara circa December 11–12, 1810, *New Orleans Louisiana Gazette*, in Arthur, *West Florida*, 144.
33. Ballinger to Toulmin, November 3, 1810, Madison Papers, LC. Most contemporary sources state that Ballinger went to Springfield to raise volunteers and that Thomas rode there himself on September 22 and led Ballinger's men back. Arthur, *West Florida*, page 105, points out that in marching on Baton Rouge, Ballinger's men covered forty miles in thirteen hours, a little better than three miles per hour, which, while certainly possible for a small party of men with little impedimenta, is still quite remarkable if true. It seems more likely, and from Thomas's point of view more practical and expeditious, that Ballinger rendezvoused his men some miles west of Springfield.
34. Statement from Bayou Sara circa December 11–12, 1810, *New Orleans Louisiana Gazette*, in Arthur, *West Florida*, 144.
35. Ballinger to Toulmin, November 3, 1810, Madison Papers, LC.
36. Ibid.
37. Ballinger to Monroe, December 26, 1811, *Territorial Papers*, Orleans, 965.
38. Benjamin Williams to Rhea, September 22, 1810, Kendall, "Documents," 488.
39. "Official Records," 716–19.
40. The precise origin of the flag is uncertain, and there seem to be no contemporary sources. In 1896 Favrot, "Incidents," pages 24–25, stated that the flag was made by "ladies" in Baton Rouge from blue wool, with a "silver star" in the center, and that Thomas only picked up the flag as he approached on the night of September 22. This seems highly unlikely, both that they would use wool rather than native cotton and that Thomas would risk detection by having the work done in Baton Rouge. Arthur, *West Florida*, page 102, states — without a source, as usual — that Melissa Johnson made the flag "several days before," then goes on to say that the five points of the star represent "five points of fellowship" of Freemasonry. Living and working in the area for many years, Arthur had access to documents and oral history that are long lost now. So Melissa Johnson may have made the flag.

   However, as stated earlier, there seems to be no contemporary source mentioning any connection of any of the rebellion leaders with things Masonic, and none of them became prominent Masons in later years. James B. Scott, *Outline of the Rise and Progress of Freemasonry in Louisiana: From Its Introduction to the Re-organization of the Grand Lodge in 1850* (New Orleans: Clark and Hofeline, 1873), pages 14 and 25, states that until 1812 there were no Masonic lodges in Louisiana other than the ones in New Orleans, and that the few scattered Masons in the West Florida parishes were not sufficient to form a lodge until 1828. Neighboring Mississippi did not get its first lodge until 1818. Of course, Isaac Johnson and others could have been Masons in 1810, but given that Arthur's assumption seems to be based on nothing more than the coincidence of Johnson using a five-pointed star — by a wide margin, the most common form of star in flags — and the "five points of fellowship" of Freemasonry, it seems too much of a leap to assert that Masonry was on Johnson's mind in designing the banner.

41. In the span of about thirty-six hours Thomas rode perhaps seventy miles to Springfield and then marched Ballinger's men forty miles back to Baton Rouge, per his report, and certainly it is theoretically possible. "Official Records," 719.

42. Ballinger to Toulmin, November 3, 1810, Madison Papers, LC. Ballinger says that Thomas reached him on the evening of September 22, but that simply is not possible, since according to Thomas he and Ballinger's men were close to Baton Rouge by 1:00 A.M., September 23. That would mean they would have marched over forty miles in just six or seven hours. If Thomas got his orders at six o'clock the morning of September 22 and rode hard, he could have covered the seventy miles from Troy to Springfield by noon perhaps, and if Ballinger's command marched as soon as Thomas arrived, they could have been within a few hours of Baton Rouge by 1:00 A.M., but the times and the distances in Thomas's and Ballinger's accounts — the only ones we have — are extremely tight, and only work out if everyone made unaccustomed speed.

43. Abernathy, "Burr," 14.

44. Ballinger to Toulmin, November 3, 1810, Madison Papers, LC.

45. Cuming, *Sketches*, 314.

46. "Official Records," 721–22.

47. José de la Peña statement, Sumario.

48. Several statements in the Sumario testify to this, but in particular see those of José de la Peña and Michael Harrold.

49. De Armas to Gil, March 15, 1811, WFP, 19, 94–95.

50. Favrot to Someruelos, January 8, 1811, Pierre-Joseph Favrot Correspondence, Tulane.

51. Statement of Artillery and Ammunition, March 29, 1811, Inventory of the Hospital, March 29, 1811, Sumario.

52. William Darby, *A Geographical Description of the State of Louisiana, the Southern Part of the State of Mississippi, and Territory of Alabama* (New York: James Olmstead, 1817), 94.

53. Arthur, *West Florida*, 105. Arthur is the only source for this episode and the colorful dialect that has been found. Though Arthur did not invent sources, he sometimes apparently invented small bits of conversation. There is no question that Larry Moore was a real and colorful character in West Florida and early Louisiana. Sparks, *Memories of Fifty Years*, pages 415–27, contains several Larry Moore stories in a similar vein, though unfortunately not this one. It seems therefore reasonable to assume that Arthur found the anecdote in some source that has eluded this author and that he quoted it accurately.

54. Carrighan, "Historical and Statistical Sketches," page 257, gives a fanciful account that has Manuel López decoying Delassus to a dinner at his home while the attack took place, but of course no one would have been having dinner at 4:00 A.M.

55. Except where otherwise cited, this and the following account of events on the Spanish side are taken from the Sumario, which contains many and often conflicting interrogations of men and officers in the command. Particularly useful are those of Francisco Galban, Francisco Morejón, Joseph Mendez, Marcos Aquelina, Francisco Ximenes, Michael Harrold, Eulogio de Casas, Antonio Balderas, Mauricio Escobar, Pedro Quinto, and Raphael Crocker.

56. Arthur, *West Florida*, page 106, says that the guard was Corporal José de la Polvora, but no soldier of that name appears in the roll of the garrison in the Sumario.

57. Sumario. The man's name was Michael Harrold.

58. "Official Records," 720.

59. Raphael Crocker to Folch, September 24, 1810, *legajo* 63, PdeC.

60. Arthur, *West Florida*, page 106, says that this volley came from Johnson's horsemen, but Favrot to Someruelos, January 8, 1811, Favrot Papers, LSU, states that it was foot soldiers who fired the volley, and Favrot is the best source we have for the defenders, though he was probably not an eyewitness.

61. Ballinger to Toulmin, November 3, 1810, Madison Papers, LC.

62. Crocker to Folch, September 24, 1810, *legajo* 63, PdeC.

63. Favrot to Someruelos, January 8, 1811, Favrot Papers, LSU.

64. Testimony of Francisco Galban, Sumario.

65. Sumario.

13. The Commonwealth of West Florida

1. Petition of Charles DeHault Delassus Praying the Repayment of a Sum of Money Forcibly Taken from Him, for Public Service, at the Capture of Baton Rouge, in 1810, United States Senate Document 401, Serial Set Vol. No. 318, 25th Congress, 2d Session (Washington, 1838), 12; "Official Records," 783.

2. Statement of Mauricio Escobar, Sumario.

3. Ballinger to Toulmin, November 3, 1810, Madison Papers, LC.

4. Petition of Charles DeHault Delassus, 12.

5. "Official Records," 800.

6. Affidavit of Jean Baptiste Metzinger, October 15, 1810, West Florida Rebellion Papers, LSU. As translated, this document appears to say that Metzinger posed his question to Brown, but at this time Brown was back at Springfield.

7. Statement of Mauricio Escobar, Sumario.

8. *New Orleans Louisiana Courier*, October 29, 1810. Another version of the eulogy written by Pierre-Joseph Favrot, September 24, 1810, is in Meneray, Favrot Papers, 5, 38–39.

9. "Official Records," 720.

10. Ibid., 783.

11. Emilio de las Casas Diary, September 29, 1810, Sumario.

12. "Official Records," 800–1.

13. Ibid., 721–22.

14. Ibid., 722–23.
15. Representatives of the Jurisdiction of Baton Rouge to the Inhabitants of St. Helena and St. Ferdinand, September 25, 1810, West Florida History Vertical File, Louisiana State Library, Baton Rouge.
16. *New Orleans Louisiana Gazette*, September 26, 27, October 3, 1810.
17. Hugh Davis to Holmes, September 25, 1810, Mississippi Territorial Archives, Administration Division, MDAH.
18. Holmes to Cushing, September 26, 1810, Proceedings of the Executive Council, Mississippi Territory, I, MDAH.
19. Walter H. Overton to Andrew Jackson, September 25, 1810, John Spencer Bassett, ed., *Correspondence of Andrew Jackson* (Washington, DC: Carnegie Institution, 1926–1935), I, 204–5.
20. Letter to Colonel William Russel, September 26, 1810, *Newport Rhode Island Republican*, December 5, 1810.
21. *New Orleans Louisiana Gazette*, September 26 and 27, 1810.
22. What appears to be the original of this document is in the West Florida History Vertical File, Louisiana State Library, Baton Rouge. A rumor soon maintained that López took no part in the convention's work after the capture of Delassus, but this is manifestly untrue. *New York Public Advertiser*, December 8, 1810.
23. *Philadelphia Weekly Aurora*, November 13, 1810. Arthur, *West Florida*, page 112, mistakes this proclamation for a preliminary version of the declaration.
24. Barrow to Bedford, October 10, 1810, *Madison Papers*, 3, 6.
25. Rhea to Holmes, September 26, 1810, *American State Papers, Foreign Relations*, 3, 396; *Portsmouth New Hampshire Gazette*, December 18, 1810; Convention to Claiborne, September 26, 1810, Kendall, "Documents," 487–88.
26. Skipwith to Graham, January 14, 1811, Padgett, "West Florida Revolution," 168–69.
27. Philip Grymes to Skipwith, October 6, 1810, Padgett, "West Florida Revolution," 89.
28. Holmes to the Convention, September 30, 1810, Kendall, "Documents," 494.
29. Holmes to Davis, September 27, 1810, Executive Council Proceedings, Mississippi Territory, MDAH.
30. Holmes to Cushing, September 28, 1810, *Territorial Papers, Mississippi*, 6, 121–22.
31. James M. Turner Oration Delivered at St. Francisville, July 4, 1811, Padgett, "West Florida Revolution," 188.
32. "Official Records," 727.
33. Brown to Folch, September 28, 1810, *legajo* 1568B, Facsimiles.
34. William Kirkland to the Convention, September 29, 1810, Kendall, "Documents," 493.
35. "Official Records," 729–30.
36. Ibid., 731–32.
37. Moses Hooker to Holmes, October 1, 1810, Mississippi Provincial Archives, MDAH.

38. Samuel Winston to Holmes, October 2, 1810, ibid.

39. Except where otherwise cited, this account of the expedition comes from Thomas to Rhea, October 9, 1810, Kendall, "Documents," 495–96. This report also appears in "Official Records," 739–40.

40. *Sag Harbor (NY) Suffolk Gazette,* December 15, 1810.

41. Samuel Winston to Holmes, October 2, 1810, Mississippi Provincial Archives, MDAH.

42. *Washington (DC) Spirit of Seventy-Six,* November 9, 1810.

43. "Official Records," 789.

44. Daniel Quilling to Thomas, October 10, 1810, Kendall, "Documents," 496–97, Abraham Spears to the Convention, October 10, 1810, 497.

45. Grand-Pré to Alexander Bookter, June 11, 1803, WFP, 4, 353, Brown to Delassus, January 9, 1810, 16, 22–23.

46. *New York Public Advertiser,* December 11, 1810; *Washington (DC) Spirit of Seventy-Six,* November 9, 1810.

47. *New York Public Advertiser,* December 11, 1810.

48. Thomas to Rhea, October 9, 1810, Kendall, "Documents," 495–96.

49. Cooper seems to disappear from the record. Arthur, *West Florida,* page 120, is the source for Cooper's death, but no contemporary record is cited, nor has one been found.

50. *New York Public Advertiser,* December 11, 1810.

51. *Washington (DC) Spirit of Seventy-Six,* November 9, 1810.

52. *Washington (DC) National Intelligencer,* October 31, 1810.

53. Ballinger to Toulmin, November 3, 1810, Madison Papers, LC.

54. *Philadelphia Weekly Aurora,* November 13, 1810; *Charlestown (WV) Farmer's Repository,* December 7, 1810.

55. *Boston Repertory,* December 7, 1810.

56. Arthur, *West Florida,* pages 125–27, publishes this document in its entirety, with numerous errors in transcription. What appears to be the original is in the Hicky Papers, LSU. It is undated, but the fact that it ends abruptly with the capture of the fort and does not mention the expedition against Shepherd Brown suggests composition shortly thereafter. Longstreth actually called Delassus "the Gawlite," a misspelling of *Gaul,* clearly a reference to French birth.

57. Folch to Someruelos, September 29, 1810, *legajo* 1568B, PdeC.

58. Moller to Crocker, August 25, 1810, WFP, 18, 311; *New Orleans Louisiana Gazette,* October 3, 1810.

59. Statement of Mauricio Escobar, Crocker to Maxent, September 24, October 12, 1810, Sumario.

60. Statement of Crocker, ibid.

61. Favrot to Someruelos, January 8, 1811, Meneray, Favrot Papers, 5, 45–49.

62. "Official Records," 732–35.

63. *Philadelphia Weekly Aurora,* November 13, 1810.

64. "Official Records," 735–38.

65. *New-York Journal,* December 12, 1810.

66. *New-York Commercial Advertiser*, November 26, 1810; *Philadelphia Weekly Aurora*, November 13, 1810.
67. Rhea to Smith, October 10, 1810, *American State Papers, Foreign Relations*, 3, 395–96.
68. "Official Records," 744.
69. Ibid., 745–46.
70. Maurice Bourezeois to Favrot, October 8, 1810, Pierre-Joseph Favrot Correspondence, Tulane.

14. Our Infant but Beloved Country

1. Letter from Baton Rouge, October 7, 1810, *New-York Journal*, December 12, 1810.
2. "Official Records," 744.
3. Ibid., 747–49.
4. Reuben Kemper to Andrew Jackson, November 17, 1815, Papers in Relation to Aaron Burr's Conspiracy, LC. Cox cites this letter three times, only once correctly, on page 478. On page 457 he dates it November 7, 1815. On page 485 he dates it 1810 and places it in the Meek Papers at MDAH.
5. Letter from Pinckneyville, October 20, 1810, *Richmond Enquirer*, November 23, 1810.
6. Samuel Baldwin to Thomas, October 12, 1810, Kendall, "Documents," 498.
7. Baldwin to Thomas, October 13, 1810, ibid., 498–99.
8. Letter from Pinckneyville, October 20, 1810, *Richmond Enquirer*, November 23, 1810.
9. *New York Journal*, October 31, 1810; *Newport (RI) Mercury*, December 1, 1810.
10. Folch to Morales and others, October 11 and 23, 1810, Perez to Folch, October 15, 1810, *legajo* 1568B, Facsimiles.
11. Perez to Folch, October 31, 1810, Folch to Someruelos, November 1, 1810, ibid.
12. *Middletown (CT) Middlesex Gazette*, December 27, 1810; *New York Columbian Gazette*, November 27, 1810.
13. Convention account with James Chauveau, September 30, 1810, "Official Records," 785; Stephen Winter to Convention, October 5 and 9, 1810, Kendall, "Documents," 494–95.
14. Francis B. Heitman, *Historical Register and Dictionary of the United States Army* (Washington: Government Printing Office, 1903), 2, 198.
15. *American State Papers, Public Lands*, 3, 63. On January 13, 1812, Cook married Elizabeth Collinsworth in St. Helena Parish, hence the supposition that he may have lived in that district.
16. James Moore to David Hutchinson, August 28, 1814, Hutchinson Family Papers, South Caroliniana Library, University of South Carolina, Columbia.
17. Ballinger to the committee, October 30, 1810, Padgett, "West Florida Revolution," 96.

18. "Official Records," 749.

19. *Newport (RI) Mercury*, December 1, 1810.

20. Ballinger to committee, October 30, 1810, Padgett, "West Florida Revolution," 96.

21. "Official Records," 749–50.

22. Ibid., 750–51; Cosas Diary, October 21, 1810, Sumario.

23. Haynie to Ballinger, October 25, 1810, Southern Historical Collection, University of North Carolina.

24. "Official Records," 751.

25. No act of the convention has been found choosing a replacement for Brown. The source for this story speaks only of "a wealthy planter" and calls him Thomas. It would be logical that Brown's replacement came from his region, and Joseph Thomas fits the bill.

26. The source describes Percy not by name but simply as a man "who once commanded a United States naval ship." Percy, of course, commanded a British privateer.

27. Henry S. Foote, *Bench and Bar of the South and Southwest* (St. Louis: Soule, Thomas and Wentworth, 1876), iv–viii. This was no doubt a popular anecdote in Mississippi legal circles that Foote must have heard far from firsthand. The account seriously confuses chronology and is probably embellished, being written more than sixty years after the fact, in 1874 or 1875. Still, there are basic elements of fact. As related, the anecdote actually suggests that the episode took place after Skipwith was elected governor in November, whereas it is established from records of the convention that the first sitting of the court took place October 22. The dashes in place of profanities are in the original.

28. *Providence (RI) Columbian Phenix*, December 1, 1810. The *New Orleans Louisiana Gazette* first carried this story, which spread around the country. The report actually stated that the convention called dragoons from Bayou Sara to handle the mutiny, but that makes no sense at all since there were already two companies of regular militia in Baton Rouge occupying the fort. In 1812 Cook was in St. Helena getting married, as cited above.

29. "Official Records," 752.

30. Barrow to Bedford, October 10, 1810, *Madison Papers*, 3, 6.

31. Leonard to Duffel, October 24, 1810, Prichard, "Original Letter," 361–62.

32. The original constitution is in the Louisiana State Archives in Baton Rouge. It is reproduced photographically in Bice, *Original Lone Star Republic*, 207–32.

33. Ballinger to Toulmin, November 3, 1810, Madison Papers, LC.

34. "Official Records," 752–53.

35. Subscription, October 28, 1810, Philip Hicky and Family Papers, LSU.

36. Committee Journal, October 30, 1810, Padgett, "West Florida Revolution," 95–96; Statement of the State of Florida in acct. with P. Hicky, Treas., November 24, 1810, Philip Hicky and Family Papers, LSU.

37. Haynie to Ballinger, October 25, 1810, Southern Historical Collection, University of North Carolina.

38. Committee to Ballinger, October 29, 1810, Padgett, "West Florida Revolution," 94–95.
39. "Official Records," 795–96, 798.
40. Kemper to Dupree, November 15, 1810, Padgett, "West Florida Revolution," 110–12.
41. In his October 28 letter cited below, Kemper said he arrived October 24. However, the October 27 James Wilkinson letter cited below says Kemper arrived the evening of October 25. It is impossible to say which is correct, if either, though Kemper ought to have known better than Wilkinson.
42. James Wilkinson near Fort Stoddert to James Innerarity, October 27, 1810, legajo 1568B, Facsimiles. This is not the General James Wilkinson of Burr conspiracy fame, who was at this time in Washington defending himself in a court of inquiry.
43. Kemper to Rhea, October 28, 1810, Padgett, "West Florida Revolution," 90–92.
44. Pintado to David Lejeune and John O'Connor, November 22, 1810, Pintado Papers, LC.
45. James Wilkinson near Fort Stoddert to James Innerarity, October 27, 1810, legajo 1568B, Facsimiles.
46. Folch to unknown, October 2, 1810, ibid.
47. Folch to Someruelos, November 1, 1810, ibid.
48. John Innerarity to Toulmin, n.d., Madison Papers, 2, 608–9n.
49. Order, October 29, 1810, Padgett, "West Florida Revolution," 93.
50. Committee to James Nielson, October 30, 1810, ibid., 96–97.
51. Richmond Enquirer, November 23, 1810.
52. Letter from Washington, Mississippi, October, Charlestown (WV) Farmer's Repository, December 7, 1810.
53. Letter from Washington, Mississippi, October 30, 1810, Washington (PA) Reporter, December 12, 1810.
54. Claiborne, Mississippi, 305.
55. Boston Columbian Centinel, December 5, 1810.
56. Madison to Jefferson, October 19, 1810, Madison Papers, 2, 585.
57. Washington (DC) National Intelligencer, December 27, 1810.
58. There would later be some confusion about what he knew, and when he knew it. In short, in later submitting documents to Congress to support his October 27 declaration, Madison included an October 17 letter from Holmes that he could not possibly have received by October 27. Since he was submitting these documents in December, he might well have been simply sending everything to support his decision. He also seems to have withheld from the copy of the Holmes letter a statement that all of West Florida was then peacefully in the convention's hands, since by the time the letter reached Washington the Mobile expedition was well known in the East. The editors of Madison Papers carefully demonstrated the sequence of communications in volume 3, 54–55n.

59. Proclamation, October 27, 1810, *Madison Papers*, 2, 595–96 and n.
60. Smith to Claiborne, October 27, 1810, *American State Papers, Foreign Relations*, 3, 397–98.
61. *Washington (DC) National Intelligencer*, July 2, 1811.
62. Smith to Holmes, October 30, 1810, *Territorial Papers, Orleans*, 901–2.
63. Thomas Rodney, "The Exploration of and Title to East and West Florida, and Louisiana, the Spanish & French Colonies in America, the Louisiana Purchase, and the Rights of Deposit, etc.," October 1810, Tracy W. McGregor Autograph Collection, University of Virginia, Charlottesville.
64. Owsley and Smith, *Filibusters and Expansionists*, 8–9.
65. Rodney to Caesar Rodney, December 10, 1810, Gratz, "Rodney," 45 (no. 2, 1921): 201.

15. The Star Will Rise and Shine

1. *Washington (DC) National Intelligencer*, December 27, 1810.
2. Ibid.
3. Rodney to William Duane, November 3, 1810, Gratz, "Rodney," 45 (no. 2, 1921): 187.
4. *New Orleans Louisiana Gazette*, October 20, 1810.
5. John Ballinger to Toulmin, November 3, 1810, Madison Papers, LC.
6. Kemper to Perez, November 3, 1810, Perez to Folch, November 6, 1810, *legajo* 55, PdeC.
7. Kemper to Rhea, November 5, 1810, Padgett, "West Florida Revolution," 101–2; Kemper to Perez, November 3, 1810, *legajo* 55, PdeC.
8. Joseph P. Kennedy to the convention, November 3, 1810, Padgett, "West Florida Revolution," 98–99.
9. Kemper to Kennedy, November 3, 1810, ibid., 101.
10. Kemper to Rhea, November 6, 1810, ibid., 103–5.
11. *Walpole (NH) Political Observatory*, November 22, 1805.
12. Toulmin to Captains of Militia in Washington County, November 4, 1810, *Territorial Papers, Mississippi*, 6, 130.
13. Toulmin to Madison, October 31, 1810, ibid., 128–29.
14. Kemper to Rhea, November 5, 1810, Padgett, "West Florida Revolution," 101–2.
15. Perez to Folch, November 6, 1810, *legajo* 55, Perez to Folch, October 31, 1810, *legajo* 63, PdeC.
16. Kemper to Rhea, November 6, 1810, ibid., 103–5.
17. Toulmin to Madison, November 6, 1810, *Territorial Papers, Mississippi*, 2, 132.
18. *Boston Gazette*, December 24, 1810; *Albany Balance, and New-York State Journal*, December 5, 1810; Rodney to Caesar Rodney, November 14, 1810, Gratz, "Rodney," 45 (no. 2, 1921): 194; *New York Spectator*, December 15, 1810.
19. *Hallowell (ME) American Advocate*, January 2, 1811; *Concord New Hampshire Patriot*, December 18, 1810.

20. *Boston Independent Chronicle,* December 27, 1810; Sterling Duprée to Kemper, November 12, 1810, Padgett, "West Florida Revolution," 109–10.
21. Kemper to Duprée, November 15, 1810, ibid., 110–12.
22. Kemper to Rhea, November 19, 1810, ibid., 113–14; Toulmin to Madison, November 22, 1810, Madison Papers, LC.
23. Toulmin to Innerarity, November 15, 1810, "West Florida and Its Attempt on Mobile, 1810–1811," 702.
24. Perez to Folch, November 14, 1810, *legajo* 63, PdeC.
25. Kemper to Rhea, November 16, 1810, Padgett, "West Florida Revolution," 106.
26. Duprée to Kemper, November 18, 1810, ibid., 118.
27. Kemper to Rhea, November 19, 1810, ibid., 113–14.
28. "Official Records," 787–88; Orders, November 2, 1810, Padgett, "West Florida Revolution," 97.
29. Brognier DeClouet to Pierre-Joseph Favrot, November 4, 1810, Meneray, *Favrot Papers,* 5, 42; Rodney to Caesar Rodney, November 14, 1810, Gratz, "Rodney," 45 (no. 2, 1921): 194.
30. *Hallowell (ME) American Advocate,* January 2, 1811.
31. Skipwith to Graham, January 14, 1811, Padgett, "West Florida Revolution," 169.
32. Frederick Kimball to Andrew Wade, December 9, 1810, Frederick Kimball Letters, LSU.
33. Order, November 12, 1810, Padgett, "West Florida Revolution," 107–9.
34. *Concord New Hampshire Patriot,* December 18, 1810.
35. "Official Records," 755–56, 766–70.
36. Skipwith to Graham, January 14, 1811, Padgett, "West Florida Revolution," 170–71.
37. Ibid., 757–58, 771–75.
38. *New York Columbian Gazette,* January 15, 1811. Also Padgett, "West Florida Revolution," 124–27.
39. *Baltimore Federal Republican and Commercial Gazette,* December 29, 1810.
40. Ibid.
41. "Official Records," 797; Bill for Supplies, November 20, 1810, Abner Duncan to John H. Johnson, November 20, 1810, Padgett, "West Florida Revolution," 115–16, Kemper to Duprée, November 21, 1810, 119.
42. James Innerarity to Toulmin, November 22, 1810, Madison Papers, LC.
43. Toulmin to Madison, November 22, 1810, ibid.
44. Toulmin to Innerarity, November 23, 1810, ibid.
45. Kemper to Rhea, November 23, 1810, Padgett, "West Florida Revolution," 120, Kemper to Alexander McMullen, November 23, 1810, 116–67.
46. McAlister, "Pensacola," 313–14.
47. Letter from Pensacola, November 23, 1810, *Richmond Enquirer,* January 5, 1811.
48. Kemper to Rhea, November 24, 1810, Padgett, "West Florida Revolution," 121–22.

49. Robert Caller to Kennedy, November 23, 1810, ibid., 117–18, Kennedy to Kemper, November 24, 1810, 117.
50. Kemper to Rhea, November 24, 1810, ibid., 121–22.
51. Toulmin to Madison, December 12, 1810, *Territorial Papers, Mississippi*, 6, 152.
52. Toulmin to Madison, November 28, 1810, ibid., 142–43.
53. Toulmin to Madison, December 6, 1810, Madison Papers, LC; Toulmin to Madison, November 28, 1810, ibid., 6, 141.
54. Toulmin to Madison, November 28, 1810, ibid., 142–43.
55. Henry Toulmin to J. Innerarity, November 26, 1810, Greenslade Papers, University of Florida, Gainesville.
56. Toulmin to Madison, November 28, 1810, Madison Papers, LC; Letter from Fort Stoddert, November 27, 1810, *Hartford Connecticut Courant*, January 16, 1811. This letter is unsigned, but context suggests that Toulmin must have been the writer.
57. Reuben Kemper to Andrew Jackson, November 17, 1815, Papers in Relation to Aaron Burr's Conspiracy, LC.
58. Toulmin to Madison, November 28, 1810, *Territorial Papers, Mississippi*, 6, 142–43.
59. Toulmin to Madison, November 28, 1810, ibid., 141.
60. Kemper to Sparks, November 27, 1810, James A. Padgett, ed., "The Documents Showing that the United States Ultimately Financed the West Florida Revolution of 1810," *Louisiana Historical Quarterly* 25 (October 1942): 945. See also *Madison Papers*, 3, 28–29n.
61. Toulmin to Madison, November 28, 1810, *Territorial Papers, Mississippi*, 6, 142.
62. Report of Dr. William Flood, January 25, 1811, Claiborne, *Mississippi*, 306–7; Statement of Joseph Collins, n.d., statement of George Farragout, n.d., *Letter Books*, 5, 88.
63. Joseph Collins to Skipwith, November 28, 1810, Padgett, "West Florida Revolution," 123–24.
64. Letter from Mississippi, November 28, 1810, *Baltimore Federal Republican and Commercial Gazette*, December 27, 1810.
65. Letter from Bayou Sara, November 28, 1810, *Richmond Enquirer*, January 5, 1811.
66. Report of military stores at St. Francisville, November 30, 1810, Padgett, "West Florida Revolution," 132–33; Mills to Skipwith, November 30, 1810, in Carrighan, "Historical and Statistical Sketches of Louisiana," 261–62; Statement of the State of Florida in acct. with P. Hicky, Treas., November 24, 1810, Philip Hicky and Family Papers, LSU.
67. Toulmin to Madison, November 28, 1810, *Territorial Papers, Mississippi*, 6, 141.
68. Folch to Someruelos, November 30, 1810, *legajo* 1568B, Facsimiles.
69. John Innerarity to John Forbes, November 29, 1810, Heloise Cruzat Papers, University of Florida, Gainesville.
70. *Newburyport (MA) Herald*, December 25, 1810.

16. *Vive la* West Floriday

1. Folch to Someruelos, August 13, 1810, *legajo* 1575, PdeC.
2. Folch to Robert Smith, December 2, 1810, *American State Papers, Foreign Relations*, 3, 398; *Charleston (VA) Farmer's Repository*, July 5, 1811.
3. Folch to John McKee, December 2, 1810, *American State Papers, Foreign Relations*, 3, 399.
4. Letter from Fort Stoddert, December 5, 1810, *Wilmington (DE) American Watchman*, January 9, 1811.
5. Toulmin to Madison, December 6, 1810, Madison Papers, LC.
6. Ibid.
7. *Providence (RI) Gazette*, January 5, 1811.
8. *Hartford (CT) American Mercury*, January 17, 1811.
9. Pickett, *Alabama*, 508. As Pickett notes on page 509, his account was based on conversations with Holmes.
10. Favrot, "Incidents," 22.
11. Pickett, *Alabama*, 508.
12. Toulmin to Madison, December 6, 1810, Madison Papers, LC. The actual route is unknown, and this is conjectural, but Toulmin did state that the boat somehow came from above Fort Stoddert.
13. House Report 189, Joseph De la França, March 3, 1845, 28th Congress, 2d Session, Serial Set Vol. 468, Session Vol. 1 (Washington, DC, 1845), 1; House Report 283, Joseph De la França, February 17, 1846, 29th Congress, 1st Session, Serial Set Vol. 489, Session Vol. 2 (Washington, 1845), 1–3; Favrot, "Incidents," 23.
14. Rodney to Caesar Rodney, December 4, 1810, Gratz, "Rodney," 45 (no. 2, 1921): 198–99.
15. *Bridgeport (CT) Republican Farmer*, January 9, 1811.
16. Toulmin to Madison, December 12, 1810, *Territorial Papers, Mississippi*, 6, 152; Pickett, *Alabama*, 508; *Montgomery (AL) Advertiser*, September 20, 1811.
17. Pickett, *Alabama*, 508.
18. Petition of Joseph P. Kennedy for Writ of Habeas Corpus, December 1 [*sic*], 1810, *Territorial Papers, Mississippi*, 6, 158–59.
19. Toulmin to Madison, December 6, 1810, Madison Papers, LC.
20. W. Brewer, *Alabama: Her History, Resources, War Record, and Public Men, from 1540 to 1872* (Montgomery, AL: Barrett and Brown, 1872), 388; Pickett, *Alabama*, 508–9.
21. Kemper to Jackson, November 17, 1815, Papers in Relation to Aaron Burr's Conspiracy, LC.
22. Toulmin to Madison, December 12, 1810, *Territorial Papers, Mississippi*, 6, 154–55.
23. Edwin Lewis to Madison, December 10, 1810, *Madison Papers*, 3, 63.
24. Toulmin to Madison, December 12, 1810, *Territorial Papers, Mississippi*, 6, 153–54, 156.
25. Toulmin to Madison, December 12, 1810, ibid., 158.

26. Pickett, *Alabama*, 509; John Nicholson to Rhea, December 17, 1810, Padgett, "West Florida Revolution," 154–55. Again, Pickett's account is based on interviews with Dr. Thomas G. Holmes, who was present at the attack, and he called the informer "an evil old man." Kemper actually later believed that Toulmin sent Folch information that led to the attack, but it seems unlikely, for even if the judge had been so disposed, chronology does not allow sufficient time for Toulmin to learn of the party at Saw Mill Creek, then get word to Folch in time for the Spaniards to attack the evening of December 9. Kemper to Jackson, November 17, 1815, Papers in Relation to Aaron Burr's Conspiracy, LC.

27. Folch to Someruelos, December 11, 1810, *legajo* 1568B, Facsimiles; Pickett, *Alabama*, 508–9; *Washington (DC) Universal Gazette*, January 11, 1811; [Toulmin] to unknown, Fort Stoddert, March 19, 1811, *Carlisle (PA) Gazette*, May 17, 1811. Holmes apparently told Pickett that there were ten prisoners including Hargraves, but Folch's report, dated two days later, must be considered the more accurate.

28. Letter of Matthew D. Willson, December 12, 1810, from Fort Stoddert, *Raleigh (NC) Star*, January 10, 1811; John Nicholson to Rhea, December 17, 1810, Padgett, "West Florida Revolution," 155.

29. Toulmin to Madison, December 12, 1810, *Territorial Papers, Mississippi*, 6, 157–58.

30. Toulmin to Madison, December 12, 1810, ibid., 158.

31. Toulmin to Holmes, February 3, 1811, Mississippi Provincial Archives, MDAH.

32. Holmes to Commanding Officer at Fort Stoddert, December 4, 1810, Executive Council Proceedings, Mississippi Territory, MDAH.

33. Toulmin to Madison, January 10, 1811, *Madison Papers*, 3, 110–14.

34. John Nicholson to Rhea, December 17, 1810, Padgett, "West Florida Revolution," 154–55.

35. *New York Columbian*, January 30, 1811.

36. Kemper to Rhea, December 16, 1810, Padgett, "West Florida Revolution," 153.

37. John Nicholson to Rhea, December 17, 1810, ibid., 154–55.

38. Address of Fulwar Skipwith, December 3, 1810, *New York Commercial Advertiser*, January 2, 1811. This also appears, undated, in Address of Skipwith to the People of West Florida, n.d. [November 29–30, 1810], Padgett, "West Florida Revolution," 158–60.

39. Philip Hicky Letter to Fulwar Skipwith, December 3, 1810, LSU; Baldwin's Appointment as Naval Agent, December 3, 1810, Padgett, "West Florida Revolution," 136, Skipwith to Collins and Baldwin, December 4, 1810, 136–37; Reuben Kemper's Comment on Suspended Claims, 1819, Padgett, "Documents," 954.

40. Philip Hicky Letter to Fulwar Skipwith, December 3, 1810, LSU; Brother's Report on Quartermaster's Stores, December 1, 1810, Padgett, "West Florida Revolution," 134.

41. Skipwith to Benjamin Collins and Charles Johnson, December 4, 1810, Padgett, "West Florida Revolution," 138, Proceedings of a Board of Militia Officers, December 1, 1810, 135, Skipwith to Ballinger, December 5, 1810, 145.

42. Arthur, *West Florida*, 129–30. Arthur is the only source for this song, and he gives no details of where he found it, mistakenly saying it was sung as the army marched out of Baton Rouge although the Mobile expedition forces never assembled in that town.

43. "Official Records," 759–62, 775–78; Frederick Kimball to Andrew Wade, December 9, 1810, Frederick Kimball Letters, LSU.

44. *New-York Gazette and General Advertiser*, December 27, 1810.

45. *Washington (DC) Enquirer*, January 10, 1811.

46. Claiborne to Smith, December 3, 1810, *Letter Books*, 5, 39–40.

47. Claiborne to Cushing, December 3, 1810, Document #7664, Parker, *Calendar*, 380.

48. Claiborne to Smith, December 2, 1810, *Letter Books*, 5, 37–38.

49. Rodney to Caesar Rodney, December 4, 1810, Gratz, "Rodney," 45 (no. 2, 1921): 198–99.

50. Rodney to Caesar Rodney, December 10, 1810, ibid., 201.

51. Claiborne to William King, December 5, 1810, *Letter Books*, 5, 79–80.

52. Claiborne to Audley L. Osborn, December 5, 1810, ibid., 45–46.

53. Claiborne to Smith, December 5, 1810, ibid., 43–44.

54. Skipwith to Graham, January 14, 1811, Padgett, "West Florida Revolution," 163; Rodney to Caesar Rodney, December 10, 1810, Gratz, "Rodney," 45 (no. 2, 1921): 202–3.

55. Proclamation, November 5, 1810, *Madison Papers*, 3, 2; Smith to Claiborne, November 5, 1810, *Territorial Papers, Orleans*, 902.

56. Rodney to Caesar Rodney, December 10, 1810, Gratz, "Rodney," 45 (no. 2, 1921): 202–3.

57. Skipwith to his Constituents, April 1, 1811, Padgett, "West Florida Revolution," 176–77.

58. Skipwith to Graham, January 14, 1811, ibid., 165.

59. Holmes to Smith, January 1, 1811, *Territorial Papers, Orleans*, 909–14.

60. Skipwith to Madison, December 5, 1810, Padgett, "West Florida Revolution," 141–44. There are two drafts of Skipwith's letter extant, both in the West Florida Miscellany, LC.

61. Claiborne to Smith, December 7, 1810, *Letter Books*, 5, 47.

62. Skipwith to Madison, December 9, 1810, Padgett, "West Florida Revolution," 147–48.

63. Reply of West Florida General assembly to Inaugural Address of Skipwith, December [6], 1810, ibid., 129–31.

64. No order recalling the Mobile expedition has been found, but it appears to have been sent late December 5, or more likely the next day.

65. Osborn to Claiborne, December 6, 1810, *Letter Books*, 5, 51–53.

66. "Official Records," 763–77, 779.

67. Osborn to Claiborne, December 6, 1810, *Letter Books*, 5, 51–53.

68. Skipwith to John H. Johnson, December 6, 1810, ibid., 50–51.
69. This quotation is a combination of Claiborne's account and Skipwith to John H. Johnson, December 6, 1810, Parker, *Calendar,* #7670. The latter is quoted in Cox, *West Florida,* page 498, but the citation is misdated December 8.
70. Claiborne to Smith, December 7, 1810, *Letter Books,* 5, 47–48.
71. Ibid. Rumor in Natchez said that after Claiborne's speech, Philemon Thomas delivered an angry harangue and then rode off to Baton Rouge declaring he would fight to defend the fort. Claiborne made no mention of any such incident in his dispatches, and the rumor clearly confuses Thomas with Skipwith and with his letter — not speech — to the legislature and their reply.
72. Frederick Kimball to Andrew Wade, December 9, 1810, Frederick Kimball Letters, LSU.
73. Holmes to Smith, January 1, 1811, *Territorial Papers, Orleans,* 909–14.
74. Claiborne to Smith, December 7, 1810, *Letter Books,* 5, 49.
75. Holmes to Smith, January 1, 1811, *Territorial Papers, Orleans,* 909–14.
76. "Official Records," 764–65. No minutes of the house of representatives' meeting at all are contained in the official journal, though it certainly met at least on December 8. Most likely the final pages are lost.
77. Mills and Audibert to Skipwith, December 14, 1810, Padgett, "West Florida Revolution," 152.
78. Holmes to Smith, January 1, 1811, *Territorial Papers, Orleans,* 909–14.
79. Skipwith to Madison, December 9, 1810, Padgett, "West Florida Revolution," 147–48.
80. Holmes to Smith, January 1, 1811, *Territorial Papers, Orleans,* 909–14.
81. Rodney to Caesar Rodney, December 10, 1810, Gratz, "Rodney," 45 (no. 2, 1921): 202–3.
82. *Wilmington (DE) American Watchman,* January 19, 1811.
83. Skipwith to Claiborne, December 10, 1810, Padgett, "West Florida Revolution," 149–50.
84. Claiborne to Smith, December 12, 1810, *Letter Books,* 5, 53–55.
85. Skipwith to his Constituents, April 1, 1811, Padgett, "West Florida Revolution," 178–79. In his account, Skipwith mistakenly recalled the surrender taking place December 9.

17. The Whole of the Mississippi Is Now American

1. "Official Records," 798–99.
2. Toulmin to Madison, January 10, 1811, *Madison Papers,* 3, 110–14.
3. Kemper to Rhea, December 20, 1810, Padgett, "West Florida Revolution," 155–56.
4. Joseph Carson to Claiborne, February 16, 1811, *Territorial Papers, Orleans,* 926.
5. John Nicholson to Rhea, December 17, 1810, Padgett, "West Florida Revolution," 155.

6. Sparks to Claiborne, December 21, 1810, *Letter Books*, 5, 73.

7. *Philadelphia Weekly Aurora*, March 5, 1811. Though unsigned, this is clearly a letter by Toulmin written at the same time as his January 10, 1811, letter to Madison.

8. Toulmin to Madison, January 10, 1811, *Madison Papers*, 3, 110–14; Sparks to Claiborne, December 21, 1810, Claiborne, *Letter Books*, 5, 74.

9. Claiborne to Sparks, December 28, 1810, ibid., 5, 77.

10. Folch to Perez, December 20, 1810, *legajo* 1569, Facsimiles.

11. Toulmin to Madison, January 10, 1811, *Madison Papers*, 3, 110–14.

12. Gaines to Perez, December 22, 1810, Perez to Gaines, December 28, 1810, *legajo* 1569, Facsimiles; *New York Columbian*, January 30, 1811.

13. These dates are approximate, based on distance and average speed of smaller sailing craft.

14. Toulmin to Madison, January 10, 1811, *Madison Papers*, 3, 110–14; Letter from Fort Stoddert, *Philadelphia Weekly Aurora*, March 5, 1811; James Callier [*sic*] to Holmes, January 15, 1811, *Wilmington (DE) American Watchman*, April 3, 1811. The letter from Fort Stoddert is almost certainly by Toulmin, and the content closely matches that of his January 10 letter to Madison, though with some additions and differences. Probably Toulmin wrote it at the same time to another addressee.

15. "Official Records," 798–99.

16. Report of Dr. William Flood, January 25, 1811, Claiborne, *Mississippi*, 306–7. A variant of Flood's report was published with other documents relating to Duprée and the affairs at Pascagoula, appearing in the *Star of Pensacola*, June 5 and 12, 1875. The documents were printed from copies in J.F.C. Claiborne's possession and differ greatly in wording from versions published in his book several years later, though with no substantive difference in content.

17. Toulmin to Madison, January 10, 1811, *Madison Papers*, 3, 110–14.

18. *Philadelphia Weekly Aurora*, March 5, 1811.

19. Ibid.

20. Innerarity to John McKee, January 21, 1811, "West Florida and Its Attempt on Mobile, 1810–1811," 704.

21. Rumor in Natchez later said that someone tore down the American flag and ran the lone star up again, but Claiborne made no mention of such an incident in his dispatches to Washington. *Salem (MA) Gazette*, January 15, 1811; *Hartford Connecticut Courant*, January 16, 1811.

22. Skipwith to Graham, January 14, 1811, Padgett, "West Florida Revolution," 165, Skipwith to his Constituents, April 1, 1811, 177.

23. Claiborne to Smith, December 12, 1810, *Letter Books*, 5, 53–55.

24. Audibert to Skipwith, December 4, 1810, Padgett, "West Florida Revolution," 139–41, December 6, 1810, 146, December 7, 1810, 146–47, December 10, 1810, 149–51.

25. Mills and Audibert to Skipwith, December 14, 1810, ibid, 152.

26. Cosas Diary, December 13, 1810, Sumario.

27. "Official Records," 786–87.

28. Robert Smith to David Holmes, November 15, 1810, *American State Papers, Foreign Relations*, 3, 398; *Alexandria (VA) Gazette*, December 8, 1810.

29. Claiborne to Smith, December 17, 1810, *Letter Books*, 5, 56–57.

30. Claiborne to Folch, December 20, 1810, with Folch to Someruelos, January 12, 1811, *legajo* 1569, Facsimiles.

31. Claiborne to Smith, December 24, 1810, *Letter Books*, 5, 62.

32. Claiborne to Smith, December 27, 1810, ibid., 68, December 24, 1810, 62.

33. Skipwith to John Graham, December 23, 1810, Padgett, "West Florida Revolution," 156–57.

34. Claiborne to Smith, December 24, 1810, *Letter Books*, 5, 62–63; Military Commission, December 22, 1810, Meneray, *Favrot Papers*, 5, 43–44.

35. Claiborne to Smith, December 24, 1810, *Letter Books*, 5, 63.

36. Claiborne, *Mississippi*, 307 and n.

37. Claiborne to Gallatin, December 24, 1810, *Territorial Papers*, Orleans, 904.

38. Squire Lee to George Poindexter, December 24, 1810, *Washington (DC) National Intelligencer*, February 16, 1811.

39. Claiborne to Smith, December 24, 1810, *Letter Books*, 5, 63.

40. Claiborne to Folch, December 27, 1810, ibid., 78, Claiborne to Smith, December 28, 1810, 66.

41. Claiborne to Smith, December 28, 1810, ibid., 66.

42. *Trenton True American*, January 14, 1811.

43. Smith to Holmes, December 21, 1810, Document #4401, Parker, *Calendar*, 223; Holmes to Toulmin, December 26, 1810, Executive Council Proceedings, Mississippi Territory, MDAH.

44. Frederick Kimball to Andrew Wade, March 5, 1811, Kimball Letters, LSU.

45. Skipwith to his Constituents, April 1, 1811, Padgett, "West Florida Revolution," 175.

46. *Baltimore Federal Republican and Commercial Gazette*, December 29, 1810.

47. Ballinger to Monroe, December 26, 1811, *Territorial Papers*, Orleans, 966.

48. Officer at Fort Adams to unknown, December 28, *Hallowell (ME) American Advocate*, February 27, 1811.

18. The Star of Florida Is Not Set

1. Rodney to Caesar Rodney, December 10, 1810, Gratz, "Rodney," 45 (no. 2, 1921): 202–3.

2. Innerarity to McKee, January 21, 1811, "West Florida and Its Attempt on Mobile, 1810–1811," 704–5.

3. Darby, *Geographical Description of the State of Louisiana*, 48, 92, 94.

4. Owsley and Smith, *Filibusters*, 63–64.

5. *New York Gazette and General Advertiser*, January 15, 1811.

6. J. P. Morier to Smith, December 15, 1810, *American State Papers, Foreign Relations*, 3, 399.

7. *Amherst (NH) Farmer's Cabinet*, July 23, 1811.

8. *Alexandria (VA) Gazette*, April 2, 1811.
9. Philadelphia, *Poulson's American Daily Advertiser*, April 1, 1811.
10. James Nielson to Madison, January 5, 1811, *Madison Papers*, 3, 101–2.
11. Claiborne to Smith, January 3, 1811, *Letter Books*, 5, 69–70.
12. Toulmin to Madison, January 23, 1811, *Madison Papers*, 3, 130–31.
13. Claiborne to William Flood, January 5, 1811, *Letter Books*, 5, 82–83. Claiborne's agent was Dr. William Flood.
14. Report of Dr. William Flood, January 25, 1811, Claiborne, *Mississippi*, 306–7.
15. Claiborne to Smith, January 6, 1811, *Letter Books*, 5, 89.
16. Claiborne to Hampton, January 6, 1811, ibid., 91.
17. Claiborne to Folch, January 7, 1811, ibid., 93.
18. Folch to Someruelos, January 8, 1811, *legajo* 1569, PdeC.
19. Claiborne to Hampton, January 9, 1811, *Letter Books*, 5, 93.
20. Hampton to Claiborne, January 12, 1811, *Hallowell (ME) American Advocate*, February 22, 1811.
21. Manuel Andry to Claiborne, January 12, 1811, ibid., February 27, 1811.
22. Ibid.
23. See several communications from Claiborne in *Letter Books*, 5, 93–100.
24. Claiborne to Philemon Thomas, January 30, 1811, ibid., 135–36.
25. Skipwith to Delassus, July 10, 1810, WFP, 18, 34ff, Skipwith to Chew and Relf, March 5, 1811, 19, 279–80, Skipwith to Louis de Gras de Vaubercey, January 24, 1811, 389; Sale Fulwar Skipwith to Richard Relf, March 5, 1811, Notary John Lynd, 7, 284–85, Fulwar Skipwith mortgage, March 5, 1811, 285–86, New Orleans Notarial Archives, Notarial Archives Research Center, New Orleans; Skipwith to Graham, January 14, 1811, Padgett, "West Florida Revolution," 167–68.
26. *Philadelphia Weekly Aurora*, March 5, 1811.
27. Skipwith to Graham, January 14, 1811, Padgett, "West Florida Revolution," 167–68.
28. *New Haven Connecticut Herald*, March 12, 1811.
29. Letter from St. Francisville, January 29, 1811, ibid.
30. *Philadelphia Weekly Aurora*, March 5, 1811.
31. *Boston New-England Palladium*, March 22, 1811.
32. Toulmin to Madison, January 23, 1811, *Madison Papers*, 3, 130–31.
33. Innerarity to John McKee, January 21, 1811, "West Florida and Its Attempt on Mobile, 1810–1811," 704.
34. Toulmin to Madison, February 6, 1811, *Territorial Papers, Mississippi*, 2, 176–77; Toulmin to Holmes, February 3, 1811, Mississippi Provincial Archives, MDAH.
35. Folch to Someruelos, January 12, 1811, *legajo* 1569, Facsimiles.
36. John McKee to Folch, January 17, 1811, Pintado Papers, LC.
37. Smith to George Matthews and John McKee, January 26, 1811, *American State Papers, Foreign Relations*, 3, 571–72.
38. Folch to McKee, February 27, 1811, Pintado Papers, LC.
39. Isaac Baker to Stephen F. Austin, February 25, 1811, Eugene C. Barker, ed., *The

Austin Papers, Part 1 (*Annual Report of the American Historical Association for the Year 1919*, 2, Washington: Government Printing Office, 1924), 185. Baker states that "Col Kemper dined with us yesterday."

40. Lemuel Henry to Gallatin, January 9, 1811, Document #4406, Parker, *Calendar*, 224.

41. Claiborne to Philemon Thomas, January 30, 1811, *Letter Books*, 5, 135–36, Claiborne to Sterling Duprée, February 16, 1811, 157.

42. Toulmin to Madison, March 6, 1811, *Madison Papers*, 3, 201.

43. Baker to Austin, February 25, 1811, Barker, *The Austin Papers*, Part 1, 2, 185.

44. Josiah Lawton to John Collins, March 10, 1811, Miscellaneous Manuscripts, LSU.

45. Frederick Kimball to Andrew Wade, March 5, 1811, Kimball Letters, LSU.

46. Ballinger to Monroe, December 26, 1811, *Territorial Papers, Orleans*, 966–70.

47. Frederick Kimball to Andrew Wade, March 5, 1811, Kimball Letters, Joseph Lawton to Collins, March 10, 1811, Miscellaneous Manuscripts, LSU.

48. *Newburgh (NY) Orange County Patriot, or The Spirit of Seventy-Six*, May 21, 1811.

49. *Natchez Chronicle*, March 18, 1811, in the *Wilkes-Barre (PA) Gleaner, and Luzerne Advertiser*, May 17, 1811.

50. Lawton to Collins, March 10, 1811, Miscellaneous Manuscripts, LSU.

51. *Newburgh (NY) Orange County Patriot, or The Spirit of Seventy-Six*, May 21, 1811.

52. Claiborne to Smith, March 22, 1811, *Letter Books*, 5, 187–88, Claiborne to Thomas, April 9, 1811, 208–9.

53. Claiborne to Smith, March 22, 1811, ibid., 187–88.

54. Skipwith to his Constituents, April 1, 1811, Padgett, "West Florida Revolution," 171–79.

55. *Bridgeport (CT) Republican Farmer*, May 22, 1811.

56. *New Haven (CT) Connecticut Herald*, March 12, 1811.

57. *New York Journal*, March 9, 1811.

58. Claiborne to Smith, March 8, 1811, *Letter Books*, 5, 174.

59. Claiborne to William Shaler, March 11, 1811, ibid., 178.

60. Claiborne to Smith, March 26, 1811, ibid., 191.

61. Someruelos to Claiborne, March 29, 1811, ibid., 225–26.

62. Claiborne to Post Master at Fort Stoddert, May 1, 1811, ibid., 249.

63. Sparks, *Memories of Fifty Years*, 415–16. Of course this anecdote may have been in some measure exaggerated or embellished in the nearly sixty years between the event and Sparks's telling of it. Sparks does confuse the context somewhat by saying this took place after Louisiana was admitted to statehood, whereas the only time that seating West Florida delegates was an issue was in the territorial stage. Sparks makes the incident responsible for the admission of West Florida's delegation, which is highly unlikely.

64. Price, "West Florida," 356–58.

65. Claiborne to Wykoff, March 26, 1811, *Letter Books*, 5, 189.

66. *New Orleans Louisiana Gazette*, July 1, 1811.

67. Kimball to Wade, May 12, 1811, Kimball Letters, LSU.
68. Toulmin to Madison, February 27, 1811, *Madison Papers*, 3, 192.
69. Toulmin to Madison, February 17, 1812, *Territorial Papers, Mississippi*, 6, 269–70.
70. [Toulmin] to unknown, March 19, 1811, *Carlisle (PA) Gazette*, May 17, 1811.
71. Innerarity to McKee, January 21, 1811, "West Florida and Its Attempt on Mobile, 1810–1811," 704–5.
72. *Richmond Enquirer*, June 21, 1811.
73. Claiborne to Sparks, April 22, 1811, *Letter Books*, 5, 215.
74. *Alexandria (VA) Herald*, June 13, 1811.
75. Caller to Holmes, April 4, 1811, Mississippi Territorial Archives, Administration Division, MDAH.
76. Toulmin to Madison, May 14, 1811, *Madison Papers*, 3, 302–3.
77. *New York Commercial Advertiser*, May 24, 1811.
78. Letter from Bayou Sara, May 26, 1811, *Richmond Enquirer*, July 16, 1811.
79. Monroe to Matthews and McKee, June 29, 1811, Document #1057, Parker, *Calendar*, 63, Monroe to Claiborne, June 29, 1811, Document #1058, 64.
80. *Kline's Weekly Carlisle (PA) Gazette*, August 9, 1811.
81. Claiborne to Monroe, July 9, 1811, *Letter Books*, 5, 300; *Richmond Enquirer*, August 13, 1811.
82. *Richmond Enquirer*, August 13, 1811.
83. *Alexandria (VA) Daily Gazette*, May 25, 1811.
84. *Charlestown (VA) Farmer's Repository*, September 13, 1811.
85. Kimball to Wade, April 9, June 23, 1811, Kimball Letters, LSU.
86. Oration Delivered at St. Francisville, July 4, 1811, Padgett, "West Florida Revolution," 179–89.
87. Claiborne to James Neilson, July 20, 1811, *Letter Books*, 5, 311.
88. Claiborne to Monroe, August 27, 1811, ibid., 344–45.
89. Claiborne to Monroe, September 2, 1811, ibid., 352–53.
90. Kimball to Wade, September 8, 1811, Kimball Letters, LSU.
91. Claiborne to Monroe, August 27, 1811, *Letter Books*, 5, 344–45.
92. Claiborne to Monroe, September 2, 1811, ibid., 352–53.
93. Articles of agreement, November 19, 1811, WFP, 19, 286.
94. Presentment by the grand jury, n.d. [November 1811], *Territorial Papers, Mississippi*, 2, 245–46.
95. George Patterson et al. to the House of Representatives, November 20, 1811, *American State Papers: Foreign Relations*, 2, 155; "Petition of the Inhabitants of West Florida, November 20, 1811" (Washington: R. C. Weightman, 1811), Mississippi Department of Archives and History, Jackson.
96. Price, "West Florida," 392.
97. Claiborne to John H. Johnson, November 27, 1811, *Letter Books*, 5, 387, December 13, 1811, *Letter Books*, 6, 6.
98. Minutes of a Public Meeting, Padgett, "West Florida Revolution," 189–90.
99. Claiborne to Johnson, December 18, 1811, *Letter Books*, 6, 10.
100. Ballinger to Monroe, December 26, 1811, *Territorial Papers, Orleans*, 965–70.

101. Claiborne to John Dawson, January 1, 1812, *Letter Books*, 6, 24, Claiborne to George Poindexter, January 6, 1812, 31; Price, "West Florida," 392–95.
102. Price, "West Florida," 400–12.
103. Memorial to Congress from Inhabitants of Feliciana County, March 17, 1812, *Territorial Papers, Orleans*, 1007–12.
104. Claiborne to Johnson, May 4, 1812, *Letter Books*, 6, 94, April 22, 1812, 88.
105. Favrot, "Incidents," 25–26; Newcombe v. Skipwith, in Francis Xavier Martin, *Martin's Reports of Cases Argued and Determined in the Superior Court of the Territory of Orleans* (New Orleans: Louisiana Supreme Court, 1846), 1, 151.
106. Price, "West Florida," 416 and n.
107. Claiborne to Gallatin, July 6, 1812, *Letter Books*, 6, 121.
108. Claiborne Circular Letter, August 25, 1812, ibid., 168.

19. The Old Hero

1. For sound reflections on this see McMichael, *Atlantic Loyalties*, 4, 174–75.
2. Pierre-Joseph Favrot to Someruelos, January 8, 1811, Meneray, *Favrot Papers*, 5, 45–49.
3. *Boston Repertory*, December 7, 1810.
4. *American Beacon and Norfolk and Portsmouth Daily Advertiser*, March 21, 1820.
5. In 1818, when Jackson took Pensacola at last, the Spanish governor Colonel José Masot engaged the ship *Peggy* to carry himself, his officers, and the official archives of West Florida to Havana. On September 9, the vessel was about fifty miles off the Cuban coast when a privateer stopped her. After robbing everyone of their money and taking provisions, the privateer moved on, but the next day the *Peggy* sailed into a severe storm that carried away anchor, masts, and boats, and then gradually broke up the ship, which went to the bottom with all the records aboard. Sea Protest, Notary John Lynd, vol. 15, 1818, 1005–7, New Orleans Notarial Archives.
6. Kendall, "Documents," part 1, 81–83.
7. *New Orleans Jeffersonian Republican*, April 3, 1845.
8. *Petition of the Louisiana Parishes of East and West Feliciana, East Baton Rouge, Livingston, St. Helena, Tangipahoa, Washington, and St. Tammany* (n.p., circa 1882), 1–3.
9. *Petition of Charles DeHault Delassus*, 4–5.
10. *Legajo* 163B, PdeC.
11. Arthur, *West Florida*, 142.
12. *Petition of Charles DeHault Delassus*, 1–2, 14; United States Senate Document 170, Report, February 15, 1843, Serial Set Vol. 415, Session Vol. 3, 27th Congress, 3d Session (Washington, 1843), 2–3; *Washington (DC) National Intelligencer*, February 4, 1835.
13. *Baltimore Commercial Transcript*, June 11, 1838; Correspondence Relating to Efforts to Acquire the "Pintado Papers," 1836–1883, Unbound Records of

the General Land Office Relating to Private Claims in Louisiana 1805–1896, M1385, NA.

14. Susanna Kneeland to Pintado, December 6, 1810, Pintado Papers, LC.
15. *New Orleans Louisiana Gazette*, February 23, 1818; *Orleans Gazette*, June 15, 1818.
16. Ancestry.com, *Mississippi State and Territorial Census Collection, 1792–1866*; *Natchez Mississippi State Gazette*, May 6, 1820, May 25, June 16, 1821.
17. Hall, *Louisiana Slave Records, 1719–1820*; *St. Francisville Louisianian*, June 5, 1819.
18. Louis E. LeBlanc et al. to Jackson, January 1815, Andrew Jackson Papers, LC.
19. Lease Agreement, March 8, 1816, Notarial Record A, 536–37, Clerk of Court, West Feliciana Parish Courthouse, St. Francisville, LA.
20. *New Orleans Louisiana Advertiser*, April 25, 1827.
21. Kemper and Wright, *Genealogy of the Kemper Family*, 65, 84–85.
22. Griffith to Kemper, September 19, 1817, Padgett, "Documents," 949–50.
23. Leonard to Duffel, October 24, 1810, Prichard, "Original Letter," 357.
24. *Portland (ME) Eastern Argus*, February 9, 1815.
25. Estate of Gov'r de Grand Pré to Samuel Fulton (as executor), May 21, 1812, Carlos de Grand-Pré Succession Papers, LSU.
26. Carrighan, "Statistical and Historical Sketches of Louisiana," 613–14.
27. *Boston Daily Courier*, October 13, 1859.
28. Willie, *History of Spanish West Florida*, 5ff. There is some disagreement as to his date of death; one obituary indicated that he died on November 17, but his gravestone says November 18. Years later he would be reinterred in the National Cemetery.
29. Carrighan, "Statistical and Historical Sketches of Louisiana," 612. At his death, his family turned over his personal papers to the Rev. W. H. Crenshaw to write a biography, which, unfortunately, he never finished.
30. *Washington (DC) Daily National Journal*, August 1, 1827; *Baltimore Patriot*, May 16, 1821.
31. Kendall, "Documents," 88–89.
32. Cox, *Skipwith*, 130.
33. McCain, "Holmes," 344–47.
34. Carrighan, "Statistical and Historical Sketches of Louisiana," 613–14; Carrighan, "Historical and Statistical Sketches of Louisiana," 257.
35. *New Orleans Daily Delta*, June 27, 1860; *Hagers-Town (MD) Gazette*, December 18, 1810.
36. Reuben Kemper to Richard M. Johnson, February 23, 1820, Documents in Relation to the Claim of James Johnson for Transportation on the Missouri and Mississippi Rivers, 72.
37. Kemper to J. F. Carmichael, June 5, 1811, Wilkinson County Land Deed Record A, 224, Chancery Court Records, Wilkinson County Courthouse, Woodville, MS.

38. Kemper to Livingston, January 21, 1812, Edward Livingston Papers, Princeton University, Princeton, NJ.

39. Ron Jackson, comp., Accelerated Indexing Systems, *Louisiana Census, 1791–1890*; Ancestry.com, *Mississippi State and Territorial Census Collection, 1792–1866.*

40. *Alexandria Louisiana Planter,* May 15, 1810. Secondary sources often assume that Reuben and even Nathan were with Samuel on the expedition, but the fact that Reuben wrote letters from Alexandria in April and May of 1813 while Samuel was still absent with the expedition seems conclusive proof that Reuben, at least, did not participate.

41. *Albany (NY) Argus,* July 2, 1813.

42. Protest, April 26, 1813, Notary John Lynd, 10, 675–76, New Orleans Notarial Archives; Kemper to Livingston, April 6, 1813, Livingston Papers, Princeton, NJ.

43. Kemper to Livingston, July 5, 1813, March 19, 1814, Edward Livingston Papers, Princeton University, Princeton, NJ.

44. John Tinkle to Reuben Kemper, August 12, 1814, Notarial Record A, 374–75, Clerk of Court, West Feliciana Parish Courthouse, St. Francisville, LA; Sale, September 9, 1814, Notary John Lynd, 11, 373–74, New Orleans Notarial Archives.

45. Smith to Pintado, March 9, 1813, Pintado Papers, LC; Charles Cosby certificate, October 19, 1814, Notarial Record A, 414–15, Clerk of Court, West Feliciana Parish Courthouse, St. Francisville, LA.

46. Reuben Kemper to George, William, and Edward Randolph, November 7, 1814, Wilkinson County Land Deed Record A, 386–88, Chancery Court Records, Wilkinson County Courthouse, Woodville, MS.

47. Kemper and Wright, *Genealogy of the Kemper Family,* 65.

48. *Albany (NY) Argus,* July 2, 1813.

49. Mrs. Dunbar [Eron] Rowland, *Mississippi Territory in the War of 1812* (Baltimore: Clearfield Company, 1968; reprint), page 160, shows Reuben was a private in Hinds's battalion, as was Samuel.

50. Arséne Lacarriére Latour, *Historical Memoir of the War in West Florida and Louisiana in 1814–15* (Gainesville: University Press of Florida, 1999; ed. by Gene A. Smith), 99–100, 126–27.

51. Treaty of Ghent Memorandum, February 19, 1815, Historic New Orleans Collection, New Orleans.

52. Kemper to Jackson, November 17, 1815, Papers in Relation to Aaron Burr's Conspiracy, LC; Reuben Kemper's Comment on Suspended Claims, 1819, Padgett, "Documents," 957.

53. Kemper to Jackson, November 17, 1815, Papers in Relation to Aaron Burr's Conspiracy, LC.

54. Register of Passport Applications, December 21, 1810–October 7, 1817, General Records of the Department of State, Record Group 59, National Archives, Washington, DC, 17.

55. It is, of course, pure speculation that Havana was Kemper's destination, but

in tandem with his November letter to Jackson and the release of the captives within a few months, it seems reasonable to assume that this is where he was going when he got his passport. There is no evidence of a trip anywhere else outside the United States, and his surviving correspondence does not reveal sufficient time for, say, a European journey.

56. Pickett, *Alabama*, page 509, says that according to Thomas G. Holmes the men were held captive for five years, which would put their release somewhere in 1815 to 1816.

57. Sibley was out of Havana by December of 1816 when he signed a petition to Congress with other Alabama planters. Petition to Congress, December 6, 1816, Land Titles in the Mississippi Territory, Walter S. Franklin and Walter Lowrie, eds., *American State Papers: Miscellaneous* (Washington: Gales and Seaton, 1832), 2, 253.

58. Reuben Kemper's Comment on Suspended Claims, 1819, Padgett, "Documents," 957.

59. Monroe to Kemper, December 30, 1815, ibid., 946.

60. *Petition of Charles DeHault Delassus*, 10. Kemper certainly seems to have had access to the papers of the convention. Their whereabouts following the takeover by the United States are cloudy. Some stayed in Hicky's hands and are in the Hicky Papers at LSU today. Near the end of the nineteenth century, the great bulk, including the journals of the convention and legislature, came into the hands of John T. Pickett and were placed in the Library of Congress, originally as a part of his extensive collection of diplomatic history documents. Cox, *West Florida*, 404n.

61. Kemper to Livingston, June 15, 1816, Livingston Papers, Princeton, NJ.

62. Kemper to Griffith, September 18, 1817, Padgett, "Documents," 948–49.

63. Henry Stuart Foote, *Texas and the Texans* (Philadelphia: Thomas, Cowperthwait & Co., 1841), 1, 187n. Foote said he was surprised at such deference to someone who had been somewhat attached to the Burr enterprise, or so he thought, adding that "I have always looked upon the incident as a little curious." His reference to Reuben as a "Texas commander" shows that in writing twenty-four years after the fact, Foote confused Reuben with brother Samuel, though Foote himself wrote one of the best early books on the history of Texas. Not too much weight should be given to someone's recollections from the age of thirteen, but it is possible that this was not a confusion and that Foote knew or heard firsthand from Reuben of Reuben's part in the Gutiérrez-Magee expedition, though demonstrably Reuben was back in Alexandria by April of 1813 and could not have participated in the taking of San Antonio.

64. Kemper to Livingston, June 15, 1816, Livingston Papers, Princeton, NJ.

65. Charles McMicken to Pintado, August 24, 1811, Receipt, February 9, 1813, Pintado Papers, LC.

66. J. A. Browder to clerk of 4th District Court, Point Coupée Parish, February 11, 1818, Reuben Kemper v. John Smith, case file, Pointe Coupée Parish Clerk of Court, New Roads, LA.

67. Jed Smith, C. McMicken, and Alexander Crawford to clerk of 4th District Court, February 14, 1818, Kemper v. Smith, Pointe Coupée Parish Clerk of Court, New Roads, LA.

68. In fact, no record has been found in the East Feliciana courthouse of the final disposition in the suit, but the fact that the sheriff was selling property related to the suit in the spring of 1819 and that Reuben had another property seized in a separate case suggest that he lost both at that time. This is supported by the complete disappearance of any mention of the suit in his subsequent correspondence with his lawyer and friend Livingston.

69. *St. Francisville Louisianian*, May 15, 1819.

70. Ibid., November 20, 1819.

71. Wilhelmy, "John Smith," 57–58.

72. *St. Francisville Louisianian*, October 30, 1819.

73. Statement of Richard Rush, May 5, 1817, Daniel Brent to Mr. Pleasanton, June 12, 1817, Padgett, "Documents," 947–48, List of Claims by the Inhabitants of West Florida, n.d., 950–52, 957, Statement of Claims, n.d., 952–53.

74. Reuben Kemper to Andrew Jackson, April 6, 1819, Andrew Jackson Papers, LC.

75. *Petition of Charles DeHault Delassus*, 21–22; Letter from the Treasurer of the United States, Transmitting the Annual Accounts of His Office, February 23, 1820, 16th Congress, 1st Session, Serial Set Vol. 39, Session Vol. 9 (Washington, DC, 1820), 68, 84, 112.

76. *Petition of Charles DeHault Delassus*, 11.

77. Carrighan, "Statistical and Historical Sketches of Louisiana," 613.

78. Kemper to Livingston, August 13, 1818, Livingston Papers, Princeton, NJ.

79. U.S. Census, Rapides Parish, Louisiana, 1820. The census shows nothing about occupation, but it does reveal a number of people in his household, including seven slaves and two white males younger than himself, one of them just a teenager. It also indicates that six people in the household engaged in agriculture and one in manufacturing of some kind. Just what to make of this is uncertain. Kemper was not married, so the white males living with him seem most likely to be boarders or hired workers. Three of the four male slaves were under the age of fourteen, and the other male was over forty-five; one female slave was over forty-five and the other two were younger, suggesting perhaps a single slave family. Reuben's statement in 1820 indicates that he stopped his barge business in 1810, so this number of people in his household seems best explained by his turning to either planting or running a boarding house and tavern.

80. Kemper to Jackson, April 6, 1819, Andrew Jackson Papers, LC.

81. John Johnston to Josiah Stoddard Johnston, November 29, December 27, 1822, Isaac Baker to Johnston, March 11, June 23, November 11, 1822, Josiah Stoddard Johnston Papers, Historical Society of Pennsylvania, Philadelphia (hereinafter cited as HSP).

82. Kemper to William Johnson, September 30, 1824, William Johnson Papers, MDAH.

83. John Johnston to Johnston, December 27, 1822, Johnston Papers, HSP.

84. Kemper to Johnston, March 18, 1824, ibid.

85. House Report 667, Joseph De La França, June 14, 1848, 30th Congress, 1st Session, Serial Set Vol. 526, Session Vol. 3 (Washington, 1848), 2.

86. Kemper to Johnston, May 19, 1826, Henry Boyer to Johnston, March 30, 1828, Johnston Papers, HSP.

87. Senate Report to accompany Bill No. 62, January 4, 1847, 29th Congress, 2d Session, Serial Set Vol. 494, Session Vol. 2 (Washington, DC, 1847), 1; Senate Report to accompany Bill No. 122, February 2, 1848, 30th Congress, 1st Session, Serial Set Vol. 512, Session Vol. 1 (Washington, 1848), 1; Favrot, "Incidents," 23–24.

88. Kemper to Livingston, January 8, 1824, Livingston Papers, Princeton, NJ; House Report 189, Joseph De la França, March 3, 1845, 28th Congress, 2d Session, Serial Set Vol. 468, Session Vol. 1 (Washington, DC, 1845), 1–2; House Report 283, Joseph De la França, February 17, 1846, 29th Congress, 1st Session, Serial Set Vol. 489, Session Vol. 2 (Washington, DC, 1845), 1–3.

89. Kemper to Livingston, January 8, 23, 1824, Livingston Papers, Princeton, NJ; Kemper to Johnston, March 18, 1824, Johnston Papers, HSP.

90. Kemper to Johnston, February 7, December 1, 1825, Reuben Kemper power of attorney, May 19, 1826, Johnston Papers, HSP.

91. For more on Bowie and his land schemes see this author's *Three Roads to the Alamo: The Lives and Fortunes of David Crockett, James Bowie, and William Barret Travis* (New York: HarperCollins, 1998).

92. Reuben Kemper to Johnston fragment, May 19, December 14, 1826, Johnston Papers, HSP.

93. Baker to Johnston, October 5, 1826, ibid.

94. Walter Overton to Johnston, December 7, 1826, ibid.

95. L. Pleasonton to Kemper, April 15, 1820, Fifth Auditor's Office, Letters Sent, 1817–1869, Record Group 217, National Archives, Washington, DC, 1, 171, Statement of the Fifth Auditor to Henry Clay, April 20, 1826, 2, 257–58.

96. Receipts and Expenditures of the United States, 1818, 88–89; 1819, 85; 1820, 62–63, Record Group 217, National Archives; Kemper to Johnston, December 14, 1826, Kemper power of attorney August 3, 1826, Johnston Papers, HSP. Note that the author's account of the de la França episode in *Three Roads to the Alamo* is incomplete and in error in several points due to insufficient sources at the time of writing.

97. The França claim continued to have a contentious history after Reuben Kemper's death. Bowie pursued it for a few more years, though Kemper's heirs argued that he never legally transferred the claim to Bowie. There was even a question at the time of whether Joseph de la França was a genuine person, though subsequent events showed that he was. The Senate claims committee had reported in favor of the claim four times by the summer of 1848, and twice it reached the House, only to fail for lack of time. Then a House committee looked at new evidence that finally gave the claim new life. At last Congress, on August 14, 1848, authorized the payment to França's estate of

the original debt of $11,850, plus interest for thirty-eight years, amounting to $26,798.78, or a total of $38,648.78. Congress did not redeem the claim in full until April 19, 1850. Davis, *Three Roads*, 220–23, 293–94; Henry Boyer to Johnston, March 30, 1828, Johnston Papers, HSP; Senate Report to accompany Bill No. 62, January 4, 1847, 29th Congress, 2d Session, Serial Set Vol. 494, Session Vol. 2 (Washington, DC, 1847), 1; Senate Report to accompany Bill No. 122, February 2, 1848, 30th Congress, 1st Session, Serial Set Vol. 512, Session Vol. 1 (Washington, DC, 1848), 1; House Report 667, Joseph de la França, June 14, 1848, 30th Congress, 1st Session, Serial Set Vol. 526, Session Vol. 3 (Washington, DC, 1848), 1–3; Favrot, "Incidents," 23–24; Reuben Kemper's Comment on Suspended Claims, 1819, Padgett, "Documents," 944–45, 970.

98. *New Orleans Louisiana State Gazette*, January 10, 1826.
99. *Natchez Mississippi State Gazette*, July 14, 1821, February 2, 1822; Kemper to William Johnson, September 30, 1824, William Johnson Papers, MDAH.
100. Kemper and Wright, *Kemper Family*, 178, 180.
101. G. C. Russell to George Potts, January 29, 1827, Claiborne, *Mississippi*, 311n; *New Orleans Louisiana Advertiser*, February 9, 1827. The multiple direct quotations from Russell's letter that appear in the obituary make it clear that he must have written that too.
102. Samuel Wells to Johnston, February 12, 1827, Johnston Papers, HSP.
103. *New Orleans Daily Delta*, June 27, 1860.
104. Reuben Kemper's Comment on Suspended Claims, 1819, Padgett, "Documents," 961.
105. *Baton Rouge Gazette and Comet*, August 29, 1863.

BIBLIOGRAPHY

The published literature on the West Florida revolt and republic is not extensive, but most of it is useful. For almost a century the standard work has been Isaac Joslin Cox's *The West Florida Controversy, 1798–1813: A Study in American Diplomacy*, a series of Albert Shaw Lectures on diplomatic history published in 1918. For its time it was an outstanding piece of scholarship and included research in domestic and foreign archives. It is full and comprehensive in the main. It suffers from a notable carelessness and inconsistency in source citations and the printer's annoyingly frequent misplacement or loss of text. Unaccountably, Cox made virtually no use of the extensive Archives of the Spanish Government of West Florida, which at that time had not yet been translated, though he certainly knew of the collection. While many of his judgments and conclusions on people and events are now open to question, Cox is still a landmark work.

An entirely different sort of approach is Stanley Clisby Arthur's *The Story of the West Florida Rebellion*, which first appeared as a series of articles in the *St. Francisville (LA) Democrat* and was subsequently collected in book form in 1935. At the outset it needs to be said that Arthur was a journalist, not an historian, though he did many great things for Louisiana history, especially his work managing the translation of the Archives of the Spanish Government of West Florida and other projects for the Work Projects Administration. Arthur paid far more attention to dramatic — often lurid — narrative than to judicious use of sources, and he frequently misread or misunderstood the sources he found. His is an entirely triumphalist account with little to offer on interpretation and contextual understanding. However, he lived in the Florida Parishes for many years at a time when he could collect oral history still current, and he seems to have found a few local sources that have since been lost, with the result that his book is now the only place to find some things of interest and even importance. To his credit, he seems not to have tampered with sources or invented anything, and consequently, his book still has value if used judiciously.

In 2004 David A. Bice published his *The Original Lone Star Republic: Scoundrels, Statesmen and Schemers of the 1810 West Florida Rebellion*. It is a straightforward popular account that contains almost nothing not found in Cox and Arthur.

Andrew McMichael's *Atlantic Loyalties: Americans in Spanish West Florida, 1785–1810,* published in 2008, is the best work to date on the subject. Only the final twenty pages deal with the events of 1810, but McMichael's extensive investigation of a quarter century of the social, political, economic, and ethnic background leading up to 1810 is outstanding. He clearly reveals the origins of the revolt in the breakdown of law and order, civil administration, land policy, the chaotic state of Spain during the Napoleonic wars, and the overwhelming American presence in West Florida. Robert V. Haynes's *The Mississippi Territory and the Southwest Frontier, 1795–1817* appeared too late to be consulted, but is an outstanding work on the neighbor with which West Florida's fortunes were so intertwined.

Primary Sources

Manuscripts

East Baton Rouge Parish Courthouse, Baton Rouge, LA
    Archives of the Spanish Government of West Florida, 1782–1816, 19th Judicial
        District Court
University of Florida, Gainesville
    Heloise Cruzat Papers
    Greenslade Papers
Historic New Orleans Collection, Williams Research Center, New Orleans, LA
    Treaty of Ghent Memorandum, February 19, 1815
Library of Congress, Washington, DC
    Aaron Burr's Conspiracy, Papers in Relation to
    James Brown Papers
    Andrew Jackson Papers
    Papeles de Cuba, Archivo General de Indias, Facsimiles from Spanish Archives,
        legajos 267B, 1566, 1567, 1568B, 1569, 1574, 2356
    Vicente Sebastian Pintado Papers
    West Florida Miscellany
Louisiana State Archives, Baton Rouge
    Constitution of the State of Florida, 1810
Louisiana State Library, Baton Rouge
    West Florida History, Vertical File
Louisiana State University, Louisiana and Mississippi Valley Collection, Hill Library, Baton Rouge
    Solomon Alston Estate Document, April 27, 1809
    Butler Family Papers
    French-Clarke Family Papers
    Carlos de Grand-Pré Succession Papers
    Philip Hicky and Family Papers
    Philip Hicky Letter to Fulwar Skipwith, December 3, 1810
    Frederick Kimball Letters
    John Lawton Letter, Miscellaneous Manuscripts

Papeles Procedentes de la Isla de Cuba, Archives of the Indies, microfilm copies *legajos* 55, 106, 163B, 176B(2), 179, 185, 594, 594A, 595
John Smith–Reuben Kemper Papers
West Florida Rebellion Papers
Mississippi Department of Archives and History, Jackson
Adams County, Mississippi Territory, Minutes of the County Court, 2, 1802–1804
William Johnson Papers
Mississippi Provincial Archives, Spanish Domination, 8 September 1802 to December 1806, Archives of the Indies, Seville, Cuban Papers
Mississippi Territorial Archives, Administration Division
Mississippi Territory Executive Council Proceedings
Mississippi Territorial Tax Rolls, Series 510, Wilkinson County, 1805
Papeles Procedentes de la Isla de Cuba, Archives of the Indies, transcripts
"Petition of the Inhabitants of West Florida, November 20, 1811" (Washington: R. C. Weightman, 1811)
National Archives, Kew, Richmond, Surrey, England
Foreign Office, General Correspondence from Political and Other Departments, General Correspondence before 1906, United States of America, Series II, FO 5/45
National Archives, Washington, DC
Correspondence Relating to Efforts to Acquire the "Pintado Papers," 1836–1883, Unbound Records of the General Land Office Relating to Private Claims in Louisiana 1805–1896, M1385, NA
Fifth Auditor's Office, Letters Sent, 1817–1869, Record Group 217
General Records of the Department of State, Record Group 59
Register of Passport Applications, December 21, 1810–October 7, 1817
Receipts and Expenditures of the United States, 1818, 1819, 1820, Record Group 217
New Orleans Notarial Archives, Notarial Archives Research Center, New Orleans, LA
John Lynd. 4, 1808–1809, Reuben Kemper et al. river protest, 512–13
———. 7, 1811, sale Fulwar Skipwith, 284–86
———. 10, 1813, Reuben Kemper protest, 675–76
———. 11, 1814, sale Reuben Kemper to Harvey Elkins, 373–74
Felix De Armas, 5, 1826, José de la França power of attorney, 72–73
University of North Carolina, Southern Historical Collection, Chapel Hill
Edward Duffel letter
Martin L. Haynie letter
Historical Society of Pennsylvania, Philadelphia
Josiah Stoddard Johnston Papers
Pierpont Morgan Library, New York, NY
Fulwar Skipwith letter, December 4, 1810, Literary and Historical Manuscripts
Pointe Coupée Parish Clerk of Court, New Roads, LA
Case of Reuben Kemper v. John Smith, 1818

Princeton University, Princeton, NJ
    Edward Livingston Papers
University of South Carolina, South Caroliniana Library, Columbia
    Hutchinson Family Papers
Tulane University, New Orleans, LA
    Pierre-Joseph Favrot Correspondence
University of Virginia, Tracy W. McGregor Library of American History, Special
        Collections, Charlottesville
    Vicente Folch, Governor of West Florida, and Juan Ventura Morales, Intendant
        of West Florida 1810, Scribe's copies of Correspondence
    Thomas Rodney, "The Exploration of and Title to East and West Florida, and
        Louisiana, the Spanish & French Colonies in America, the Louisiana Pur-
        chase, and the Rights of Deposit, etc."
West Feliciana Parish Courthouse, St. Francisville, LA
    Notarial Record A, Clerk of Court
Wilkinson County Courthouse, Woodville, MS
    Wilkinson County Land Deed Record A, Chancery Court Records

Newspapers

Albany (NY) Argus, 1813
Albany (NY) Balance, and New-York State Journal, 1810
Alexandria (LA) Louisiana Planter, 1810
Alexandria (VA) Advertiser, 1805
Alexandria (VA) Daily Gazette, 1811
Alexandria (VA) Gazette, 1810, 1811
Alexandria (VA) Herald, 1811
Amherst (NH) Farmer's Cabinet, 1811
Augusta (ME) Kennebec Gazette, 1803
Baltimore Commercial Transcript, 1838
Baltimore Federal Republican and Commercial Gazette, 1810
Baltimore Patriot, 1821
Baton Rouge (LA) Gazette and Comet, 1863
Boston Columbian Centinel, 1810
Boston Daily Courier, 1859
Boston Democrat, 1805
Boston Gazette, 1810
Boston Independent Chronicle, 1805, 1810
Boston New England Palladium, 1805, 1808, 1811
Boston Repertory, 1805, 1810
Brattleborough (VT) Reporter, 1806
Bridgeport (CT) Gazette, 1810
Bridgeport (CT) Republican Farmer, 1811
Burlington Vermont Centinel, 1807
Carlisle (PA) Gazette, 1811

Carlisle (PA) Kline's Weekly Carlisle Gazette, 1811
Charleston (SC) City Gazette, 1805
Charleston (SC) Courier, 1804
Charlestown (VA, later WV) Farmer's Repository, 1810, 1811
Cincinnati Liberty Hall and Cincinnati Mercury, 1808
Concord New Hampshire Patriot, 1810
Doylestown Pennsylvania Correspondent, 1805
Easton (MD) Eastern Shore Republican Star or General Advertiser, 1802
Frankfort (KY) Western World, 1806
Frederick (MD) Hornet or Republican Advocate, 1810
Frederick-town (MD) Hornet, 1804
Hagers-Town (MD) Gazette, 1810
Hagerstown Maryland Herald, 1804
Hallowell (ME) American Advocate, 1811
Harrisburg (PA) Oracle of Dauphin, 1804
Hartford (CT) American Mercury, 1811
Hartford Connecticut Courant, 1804, 1811
Lexington (KY) Reporter, 1808
Middletown (CT) Middlesex Gazette, 1810
Montgomery (AL) Advertiser, 1911
Morristown (NJ) Palladium of Liberty, 1810
Nashville Tennessee Gazette, 1804
Natchez (MS) Chronicle, 1811
Natchez Mississippi Herald and Natchez Gazette, 1804, 1805
Natchez Mississippi State Gazette, 1821, 1822
Natchez (MS) Weekly Chronicle, 1810
Newburgh (NY) Orange County Patriot, or The Spirit of Seventy-Six, 1811
Newburyport (MA) Herald, 1805, 1810
Newburyport (MA) Statesman, 1809
New Haven Connecticut Herald, 1811
New Haven Connecticut Journal, 1810
New Orleans Daily Delta, 1860
New Orleans Jeffersonian Republican, 1845
New Orleans Louisiana Advertiser, 1827
New Orleans Louisiana Courier, 1808, 1810
New Orleans Louisiana Gazette, 1810, 1811, 1818
New Orleans Louisiana State Gazette, 1826
New Orleans Orleans Gazette, 1805, 1818
Newport (RI) Mercury, 1810
Newport Rhode Island Republican, 1810
New York American Citizen, 1805
New York Columbian, 1810, 1811
New York Commercial Advertiser, 1804, 1806, 1810, 1811
New York Daily Advertiser, 1803, 1805
New York Evening Post, 1810

New-York Gazette and General Advertiser, 1810, 1811
New-York Herald, 1804, 1805, 1809
New-York Journal, 1810, 1811
New York Mercantile Advertiser, 1804
New York Northern Post, 1805
New York Public Advertiser, 1810
New York Republican Watch-Tower, 1804
New York Spectator, 1805
New York Spy, 1807
New York Weekly Museum, 1804
Norfolk (VA) American Beacon and Norfolk and Portsmouth Daily Advertiser, 1820
Norwich (CT) Courier, 1804, 1806, 1810
Otsego (NY) Herald, 1804
Peacham (VT) Green Mountain Patriot, 1804
Pensacola (FL) Star of Pensacola, 1875
Petersburg (VA) Intelligencer, 1808
Philadelphia Aurora General Advertiser, 1804
Philadelphia Poulson's American Daily Advertiser, 1811
Philadelphia United States Gazette, 1804
Philadelphia Weekly Aurora, 1810, 1811
Pittsfield (MA) Sun, 1805
Portland (ME) Eastern Argus, 1815
Portland (ME) Jenks' Portland Gazette, 1804
Portsmouth New-Hampshire Gazette, 1810
Portsmouth (NH) United States Oracle and Portsmouth Advertiser, 1803
Providence (RI) Columbian Phenix, 1810
Providence (RI) Gazette, 1811
Providence (RI) Phenix, 1804
Providence Rhode Island American, and General Advertiser, 1810
Raleigh (NC) Star, 1810, 1811
Richmond Enquirer, 1804, 1806, 1807, 1810, 1811
Richmond and Manchester Advertiser, 1804
Richmond Virginia Patriot, 1810
Rutland (VT) Herald, 1806, 1807
Sag Harbor (NY) Suffolk Gazette, 1804, 1810
Salem (MA) Gazette, 1804, 1811
Springfield (MA) Hampshire Federalist, 1806
St. Francisville Louisianian, 1819
Suffolk (NY) Gazette, 1805
Trenton (NJ) True American, 1811
Walpole (NH) Political Observatory, 1804, 1805, 1807
Washington (DC) Daily National Journal, 1827
Washington (DC) Enquirer, 1811
Washington (DC) Expositor, 1808
Washington (DC) Federalist, 1804

Washington (DC) Monitor, 1808
Washington (DC) National Intelligencer, 1804, 1810, 1811, 1835
Washington (DC) Spirit of Seventy-Six, 1810
Washington (DC) Universal Gazette, 1805, 1810, 1811
Washington (PA) Reporter, 1810
Wilkes-Barre (PA) Gleaner, and Luzerne Advertiser, 1811
Wilmington (DE) American Watchman, 1811
Windsor (VT) Spooner's Vermont Journal, 1808, 1810

Official Documents

Carter, Clarence Edwin, comp. *The Territorial Papers of the United States.* Vol. 5, *The Territory of Mississippi 1798–1809.* Washington, DC: Government Printing Office, 1937.

———. *The Territorial Papers of the United States.* Vol. 6, *The Territory of Mississippi 1809–1817.* Washington, DC: Government Printing Office, 1938.

———. *The Territorial Papers of the United States.* Vol. 9, *The Territory of Orleans 1803–1812.* Washington, DC: Government Printing Office, 1940.

Documents in Relation to the Claim of James Johnson for Transportation on the Missouri and Mississippi Rivers, March 1, 1821, House Document 110, Serial Set Vol. 55, Session Vol. 8. Washington, DC: United States Congress, 1821.

Franklin, Walter S., and Walter Lowrie, eds. *American State Papers: Foreign Relations.* 6 vols. Washington, DC: Gales and Seaton, 1832.

———. *American State Papers: Miscellaneous.* 2 vols. Washington, DC: Gales and Seaton, 1832.

———. *American State Papers: Public Lands.* 8 vols. Washington, DC: Duff Green, 1834.

Hamilton, William Baskerville. *Anglo-American Law on the Frontier: Thomas Rodney and His Territorial Cases.* Durham, NC: Duke University Press, 1953.

House Report 189, Joseph de la França, March 3, 1845, 28th Congress, 2d Session, Serial Set Vol. 468, Session Vol. 1. Washington, DC: United States Congress, 1845.

House Report 283, Joseph de la França, February 17, 1846, 29th Congress, 1st Session, Serial Set Vol. 489, Session Vol. 2. Washington, DC: United States Congress, 1845.

House Report 667, Joseph de La França, June 14, 1848, 30th Congress, 1st Session, Serial Set Vol. 526, Session Vol. 3. Washington, DC: United States Congress, 1848.

Letter from the Treasurer of the United States, Transmitting the Annual Accounts of His Office, February 23, 1820, 16th Congress, 1st Session, Serial Set Vol. 39, Session Vol. 9. Washington, DC: United States Congress, 1820.

Martin, Francis Xavier. *Martin's Reports of Cases Argued and Determined in the Superior Court of the Territory of Orleans.* 10 vols. New Orleans: Louisiana Supreme Court, 1846.

Petition of Charles DeHault Delassus Praying the Repayment of a Sum of Money Forc-

ibly Taken from Him, for Public Service, at the Capture of Baton Rouge, in 1810, United States Senate Document 401, Serial Set Vol. No. 318, 25th Congress, 2d Session. Washington, DC: United States Congress, 1838.

Rowland, Dunbar. Official Letter Books of W.C.C. Claiborne, 1801–1816. 6 vols. Jackson: Mississippi Department of Archives and History, 1917.

Senate Report to accompany Bill No. 62, January 4, 1847, 29th Congress, 2d Session, Serial Set Vol. 494, Session Vol. 2. Washington, DC: United States Congress, 1847.

Senate Report to accompany Bill No. 122, February 2, 1848, 30th Congress, 1st Session, Serial Set Vol. 512, Session Vol. 1. Washington, DC: United States Congress, 1848.

United States Census, Rapides Parish, Louisiana, 1820.

United States Senate Document 170, Report, February 15, 1843, Serial Set Vol. 415, Session Vol. 3, 27th Congress, 3d Session. Washington, DC: United States Congress, 1843.

Letters, Diaries, and Memoirs

Barker, Eugene C., ed. The Austin Papers. Part 1: Annual Report of the American Historical Association for the Year 1919. 2 vols. Washington, DC: Government Printing Office, 1924.

Bassett, John Spencer, ed. Correspondence of Andrew Jackson. 7 vols. Washington, DC: Carnegie Institution, 1926–1935.

Coker, William, and G. Douglas Inglis. The Spanish Census of Pensacola, 1784–1820: A Genealogical Guide to Spanish Pensacola. Pensacola: Perdido Bay Press, 1980.

Cuming, Fortescue. Sketches of a Tour to the Western Country. Pittsburgh: Cramer, Spear and Eicheuam, 1810.

Darby, William. A Geographical Description of the State of Louisiana, the Southern Part of the State of Mississippi, and Territory of Alabama. New York: James Olmstead, 1817.

Flint, Timothy. Recollections of the Last Ten Years in the Valley of the Mississippi. Carbondale: Southern Illinois University Press, 1968; reprint of 1926 edition edited by George R. Brooks.

Ford, Paul Leicester, comp. The Writings of Thomas Jefferson. 10 vols. New York: G. P. Putnam, 1897.

Kendall, John S. "Documents Concerning the West Florida Revolution, 1810." Louisiana Historical Quarterly 17 (January 1934): 80–95; (April 1934): 306–14; (July 1934): 474–501.

Latour, Arséne Lacarriére. Historical Memoir of the War in West Florida and Louisiana in 1814–15. Ed. by Gene A. Smith. Gainesville: University Press of Florida, 1999.

Meneray, Wilbur E., ed. The Favrot Family Papers: A Documentary Chronicle of Early Louisiana. 5 vols. New Orleans: Howard Tilton Memorial Library, 1997.

Ordinance Adopted by the Convention of West Florida. Natchez: John W. Winn, 1810.

Padgett, James A., ed. "The Constitution of the West Florida Republic." *Louisiana Historical Quarterly* 20 (October 1937): 881–94.

———. "The Documents Showing that the United States Ultimately Financed the West Florida Revolution of 1810." *Louisiana Historical Quarterly* 25 (October 1942): 943–70.

———. "Official Records of the West Florida Revolution and Republic." *Louisiana Historical Quarterly* 21 (July 1938): 685–805.

———. "The West Florida Revolution of 1810, as Told in the Letters of John Rhea, Fulwar Skipwith, Reuben Kemper, and Others." *Louisiana Historical Quarterly* 21 (January 1938): 76–202.

Petition of the Louisiana Parishes of East and West Feliciana, East Baton Rouge, Livingston, St. Helena, Tangipahoa, Washington, and St. Tammany. N.p., circa 1882.

Robin, C. C. *Voyages dans l'Intérieur de la Louisiane.* Gretna, LA: Firebird Press, 2000; reprint, trans. by Stuart O. Landry Jr.

Schultz, Christian. *Travels on an Inland Voyage.* New York: Isaac Riley, 1810.

Sparks, William Henry. *The Memories of Fifty Years.* Philadelphia: E. Claxton and Co., 1870.

Stagg, J.C.A., Jeanne Kerr Cross, and Susan Holbrook Perdue, eds. *The Papers of James Madison: Presidential Series.* Vol. 2, *October 1809–2 November 1810.* Charlottesville: University Press of Virginia, 1992.

———. *The Papers of James Madison: Presidential Series.* Vol. 3, *3 November 1810–4 November 1811.* Charlottesville: University Press of Virginia, 1996.

State Papers and Correspondence Bearing upon the Purchase of the Territory of Louisiana. Washington, DC: Government Printing Office, 1903.

Wilkinson, James. *Memoirs of My Own Times.* 3 vols. Philadelphia: Abraham Small, 1816.

Articles

Carrighan, J. W. "Historical and Statistical Sketches of Louisiana." *DeBow's Review of the Southern and Western States* 11, New Series 4 (September 1851): 252–63.

———. "Statistical and Historical Sketches of Louisiana." *DeBow's Review of the Southern and Western States* 11, New Series 4 (December 1851): 611–17.

Clark, Daniel. "Remarks on the Population, Culture, and Products of Louisiana." *Literary Magazine and American Register* 7 (1807): 45–57.

Gratz, Simon, ed. "Thomas Rodney." *Pennsylvania Magazine of History and Biography* 44, 1920, no. 1, 47–72; no. 2, 170–89; no. 3, 270–84; no. 4, 289–308; 45, 1921, no. 1, 34–65; no. 2, 180–203.

Prichard, Walter. "An Original Letter on the West Florida Revolution of 1810." *Louisiana Historical Quarterly* 18 (April 1935): 354–62.

Van Cleve, Benjamin. "Memoirs of Benjamin Van Cleve." *Quarterly Publication of the Historical and Philosophical Society of Ohio* 17 (January–June 1922): 7–71.

"West Florida and Its Attempt on Mobile, 1810–1811." *American Historical Review* 2 (July 1897): 699–705.

Websites

Ancestry.com. *Louisiana Marriages to 1850.*

———. *Mississippi State and Territorial Census Collection, 1792–1866.*

"Descendants of Alexander Stirling," March 16, 2002, http://www.clanstirling.org/Main/families/USA/pdf/alexanderstirlinglouisana.pdf.

Hall, Gwendolyn Midlo, comp. Ancestry.com. *Louisiana Slave Records, 1719–1820.*

Jackson, Ron V., Accelerated Indexing Systems, comp. Ancestry.com. *Mississippi Census, 1805–1890.*

———. Ancestry.com. *Louisiana Census, 1791–1890.*

———. Ancestry.com. *Ohio Census, 1790–1890.*

Secondary Sources

Books

Arthur, Stanley Clisby. *The Story of the Kemper Brothers.* St. Francisville, LA: St. Francisville *Democrat*, 1933.

———. *The Story of the West Florida Rebellion.* Baton Rouge: Claitor's Publishing, 1975; reprint of 1935 edition.

Beers, Henry Putney. *French and Spanish Records of Louisiana: A Bibliographical Guide to Archive and Manuscript Sources.* Baton Rouge: Louisiana State University Press, 1989.

Bice, David A. *The Original Lone Star Republic: Scoundrels, Statesmen and Schemers of the 1810 West Florida Rebellion.* Clanton, AL: Heritage Publishing Consultants, 2004.

Brewer, W. *Alabama: Her History, Resources, War Record, and Public Men, from 1540 to 1872.* Montgomery, AL: Barrett and Brown, 1872.

Brown, William Horace. *The Glory Seekers.* Chicago: A. C. McClurg, 1906.

Claiborne, J.F.C. *Mississippi As a Province, Territory, and State, with Biographical Notices of Eminent Citizens.* Jackson, MS: Powers and Barksdale, 1880.

Clark, Thomas D., and John D. W. Guice. *Frontiers in Conflict: The Old Southwest, 1795–1830.* Albuquerque: University of New Mexico Press, 1989.

Cox, Henry Bartholomew. *The Parisian American: Fulwar Skipwith of Virginia.* Washington, DC: Mount Vernon Publishing Co., 1964.

Cox, Isaac Joslin. *The West Florida Controversy, 1798–1813: A Study in American Diplomacy.* Baltimore: Johns Hopkins Press, 1918.

Davis, William C. *Three Roads to the Alamo: The Lives and Fortunes of David Crockett, James Bowie, and William Barret Travis.* New York: HarperCollins, 1998.

Foote, Henry Stuart. *Bench and Bar of the South and Southwest.* St. Louis: Soule, Thomas and Wentworth, 1876.

———. *Texas and the Texans*. 2 vols. Philadelphia: Thomas, Cowperthwait, 1841.

Gayarré, Charles. *History of Louisiana: The American Domination*. Gretna, LA: Pelican Publishing, 1998; reprint of the 1882 edition.

———. *History of Louisiana: The French Domination*. New York: William J. Widdleton, 1866.

Geggus, David, ed. *The Impact of the Haitian Revolution in the Atlantic World*. Columbia: University of South Carolina Press, 2001.

Goss, Charles Frederic. *Cincinnati, the Queen City, 1788–1912*. Chicago: S. J. Clark Co., 1912.

Groves, Joseph. *The Alstons and Allstons of North Carolina*. Atlanta: Franklin Printing and Publishing, 1901.

Haynes, Robert V. *The Mississippi Territory and the Southwest Frontier, 1795–1817*. Lexington: University Press of Kentucky, 2010.

Heitman, Francis B. *Historical Register and Dictionary of the United States Army*. 2 vols. Washington: Government Printing Office, 1903.

Hoffman, Paul E. *Florida's Frontiers*. Bloomington: Indiana University Press, 2002.

Hyde, Samuel C., Jr. *Pistols and Politics: The Dilemma of Democracy in Louisiana's Florida Parishes, 1810–1899*. Baton Rouge: Louisiana State University Press, 1996.

———, ed. *A Fierce and Fractious Frontier: The Curious Development of Louisiana's Florida Parishes, 1699–2000*. Baton Rouge: Louisiana State University Press, 2004.

Kemper, Willis Miller, and Harry Linn Wright. *Genealogy of the Kemper Family in the United States, Descendants of John Kemper of Virginia*. Chicago: George K. Hazlitt and Co., 1899.

Kennedy, Roger G. *Mr. Jefferson's Lost Cause: Land, Farmers, Slavery, and the Louisiana Purchase*. New York: Oxford University Press, 2003.

Kerr, Derek N. *Petty Felony, Slave Defiance, and Frontier Villainy: Crime and Criminal Justice in Spanish Louisiana, 1770–1803*. New York: Garland Publishing, 1993.

Lomask, Milton. *Aaron Burr: The Conspiracy and Years of Exile, 1805–1836*. New York: Farrar, Straus and Giroux, 1982.

McMichael, Andrew. *Atlantic Loyalties: Americans in Spanish West Florida, 1785–1810*. Athens: University of Georgia Press, 2008.

Monette, John W. *History of the Discovery and Settlement of the Valley of the Mississippi*. New York: Harper and Brothers, 1848.

Owsley, Frank Lawrence, Jr., and Gene A. Smith. *Filibusters and Expansionists: Jeffersonian Manifest Destiny, 1800–1821*. Tuscaloosa: University of Alabama Press, 1997.

Parker, David W. *Calendar of Papers in Washington Archives Relating to the Territories of the United States (to 1873)*. Washington, DC: Carnegie Institution, 1911.

Patrick, Rembert. *Florida Fiasco: Rampant Rebels on the Florida-Georgia Border, 1810–1815*. Athens: University of Georgia Press, 1954.

Perez, Luis Marino. *Guide to the Materials for American History in Cuban Archives*. Washington, DC: Carnegie Institution, 1907.

Pickett, Albert James. *History of Alabama and Incidentally of Georgia and Missis-*

sippi, from the Earliest Period. Birmingham, AL: Birmingham Book and Magazine Co., 1962; reprint of 1851 edition.

Rowland, Dunbar. *Mississippi, Comprising Sketches of Counties, Towns, Events, Institutions, and Persons, Arranged in Cyclopedic Form.* 3 vols. Atlanta: Southern Historical Publishing Association, 1907.

Rowland, Mrs. Dunbar [Eron]. *Mississippi Territory in the War of 1812.* Baltimore: Clearfield Company, 1968; reprint.

Scott, James B. *Outline of the Rise and Progress of Freemasonry in Louisiana: From Its Introduction to the Re-organization of the Grand Lodge in 1850.* New Orleans: Clark and Hofeline, 1873.

Shepherd, William R. *Guide to the Materials for the History of the United States in Spanish Archives.* Washington, DC: Carnegie Institution, 1907.

Smith, Joseph Burkholder. *James Madison's Phony War: The Plot to Steal Florida.* New York: Arbor House, 1983.

Tennessee Old and New: Sesquicentennial Edition, 1796–1946. Nashville: Tennessee Historical Commission, 1946.

Walker, Alexander. *The Life of Andrew Jackson.* Philadelphia: Davis, Porter and Coates, 1866.

Whitaker, Arthur Preston. *The Mississippi Question 1795–1803, a Study in Trade, Politics, and Diplomacy.* New York: D. Appleton-Century, 1934.

White, David Hart. *Vicente Folch, Governor in Spanish Florida, 1787–1811.* Washington, DC: University Press of America, 1981.

Willie, LeRoy E., comp. *History of Spanish West Florida and the Rebellion of 1810 and Philemon Thomas, Patriot.* Baton Rouge: General Philemon Thomas Chapter, Sons of the American Revolution, 1991.

Works Project Administration of Louisiana. *Index to 18 Volumes of Spanish West Florida Records.* N.p.: Baton Rouge, 1939.

Articles

Abernathy, Thomas Perkins. "Aaron Burr in Mississippi." *Journal of Southern History* 15 (February 1949): 9–21.

Brooks, Philip. "Spain's Farewell to Louisiana, 1803–1821." *Mississippi Valley Historical Review* 27 (June 1940): 29–42.

Butler, Louise. "West Feliciana — A Glimpse of Its History." *Louisiana Historical Quarterly* 7 (January 1924): 90–120.

Casey, Powell A. "Military Roads in the Florida Parishes of Louisiana." *Louisiana History* 15 (Summer 1974): 229–42.

Chambers, Henry E. "A Short-Lived American State." *Magazine of American History* 27 (January 1891): 24–29.

Egan, Clifford. "The United States, France, and West Florida, 1803–1807." *Florida Historical Quarterly* 47 (January 1969): 227–52.

Favrot, Henry L. "Some of the Causes and Conditions that Brought about the West Florida Revolution in 1810." *Publications of the Louisiana Historical Society* 1, part 2 (1895): 37–46.

———. "The West Florida Revolution and Incidents Growing Out of It." *Publications of the Louisiana Historical Society* 1, part 3 (1896): 17–30.

Hyde, Samuel C., Jr. "Seventy-Four Days a Nation: Louisiana's Florida Parishes, the Original Lone Star Republic." *Louisiana Cultural Vistas* 15 (Winter 2004–2005): 79–89.

McAlister, L. N. "Pensacola During the Second Spanish Period." *Florida Historical Quarterly* 37 (January–April 1959): 281–327.

McCain, William. "The Administrations of David Holmes." *Journal of Mississippi History* 29 (1967): 328–47.

McMichael, Andrew. "The Kemper 'Rebellion': Filibustering and Resident Anglo American Loyalty in Spanish West Florida." *Louisiana History* 43 (Spring 2002): 133–65.

Pitcher, M. Avis. "John Smith, First Senator from Ohio and His Connections with Aaron Burr." *Ohio History* 45 (January 1936): 68–88.

Sterkx, Henry Eugene, and Brooks Thompson. "Philemon Thomas and the West Florida Revolution." *Florida Historical Quarterly* 39 (April 1961): 378–86.

Taylor, Robert. "Prelude to Manifest Destiny: The United States and West Florida, 1810–1811." *Gulf Coast Historical Review* 7 (Spring 1992): 45–62.

"West Florida and Its Attempt on Mobile, 1810–1811." "Documents," *American Historical Review* 2 (July 1897): 699–705.

Wilhelmy, Robert W. "Senator John Smith and the Aaron Burr Conspiracy." *Cincinnati Historical Society Bulletin* 28 (Spring 1970): 38–60.

Theses and Dissertations

Price, Grady Daniel. "The United States and West Florida, 1803–1812." PhD diss., University of Texas, Austin, 1939.

INDEX

Tombigbee R.

MISSISSIPPI

TERRITORY

McIntosh's
Bluff

Alabama R.

Fort Stoddert

McCurtin's
Bluff
(Bunker Hill)

- - - ELLICOTT LINE - - -

Saw
Mill
Creek

Tensaw R.

SPANISH

Mobile R.

White
House

WEST

Mobile

Minette
Bay

Spanish
Fort

FLORIDA

Mobile Bay

Pascagoula R.

Pascagoula

Petit Bois Island

Dauphin
Island